D0893478

Family Assessment: Integrating Multiple Perspectives

Family Assessment

Integrating Multiple Perspectives

Edited by

Manfred Cierpka
Volker Thomas
Douglas H. Sprenkle

Library of Congress Cataloging-in-Publication Data
is available via the Library of Congress Marc Database under the
LC Control Number 2002102110

Library and Archives Canada Cataloguing in Publication

Family assessment : integrating multiple clinical perspectives / M. Cierpka, V. Thomas, D. Sprenkle (eds.).

Includes bibliographical references and index.
ISBN 0-88937-240-3

1. Family assessment. 2. Family psychotherapy.
I. Cierpka, M. (Manfred) II. Thomas, Volker III. Sprenkle, Douglas H.

RC488.53.F34 2005   616.89'156   C2004-906042-2

PUBLISHING OFFICES
USA: Hogrefe & Huber Publishers, 875 Massachusetts Avenue, 7th Floor,
               Cambridge, MA 02139
               Phone (866) 823-4726, Fax (617) 354-6875; E-mail info@hhpub.com
EUROPE: Hogrefe & Huber Publishers, Rohnsweg 25, 37085 Göttingen, Germany
               Phone +49 551 49609-0, Fax +49 551 49609-88, E-mail hh@hhpub.com

SALES & DISTRIBUTION
USA: Hogrefe & Huber Publishers, Customer Services Department,
               30 Amberwood Parkway, Ashland, OH 44805
               Phone (800) 228-3749, Fax (419) 281-6883, E-mail custserv@hhpub.com
EUROPE: Hogrefe & Huber Publishers, Rohnsweg 25, 37085 Göttingen, Germany
               Phone +49 551 49609-0, Fax +49 551 49609-88, E-mail hh@hhpub.com

CORPORATE OFFICE
Hogrefe & Huber Publishers, Inc., 218 Main Street, Suite 485, Kirkland WA 98033

OTHER OFFICES
CANADA: Hogrefe & Huber Publishers, 1543 Bayview Avenue, Toronto, Ontario M4G 3B5
SWITZERLAND: Hogrefe & Huber Publishers, Länggass-Strasse 76, CH-3000 Bern 9

Hogrefe & Huber Publishers
Incorporated and registered in the State of Washington, USA, and in Göttingen, Lower Saxony, Germany

Printed and bound in Germany
ISBN 0-88937-240-3

CONTENTS

Preface

This book presents several unique perspectives of family diagnostics and assessment. First, it integrates the views of family therapists from Germany and the United States by offering a glimpse of systemic thinking from two cultures, two languages, and two historical contexts. Second, the book offers multiple theoretical perspectives integrated into one comprehensive approach that has the overarching goal to match the assessment process with the family's needs. These perspectives include psychodynamic and systemic theories that require different assessment procedures. The interaction effects between the two approaches and their integration contribute to the unique contribution of this work in providing new assessment procedures.

The book is conceptualized to view families through different lenses, similar to looking through a window into the inside of a house. Each chapter offers a special perspective into the family's house as illustrated in Figure 1. The personal theories of the diagnostician, his or her scientific theories of how a family works, and the social context in which the assessment of the family takes place, all influence the definitions, the observations, and the formation of a clinical assessment. In Figure 1 these influencing factors are shown in the outer ring that surrounds the diagnostic window and the concrete implementation of the first interview. *Chapter 1* presents definitions of family and family assessment. Advantages and disadvantages of the assessment procedures are discussed. "The Three-Level Model of Family Assessment" in *Chapter 2* is an attempt to integrate the various perspectives like psychodynamic and systemic thinking by looking at the level of the individual, dyadic and triadic relationships, and the family as a whole. These two introduction chapters constitute the theoretical framework of our understanding of family assessment.

The diagnostic/assessment process as outlined in the center box of Figure 1 illustrates the stages for carrying out the assessment interviews. Three chapters describe, step-by-step, and as practice-oriented as possible, the assessment process from the first contact (usually a telephone conversation) with the family to the problem definition and the formulation of the therapy goals. *Chapter 3* "First Contacts and Preconditions for the Initial Interview" describes the establishment of contacts between the systems of the family and that of the therapists. During the initial interviews family members formulate their perceptions of the problems and express the changes they desire. Problem definition and treatment goals are central issues in this stage of the process. *Chapter 4* called "A Problem Well Stated is a Problem Half Solved" explores more formal assessment procedures. *Chapter 5* presents the case example of assessment interviews with a family. This chapter "Conducting the First Interview with the Family" contains guidelines for first interviews. In the course of the first sessions, the therapist explains, in concrete terms, how the assessment process will proceed. In addition, the commentary to the interview discusses theoretical considerations regarding the clinical material from various, individual and systemic diagnostic points of view.

The outer layer of Figure 1 represents the different elements of the diagnostic/assessment window through which the information of the assessment interviews is gathered, connections are found and, finally, results are interpreted. The elements themselves are located on different levels of abstraction. *Chapter 6* "Family Assessment in Context" describes the framework in which first family interviews take place and the variables that

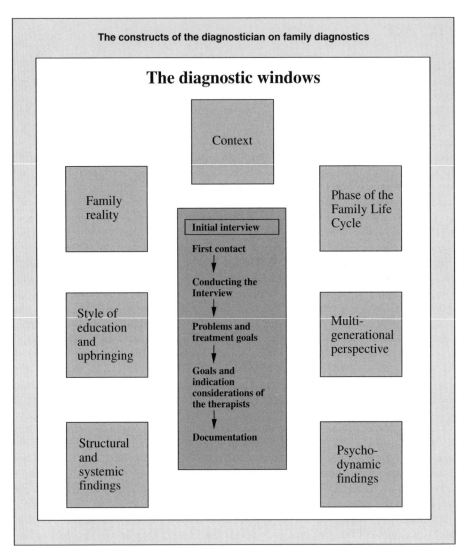

Figure 1. The diagnostic windows of the family interview.

influence the presentation of the family problems. The social environment of the family or partnership has an effect on the diagnostic/assessment and therapeutic process. *Chapter 7* "The Family's Social World" discusses the assessment of the social realities of families. Families have histories extending back for many generations and cultural contexts in which they have been embedded. *Chapter 8* entitled "The Multigenerational Perspective of Family Assessment" focuses on diagnosing/assessing the psychodynamics of families over several generations as a contributing factor in the present, ongoing relationships of a family. Family dynamics are a result of the growth processes of the individuals and the adaptation of the family life cycle in response to them. Families proceed through lifecycle stages that greatly influence the environment and the tasks that characterize their communal lives. *Chapter 9* "The Family Life Cycle and the Genogram" synthesises the family's context and environment into the visual diagnostic/assessment tool of the genogram. Behavior management with regard to education and parenting plays an important role in many family problems. *Chapter 10* "Assessment of Parenting Styles and Behavior" provides the family therapist with another angle into a diagnostic window of family assessment.

In family assessment, the connections between the presenting problems and the family dynamics can be viewed as a reciprocal interaction between systemic-structural and psychodynamic factors. From our point of view, comprehensive family assessment integrates psychodynamic and systemic-structural findings into a summary of its clinical diagnosis.

The systemic dimension constitutes the first theoretical element that highlights the structure of the family – the transactional patterns that manifestly regulate desires and fears at the relational and behavioral levels. The family therapist can form a picture of the systemic-structural components by, for example, observing and assessing the structure of role assignments and the appropriateness of these roles with regard to generational and gender alliances and limitations. The therapist must observe the reciprocal relationships between the subsystems and the family as a whole with other systems and place these in relationship to the current development status of the individual family members and the current life-cycle stage of the family. *Chapter 11* "The Systemic Assessment" summarizes assessment information from the longitudinal life-history perspective and from the ongoing, present-related systemic perspective, respectively. The psychodynamic window adds an assessment element of the desires and fears of the individual family members as they influence (mostly unconsciously) the relationship dynamics. The therapist must also discover the unconscious dynamics of the "whole family." The object relationships of individual family members produce a network of conscious and unconscious desires and anxieties that emerge in the framework of these object relationships and constitute both the family dynamics of the whole family as well as the inner images of the family for each individual. *Chapter 12* "Psychodynamic Assessment" gives an overview of the guidelines for assessing psychodynamic constructs in family life. The family therapist assesses the tension between the constructive and destructive components between the individual, inner world of the family members and the family relationship patterns. The flexibility of the family, that is, the extent of possible change, will depend mostly on these parameters. Finally, *Chapter 13* applies both theoretical perspectives illustrating some "Family Sculpture Procedures" that are particularly helpful in the assessment process.

We would like to thank the 7 German and 13 US authors for taking on the challenging task of writing a book that attempts to bridge two cultural and two theoretical worlds. Their enthusiasm, respect for each other, and patience made this book a pleasure to conceptualize, put together, and look through to its completion. Thanks to Hogrefe's Lisa Bennett who kept us on track when the transatlantic communication among the editors appeared interrupted. We hope that the reader will enjoy this book as much as we did working on it.

Manfred Cierpka, Volker Thomas, and Douglas Sprenkle

Introduction

1

Introduction to Family Assessment

Manfred Cierpka

Summary

In this book, the family and other forms of living together are described as special types of relationship, characterized by their joint aims, the intimacy between the partners and their shared life plans. The perspectives of family assessment are oriented towards this view of the family. The definition of family assessment used in this handbook emphasizes that the present interactive behavior of family members and the conflicts it implies must be seen as a point of intersection between multigenerational relationships and current relationship patterns.

In medical terms, *physical health* is a standard concept that can be applied to everyone. As far as psychic problems, disorders, and illnesses are concerned, however, the boundaries between illness and health are rather more fluid and more difficult to define. On the one hand, the context often governs what is described as illness and what as health; on the other hand, health and illness are often too quickly misinterpreted as normality and abnormality. Assessment in a psychosocial setting is often in danger of being seen as a labeling and stigmatizing of outsiders, of people who are unusual or strange. Reluctance towards being judged by others is of course partly justified – assessment is sometimes used as a powerful instrument within society to demarcate or even confine the mentally ill or the handicapped. Totalitarian regimes tend to use this kind of labeling assessment. Thus it is understandable that, assessment and giving a diagnosis has far-reaching consequences, democratic controls must be introduced by society. During the last three decades, a large group of psychiatrists has been working on internationally recognized classifications in a democratic and (more or less) transparent systematic process. Their aim is to find a consensus for the definition and classification of psychic phenomena in a way that is as free of ideology and as practice-oriented as possible. Whatever opinion one may have towards such a standardized and operationalized classification system, family diagnostics does not yet have this kind of democratic process of consensus at its disposal. For example, a family therapist may view a relational disorder from a completely different perspective than therapists from other schools of thought. In this way, the concepts of family assessment presented in this book should not always be taken at face value – they remain provisional in character, having not yet received the scientific community's seal of approval.

In the field of family assessment, an opinion is reached in the same way as in all other areas of medicine and psychotherapy – by means of examination and comparison. Assessment consists of several tasks such as description, classification, explanation, prognosis, documentation etc. (Laireiter, 2001). The main aim of family assessment is to describe and explain functional and less functional processes on the level of relationships. The classifications are not concerned with the differences between a normal and an abnormal family, but with the recording of dysfunctional (i.e., less than optimal) processes and the strength of resources that could be put to use to encourage positive developments and changes in individuals, couple relationships, or the family as a whole and to work through the problems.

On a clinical level, assessment paves the way for therapy. This book is based on the theory that family assessment can be extremely valuable for family therapy and other forms of psychotherapy. In the end, the practical use of assessment methods will determine whether family therapy is able to make use of family assessment. In the last few decades, there has been a tremendous increase in the amount of scientifically based knowledge available for family assessment. This book presents and discusses the diagnostic possibilities available.

Family Assessment: A Form of Theory Based Assessment

In the following chapters, family assessment is discussed within the context of clinical psychotherapeutic evaluation. It may therefore be grouped under psychotherapeutic assessment (Cierpka, 2000). Laireiter (2000, p. 6) defines four diagnostic concepts that are useful in modern psychotherapy – clinical psychiatric assessment, somatic-medical assessment, psychological assessment, and assessment related to certain schools or fields of orientation. In this book family assessment is mainly theory-related (Baumann & Stieglitz, 1994) or theory-based (Bastine, 1992) on an interpersonal level. Disorders, individuals, or relationship systems are described and defined according to elaborate family theoretical models using assessment criteria and explained with the help of theoretical constructs.

The aim of this form of interpersonal assessment is to identify, describe, and quantify relational processes that may be functional or dysfunctional for the development of the individual or the system of relationships. Within the context of psychotherapy, interpersonal assessment becomes *clinical family assessment*, as the various schools of family therapy work on the assumption that interpersonal relations and specific conflicts or disorders in dyads, triads, or the family as a whole are related to or even cause the development and persistence of problems, complaints, and symptoms in individuals. The aim of family therapy is to try to change the dysfunctional relationships that lead to the manifestation and persistence of disorders.

In this way, family assessment can be a form of *psychological assessment* when dimensions related to the family are defined using reliable and valid instruments such as rating scales or questionnaires in order to compare the strengths and weaknesses of certain families with, for example, a sample consisting of "normal" families. This book introduces this form of assessment, which is usually practiced at the beginning of a therapy, from a clinical point of view. It is used to identify and quantify family (dys)functionality, providing further insight into the connection between individual symptoms and relationship disorders.

Family assessment provides a *status evaluation* and an evaluation *change*. It is helpful to make a status definition at certain points in time, e.g., at the beginning and at the end of therapy, in order to identify the problems or symptoms and to define the degree of their severity. This implies an assessment of all the factors that could contribute to the persistence or the disappearance of the symptoms. The status assessments also classifies the complaint, problem or symptom within an overall classification system. The assessment of change describes the process that brings about changes in individuals and/or in the family system during therapy. For research purposes, the question of how effects of change can be defined and described so as to identify effective mechanisms in psychotherapy is becoming more and more of an urgent issue. Information relating to the process is registered under adaptive indications in the interplay between the family system and the therapist system. In this way, suitable intervention strategies can be developed. The aim here is to advance the therapeutic process as much as possible. In every family therapy there is a specific course of progress, starting from the first interview and ending with the completion of therapy. Just as in other forms of psychotherapy, an assessment *of progress* can be made following Schacht and Strupp's (1984) principle of *problem–treatment–outcome–congruency*. This general heuristic guideline signifies that there must be a similarity, an isomorphism, or congruence between the assessment of the clinical problem, the conceptualization of the process of therapeutic change and the description of clinical success. Thus, what may be described as success (this can be measured using various objective questionnaires) should be reflected by the results of an analysis of clinical success (see also Strupp et al., 1988). The common language alone allows a connection to be made between the problem, the process of intervention, and the result of family therapy treatment. For this reason, we sometimes resort to the use of problem lists in addition to the definition of the problem as established during the first interview. With the help of such lists it is possible to quantify problems according to their degree of severity during the course of treatment. A wide variety of rating scales and self-assessment instruments are also available which are considered reliable and valid enough to be used in objective progress diagnostics (see Grotevant & Carlson, 1989; Sprenkle & Moon, 2004).

Assessment and Therapy

Clinical family assessment is relational, applied within the context of interpersonal relationships – not only the relationships between individual family members but also between the therapist and the family. Interaction between the therapist and the family can be described in terms of a touching of two larger systems – the therapist system and the family system. The information required by the therapist and the family to understand the problems at hand is found within this system made up of family and therapists.

> The therapist system consists of the therapist and all other systems participating in the treatment of the family. Rather than using the term family system, it is more helpful to speak of the problem system. The concept of the problem system incorporates the psychotherapeutic question of which members of the system should be involved in sessions at what point of the diagnosis, and later at which phase of the treatment, in order to gain specific information or to encourage specific processes of change. The problem system includes all individuals who may have an influence on the persistence of the current problem or its solution.

In psychodynamic relational assessment, three sources of information are available. Firstly, the family members provide the therapists with their own accounts of relationships within and outside of the family; secondly, familial relationships may be observed in the present therapy situation, and thirdly, information may be gathered from the development of the current relationship between the therapists and the family. The third source of information implies the dynamics of transference and counter transference between the two systems.

The development of a relationship between the therapist and family systems means that it is difficult to draw a clear boundary between assessment and therapy. A relationship between the therapists and the family begins to develop from the first moment of the contact onwards. The family experiences this relationship as supportive and, as such, it has a therapeutically effective character from the very beginning. Hence, any division drawn between the assessment and therapeutic phases of treatment is destined to be artificial in nature. The only form of family assessment that could be described as pure evaluation would have to consist of psychological tests performed in a laboratory, where the family performs interactive tasks or fills out questionnaires.

It is not only the relationship within the therapist-family system that proves to be an effective therapeutic factor from the beginning of treatment onwards. The therapist's questions also trigger a process of self-reflection within the family, so that family members begin to become aware of their situation and to initiate changes. Often for the first time, the family begins to think about the circumstances that have led to the development of a symptom and why it persists. The possibility of speaking openly under the therapist's protective wing gives the family strength and motivates them to try to change the situation.

In spite of the arguments against family assessment, there are good reasons to continue to make a distinction between assessment and therapy. Real clinical family assessment takes place before family therapy treatment begins. It offers both the therapists and the family the opportunity to decide whether or not they wish to embark on a process of therapy with one another. The family has time to consider whether they wish to engage in a therapeutic process with these therapists. They may decide to seek the help of a different agency. The family is also given the chance to think about whether they really wish to tackle the changes that are suggested in the first interview. Individual members of the family can decide whether they wish to approach their problems with the rest of the family or, if they would perhaps prefer, to undergo therapy alone, or even not at all. The initial assessment phase also makes the official start of the main therapy process more binding in character. The family takes on more responsibility for initiating certain changes on their own. The family co-operates closely with the therapist, helping to make decisions concerning what should be achieved during the phases of assessment and therapy. Following the assessment phase, the family and the therapists can discuss the goals of therapy. Stierlin (2001) emphasized the importance of the democratic nature of this process, providing that therapists put their cards on the table and speak openly about their view of the family's problems. Goals set by the therapist and the family together result in a greater degree of transparency in the assessment process.

Therapists may also find it helpful to distinguish between assessment and therapy, thus giving themselves time to consider the question of the indications for psychotherapy. Clinical family assessment is not an end to itself, but should always be seen, as an *indicator of the direction therapy should take*. This is true of both status evaluation and evaluation of change. In the case of status evaluation, therapists have the task of making an indication after the phase of family assessment. Systemic therapists often express reservations towards family assessment (Stierlin, 2001; White & Epston, 1990). A group of these therapists doubt whether it is of any use at all in a clinical sense. Their argument, which appears quite feasible, makes a distinction between problem patterns and solution patterns in the treatment of families. In order to stimulate changes in the process, it is not necessary to analyze problem situations in detail; indeed, this can sometimes even be detrimental to the development of the therapy (Schiepek et al., 2000). This line of thought is process-oriented and logical if we consider that a system requires stimulation in order to change. However, the *analysis of problem patterns* allows a more detailed description of dysfunctional ties to be made, thus providing sufficient information on which to base indication decisions. Modern psychotherapy has so many procedures, methods, techniques, and setting variations at its disposal that we consider an analysis of problems to be indispensable. Of course, equal importance should be attached to solution patterns and a focus on pathology-based aspects should be avoided.

In *indicationally oriented assessment,* the description and explanation of problems is followed by the question of the appropriate method or the right setting, i.e., ideas on differential indications. As well as the (sometimes very personal) question of whether the therapists think they can work with this particular family, it is sometimes extremely useful to introduce a distinction between the phases of assessment and therapy for indicational reasons.

Assessment Perspectives

In psychiatry, just as in organic medicine, symptoms are grouped under various forms of illness, which in their turn infer therapeutic intervention. Descriptive-phenomenological assessment classifies illnesses or psychic disorders according to standard criteria, for example on the basis of ICD-10 or DSM-IV. Here, assessment is performed within a clear-cut pattern of relationships – the psychiatrist is the assessor, the person who is being assessed is the patient. The psychopathological results should be reported as objectively as possible – the patients and their psychic difficulties are objects that must be accurately described. This splitting between observer and object is found everywhere in somatic medical assessment.

Clinical family assessment is not concerned with this kind of *topographical diagnostic model* based on objective reality. Therapists do not only observe the family as an object from the outside, in order to assess the problem and make a diagnosis. The evaluator becomes a component of the system and extracts assessments from his or her own feelings, thoughts, and behavior as a member of the therapist-family system. Thus the therapist assesses a process at a certain point in time, a process of which he or she forms a part and which is in a constant state of change. The information gained in the assessment is based on the constructions of the therapists and the family, so that all parties involved are able to understand the dynamics of the family. All assessments are working hypotheses that must be reviewed or rejected in the dialogic process. This means that:
- no assessment information can be objective, it is always subject to the influence of the therapist and his or her contexts, and
- the information gathered during the process of assessment is "statically" impressive, as all data are put together to form a family item. In fact, however, the assessment of the family structure, organization and dynamics can only provide a cross-sectional view of the processes at work in a developing therapist-family system.

Specificity versus Non-Specificity

A classification of families along the lines of psychiatric diagnosis appears unsuitable for the purposes of family assessment. The effect of disturbed couple and family relationships on the development of specific illnesses has been the topic of much controversial discussion, especially since the publication of the book on the "psychosomatic" family by Minuchin and colleagues (Minuchin, Roseman, & Baker, 1978). The debate is centered around differences of opinion on specific forms of family dysfunctionality that are said to be characteristic in so-called psychosomatic families. The term specificity is used to describe theoretical ideas assuming a close causal relationship between certain specific family interactions or configurations and certain forms of illness in a patient.

The term specificity originates from somatic medicine. An infection with a specific cause, e.g., the tubercle bacillus, leads to a certain morphological change in the tissues, i.e., tuberculosis. Even though we must assume that certain other conditions must be fulfilled if the infection is to take a grip, we may say that the tubercle bacillus is the specific cause. As far as the development of psychic illnesses are concerned, Freud pointed out that we may only speak of a certain specific cause if "its presence is an absolute prerequisite for the realization of the effect ..." (Freud, 1895f, p. 375). A hypothesis of specificity for psychosomatic illnesses was formulated by Alexander et al. (1968). For each of the seven illnesses they investigated (bronchial asthma, rheumatic arthritis, colitis ulcerosa, essential hypertension, hyperthyroidism, gastric ulcer, and neurodermatitis), it was assumed that, apart from the predisposed somatic x factor and the subjectively significant life situation that can act as a trigger, there is a specific psychodynamic configuration that develops in childhood along with respective defense procedures. A vivid discussion arose on the topic of specificity vs. non-specificity, a discussion that still continues up to the present day.

During the course of the development of family therapy models, three types of specificity hypotheses relating to the connection between the clinical picture of a family member and a particular disorder within family interaction have emerged (Cierpka, 1989). Circular models followed linear concepts and, finally, concepts based on the construct of *expressed emotions* were introduced. None of these concepts have been able to provide clear evidence of specificity. Empirical studies on the typology of families, e.g., so-called psychosomatic (Wirsching & Stierlin, 1982), schizophrenic (Stierlin, 1975), and manic depressive (Stierlin et al., 1986) families are too unreliable in their methodology to be considered convincing (Cierpka, 1991).

In this book, the so-called dimensional model is used. This model does not categorize families according to illnesses; rather, they are classified on a continual basis on various dimensions providing information on their strengths and weaknesses.

Assessment Based on Pathology Versus Resource-Oriented Assessment

Medical assessment is pathology based. The term diagnostics is taken from the Greek word *diagnoskein*, which means investigate or differentiate. By differentiating between the healthy and the unhealthy and researching into the causes of illnesses, this form of assessment follows the scientific model that links cause and effect together in a linear, causal relationship. Because a tubercle bacillus has to be present in every case of tuberculosis, of course doctors will try to identify the bacillus in their assessment if they suspect that a patient is infected. Even if this kind of simple linear relationship is not always found in other illnesses, the medical diagnostician always concentrates primarily on a cause, a pathological substrate, or a functional disorder that has triggered the outbreak of the symptoms and disorder.

It is not until recent times that medicine has begun to seriously consider the question of how a clinical picture can be changed by the resources available within the body (Engel, 1977), a question that has been quite accepted in homeopathy for centuries. In cancer research, medicine is looking more and more towards reinforcing the body's own defenses to fight against pathologically changed cells. The resources of immunological defense and auto-regulation are put to use.

One of the main aims of clinical family assessment is to form hypotheses to explain the relationship between the development of the symptoms or problem and intrafamilial relational conflicts. This means that the family therapist's view is also primarily defect or pathology-oriented when identifying dysfunctional patterns. A certain level of disorder orientation is essential in order to stimulate purposeful processes of change and to find the direction the therapeutic process is to take. Otherwise, there is a danger of disorientation during the course of the therapy.

However, family therapists also take into account the systemic interactive processes of the many factors that can lead to stagnation in the developmental process of a family. There are no clear causal, linear explanations for the contextual circumstances leading to the development and continuation of a symptom. A diagnosis based on pathology, focusing on causes, does not reach far enough. Therefore, practice-related assessment must bear in mind the contextual circumstances that can, for example, encourage a developmental process to take place within the family. This means that the assessment process must focus on resources. Symptoms always have a stabilizing function and this should be recognized by the family. It is much more helpful to place emphasis on this positive aspect, pointing out the effectiveness of the system's inherent strengths. The family then feels competent as opposed to unhealthy and helpless. For this reason family assessment concentrates far more on resources than is common in medicine and all other kinds of psychotherapeutic methods, with the aim of using the family's resources to activate its own powers of self-regulation. In resource-oriented family assessment, the most important task is to identify the strengths that could contribute to effecting a positive change. In this case, family assessment looks towards the process-oriented developmental possibilities present within the family and uses these resources to introduce developmental steps.

In this book it is assumed that diagnosis based on pathology and resource-oriented assessment complement one another. As we all know, the half full glass of water is also half empty, and vice-versa. It is not advisable to take only one orientation into consideration. Perspectives must remain flexible, so that each case presents a new opportunity for the clinicians to change the pair of glasses they were wearing in order to gain optimal information concerning the family.

The Definition of the Family

The clinical phenomena to be defined in family assessment depend partly on what a family is considered to be. The social concept of the family is by no means easy to define, as it has a different meaning in each scientific discipline. This basic difficulty – even for the purposes of this book – is demonstrated by the following normative definitions of family.

Family sociologists generally focus on the socialization process of the children as a crystallization point for the family. A family is described in terms of the social relations between parents and children, which are socially recognized as such. This takes into consideration the fact that human children require a high level of care and attention for a relatively long period of time in order to survive. Intrafamilial relations and identification with these are considered highly important for the psychic development of children.

The legal definition of family also focuses on the principle of filiation, along with the principle of care and custody. The term family can be used if "two generations are bound to one another through biological and legal parenthood and the question of care or custody has been settled for the child generation" (Schneewind, 1987, p. 972). Compared with the legal term of family, the genealogical definition of family, based on the principal of relatedness, incorporates a far wider variety of family forms. An individual's family is described as "the group of people (...) who are related, married, or related by marriage, regardless of whether they live together or not, and whether the individual members are still alive or – if deceased – have played a part in the creation of the family" (Scientific advisory board for questions of family at the Federal Ministry of Young People, Family and Health, Germany, 1984, p. 27).

Psychotherapists define the family as a system of intimate relationships. Frevert (1992) follows on from Schneewind (1987), defining the family as "a system of intimate relationships involving two or more people who share a way of life together. The shared way of life is determined by the criteria of demarcation, privacy, permanence, and closeness or intimacy and emotionality" (p. 8).

Clinical family assessment requires a definition of family that is oriented towards the living together of individuals in a special small group – the family. The specific relationships within the family characterize the form of living.

Definition of the Family

A family (with one or two parents) consists of several people who live together, normally the two generations represented by the (real, adoptive, foster, or step) parents and the (real, adopted, foster, or step) children. Life together in the family is characterized by joint tasks, the wish for intimacy and privacy, and by the family's utopia. When a family is founded, each partner contributes his own personal notion of family utopia, which is realized as a life form and adapted to incorporate the partner's ideas and social reality. Thus a framework is created for the developmental and life tasks that are to be fulfilled by the family.

This definition of family serves as a guideline for the family assessment perspectives and the evaluation criteria that are used in various parts of the book to assess familial relationships, structures, and processes. As well as the fact that several generations live together, usually the parents and children, the main emphasis of the definition is placed upon current relationships and family interaction. Demographic surveys show that people seek a family as a place of emotionality, a place where privacy and intimacy can be experienced (Emnid Institute, 2004).

Today it has become uncommon for more than two generations to live together in the same household. Kaufmann (1994) describes the present ideal typical form of life as a *multilocal multigenerational family*. This definition expresses the fact that family relationships are withheld over at least three generations. However the three generations no longer live together under the same roof, but more usually in different households in different locations. Along with the living together of two or more generations and the search for intimacy and privacy there is a third criterion for the definition of the family – its concept of a shared future – the family's utopia and life plans.

When young people have children they wish to start a family that may – in their life plan – be described as the nuclear family. This aim is usually pursued with the personal utopia of a mostly harmonious, ideal typical family. The personal ideas of family are present when the family is founded. The life plans of couples are based on joint but at the same time sometimes very different historical foils from their own families of origin. When they join forces a new framework is introduced, within which the partners – or, if they have children, the family – live together. The discrepancy between the kinds of family the individual partners imagined they would have and how their family actually turns out to be forms a part of the family's identity.

Our society accepts various ways of life; various basic conditions for living together in intimacy and privacy are possible. The plurality of lifestyles mainly applies to the time before a couple has children (Bertram et al., 1993). Divorce rates reach a peak after the birth of the first child and after the last child has left home (Kraul et al., 2003). The period involving the children's socialization process is the time when the traditional nuclear family is at its most stable.

As far as various forms of living are concerned, couples seek relationships that correspond with the personal utopias of the individuals concerned. Often, alternatives to traditional family life offer individuals more freedom to balance their personal needs, for example the need for autonomy and the need for dependence upon a partner. For example, some couples cannot or do not choose to live together; they live in different locations and see each other only on weekends. Our modern world allows partnership and family constellations that would not have been possible in earlier times. Although such forms of living do not provide the same level of security as traditional models, they can offer greater potential for personal development and the fulfillment of relationship needs.

The Definition of Family Assessment

Family assessment is defined as follows:

> Family assessment examines and describes interactions and changes between the members of a family and its subsystems, and analyses family dynamics as a systemic whole. It examines the unconscious fantasies, wishes, and fears of the family against the background of family history and future life plans, in order to gain an insight into the significant interactive sequences and their functionality. (Cierpka, 1987, p. 2)

This definition contains several statements that play an important role in clinical family assessment:
1. The object of analysis is the interaction of the family members and changes in this interaction following intervention. In the first clinical interview a characteristic network of relationships is examined. This can be defined by means of a so-called structural picture of the family in a cross-sectional view (horizontal perspective).

The structure of the family is made up of individual, personal needs on the one hand and the demands of the family on the other.

2. However, families are not only defined in terms of current relationships in a cross-sectional view. All families have a past that goes back over several generations. This refers to family tradition and its cultural context. A family's background and history and life plans for the future are examined in a longitudinal section (vertical perspective). This is known as the multigenerational perspective.

3. Current family dynamics are characterized by the crossing over of the structural, horizontal perspective and the longitudinal, vertical perspectives. Every interaction is defined by the structure of the family and its history at a specific point in time, just as each interaction in its redundancy influences the structure of the family and its future. Carter and McGoldrick (1988) illustrate how the development-related demands that families are faced with, particularly during phases when changes in the lifecycle take place, are made up of both vertical (longitudinal) and horizontal (structural) stress factors. This stress model is just one explanation for the basic assumption that all processes relating to family dynamics are both structurally and historically determined.

4. The clinician looks for explanations for the behavior of the family members and the development of any crises within the family. Here again, the vertical and horizontal perspectives cross paths.

5. Family assessment must be carried out on at least three levels – on the level of the individuals, the level of dyads and triads and the level of the family system. Only if these various levels are taken into account can statements concerning the different weighting of individual, dyadic and familial factors be made. The family diagnostician must always bear these various levels in mind, as he must make assessments based on each individual level and interactions between it and the other levels.

6. Furthermore, the clinician must gain an insight into the family's embeddedness in the socio-cultural context in order to understand the values and norms that influence the family system. He or she must direct his attention towards the family's social network and the basic socio-cultural and economic conditions surrounding it.

References

Alexander, F., French, T., & Pollock, G. (1968). *Psychosomatic specifity*. Chicago: University Chicago Press.

Bastine, R. (1992). Klinische Psychodiagnostik [Clinical Psychodiagnosis]. In R. Bastine (Ed.), *Klinische Psychologie*, Band 2 [Clinical Psychology] (pp. 1–55). Stuttgart: Kohlhammer.

Baumann, U., & Stieglitz, R. D. (1994). Psychodiagnostik psychischer Störungen: Allgemeine Grundlagen [Psychodiagnosis of psychic disorders: General principles]. In R. D. Stieglitz & U. Baumann (Eds.), *Psychodiagnostik psychischer Störungen* [Psychodiagnosis of psychic disorders] (pp. 3–20)]. Stuttgart: Enke.

Bauriedl, T., Reich, G., Cierpka, M., & Neraal, T. (2002). Psychoanalytische Paar- und Familientherapie [Psychoanalytical couple and family therapy]. In M. Wirsching & P. Scheib (Eds.), *Lehrbuch der Familientherapie* [Textbook of family therapy] (pp. 79–106). Heidelberg: Springer.

Benjamin, L. S. (1974). A structural analysis of social behavior (SASB). *Psychological review, 81,* 392–425.

Bertram, H., Bayer, H., & Bauereiss, R. (1993). *Familien-Atlas. Lebenslagen und Regionen.* [Family atlas. Life circumstances and regions] Opladen: Leske & Budrich.

Carter, B., & McGoldrick, M. (1988). *The changing family life cycle* (2nd ed.). New York: Gardner Press.

Cierpka, M. (1987). (Ed.). *Familiendiagnostik* [Family diagnosis]. Heidelberg: Springer.

Cierpka, M. (1989). Das Problem der Spezifität in der Familientheorie [The problem of specificity in family theory]. *System Familie, 2,* 197–216.

Cierpka, M. (1991). Entwicklungen in der Familientherapie [Developments in family therapy]. *Praxis Psychotherapie und Psychosomatik, 36,* 32–44.

Cierpka, M. (2000). Diagnostik in der Familientherapie. In A.-R. Laireiter (Ed.), *Diagnostik in der Psychotherapie* [Diagnosis on psychotherapy] (pp. 217–234). Springer: Vienna.

Emnid-Institut. (2004). *Repräsentativerhebung* [Representative survey]. Bielefeld.

Engel, G. (1977). The need for a new medical model: A challenge for biomedicine. *Science, 196,* 129–136.

Freud, S. (1895f). *Zur Kritik der Angstneurose* [The problem of anxiety] (pp. 357–376], GW Vol. 1.

Frevert, G. (1992). *Der Dialog zwischen Therapeuten- und Familiensystem. Eine textanalytische Untersuchung von Familiengesprächen.* [The dialog between therapists and family system. A text analysis of family dialogs]. Unpublished dissertation, University of Ulm, Germany.

Grotevant, H. D., & Carlson, C. I. (1989). *Family assessment: A guide to methods and measures.* New York: Guilford.

Kaufmann, F.-X. (1994). *Die ökonomische und soziale Bedeutung der Familie* [The economic and social significance of the family]. Presented at the Symposium of the BmFSFJ "Zukunft der Familie" [The future of the family], Bonn, Germany.

Kraul, A., Ratzke, K., Reich, G., & Cierpka, M. (2003). Familiäre Lebenswelten [Familiar life worlds]. In M. Cierpka (Ed.), *Handbuch der Familiendiagnostik* (pp. 225–250). Heidelberg: Springer.

Laireiter, A.-R. (2001). Diagnostik in der Psychotherapie [Diagnosis in psychotherapy]. *Psychotherapeutiks, 46,* 90–101.

Laireiter, A.-R. (Ed.) (2000). *Diagnostik in der Psychotherapie* [Diagnosis in psychotherapy]. Vienna: Springer.

Minuchin, S., Rosman, B., & Baker, L. (1978). *Psychosomatische Krankheiten in der Familie* [Psychosomatic illnesses in the family]. Stuttgart: Klett-Cotta.

Schacht, T. E., & Strupp, H. H. (1984). *Psychotherapy outcome. Individualized is nice, but intelligible is beautiful.* Presentation at the Society for Psychotherapy Research Conference, Lake Louise, Canada.

Schiepek, G., Ludwig-Becker, F., Helde, A., Jagdfeld, F., Petzold, E. R., & Kröger, F. (2000). Synergetik für die Praxis [Synergetic for the praxis]. *System Familie, 13,* 169–177.

Schneewind, K. A. (1987). Das "Familiendiagnostische Testsystem" (FDTS). Ein Fragebogeninventar zur Erfassung familiärer Beziehungsaspekte auf unterschiedlichen Systemebenen [The"Family DiagnosisTest System" (FDTS). A questionnaire to ascertain aspects of family relationships on different system levels]. In M. Cierpka (Ed.), *Familiendiagnostik* (pp. 320–342). Berlin: Springer.

Sprenkle, D. H., & Moon, S. M. (2004). *Research methods in family therapy* (2nd ed.). New York: Guilford.

Stierlin, H. (1975). *Von der Psychoanalyse zur Familientherapie* [From psychoanalysis to family therapy]. Stuttgart: Klett-Cotta.

Stierlin, H. (2001). Welche Rolle spielt die Diagnostik in der systemischen Psychotherapie? [What role does diagnosis play in systemic psychotherapy]. *Psychotherapeutik, 46,* 134–139.

Stierlin, H., Weber, G., & Simon, F. B. (1986). Zur Familiendynamik bei manisch-depressiven und schizoaffektiven Psychosen [The family dynamics in manic-depressive and schizo-affective psychoses]. *Familiendynamik, 11,* 267–282.

Strupp, H. H. (1980). Success and failure in time-limited psychotherapy: A systematic comparison of two cases (Comparison I). *Archives of General Psychiatry, 37,* 595–603.

Strupp, H., Schacht, T., & Henry, W. (1988). Problem-treatment-outcome congruence: A principle whose time has come. In H. Dahl, H. Kächele, & H. Thomä (Eds), *Psychoanalytic process research strategies* (pp. 1–14). Berlin: Springer.

White, M., & Epston, D. (1990). *Narrative means to therapeutic ends*. Adelaide: Dulwich Centre Publication.

Wirsching, M., & Stierlin, H. (1982). *Krankheit und Familie* [Illness and the family]. Stuttgart: Klett-Cotta.

2

The Three-Level Model of Family Assessment

Manfred Cierpka

Summary

The three-level model in family diagnostics differentiates between the levels representing the individual, dyads or triads, and the family system. These levels are functional systems that may be organized and described according to certain dimensions (functions). In family diagnostics, various steps must be taken to determine the connections between the problem or symptom and interpersonal disorders within the family:

1. Each level must be assessed separately. The diagnostician must examine the family through different "pairs of glasses," i.e., from the point of view of various theoretical models.
2. The dimensions that are relevant for family diagnostics are assessed for functionality or dysfunctionality on each level.
3. The diagnostician must ascertain which interactive processes between the levels lead to the weakening or strengthening of dysfunctional processes on one or several levels.
4. For each complaint/problem/symptom/illness and for every patient, key concepts for the interfaces between individual, familial, and social factors must be identified and described.

The Levels of the Family

It has proven clinically useful to record phenomena on various system levels. At least three levels are relevant in family diagnostics – these levels relate to the individual, the dyad, and the family as a whole. As clinical experience shows, restricting a view to just a few levels implies simplifying complex situations in order to describe them. Of course, one must bear in mind that this procedure differentiates between systems that cannot really be viewed separately, as they are in a continual state of interaction with one another. Family life takes place on several parallel levels. This parallelism means that diagnosticians have to refocus their lenses according to the level they wish to view (Retzer, 1996). For example, if the therapist directs his or her attention towards intrapsychic structures on the level of the individual, he or she does so against a background of associations with superordinate systems such as dyadic or social processes. If the therapy concentrates on familial relationship patterns on the perspective of the system, the question also arises as to how the individual family members contribute to the maintenance of the system. The decision on which levels to focus in therapy is extremely relevant for the assessment process and for the selection of an appropriate setting (see Chapter 5).

What does *level* mean? The term denotes integrative levels or steps that differ from one another in the system-theoretical paradigm of systems of varying complexity. The universe can be described as a multitude of systems ordered in a hierarchy, whereby each "higher" or more advanced level consists of systems of lower or less advanced complexity (subsystems). The term level sounds static and unsuitable for the description of interactive processes in human systems. In fact, *levels* refer to systems that can be described in terms of their functions which distinguish them from other functional systems and which interact with one another. For example, on the one hand, the family system forms a part of a larger system (the surrounding community, society, culture) and, on the other hand, it is placed above the various subsystems beneath it (triads/dyads/the individual) in a hierarchical sense.

Theoretical views relating to system theory can be put to good use in the three-level model in family assessment, particularly first-degree cybernetics. This theory is particularly suitable for defining individual elements (levels) and placing these in their interactive setting in an overall, integrative system. These fundamental principles are based on the General-System-Theory[1] formulated by von Bertalanffy (1956, 1962) for living organisms. Bertalanffy describes the human being and other social institutions as open and dynamic systems that are in a continual state of exchange with their environment. Social entities are governed by the same principles of organization as simple organisms. Hall and Fagen (1956) define each system as a group of elements that is associated with other elements through relations, where the behavior of the elements is explained in terms of the relations rather than by the inherent characteristics of the individual elements (see Chapter 11). These characteristic relations between the elements of a subsystem lead to boundaries being drawn (differentiation) between themselves and other elements. These boundaries imply that the relations between the elements within one group are closer than its relations with the elements that lie outside of the boundary (Luhmann, 1984). The boundaries between groups of elements also demarcate "levels".

---

[1] The following fundamental principles are found in the GST (General-System-Theory):

1. Life is organised in organismic entities, governed by a holistic principle – the system as a whole has many conditional factors. Therefore biology, behavioural sciences and sociology are concerned with a multivariate system.
2. Complex phenomena are more than the sum of isolated causal chains. This holistic principle was taken from form psychology.
3. Consequently, not only individual parts of an organismic system must be investigated but also the relationships between the components. These relationships are considered to be system constituents.
4. Living organisms are basically seen as "open systems". i.e., they exchange information and energy with the environment. Only open systems are in a position to adapt to environmental changes and remain functional.

This theory, which originally related mainly to biology, was influenced by interdisciplinary, particularly philosophical trains of thought during the course of the 1950s, and became integrated in the definition of social systems. Finally in the 1960s in America it was adopted by family therapy research in Palo Alto (Bateson, Watzlawick et al.).

Miller (1978) names seven organizational levels relating to living systems, whose structural similarities give rise to a hierarchical order – cell, organ, organism, organization, group, society, supranational systems. Scheflen (1981) follows on from this concept, elaborating the ideas on each of these levels using the example of dysfunctional processes and interaction in schizophrenic illnesses. Dysfunctionality culminates synergistically at the outbreak of the illness. This means that, as far as such processes on several levels are concerned, therapists are ill-advised to concentrate on one level only, for example by using psychopharmacological treatment alone. It is essential to consider various levels simultaneously.

For several reasons, it is justifiable to divide the various functional systems within families into three levels. As Simmel (1922) pointed out in his sociological research, the family plays an important mediatory role between the individual and society. Simmel describes a structure consisting of three parts – the individual, the family, and society. He also specifies the dual role of the family – on the one hand it is an extension of one's own personality, a unit, and on the other hand it is a complex in which each individual is different from all the others (p. 537).

In psychoanalytical literature, Balint (1957) identifies the three levels arising from the dual union between mother and child. In a point of view that is centered around the individual, he follows on from an idea formed by Rickman (1951), envisaging a splitting of the human soul into three parts based on the number of its relationships with the object world: a) the relationship involving one person or the intrapsychic level, b) the relationship involving two persons, i.e., the dyad, and c) the relationship involving three or more persons.

In family therapy, structural family therapy (Minuchin, 1974; Minuchin & Fishman, 1981) particularly stresses that the structure of the family is hierarchical in nature. This applies to the differences in the roles of parents as opposed to children and resultant family rules. The various rules come into play as far as the assertion of authority and influence is concerned, for example, and contribute to a distinction being made between the hierarchical levels. The differences between the assignment of roles and role behavior serve to differentiate between the three levels. The recurrence of certain interactive patterns points towards rules that are inherent to the structure and whose redundancy governs the structure of the various levels.

In family research, it has also proved useful to assume a division of the family organization into three hierarchical levels (Gurman & Kniskern, 1978a, 1978b; Cromwell & Peterson, 1983; Steinhauer et al., 1984; Cierpka, 1987, 1990; Skinner et al., 2000).

> To summarize, it may be said that the three-level model in family assessment is well founded as a heuristic guideline, and serves to illustrate various functions. Distinctions are made between the individual, the dyadic or triadic levels and the dynamics of the system as a whole, which are organized in a hierarchical fashion. When using this type of model, which reduces the complexity of the overall situation, one must always bear in mind the fact that the family is embedded in a socio-cultural context. Environmental circumstances must be taken into consideration and treated to some degree as an additional functional system.

The biological processes of the organism are an independent, active system that influences its environment and its own contextual circumstances. Seen in a historical perspective, the interactive processes between the organism and the psychosocial processes in family therapy were neglected for a long period of time. Minuchin's theory on the "psychosomatic family" is one of the most influential, most frequently quoted works in family therapy. In this book, the child psychiatrist Minuchin, the psychologist Rosman and the psychiatrist Baker present their experiences in the treatment of children with diabetes mellitus, bronchial asthma, and later anorexia nervosa. They then develop a model to explain the dysfunctionality of families in which a young person has developed a psychosomatic illness (Minuchin et al., 1978). Continuing on from this, Wood (1991, 1994) presents a theoretical model of the psychosomatic family within a broader framework. She names her concept the "bio-psychosocial developmental model." Here, the fact that psyche and body are seen as a united entity is emphasized in the original term of *psychosomatics*. The model is less disorder-oriented and contains relevant individual developmental psychological factors and other social context variables such as the influence of schools. All these factors contribute to the well-being of the child and the family in interactive processes.

Psychosomatic models are concerned with the problem of the relationship between the organism and its environment. Models such as Freud's concept of drives and Pawlow's theory of behavioral conditioning show that psychic phenomena can be coupled with physical ones. The concept of the various levels gains greater relevance when the question of the interconnection between biological, psychological, and social processes is raised. The interactive processes of these multi-level models in the event of individuals developing illnesses or being restored to health are addressed in Engel's (1977) developmental *biopsychosocial model* or in the *situation circle* by von Uexküll (1986). In these models the individual as a biopsychosocial being is seen as one component of an extensive complex of systems; however it is also in itself a system consisting of many subsystems.

The diagnostic concepts and therapeutic theories found in bio-psychosocially oriented medicine are governed by many factors and linked together in an integral system. Biological, psychological, and social factors should be seen as synergetic in relation to processes of human maturing and growth, but also with regard to the pathogenesis of disorders.

Co-Evolving Development in Relationship Systems

The development of relationship systems is largely subject to individual growth and processes of psychic maturing. For example, the life cycle determines an individual's existence and often also family life. Individual experiential development is only possible in association with contextual development. Through experiences made within one's own family, an impression of childhood becomes engraved on one's memory. These experiences influence what is known as the family feeling (Cierpka, 1992). Family experiences are internalized to form family representations that go hand in hand with the acquisition of family feeling. We are unconsciously guided by these internalized experiences made in our family of origin when founding a family of our own in later life. The theory behind the acquisition of family feeling also makes use of systems theory, for example to describe contextualization in the development of the sphere of relationships of a child in a kind of open system.

The individual intuitively seeks the contexts he or she needs in order to develop. Research shows that the experiences necessary for a child's development in relation to his or her primary persons of reference, usually the family, are gained during the first three years of life (to a lesser degree up to the age of 16). These developments alone demand continual reorganization on the part of the family system – it is continually faced with specific developmental tasks. At the same time, changes within the family also influence individual experiential development, including neurobiological maturing processes (Roth, 2001).

Organizational processes in families, partnerships, and individuals can be described using the model of co-evolution (Willi, 1985) and the theory of autopoiesis (Maturana & Varela, 1980). Maturana assumes the existence of a structural "union" between the environment (external world) and the psyche (internal world) in as far as that these areas mutually interact with one other. He stresses the importance of the interaction of these functional procedures in a circular understanding between the systems. The family may also be viewed as a self-organizing system in terms of the co-evolution of several members in a structural union with its socio-cultural context. The image chosen to demonstrate the process of co-evolution is usually a spiral, symbolizing the fact that processes give rise to one another, mutually influence one another, and, most importantly, are able to regenerate themselves. This characteristic is described as *autopoiesis* (Greek = "self-creation").

Living systems are also subject to rhythms and non-linear processes of change, although the system always tries to organize itself and strives towards stability. One characteristic of non-linear systems is that a small change in one of the variables – particularly in its original state – effects the other variables and their changes in a way that is often quite out of proportion and unforeseeable. Non-linear systems are also created by the interaction of several variables. This interaction can amplify, weaken, or cancel out the function of the first variables.

Clinicians following the bio-psychosocial model attempt to define dysfunctional processes on biomedical, psychological, and social levels. If dysfunctionalities on these various levels reinforce one another, so that disorders or illnesses arise or are sustained, the processes are said to be co-evolving. However, components can only be said to codetermine one another in a co-evolving process if they fit together like a lock and key – this is why we speak of key concepts (Cierpka et al., 1998). Patterns emerging as a result of interaction between dysfunctional components and the co-evolving process change the structure of the systems; this can be observed, for example, when an acute illness begins to become chronic. In the course of time and through repetition the new bio-psychosocial patterns are given a new meaning, which helps to stabilize them. For each problem or symptom therapists require a developmental model, characterized by completely different dysfunctional processes.

> The assessment process must define not only the functional systems, but also all interactive processes between them. Parts of the whole (the levels) must be assessed but also – more importantly – the interaction among them. This interaction can serve to amplify or weaken the functions of a level.

Family Assessment Using the Three-Level Model

Strauss (1973) preferred to use a dimensional model rather than the topographical assessment model for the purposes of individual assessment. The dimensional view allows therapists to evaluate a family more or less separately from the individual and his or her symptoms. Families are classified along a continuum with respect to strengths and weaknesses. The strengths and weaknesses appear to varying degrees on the various dimensions, so that a profile can be drawn up providing a description of any family or even groups of families. The classification of a family is based on multidimensional observations. When groups of families are categorized according to the functionality or dysfunctionality of the dimensions, family types emerge. Fisher's (1977) research was based on the dimensional definition of strengths and weaknesses in families. He was able to show that family typologies arising in this way do not depend upon medical diagnostic classification systems.

The dimensional model is also used in this handbook of family assessment. However it only partly solves the problem of the classification of healthy and unhealthy; this problem rather tends to become displaced. In most cases, a second step is required, in which cut-off values are determined to mark the transition from functionality to dysfunctionality on the dimensions.

The relevant dimensions are the *functions* that contribute to self-organization on each level and characterize the functional system. The paradigm of self-organization is particularly appropriate for explaining these processes (Schiepek, 1999).

The functional perspective is crucial in assessment. The following questions for diagnosis should be asked – which functions are necessary on each level, in order to maintain the respective functional system? How can these functions be qualified and quantified with regard to functionality and dysfunctionality?

For family assessment this means that the relevant dimensions (functions) on each level must be identified, described, assessed, and then judged with regard to functionality or dysfunctionality. In the three-level model, this implies four large complexes of questions for assessment:

1. How does the individual organize himself or herself within the system of relationships?
2. How are the dyadic or triadic relationships organized within the family?
3. How does the family organize itself as a family?
4. How does the family organize itself within the context of social surroundings and society?

Below, this procedure is examined more closely for each of the separate levels. In a further step, the interactive processes are examined at the connecting points between the levels, which can be said to be responsible for the development, maintenance, and solving of a problem.

How does the individual organize himself or herself within his system of relationships?

The individual is in a constant state of exchange with the environment, both in a physical and in a psychological sense. The human child, more than any other living being, is dependent on persons of reference for a long period of psychological and physical maturing. Each individual also has his/her own specific characteristics (e.g., temperament) that also influence the family and contribute towards family dynamics. Organism-related circumstances (e.g., physical stability and health or the plasticity of the neuronal networks in the brain) play quite a considerable role. Today, the interaction between nature and nurture is taken far more seriously than in times gone by. Genetic conditions seem to be a given standard, the construction and coding of the human genome has been decoded. Which genes express effects at what point in time is triggered by environmental stimuli and surrounding circumstances, so that the interaction between the individual and the immediate and most important environment, i.e., the family, is extremely important for the development of the organism, even for neuronal networks and the structures of the brain. In the case of illness, the object of medical somatic diagnosis is to examine physical functions.

The theories of individual psychology describe the cognitive (intelligence, giftedness, attentiveness, concentration, fantasies, etc.), emotional (e.g., emotional strength, affective patterns, anxiety level etc.), and motivational (visions of the future, aims, expectations, values, wishes, interests) aspects of the individual. The individuals who make up a family differ from one another on these dimensions. The dimensions can be diagnosed on the level of the individual with the help of various theories (e.g., theory of learning, behavioral theory, cognitive psychology, affect theory; see Laireiter, 2000).

The psychoanalytical view describes the internal psychic world of the individual, which develops through interactions with the primary persons of reference, usually the parents, in childhood and is in a state of constant exchange with the environment throughout his or her life. By developing representations as internalizations of relational experience and all learning processes, the child conquers the world; at the same time it also becomes part of the world. Psychoanalysis asks how the structure of the intrapsychic world in these representations, which can also be grouped together and called the self, functions in interaction with the environment ("objects").

Dimensional descriptions of the individual can be qualified and quantified. The diagnostic instrument known as Operationalized Psychodynamic Diagnostics (OPD Task Force, 2000), for example, can be used to describe relational behavior, intrapsychic conflicts, and the structural level of the psychic processes in an individual, always from the perspective of a continual exchange process between the internal and external world. Internal conflicts and the internal structure can be recorded only in terms of communication with others on an interactive level. Internal conflicts, for example, influence the relationships within a family, where they may be observed as interactive strategies. The structure axis of OPD allows a definition of the *structural level* to be made, which indicates the functional quality of the self in interaction with objects (e.g., other members of the family). The intrapsychic structure may be understood as a disposition of experience and behavior that is typical for an individual. The given structural patterns manifest themselves in interactive behavior, where they become visible for others.

How are dyadic and triadic relationships organized within the family?

Slow motion films can be made of dialogic interactive behavior between partners, with the aim of showing the intuitive synchronization processes that take place within a dyad. In these films a subtle dance between the speaker and the listener can be observed, a rhythmic movement from one partner to the other, as if a detailed choreography were at work. This choreography can perhaps be most clearly observed between mother and child, as Stern (1985) pointed out in his research on dyads and Fivaz-Depeursinge and Corboz-Warnery (1999) on familial triads. The observer has the impression of seeing a single organism, two or three different autonomous individuals who are dependent upon one another to such a degree that they seem to form a whole. Research shows what an important part affect of the interactive partners play in interpersonal synchronization (Krause & Merten, 1999). Clinically relevant affect – which can also be read from facial expressions – include interest, surprise, joy, anger, disgust, sadness, and shame. The affective system, like the attachment seeking behavior, is already biologically present at birth. However interactive strategies guided by affect, which work on an unconscious level, are developed within the context of the early relationship between mother and child. Sander (1985) speaks of a system consisting of child and person of reference, which has its own unique configuration and regulation. This special system governs the child's ability to gain access to the consciousness of its own inner states, its internal experiences and activities, so as to organize self-regulatory behavior. These configurations subsequently become a repertoire of lasting co-ordination and adaptation strategies, which, in their turn, can be repeated and recognized in relationships with others. Internal psychic representations are linked with the internalized experiences of this early relationship (so-called RIGs = representations of interactions that have been generalized"; Stern, 1985) and are stored in the episodic memory. RIGS have a significant effect on relationship behavior and experience in adulthood, in that the individual tries to repeat central relationship themes with other partners in a process of transference (Luborsky & Crits-Christoph, 1990; Stasch et al., 2002). In this way, experiences from early childhood are continually repeated and confirmed via other experiences. These patterns can characterize the behavior of an individual for his or her whole life. Since the beginning of the 1970s, many researchers and clinicians have worked on projects to find systematic formulations for the description or illustration of interpersonal problems, particularly individual psychotherapeutic therapist-patient constellations (overview available from Schauenburg & Cierpka, 1994). All procedures assume the existence of one or perhaps several interpersonal patterns in lasting relationships.

The assessment of dyads and triads in family assessment is extremely interesting. Family therapy has many concepts at its disposal in this area. A clinical assessment of dyads is made on the basis of schools of thought in family therapy and ranges from communication analysis to the search for unconscious collusion.

The assessment of a partnership or a relationship between parents is a vital aspect of family assessment. Concurrence in the parents' methods and aims in bringing up children can be identified and examined (see Chapter 10). The diagnostic methods available cannot be described in detail here; a separate handbook would have to be written to accommodate them. Summaries can be found under Hiebert, 1993; Gottman, 1995; Groth-Marnat, 2003; Sperry, 2004; Sprenkle and Moon, 2004.

The sibling dyads and the dyads consisting of one parent and one child (mother and child or father and child) must also be taken into consideration; they can differ considerably from the dyads consisting of the same parent and another child. Research projects in the field of behavioral genetics (reviews by Joraschky & Cierpka, 1990; Hetherington et al., 1994) are concerned with genetic and psychosocial factors in connection with the contraction of illnesses. Here it could be shown that the majority of variance in environmental factors was due to the children's non-shared environment variables. The dyadic experiences of a child are evidently highly specific. Dyadic experiences are also crucial to how a child develops within a family. These experiences point towards the fact that dyads within a family are almost as different as dyads consisting of individuals from completely different families.

How are triads organized within families? Human relationships have a basic triangular form; at just a few weeks old, babies are able to form relationships with both parents as well as other persons, whom they are able to distinguish from one another and store in the form of memory available to them. These representations of triadic patterns guide relationship strategies in relationships involving several people to a considerable extent. Family therapists with a psychodynamic orientation examine triadic relationship patterns and the solving of triangular conflicts against a background of oedipal theories (see Bauriedl et al., 2002).

Psychoanalytic concept formation describes developmental processes in dyadic and triadic systems. However these processes do not provide a full picture of family dynamics. One should point out the narrowing that occurs in psychoanalysis if the family is seen only as the nuclear family, i.e., the father-mother-child triangle. Sibling relationships, peer relationships, and the influence of secondary socialization institutions such as schools or career training centers are often disregarded. The areas and relationship contexts that tend to be ignored are those related to the process of exchange between society and the family. Social embeddedness is threatening to become obsolete; the focus on the nuclear family sometimes appears to be a kind of cut-out construct in psychoanalytical theory formulation.

How Is the Family Organized as a System?

How does a family work? What should a family provide? In order to identify the central dimensions and functions that allow a family to organize itself as a system, we must first ask ourselves what the obligations of a family are. It performs several tasks:

Coping with Everyday Life

First and foremost, a family must provide for itself in a material sense, i.e., food, protection, health, etc. The family normally provides a child with the context for somatic integrity (nature) and emotional security (nurture). The family provides a cohesive atmosphere that enables the family members to live together.

Allowing the Development of the Individual While Respecting the Family as a Whole

A central task of the family is to supply a child with the conditions it needs to mature and psychically develop in a satisfactory way. The family member is provided with the supportive environmental conditions it needs to mature in the best possible way (Winnicott, 1974). Psychological processes of development and growth that are favorable for a child contribute largely to its psychic stability in adulthood (Johnson et al., 1999; Felitti, 2002).

Today we still agree with Erikson's (1968) assumption that an individual continues to develop throughout life. The family must be in a position to accommodate for these changes. A "functional" family fulfils its function when it fulfils its developmental tasks, i.e., enabling the child or young person to achieve the maturity and psychic growth it requires to master transitional situations (first steps towards independence at pre-school and school, changes during adolescence, leaving the family home). When "dysfunctional" families fulfill these tasks to an unsatisfactory degree, family members are not provided with the developmental opportunities appropriate to their age group.

Living Together in Intimacy

Families are characterized by togetherness over the generations. Ideally, the family – usually the parents and children – live together in an atmosphere of intimate togetherness. There is generally no other way of life that offers such a high degree of security, affect tolerance, and possibilities for regression.

The fulfillment of tasks may be operationalized on various dimensions. Against a background of various family theoretical ideas, several process models form categories that allow statements to be made on the functionality of this dimension. For example, Beavers and his colleagues aimed to develop a process model to distinguish between "clinical" and "normal" families (Beavers, 1982; Beavers & Voeller, 1983; Beavers, Hampson, & Hulgus, 1985). The Beavers Interaction Scales refer to two basic dimensions: family competence and family style (centripetal or centrifugal family style). Family competence describes how a family is organized as an interactive unit. The assessment of a family's competence leads to a statement on the resources, i.e., abilities, available within a family.

The Process Model of Family Functioning (Steinhauer et al., 1984) investigates seven dimensions to operationalize how a family is organized as a family, giving individuals the freedom to develop without endangering the maintenance of the family as a whole. A successful mastery of tasks demands the *differentiation of roles* within a family and consequently the willingness of family members to assimilate the roles assigned to them. For the assignment and performance of roles, effective *communication* is required. The intensity of feelings, *emotionality,* can either hinder communication or contribute to a successful fulfillment of roles. The emotional interest of the individual family members for one another is expressed in the dimension *affective involvement*. The process by which individual family members influence one another is described as *control*. Family members should be able to reliably maintain certain functions, while being ready to change others in a more flexible way. Social *values* and *norms* are adopted by the family and take effect on all of these dimensions.

Can the functionality or dysfunctionality of these dimensions of the various process models be quantified? Is it possible to assess the degree of a disorder or a "structural plane" in these function systems?

The functionality of the family system may be linked with the question of *how* the development and maturation of the individual is realized alongside the coevolving development of the family. According to the degree to which basic functions are secured, allowing psychic growth or psychic maturing of the individual on the one hand and family life to develop on the other, the degree of disorder or structural plane can be examined and thus quantified. The structural plane is made up of the relation between functionality and dysfunctionality. The question of how, e.g., the need for attachment and affective togetherness with the highest possible level of security can be guaranteed within a family can be answered using the dimensions of the Process Model of Family Functioning. The structural plane is derived from how well, how efficiently, how appropriately the family functions on the dimensions of "emotionality" and "affective involvement." Strengths and weaknesses are assessed for each dimension and then quantified and graphically represented, e.g., in a profile. Rating instruments or questionnaires can be used in family interviews and for research purposes to define the degree of functionality/dysfunctionality (Grotevant & Carlson, 1989; Skinner et al., 2000).

How Is the Family Organized Within the Social Context?

Families are embedded in the social context of the neighborhood, the community, the town, and in wider cultural and social contexts. The family must be able to adapt to its environment, or find favorable environmental circumstances that allow it to develop in an atmosphere of fruitful exchange. However the family itself is also a basic unit of society and develops values and norms that are assimilated by society. Values and norms continue as part of family tradition over the generations. This is especially true of moral and religious standards, which determine what is morally or ethically acceptable. The aims and standards of a family are derived from this. Many of these moral or religiously influenced values are reflected in the (explicitly or implicitly formulated) set of family rules. The norms of a family describe, in a cross-section, the sum of the values that it considers acceptable. This lays down the minimum standard requirements for the individual family members. Thus, individuation processes are influenced by these norm values, for example the time of life at which detachment is considered acceptable varies greatly from family to family. The age at which people get married also depends on familiar and socio-cultural ideas. This is reminiscent of the interrelation of identification and emotional attachment as described by Freud (1923). Interrelating identification assumes the existence of joint ideals within the family that are recognized and shared by all family members. In a multicultural society, family assessment must always take the values and norms of a family into consideration.

A family is a part of society, but also an independent entity. The level of the "family as a whole" includes the organization of family functions contributing to its independence and distinguishing it from other families. From a sociological point of view, families are small groups. Sociological and socio-psychological theories describe the role behavior or organization of small groups. Families differ from other small groups in view of the so-called multigenerational perspective and the biologically common ground it infers. Families have their own history that is linked with ideologies, certain values and norms, but also with family myths. Of course, family members are bound to one another not only because of their past but also through the life context they share in the present. The material as well as the psychic needs of the family members must be satisfied to a satisfactory degree.

System therapists examine the communication process, family rules, self-organization processes, or the constructions of family reality within a given context. They emphasize that families can never be seen independently from their environmental circumstances. According to the basic family theory used, they describe the dimensions that are relevant for this level. They ask themselves how a family is organized within the social context and how it differs from its surroundings.

The familial system can be very open (centrifugal, detached) or very withdrawn (centripetal, rigidly enmeshed) towards its environment. Other more empirically oriented family researchers describe the state of these system features using the familial dimensions of cohesion and adaptability. Olson (1983) developed a model defining cohesion as the emotional bonding of the family members. Olson uses the term enmeshment to describe an extremely high level of cohesion that causes over-identification with the family and stands in the way of the family members' individuation. Extremely low cohesion is characterized by the unrelatedness of the family members and is known as disengagement. Between these two poles lie the areas of separateness and closeness, which describe forms of more or less appropriate emotional relationships between the members of a family.

Adaptability is the name given by Olson (1983) to the ability of a couple or a family system to change its power structures, role relationships, and relationship rules according to the level of situational and developmental stress. This dimension is essentially based on the concept of "dynamic change" (Olson 1983, p.77), moving along a continuum of morphogenesis (gradual change) to morphostasis (no change, stability).

Interfaces and Connections Between the Levels

Up to now, we have not been concerned with the interactive processes between the levels. In a conceptualization of the theoretical connections between the levels representing individual, dyad, family, and external world/society, we continue on from a description of the dimensions themselves to examine the interactions between them. In order to make statements concerning these interfaces it is necessary to consult and partly to integrate various theoretical approaches. A pluralistic approach is the only way to deal with the complexity of the family and the interactive associations between the levels.

Some psychoanalysts have made links between the individual-oriented theory of psychoanalysis and systemic concepts, in an attempt to understand the individual within the context of the relationship systems in which he or she lives. Particularly Bowen (1965) and then Marmor (1975), Havens (1973), Slipp (1980), Flomenhaft and Christ (1980), Kantor (1980), Framo (1981), and Steinhauer (1984, 1986) call for a homogenous conceptual framework that allows room for differing theoretical ideas. In Germany Fürstenau (1992, 2001) and Buchholz (1990a, 1990b, 1993) have suggested the acceptance of an integrative viewpoint for psychotherapeutic treatment.

Steinhauer (1986) speaks of an "interface" at the meeting point of two different levels. For example he names interfaces in the intrapsychic area between the ego and the superego, on the interpersonal level between man and woman, parents and children, or between the family and the environment.

Generally the control functions of these interfaces, which protect the boundaries between the systems, are in a state of balance. In this equilibrium no energies are released that press for changes to be made. There is no consciousness of tension and subjective, experienced anxiety. For example, the intrapsychically determined demands of one family member on another do not represent a problem as long as these wishes are fulfilled by the other person and all the remaining family members are in consent.

As may be expected, disorders in the balance of a system that lead to tension at the interfaces with other systems and to changes in the balance of the control functions can cause strain on the neighboring systems (Steinhauer & Tisdall, 1984). If these disorders are not corrected, they must be compensated for by the systems that are higher in the hierarchy. A father with a severe depression where neurobiological causes are suspected will place a strain on other subsystems in the family (e.g., the marriage), although his problem is primarily an individual one. This kind of functional disorder, if lasting and severe, can lead to changes in the family structure on another, more complex level; the family must adapt to the situation. The model of the interfaces between the levels allows clinical statements to be made relating to the indication, as the identification of dysfunctionality on the various levels is a vital factor in deciding which setting should be used in therapy (see Chapter 5).

Key Concepts

The mysterious leap in the body-mind problem leads us to the question of how psychic processes influence physical ones and vice-versa. As described above, the study of psychosomatics has produced several theoretical models relating to this question (see e.g., von Uexkuell, 1986; McDaniel et al., 1992). For every psychosomatic illness a developmental model of the disorder is required, characterized by the various dysfunctional processes it implies.

The interfaces between biological and psychological factors should be understood in terms of feedback processes between the family system and the immunological and endocrinological parameters of the human being, using systems theory. For example, family dynamics resulting in stressful life events influence the immune status, manifesting themselves in the form of a higher incidence of infections and neoplasm (Ramsey, 1989; Cierpka et al., 2001). In endocrine feedback cycles, family dynamics stimulate information processes, from the brain to humorally governed end organs. Family conflicts act as stress stimuli, influencing metabolism, growth, and reproduction processes.

In this procedure, which consists of several steps, it is essential to consider the symptom context. Of primary interest are determinants that may have triggered, aggravated, or stopped the physical symptoms at a certain point in the developmental history of the individual or family. Only in this way, by identifying and processing the factors that release the problem, can the clinician gain a practical view of the key concepts.

The influence of psychological parameters on biological factors may be illustrated using the example of the emergence of atopic illnesses in small children. A high percentage of cases of atopic dermatitis break out during early infancy, which means that the family is faced with considerable problems in dealing with the child's symptoms right at the beginning of the familial life cycle. This happens at a time when the demands on the family system's adaptability are at their highest, i.e., at the interchange between partnership and becoming a family (in the case of a first child). The treatment of the child demands a relatively high level of care. Medication must be given; cream must be applied to the child's skin at regular intervals. Often, a special diet must be adhered to or the child must be kept away from allergens. For the parents, who are sometimes still young themselves, this implies a high level of responsibility. Presumably functional families who are not under a great deal of stress in other areas are more capable of providing this intensive medical care.

Studies have proven that emotional strain and familial stress cause the child to scratch more, which can make the condition worse (Jordan & Whitlock, 1972; Faulstich et al., 1985; Faulstich & Williamson, 1985). For example if the autonomous level of activation is changed, disorders of the vascular microcirculation arise, which in turn exacerbate itching and scratching. On the other hand, the chronic disease and the child's worsening symptoms represent a great strain on the family, which can again influence the individual as described above, resulting in a vicious circle.

This model for family assessment on several levels comprises a number of statements that are relevant for the *weighting* of various factors when problems and symptoms develop or persist:

- Individual psychological and/or biological factors can be in the foreground when assessing dysfunctionality on the various levels, whilst familial dimensions appear impressively strong. In such cases, the family can help in coping with the disorder of the individual family member. Resource-oriented family medical strategy (McDaniel et al., 1992, 1997; Cierpka et al., 2001) is based on the modus of individual biomedical pathology becoming weakened when the partners or the family take over the task of providing the patient with new solutions.

- On the other hand, dysfunctional family dynamics can be in the foreground, while the individual appears largely healthy. In this case an indication for family interviews or family therapy should be made in order to provide the individual with new developmental opportunities.
- Other interactive processes and key concepts should be defined for interfaces with the social environment.
- Individual, partnership, familial, and social factors can reinforce one another in processes of escalation. In such cases, intervention should be directed at as many factors as possible on various levels, with the aim of achieving synergetic effects.

References

Balint, M. (1957). *Problems of human pleasure and behaviour*. London: Hogarth.

Bauriedl, Th., Reich, G., Cierpka, M., & Neraal, T. (2002). Psychoanalytische Paar- und Familientherapie [Psychoanalytical couple and family therapy]. In M. Wirsching (Ed.), *Lehrbuch der Familientherapie* (pp. 79–106). Heidelberg: Springer.

Beavers, W. R. (1982). Healthy, midrange, and severely dysfunctional families. In F. Walsh (Ed.), *Normal family processes* (1st ed.) (pp.45–66). New York: Guilford Press.

Beavers, W. R, Hampson, R. B., & Hulgus, J. F. (1985). Commentary: The Beavers Systems approach to family assessment. *Family Process, 24,* 398–405.

Beavers, W. R., & Voeller, M. (1983). Family models. Comparing the Olson Circumplex Model with the Beavers Systems Model. *Family Process, 22,* 85–98.

Bertalanffy, L., von (1956). General system theory. *General Systems, 1,* 1–10.

Bertalanffy, L., von (1962). *General system theory – A critical review. General Systems,* 7, 1–20.

Bowen, M. (1965). Family psychotherapy with schizophrenia in the hospital and private practice. In I. Boszormnyi-Nagy & J. Framo (Eds), *Intensive family therapy*. New York: Harper & Row.

Buchholz, M. B. (1990). Die Rotation der Triade [Rotation of triades]. *Forum Psychoanal, 6,* 116–134.

Buchholz, M. B. (1990). *Die unbewußte Familie. Psychoanalytische Studien zur Familie in der Moderne* [The unconscious family. Psychoanalytical studies of families in modernism]. Berlin: Springer.

Buchholz, M. B. (1993). *Dreiecksgeschichten* [Triangular histories]. Göttingen: Vandenhoeck & Ruprecht.

Cierpka, M. (1987). (Ed.). *Familiendiagnostik* [Family diagnosis]. Heidelberg: Springer.

Cierpka, M. (1990). *Zur Diagnostik von Familien mit einem schizophrenen Jugendlichen* [Diagnosis of families with a schizophrenic adolescent]. Heidelberg: Springer.

Cierpka, M. (1992). Zur Entwicklung des Familiengefühls [The development of family feelings]. *Forum der Psychoanalyse, 8,* 32–46.

Cierpka, M. (2001). Geschwisterbeziehungen aus familientherapeutischer Perspektive –

Unterstützung, Bindung, Rivalität und Neid [Sibling relationships from a family therapy perspective – Support, attachment, rivalry, and envy]. *Prax. Kinderpsychol. Kinderpsychiat., 50,* 440–453.

Cierpka, M. (2002). Organisiationsprozesse und ihre Funktionalität in Familien [Organistion processes and their functionality in families]. In G. Rudolf (Ed.), *Die Struktur der Persönlichkeit* (pp. 145–156). Stuttgart: Schattauer.

Cierpka, M., Krebeck, S., & Retzlaff, R. (2001). *Arzt, Patient und Familie* [Doctor, patient and family]. Stuttgart: Klett-Cotta..

Cierpka, M., Reich, G., & Kraul, A. (1998). Psychosomatic medicine and family psychopathology. In G. L'Abate (Ed.), *Handbook of family psychopathology* (pp. 311–332). New York: Guilford Press.

Cromwell, R. E., & Peterson, G. W. (1983). Multisystem-multimethod family assessment in clinical contexts. *Family Process, 22,* 147–163.

Egle, U., & Cierpka, M. (1991). *Die Bedeutung von sozialer Situation und familiärer Interaktion für Ätiopathogenese, Verlauf und Prognose atopischer Erkrankungen bei Kleinkindern* [The significance of social situation and familial interaction for etiopathology: Course and prognosis of atopic illness in small children]. Unpublished research project, University of Mainz, Germany.

Engel, G. (1977). The need for a new medical model: A challenge for biomedicine. *Science, 196,* 129–136.

Erikson, E. H. (1968). *Identity. Youth and crisis.* New York: Norton.

Faulstich, M. E., & Williamson, D. A. (1985). An overview of atopic dermatits: Towards a bio-behavioral integration. *Journal of Psychosomatic Research, 29,* 647–654

Faulstich, M. E., Williamson, D. A., Duchmann, E. G., Conerly, S. C., & Brantley, P. J. (1985). Psychophysiological analysis of atopic dermatitis. *Journal of Psychosomatic Research, 29,* 415–417.

Felitti, V. J. (2002). The relationship of adverse childhood experiences to adult health: Turning gold into lead. *Z Psychosom Med Psychother, 48,* 359–69.

Fisher, L. (1977). On the classification of families. *Archives of General Psychiatry, 34,* 424–433

Fivaz-Depeursinge, E., & Corboz-Warnery, A. (1999). *The primary triangle.* New York: Basic Behavioral Science.

Flomenhaft, K., & Christ, A. E, (1980). *The challenge of family therapy: A dialogue for child psychiatric educators.* New York: Plenum Press.

Framo, J. L. (1981). The integration of marital therapy with sessions with family of origin. In A. S. Gurman & D. P. Kniskern (Eds.), *Handbook of family therapy.* New York: Brunner-Mazel.

Freud, S. (1923). *Das Ich und das Es* [The ego and the id]. *Gesammelte Werke, Band 13* (Vol. pp. 235–289). Frankfurt: Fisher.

Fürstenau, P. (1992). *Entwicklungsförderung durch Therapie. Grundlagen psychoanalytisch-systemischer Therapie* [Developmental promotion through therapy. The basic principles of psychoanalytical-systematic therapy]. München: Pfeiffer.

Fürstenau, P. (2001). *Psychoanalytisch verstehen, Systemisch denken, suggestiv intervenieren* [Psychoanalytical understanding, systemic thinking, suggestive intervention]. München: Pfeiffer.

Gottman, J. (1995). *Why marriages succeed or fail: And how you can make yours last.* New York: Simon & Schuster.

Grotevant, H. D., & Carlson, C. I. (1989). *Family assessment: A guide to methods and measures*. New York: Guilford.

Groth-Marnat, G. (2003). *Handbook of Psychological Assessment*. New York: Wiley.

Gurman, A. S., & Kniskern, D. P. (1978). Deterioration in marital and family therapy. Empirical, clinical and conceptual issues. *Family Process, 17*, 3–20.

Hall, A., & Fagen, R. (1956). Definition of systems. In v. L. Bertalanffy, & A. Rapaport, (Eds.), *General systems yearbook*. Ann Arbor, MI: University of Michigan Press.

Havens, L. L. (1973). *Approaches to the mind*. Boston: Little Brown.

Hetherington, E. M., Reiss, D., & Plomin, R. (1994). Separate social worlds of siblings: The impact of nonshared environment on development. Hillsdale, NJ: Lawrence Erlbaum.

Hiebert, W. J. (1993). *Dynamic assessment in couple therapy*. New York: Lexington Books.

Johnson, J. G., Cohen, P., Brown, J., Smailes, E. M., & Bernstein, D. P. (1999). Childhood maltreatment increases risk for personality disorders during early adulthood. *Archives of General Psychiatry, 56*, 600–606.

Joraschky, P., & Cierpka, M. (1990). Von der geteilten zur nichtgeteilten Konstruktion der Realität [The divided and nondivided construction of reality]. *Familiendynamik, 15*, 43–61.

Jordan, J. M., & Whitlock, F. A. (1972). Emotions and the skin: The conditioning of scratch responses in cases of atopic dermatitis. *British Journal for Dermatitis, 86*, 574–585.

Kantor, D. (1980). Critical identity image: A concept linking individual, couple, and family development. In J. K. Pearce & L. J. Friedman (Eds.), *Family therapy: Combined psychodynamic and family systems approaches* (pp 137–167). New York: Grune & Stratton.

Krause, R., & Merten, J. (1999). Affects: Regulation of relationship, transference and countertransference. *International Forum of Psychoanalysis, 8*, 103–114.

Laireiter, A.-R. (Ed.) (2000). Diagnostik in der Psychotherapie [Diagnosis in psychotherapy]. Springer: Vienna.

Luborsky, L., & Crits-Christoph, P. (1990). *Understanding transference*. New York: Basic Books.

Marmor, J. (1975). The nature of the psychotherapeutic process revisited. *Journal of the Canadian Psychoanalytical Association, 20*, 557–565.

Maturana, H. R., & Varela, F. J. (1980). Autopoiesis: The organization of the living. In H. R. Maturana & F. J. Varela (Eds.), *Autopoiesis and cognition: The realization of living* (pp 59–140). Dordrecht: Reidel.

McDaniel, S. H., Hepworth, J., & Doherty, W. J. (1997). *The shared experience of illness*. New York: Basic Books.

McDaniel, S. H., Hepworth, J., & Doherty, W. J. (1992). Medical family therapy: A biopsychosocial approach for families with health problems. New York: Basic Books.

Miller, I. G. (1978). *Living systems*. McGraw-Hill, New York.

Minuchin, S. (1974). *Families and family therapy*. Cambridge, MA: Harvard University

Minuchin, S., & Fishman, H. C. (1981). *Family therapy techniques*. Cambridge, MA: Harvard University Press.

Minuchin, S., Rosman, B., & Baker, L. (1978). *Psychosomatic families: Anorexia in context*. Cambridge, MA: Harvard University Press.

Olson, D. H., McCubbin, H. J., Barnes, H. L., Larsen, A. S., Muxen, M. J., & Wilson, M. A. (1983). *Families: What makes them work.* Beverly Hills, CA: Sage.

OPD Task Force. (2000). *Operationalized psychodynamic diagnostics.* Göttingen: Hogrefe & Huber.

Ramsey, C. N. (1989). *The science of family medicine.* In C. N. Ramsey (Ed.), Family systems in medicine (pp. 3–17). New York: The Guilford Press.

Reiss, D., Neiderhiser, J. M., Hetherington, E. M., & Plomin, R. (2000). *The relationship code: Deciphering genetic and social influences in adolescent development.* Harvard University Press, Cambridge MA.

Retzer, A. (1996). *Familie und Psychose* [The family and psychosis]. Stuttgart: Fischer.

Rickman, J. (1951). *Psycho-analysis and culture.* New York: Internal University Press.

Roth, G. (2001). *Fühlen, Denken, Handeln* [Feeling, thinking, action]. Frankfurt: Suhrkamp.

Sander, L. W. (1985). Toward a logic of organization in psychobiological development. In H. Klar & L. Siever (Eds.), *Biologic response styles: Clinical implications.* Washington: The Monograph Series of the American Psychiatric Press.

Schauenburg, H., & Cierpka, M. (1994). Methoden zur Fremdbeurteilung interpersoneller Beziehungsmuster [Methods of externally rating interpersonal relationship patterns. *Psychotherapeutics, 39,* 135–145.

Scheflen, A. E .(1981). *Levels of schizophrenia.* New York: Brunner & Mazel.

Schiepek, G. (1999). *Die Grundlagen der systemischen Therapie. Theorie. Praxis. Forschung.* [The basic principles of systemic therapy: Theory, praxis, research]. Göttingen: Vandenhoeck & Ruprecht.

Simmel, G. (1922). *Soziologie. Untersuchungen über die Formen der Vergesellschaftung.* [Sociology: Investigations of the forms of socialization]. Duncker & Humblot: München.

Skinner, H. A., Steinhauer, P. J., & Sitarenios, G. (2000). Family assessment measure and process model of family functioning. *Journal of Family Therapy, 22,* 190–210.

Slipp, S. (1980). Interactions between the interpersonal in families and individual intra-psychic dynamics. In J. K. Pearce & L. J. Friedmann (Eds.), *Family therapy.* New York: Grune & Stratton.

Sperry, L. (2004). *Assessment of couples and families: Contemporary and cutting-edge strategies.* New York: Brunner-Routlledge.

Sprenkle, D. H., & Moon, S. M. (2004). *Research methods in family therapy* (2nd ed.). New York: Guilford.

Stasch, M., Cierpka, M., Hillenbrand, E., & Schmal, H. (2002). Assessing re-enactment in inpatient psychodynamic therapy. *Psychotherapy Research, 12,* 355–368.

Steinhauer, P. D. (1986). *Beyond family therapy – Towards a systemic and integrated view.* Unpublished manuscript, University of Toronto, Canada.

Steinhauer, P. D., Santa-Barbara, J., & Skinner, H. A. (1984). The process model of family functioning. *Canadian Journal of Psychiatry, 29,* 77–88.

Steinhauer, P. D., & Tisdall, G. W. (1984). The integrated use of individual and family psychotherapy. *Canadian Journal of Psychiatry 29,* 89–97.

Stern, D. N. (1985). *The interpersonal world of the infant: A view from psychoanalysis and developmental psychology.* New York: Basic Books.

Strauss, J. S. (1973). Diagnostic models and the nature of psychiatric disorder. *Archives of General Psychiatry, 29,* 445–449.

Uexküll, T., von (1986). *Psychosomatische Medizin* [Psychosomatic medicine]. München: Urban & Schwarzenberg.

Willi, J. (1985). *Koevolution. Die Kunst gemeinsamen Wachsens* [Coevolution: The art of mutual growth]. Hamburg: Rowohlt

Winnicott, D. W. (1990). *The maturational processes and the facilitating environment.* London: Karnac Books.

Wood, B. (1991). Beyond the "psychosomatic family": A biobehavioral family model of pediatric illness. *Family Process, 32,* 261–278.

Wood, B. (1994). One articulation of the structural family therapy model: A biobehavioral family model of chronic illness in children. *Journal of Family Therapy, 16,* 53–72.

Part I:
The Initial Interview

3

First Contact and Preconditions for the Initial Interview

Conducting the First Interview

Joseph L. Wetchler and Gina Gutenkunst

Summary
This chapter presents a model for using the initial client telephone call and the first session as an assessment tool. It divides the assessment process into evaluation of the family and evaluation of the therapist/client relationship.

This chapter presents an overview of the initial therapeutic contact and the first interview in family therapy. It discusses how the therapist conducts these encounters and how they are used to gather specific assessment information. While both authors follow an integrative family therapy approach that includes many theories, this chapter will be heavily influenced by the structural (Minuchin, 1974; Minuchin & Fishman, 1981), strategic (Haley, 1987; Watzlawick, Weakland, & Fisch, 1974), solution-focused (de Shazer, 1985, 1988), and Milan systemic (Boscolo, Cecchin, Hoffman, & Penn, 1987; Selvini Palazzoli, Boscolo, Cecchin, & Prata, 1980) schools of family therapy. Other theoretical schools will be noted as they pertain to specific aspects of our work.

Haley (1987) has stated that the primary goal of the first session is to get the family to return for the second session. While this statement may sound a bit flippant at first, it is quite profound when one thinks about it. The initial contact, typically by telephone, and the first session represent the first encounters between the client family and the therapist. Not only will therapists use these encounters to assess what is happening in the family, but also to develop a therapeutic relationship with each member of the family. This initial sense of relationship to their therapist may impact the outcome of therapy (Alexander, Barton, Schiavo, & Parsons, 1976) and may be the impetus for helping reluctant family members to continue with treatment. Therefore, our assessment scheme focuses not only on what is happening in a family that maintains the problem, and how we can intervene in that process, but also how we need to relate to individual family members to make them therapy customers (Fisch, Weakland, & Segal, 1983; de Shazer, 1988).

Overview of the Literature on First Contacts and Initial Interviews

Much of what has been written about initial contacts in family therapy has been presented in introductory textbooks (Brock & Barnard; 1999, Lukas, 1993; Patterson, Williams, Grauf-Grounds, & Chamow, 1998; Worden, 1994). While all of these are excellent sources, they inadvertently present the illusion that this is an area more suited for beginners and not advanced clinicians. Further, the step-by-step presentation of these discussions may lead readers to assume that these are ritualized encounters that must be performed in a specific manner. Finally, the behavioral nature of these presentations tends to separate the practice of family therapy from its theoretical underpinnings.

What we emphasize in this chapter is that all initial encounters between a therapist and family are first and foremost theory driven endeavors that emanate from a therapist's core assumptions of therapy and drive all subsequent hypotheses that may develop from these interactions. In other words, a therapist's theoretical orientation will determine how he or she will conduct these initial encounters and determine those aspects of the interview that are clinically relevant to his or her assessment. Theoretically, we use these first encounters to develop hypotheses that enable us to engage our families and evaluate the nature of their problems (Worden, 1994). To expand on this idea, we will separately discuss the issues of clinical hypotheses, client engagement, and the assessment of family interaction. We realize that these activities typically occur simultaneously, and that engaging in them also serves as potential interventions (Minuchin, 1974). Therefore we separate them for the sake of clarity and not as a description of a step-by-step process.

Clinical Hypotheses

We believe that the initial session, as well as therapy in general, is a theory-driven endeavor. It is impossible to develop a coherent assessment without a framework to organize the data one encounters in the therapy room, as well as on the telephone. Ideally, when using an assessment instrument, the therapist chooses one that is theoretically valid and reliable. When conducting an initial session, the therapist must be that instrument. Therefore, his or her questions must be valid, in that they fit within his or her theoretical orientation, they are relevant to the problem the family brings to therapy, and they can lead to interventions that help a family solve its problem. Further, his questions must be reliable, in that there is a degree of theoretical consistency across different client families and a certain degree of similarity in the questions asked.

The Milan Associates (Selvini Palazzoli et al., 1980) provide a compelling discussion on the role of hypotheses in therapy. Starting with the first initial encounters, therapists begin to organize their clients' stories into potential hypotheses that drive their subsequent questions. It is the feedback they receive from their clients that allows them to either refine their initial impressions or develop new hypotheses. If therapist questions are randomly presented, then it will be difficult to organize clients' responses into a meaningful whole. It is only through a well-developed sense of theory that a therapist can coherently generate hypotheses and test them in the therapy room.

Murray Bowen (1978), a transgenerational therapist, expands on the importance of theory with two central axioms. First, if therapists have a strong personal theory they will know how to handle diverse clinical situations. In other words, therapists' theories drive how they behave in therapy. Both in terms of what questions they ask and the way they intervene.

Second, therapists will be more effective if they treat all of their client families as research families. This means that if therapists are willing to engage in an assessment process and develop hypotheses, rather than operating from preconceived assumptions, they can develop a better feel for what is happening in the family and better assess whether their interventions are on target or not.

Engagement of Treatment Families

If one of the primary goals of the first interview is to get the family to return, then it is crucial that the therapist engage them in the therapy process. Joining is the active process by which therapists let their treatment families know they understand them and are working on their behalf (Minuchin & Fishman, 1981). This is not accomplished by simply having good manners and putting people at ease. While, this is certainly a part of the process, it also stems from therapists developing accurate hypotheses about how their clients think about their problems and the world, in general. For the members of the MRI, this involves identifying the words the family members use to describe their problems. They then use them to develop an interactional picture of the problem and to explain interventions in a manner similar enough to the family's views to enhance the probability that they will comply with them (Fisch, Weakland, & Segal, 1983).

Minuchin (1974) uses the term "accommodation" to describe how therapists adjust themselves to achieve joining. He states:

> To join a family system, the therapist must accept the family's organization and blend with them. He must experience the family's transactional patterns and the strength of those patterns. That is, he should feel a family member's pain at being excluded or scapegoated, and his pleasure at being loved, depended on, or otherwise confirmed within the family. The therapist recognizes the predominance of certain family themes and participates with family members in their exploration. He has to follow their path of communication, discovering which ones are open, which are partly closed, and which are entirely blocked. When he pushes beyond the family thresholds, he will be alerted by the system's counterdeviation mechanisms. The family's impingements on the therapist are the factors that make known the family to him. (Minuchin, 1974, pp. 123-124)

In other words, therapists use the initial therapeutic encounters to develop a preliminary map of how they can phenomenologically relate to their clients. These tentative hypotheses set the groundwork for how they understand and communicate with their treatment families. Of course, these early hypotheses may change as therapists get further feedback from their clients. New ways of relating and explaining will then be needed to facilitate the therapy process.

de Shazer (1988) operationally defines the therapist/client relationship into one of three categories: visitor, complainant, and customer. These categories are more an assessment of the therapeutic relationship than a diagnosis of the client. They inform therapists about the best options for relating, communicating, and intervening with their clients. In fact, de Shazer (1984) views client resistance as more a facet of therapists misunderstanding their clients' pace and world view than to any intention on the part of their clients. Therapy can only proceed if therapists fit their clinical behaviors and communications to those of their clients (de Shazer, 1988).

Visitor Relationship

A visitor relationship often exists when a client is reluctant to discuss a complaint, or even is reluctant to come to therapy. In this therapeutic relationship, the client may be forced to come to therapy, perhaps by a probation officer or even a parent, but does not feel he or she has a problem. Other times, clients, for whatever reason, may not initially feel comfortable disclosing personal information to their therapist. Perhaps it is because they do not initially trust this strange individual with their problems, or, perhaps they consider their complaint to be too personal to share at this time.

A common mistake that therapists may make with this type of relationship is to push clients to discuss their problems or to label them as resistant. What this typically does is create a repetitive avoider/pursuer pattern, in which the therapist pushes the client to disclose more information, while the client attempts to close up. When confronted with this situation, de Shazer (1988) recommends that therapists accept that their clients do not want to talk about a problem at this time. Rather than confront their clients, they should attempt to side with them in their view of their situation. Finally, therapists should compliment these clients on some positive aspects the therapist identifies in their encounter. It is only when clients feel that their therapist supports them and understands them that therapy can move forward to the discussion of problems.

Complainant Relationship

In a complainant relationship, the client wants to talk about a specific problem, but may not be ready or able to do something about it. This does not mean that the client is unwilling to do something, but for whatever reason is not ready. For example, many people who suffer loses or have been abused need to talk about their experience, and have their feelings validated before they are able to move on with their lives. Pushing clients to get over problems like these before they have adequately discussed them (which can take a substantial period of time for some people) will only lead to their feeling unheard and slowing down any therapeutic movement.

Therapist behaviors that are most helpful in complainant relationships are to listen to their clients' stories, validate their clients' experience, identify, and compliment their clients' strengths, and to give assignments in which they observe their process. These assignments may include identifying their own strengths, when their problem happens, and times the problem does not exist. Many schools of therapy make similar assignments to these. For example, journaling one's feelings and baselining behaviors are common complainant assignments that cross many theoretical orientations. What these interventions have in common is that they allow clients to deepen their experience and discussion of the problem and provide therapists with important assessment information. Further, they promote client readiness to engage in tasks that lead to change.

Customer Relationship

In a customer relationship, the client is not only willing but wants to do *something* about the complaint (de Shazer, 1988). One of the diagnostic criteria for assessing a customer relationship is that the client will talk about things he or she has attempted to resolve the problem. The therapist can now begin to assign tasks that direct the client to either do more of the things that work, or to do something different. A good clue as to how to assign tasks can be found in client descriptions of how they attempt to resolve their problems. Clients that describe their attempts in behavioral terms should be assigned behavioral tasks, while those that describe their attempts in perceptual or conceptual terms should be assigned feeling or thinking tasks. If clients continue to follow a therapist's assignments, he or she can assume that a customer relationship continues to exist; however, if a client stops following tasks, a therapist should reassess to see if the relationship has moved to either complainant or visitor status. In those cases, the therapist should also switch to the appropriate relationship.

Assessment of Problem-Maintaining Patterns

If family therapy was simply a matter of developing a strong relationship with a client family, then we could stop our discussion right here. But, if therapists are going to be of service to their clients, they must also develop hypotheses about what patterns are maintaining their client's problem, and how they can alter them. More than any other aspect of our discussion, a therapist's personal theoretical orientation will play a major role in what he or she considers important problem-maintaining patterns. A discussion of what all the various theoretical orientations consider to be relevant to keeping a client stuck is beyond the scope of this chapter. Therefore, we will briefly cover important assessment information for structural, strategic, and solution-focused family therapy.

Assessment of Family Structure

The assessment of family structure is especially helpful for families with a child or adolescent/focused problem (Fishman, 1988) and for families experiencing child abuse and incest (Trepper & Barrett, 1989). In these instances we are most concerned with assessing the presence or absence of a parent/child hierarchy, triangles, and interpersonal boundaries.

When assessing for the presence or absence of a parent/child hierarchy, the therapist is essentially trying to observe if the parents are in charge of their child's life (Minuchin, 1974). Do parents make appropriate rules and follow through when their children disobey? Do parents act in a responsible manner with their children, or do they act more like peers with their child? For example, a parent/child relationship in which the parent appropriately breaks up a fight between his or her children, while also being caring and nurturing in the process would demonstrate the presence of a parent/child hierarchy. However, a situation in which a parent was unable to stop his or her children from fighting, or got into a shouting match with the children might show a lack of a parent/child hierarchy.

Triangles typically exist in parent/child relationships when a child is caught in the middle of a disagreement between two adults. The adults could be from the same generation, such as two spouses, or they could be from different generations, such as a grandmother and a father (Haley, 1987). An example we often encounter happens when two parents disagree on how to discipline their child. One parent argues that the child needs more love, while the other argues that the child needs more punishment. More often than not, the couple are so caught up in this argument that neither partner follows through appropriately with the child, and if one does, the other will respond to the child by doing the opposite.

Boundaries are invisible lines of demarcation between two or more family members (Minuchin, 1974). Clear boundaries provide both personal autonomy and the ability to communicate needs and desires appropriately between people. Enmeshed boundaries tend to be diffuse in that people become over responsible for each other. In rigid boundaries, individuals can be so emotionally distant as to be non-communicative with each other. It is not uncommon in a triangle to see one parent over involved with the child while the other parent remains distant. The over involved parent will constantly worry about the child, overly monitor the child, and be involved in all aspects of the child's life. The distant parent will tend to have no idea what is going on in the child's life and take little responsibility for dealing with the child.

Assessment of Family Interaction

No problem exists in isolation, but is more likely to be a component within a string of problem-maintaining behaviors (Watzlawick et al., 1974). Assessing interactional sequences can be helpful in both couple and parent/child problems. A common sequence in certain marital problems involves one spouse constantly in the role of the pursuer while the other spouse tries to maintain distance. The more the pursuer tries to gain closeness by chasing after the avoider, the more the avoider tries to maintain greater distance. Very little can be resolved by this couple because each attempt to discuss things by the pursuer leads to an attempt to distance by the avoider, and each move by the avoider to maintain distance leads to a greater attempt at closeness by the pursuer. In identifying a problem of this nature, the therapist would then try to alter the pattern by bringing the pursuer out of his or her shell while simultaneously blocking the pursuer. When the pursuer feels safe enough to begin talking about his or her issues, then the therapist can allow the pursuer to start talking.

Assessment of Solutions

When couples or families experience a persistent problem, they often are so overwhelmed that they are unable to identify those rare occasions when they actually exert control over the problem. It is as if the problem takes up so much of their consciousness that they are unable to see their successes. When assessing solutions, the therapist asks clients to identify times when the problem does not exist and then to figure out what they did to solve it. Many times the identification of these exceptions (de Shazer, 1985) leads to assignments to do more of these behaviors which may lead to problem solution.

The First Phone Contact

If the primary goal of the first interview is to get the family to return for a second session, then the primary goal of the first phone contact is to get the family to come to the first session. The therapist's primary tool is his or her own person. It is his or her ability to develop tentative hypotheses about how to engage the client and about what might be happening that is maintaining the problem. These initial hypotheses will help therapists conduct the initial phone call, decide who to invite for the first session, and how to explain this decision to their clients. Further, tentative hypotheses derived from the initial phone call are useful for asking opening questions during the first session. In essence, the therapist's theoretical orientation plays an important role in even the most preliminary context. It will guide him or her through the initial stages of therapy. Of course, therapists need to remind themselves that these are tentative hypotheses, at best, and should avoid becoming wedded to them, lest they limit their options for discovering more useful hypotheses (Boscolo et al., 1987).

Even before a client calls for family therapy, we have some tentative hypotheses that guide how we conduct our initial phone contact. First, we assume that people who call for therapy are very distressed about their problem. It typically takes a relatively high level of discomfort for a person to make the decision to call for therapy. By the time they make an initial phone call, many clients need to tell some part of their story to relieve their stress. For that reason alone, we believe that initial phone calls are best conducted by a therapist (preferably the one who will be their therapist) and not a secretary. Simply allowing clients to tell their story begins the development of a therapist/client relationship. Further, therapist curiosity (Cecchin, 1987) about a problem opens the gateway for new hypotheses.

Second, we assume that most clients who call for therapy are still ambivalent about whether or not they will actually attend. Again, it is crucial that therapists be courteous, compassionate, and attentive to their clients needs. The development of a caring connection can be just enough to facilitate an ambivalent client to enter therapy (Brock & Barnard, 1999).

We divide the initial telephone contact into five components: 1) listening to the client; 2) having them identify the problem and who is part of the problem system; 3) negotiating with the client about who will attend the first session; 4) informing the client about the therapist's or agency's policies, and what to expect in the first session; and 5) allowing the client to ask questions or share any concerns they may be having. Following through with these elements, will help ease a client's anxieties, as well provide therapists with some tentative hypotheses to begin the first session.

Listen to the Client

Listening to a client is less a component than an overarching stance during the entire phone contact. Clients are often confused, frustrated, and unsure of themselves during this initial contact, listening and reflecting with a prospective client, can help them feel understood and important (Andersen, 1991). Further, engaging in a brief dialogue may begin to move a stuck problem forward (Andersen, 1991; Anderson, 1997). Talking with a client in this way can engender a sense of hope that they can resolve their problem (Patterson et al., 1998), leaving them with feelings of optimism and eagerness for their first therapy session.

For the therapist, taking the time to listen to a client allows them to develop some tentative initial hypotheses about what might be maintaining a family's problem, who might be appropriate to attend the first session, and how they might begin the joining process with other family members. It is at the point that therapists start to lose their initial curiosity over first phone calls that they begin to reify clients and their situations. When listening to client stories becomes routine, then human contact is lost and the development of client specific hypotheses is hindered.

The Problem

We typically ask our clients to give us a brief description about the presenting problem and who in the system is involved with the problem. It is important to keep this information gathering time brief, getting just enough information to begin hypothesizing, preparing for the first session, and collecting relevant information to help decide who should attend therapy. We typically ask the client to describe the problem and how it has impacted his or her lives. We also ask for concrete information on those members who live in the home, their relationship to the identified patient, and their ages. Finally, it is important to find out how the caller feels about the problem. This helps the client feel understood by the therapist and helps the therapist develop an emotional attachment to the client. Often the way a caller describes the problem and his or her feelings about it helps the therapist develop hypotheses about how to relate to that client in the initial session.

Negotiate Who Attends The First Session

While some family therapists believe that all family members must be present at the first session (e.g., Whitaker, 1989), we take a more conservative view. We find it best to negotiate with our clients about who will attend the first session. While having all family members present in the first session can often be helpful, it is not always the best way to begin. The idea of having all family members at the first session is one that has become more ritualized than theoretically based. Demanding that all family members attend the first session not only creates a power struggle between the therapist and family members, but the routine nature of starting all therapy sessions the same way diminishes one's ability to develop hypotheses that may be unique to a specific problem system.

It is often more helpful to decide who to invite after finding out about the problem and who is involved. We then tentatively recommend who we think would be most useful to attend the first session. It is then useful to find out if the caller agrees or disagrees with this recommendation. If the caller agrees, then we move to the next step. If not, we get more information about the caller's concerns. We might then provide a clearer rationale, based on this new information, or we might agree with who the caller thinks is appropriate for the first session. This is crucial information in developing a greater sense of fit and understanding with the family system. For example, a woman wanting marital therapy asked that she be seen alone in the first interview. During this interview, she discussed how she had felt blamed by her previous therapist for her marital difficulties. She also said that she was currently involved in an extramarital affair. Her therapist was able to assure her that he would be able to work in a non-blaming manner with her, and was able to negotiate with her to end the affair prior to beginning couple therapy. Needless to say, this was crucial information that might not have come out if the couple had been seen conjointly in the first session.

The Therapist's Policies

An explanation of the therapist's or agency's policies is an important element of the initial phone contact. Simple clarification of fees, how appointments are made, confidentiality, whether or not child care is provided, guidelines for keeping and canceling appointments, directions, and any other information that is pertinent to the therapeutic agreement should be discussed with the client before their first session. Discussing these policies with a client during the initial phone contact enables them to understand their rights as a client and what is expected of them, as well what they can expect throughout the therapeutic process. Addressing these issues over the phone can minimize any confusion or concerns, helping to decrease cancellations and no-shows in the future.

Questions and Concerns

Finally, it is helpful to ask the caller if they have any questions or concerns. Client responses can be as simple as asking for directions to the clinic, or as important as sharing crucial information that had not previously been mentioned. For example we have had clients add share that a key member has an alcohol problem or that someone was abused. We are then able to refine our initial hypotheses and even make changes in who should attend the initial session. It also is important to assure the client that they have the right to ask questions or share any concerns they might have throughout the entire therapy process. This leads to a more collegial therapy, which has the potential for more information to be shared with a therapist.

The following case examples show how the initial phone contact can both help and hinder therapy. The first example shows how a reluctant client was helped to attend therapy, and the second shows how the therapist's reluctance to listen to a client led to a premature termination.

Example A

A client called her employee assistance program (EAP) for therapy concerning sexual abuse she had endured as a child. The client seemed to be very nervous over the phone and unsure that the therapist could help. Through listening to the client and reflecting back her fears about seeking therapy the therapist was able to calm her and answer some of the questions she had. The client had heard that EAPs only provided 3 sessions and did not think this would be enough sessions. The therapist told the client about the agency's policies, including the fact that their agency provided 10 sessions for clients and would extend these sessions in special circumstances such as sexual abuse. The therapist continued to empathize with the client that sexual abuse was a very traumatic event to endure and that her treatment in therapy would go as slow as she needed. The therapist explored with the client if there were any other individuals that were circumstantial to her treatment, such as her husband or a sibling. The client explained that her relationship with her husband was affected by her history of being sexually abused, but she felt that she needed to explore her own feelings and memories about the sexual abuse before involving her husband. The therapist agreed with the client, but confirmed that her husband knew about the sexual abuse and that she was seeking therapy. When asked if the client had any more concerns, she discussed her hesitancy to share such important information a stranger. Her therapist again reassured her that she would be in charge and would only share what she felt comfortable disclosing. This contact had a positive effect on the woman, because at the start of the first session, the client stated that their phone conversation had helped her to feel confident in seeking therapy for herself. In fact, it was a positive start to what would be a productive therapeutic relationship.

Examble B

A mother called for therapy for her teenage son who was experiencing drug problems. The family was relatively affluent and was concerned about people knowing about their son's problem. When the therapist stated that all members of the family should attend, the mother asked that her other children not attend as it was not their problem. The therapist responded by telling the mother it was her policy that all family members come to the first session. The mother agreed, but said she resented the therapist telling her how best to deal with her daughter's problem when she hardly knew the family. The therapist still insisted, and the mother reluctantly agreed. Needless to say, the family began the first session by grilling the therapist about her credentials, and dropped out after the fourth session saying the therapist was not qualified to help them.

Clearly, had the therapist in the second example been as attentive to the caller's concerns as the therapist in the first example, the first session might have got off to a better start. At least, the client would have learned that the therapist respected her opinion, which might have lessened the competitive atmosphere of the first session. Further, had the therapist listened to the client, she might have developed more specific hypotheses to relate better to her.

The First Session

As with the initial phone call, we will outline the first interview as a series of steps; however, we view this type of assessment more as an overall theoretical process than a grouping of discrete tasks. Further, the initial session process may take more than one session to complete. In fact, we often find that two or three sessions are needed to develop an adequate grasp of what maintains a family's current problem and to develop an adequate therapist/client emotional bond. Finally, all hypotheses developed during the initial sessions are tentative at best. Assessment is an ongoing process throughout the course of therapy. The therapy process is an ongoing feedback cycle. Every intervention, and even every comment, is a potential source of assessment information.

Listen and Observe

As with the initial telephone contact, we view the processes of observing and listening as an overall heuristic for the first session. While the observer can never completely be separated from what he or she is observing, the development of more useful hypotheses is best achieved when the therapist actively tunes in to what client families are saying and doing (Anderson, 1997). This means actively paying attention to one's clients and not allowing one's initial hypotheses to cloud one's vision. So often, what we think is going on with a family can change radically when we allow them the time to further explain themselves, or when we take a moment to observe how they interact together.

Further, we may enhance the therapist/client relationship by actively listening to our treatment families. We not only develop a better understanding of our clients, but they are more likely to bond with us when they discover we truly are concerned with what they have to say.

Social Period

Typically, the first few minutes of an initial session are devoted to getting to know the family members and allowing them to get to know the therapist. When we meet the family in the waiting area, we prefer to immediately make brief contact with the person who made the initial phone call, and have him or her introduce us to the other family members. We shake hands with everyone and share our names. After everyone is seated in the therapy room, we ask social questions about where people work and where they go to school. We then tell them a bit of professional information about ourselves (e.g., degrees and licenses) and some personal information (e.g., marital status and number of children). We then allow them to ask any questions they wish to know about us. While most families do not have any questions at this time, giving them the option to ask makes for a more egalitarian relationship and opens the possibility for a freer give and take of ideas (Anderson, 1997). Finally, we tell them that they are free to ask us any questions about any of the procedures we employ in their therapy.

We attempt to get a preliminary feel for the family during this phase. For example, we observe which family members sit closer and further away from each other. This can provide tentative hypotheses about family alliances and coalitions (Minuchin, 1974; Minuchin & Fishman, 1981). We also pay attention to the words family members use to describe their lives, their work, and their relationship to each other. These words may be helpful in learning how to explain things to the family (Fisch et al., 1983) and to help us better relate to them. Of course, all of our observations must be very tentative, as we have only had a few minutes to interact with the family.

Statement of the Problem

We then ask each family member to give a brief statement of the problem. We first state what the family member who made the call said about the problem. Then we ask the others to share their views. We then invite the person who made the call to briefly share any further views.

There are several reasons for proceeding in this manner. First, we give a message that we are not already aligned with the initial caller's view of the problem. We want to hear from every member of the family. Second, speaking with each family member enhances the therapist/client bond. While some family therapists speak about the family as an organism (e.g., Whitaker, 1989), it still is made up of individuals with different views, beliefs, and feelings about the problem. Making contact with each family member not only heightens the bond with each member, but it enhances the overall relationship between the therapist and the family. Third, making contact with each member allows therapists to assess who is involved with the problem and who is invested in doing something about it.

Assessment of Problem Maintaining Sequences and Attempted Solutions

It is here that one's theoretical orientation plays the largest role in what he or she considers important diagnostic information. Research suggests that in outcome studies, effectiveness is related less to a particular family therapy orientation, than to the manualization of that orientation (Pinsof & Wynne, 1995; Shadish, Ragsdale, Glaser, & Montgomery, 1995). This means that the more a treatment is standardized across a number of therapists, the better the chance it will be effective over a number of cases. With a bit of a stretch, it might then follow that the more theoretically organized and consistent a family therapist, no matter his or her theoretical orientation, the better the chance he or she will be effective across a range of families.

Each family that enters treatment becomes an "n of one" study for how that therapist conducts therapy with that family. The therapist becomes the diagnostic and intervention instrument in the relationship. How theoretically reliable and valid a therapist is within one particular therapy and across a number of therapies depends on how theoretically grounded he or she is in his or her approach. In other words, we need to be able to make consistent sense of what we observe, and to know what to do with this information once we understand it.

As stated earlier, our theoretical orientation tends to be an integration of structural (Minuchin, 1974), strategic (Haley, 1987; Watzlawick et al., 1974), solution focused (de Shazer, 1985, 1988), and Milan systemic (Boscolo et al., 1987, Selvini Palazzoli et al., 1980) family therapies. Thus, we tend to assess for family structure, family interaction patterns, and specific strengths and solutions families have to resolve their problems. Since we previously discussed the theoretical tenets of those approaches, we will instead focus on how we assess for that information.

Discussion of How a Problem Is Maintained and Solved

After we get a brief statement of the problem from all family members, we then have the family tell us about the problem. We gather interactional information about how they unsuccessfully and successfully try to resolve the problem, and how they relate to each other in the process (Depending on one's theoretical orientation, other information may be more appropriate for a particular therapist.). We attempt to get as many perspectives on the situation as possible, with the understanding that some family members may be more invested in talking to us than others. Further, our hypotheses become more refined as we gather more perspectives from different family members.

Therapists must keep in mind that their ability to develop meaningful hypotheses starts with their ability to ask meaningful questions (Tomm, 1987a, 1987b, 1988). Therapists can best develop meaningful questions by starting with their tentative hypotheses. They then need to ask enough questions to see whether that hypothesis fits or needs to be refined. Two of the better measures of whether or not a hypothesis fits, is how many family members tend to agree with the hypothesis and how long the family will respond in the affirmative to questions related to that hypotheses. For example, if a mother, father, and adolescent all agree that the parents try to deal with the child in different ways, and discuss this pattern for a sustained length of time, then the therapist can be relatively sure that his or her hypothesis of a family triangle is appropriate. However, if questions about how the parents attempt to deal with their child go nowhere, or the family keeps trying to talk about a different subject, the therapist had better begin working with a different hypothesis.

To assess if a hypothesis fits, a therapist needs to ask a sufficient amount of related questions over a sustained period of time. It is the ability to get consistent feedback over time that lets him or her know whether he or she is on track. This means that therapists need to ask questions in an organized fashion. Random questions do not provide enough sustained information to let either the therapist or client know if a hypothesis is valid or not. In fact, random questions typically lead to greater confusion for both the therapist and client. In these situations, the client's initial hypotheses, which typically maintain the problem, will remain in the forefront, and therapy will be stalled. In fact, the therapist will often take on the client's hypotheses in these situations, as no new ideas are available to move to the forefront.

Piaget's (e.g., 1930, 1950) concepts of scheme, assimilation, and accommodation might best explain this process. Piaget believes that individuals' cognitive schemes develop through interaction with the environment. We believe the same applies for client and therapist hypotheses. In fact, we consider the terms *scheme* and *hypothesis* to be relatively synonymous. Hypotheses tend to be strengthened through the process of assimilation when the same conclusions can be drawn from the same repeated interactions. They are changed through accommodation, or when a novel experience leads to a new way of thinking about the world. This new hypothesis then becomes strengthened through repeated experiences that lead to the same results.

Existing schemes, or hypotheses, tend to remain in the forefront through three means. Repeated experiences that lead to the same outcome is the most commonly known process; however two other processes also lead to the strengthening of a hypothesis. One way is for an individual to experience a phenomenon that is so discrepant from his or her way of thinking that he or she shuts down the ability to process that experience as new. This is seen when babies are so over stimulated that they either begin to cry or go to sleep. This also can be seen in clients who when presented with a therapist suggestion that is so discrepant from their way of thinking, dig in their heels and resist the suggestion. We once observed a therapist struggle with an angry father who refused to accept that his daughter's problem was representative of a family problem; however, he readily agreed to come to therapy when the therapist explained things in a way that made sense to the father. The therapist simply said that the daughter's problem was so severe, that it would take both the mother and father attending therapy to get her under control.

The other way that a hypothesis can be maintained is by subjecting an existing scheme to a random experience. If a client family experiences a series of random questions, there is not enough sustained interaction for them to accommodate to a new way of thinking. With nothing new to notice or to hang on to, the old way of thinking will predominate. This is also the same for the therapist. If the therapist's questions are random, he or she will not have enough information to develop a hypothesis, and will then run the risk of following the most dominant hypothesis in the room, which is that of the client's.

In most cases, asking a series of sustained questions allows therapists to assess if a hypothesis is on track or not. However, in some cases verbal information may not be enough. For example, a family's existing hypothesis may be so strong that all of their verbal descriptions simply serve to reinforce how they view their problem. Further, some people may be so verbally adept that they can always move a provoking question back to their original way of viewing things. In those cases, a therapist may have to rely on observational methods for eliciting new ideas.

Observation of Family Interactions

Observing how family members interact is a useful addition to developing hypotheses through discussion. Further, it also might provide the key when verbal descriptions go nowhere. By watching how family members relate to each other, therapists can get useful information they might never get through verbal description. For example, one of our clients consistently stated that he was open to his wife's suggestions; however, whenever she spoke to him in sessions, he turned away from her or gave her a dirty look. It is this type of information that can open up a world of possibility for assessment and intervention. In the case of our husband, confronting him with this discrepancy in his behavior and then helping him to look at his wife when she spoke to him facilitated his ability to become more attentive to his wife and led to greater intimacy between them.

Haley (1987) recommends having family members enact how they attempt to resolve their problem during the initial session. He believes that this is an excellent way to see what actually goes on in their lives at home. We disagree with this procedure as we have found that people often feel self-conscious role-playing their behaviors in the therapist's office. Instead of getting a more realistic appraisal of what happens, we are more likely to get a constrained view of what goes on at home. Further, we run the risk of people feeling uncomfortable in the first session and not returning.

We prefer to observe spontaneous behavior as it happens in our office. For example, a couple that complains of constant bickering will eventually begin arguing over their different views of a therapist's questions. Or a parent with a defiant adolescent will eventually have to deal with that adolescent's behavior at some point during the session. It is at these moments that we can get the information we need about what happens, but also gain some insight about how to relate to the family members. For example, if the parent in the second example responds with frustration to the child's defiance, we can reflect how frustrated the parent feels with this behavior. Or with the arguing couple, we can empathize with each of them how difficult it is when "you can't see eye-to-eye with your partner."

For those times when verbal descriptions are not productive and the family is too constrained to spontaneously interact with each other, we might use an experiential technique like sculpting (Duhl, Kantor, & Duhl, 1973) to elicit the information we need. The advantage of sculpture over asking people to enact what they do at home, is in the artistic, make-believe, nature of the sculpture. People are less self conscious about creating sculptures because they are a metaphor of their behavior rather than an actual representation of their behavior. For some clients, there is a greater level of security in speaking in metaphor than in actually describing what is happening (Haley, 1987). The less vulnerable a client feels during an initial interview, the greater the chance that he or she will return for another session.

Assessment of Client-Therapist Relationship

We find that assessment of the client-therapist relationship is as important as assessment of problem maintaining and problem solving behaviors. Our interactions with our clients are designed as much to develop hypotheses about the best way to relate to them as they are about the best way to treat them. We find de Shazer's (1988) classification of visitor, complainant, and customer relationships to be the most useful to date.

As we develop our relationship hypotheses, we especially pay attention to: 1) which family members are more interested in attending therapy and which family members are less interested; 2) which family members talk more about the problem and which family members talk less; and 3) which family members are more active in attempting to resolve the problem and which family members are less active. This information helps us determine how we should initially relate to the different family members.

We consider those family members who are highly interested in attending therapy, talk a great deal about the problem, and are actively involved in resolving the problem to be customers. We tend to be more interactive and directive with customers. In fact, we find that customers almost demand this behavior from us.

We classify those family members who are highly interested in attending therapy and actively talk about the problem, but are not actively involved in resolving the problem, as complainants. While we tend to be highly interactive with complainants, we avoid being directive. If we do assign a task, it will be one in which they observe some aspect of what is happening with their family. This type of assignment is consistent with their high level of concern, but low level of activity.

Visitors typically are not interested in attending therapy, do not actively talk about the problem, and have little investment in problem resolution. While we are emotionally engaged with visitors, we do not talk much with them about the problem, or assign them anything to do about it. We do not consider visitors to be any less important than customers or complainants, only that they relate differently to the problem. In fact, we are as highly emotionally involved in our visitor relationships as we are with our customer and complainant relationships.

An excellent example of how all three relationship categories can exist in a single family is found in the Smiths, who saw us for a substance abuse problem with their adolescent son. Mrs. Smith began the session by stating how concerned she was with her son's behavior and was an active participant throughout. She believed that therapy was his last chance and worried that her son did not see himself as having a problem. She felt her husband's plans to punish her son were too punitive, yet, when asked how she wanted to handle the problem, replied, "I have no idea what to do?" We diagnosed Mrs. Smith as a complainant since she was invested in therapy and was very concerned about her son's problems; however, she was not actively involved in trying to resolve the problem at the time of the initial interview.

Mr. Smith was the first person in the family to identify his son's problem. He noticed that he seemed to have less money at home than he thought on several occasions. To solve the problem, he put a specific amount of money in his dresser drawer, and discovered that half of it was missing. He confronted his son and discovered his son had been using the money to buy drugs. Mr. Smith grounded his son, but found out that his son again began taking money for drugs after his grounding had ended. He again wanted to ground his son, but wanted to talk to a therapist to make sure he was on the right track. We diagnosed Mr. Smith as a customer since he was invested in therapy, was concerned about the problem, and was actively trying to solve the problem.

The adolescent son admitted to using drugs but did not want to come to therapy. He said he enjoyed doing drugs and had no plans to stop. He told his parents that no matter what they did, he would continue to use drugs, and he told the therapist he did not believe in therapy. We diagnosed the son as a visitor since he was not invested in therapy, did not believe he had a problem, and had done nothing to change his behavior. Based on our relationship diagnosis, we focused most of our attention on helping Mr. and Mrs. Smith develop an effective plan for controlling their son's stealing and drug abusing behavior. We also continued to see the son individually to support him in adjusting to his parents' new ways of dealing with him.

Assessment of Family Strengths

During the last quarter of the initial session we ask each family member what they like about the family, and what they feel are the strengths the family possesses to resolve the problem. This often makes a dramatic shift in the session as each member listens to the others describe their family in positive terms. Much of the heaviness leaves the room as the family members realize that everyone sees something positive about the family. Even the identified patient typically has something positive to say about the family.

We find this ritual to be an important source for identifying positive aspects and potential solutions within the family that we might have missed during the session. Further, it helps our overall relationship to the family as we get a better feel for its strengths and what each member likes about the family. Finally, we find that the family members tend to feel more secure with us when they discover that we do not see them as simply a grouping of problems, but also want to see their strengths as well.

Therapist Review of Family Strengths and Compliments

Prior to ending our first session, we give the family feedback on what we discovered that might aid them in solving their problem. We compliment each family member on the strengths we noticed during the session and how they impacted us personally. This stems from de Shazer's (1988) technique of complimenting clients at the end of each session. We find that this sets a positive tone for the therapy and instill hope that the problem can be resolved. More importantly, it lets the family members know that we see them in a positive light and helps them bond to us. Further, it helps us develop a positive relationship with our clients as it disciplines us to notice their strengths and avoid getting caught in the negative aspects of a problem-focused discussion. Finally, for many of our families, it is the first time they have received praise from a professional. This experience alone may be enough to start a positive movement toward problem resolution.

Plan for Future Sessions

We conclude our sessions by setting a time for our next meeting and negotiating who will attend the next session. As with the initial session, we give our ideas about who should attend the next meeting, but keep an open mind regarding any thoughts the family has. We typically comply, if the family members have any strong concerns about who should attend the following sessions. After all, the primary goal of the first session is to get the family to return for the second session.

Conclusion

This chapter presented a theory-driven model for conducting the initial contacts in family therapy. Since the therapist is the sole assessment tool in these encounters, it is important that he or she is theoretically valid and reliable. Rather than viewing the various components of our model as a step-by-step procedure, we hope that our readers will use this as a guideline for organizing their own theoretically based assessments. We remind our readers that hypotheses are limited when therapy is reduced to a set of reified techniques.

References

Alexander, J. F., Barton, C., Schiavo, R. S., & Parsons, B. V. (1976). Systems-behavioral intervention with families of delinquents: Therapist characteristics, family behavior, and outcome. *Journal of Consulting and Clinical Psychology, 44,* 656-664.

Andersen, T. (1991). *The reflecting team: Dialogues and dialogues about the dialogues.* New York: Norton.

Anderson, H. (1997). *Conversation, language, and possibilities: A postmodern approach to therapy.* New York: Basic Books.

Boscolo, L., Cecchin, G., Hoffman, L, & Penn, P. (1987). *Milan systemic family therapy: Conversations in theory and practice.* New York: Basic Books.

Bowen, M. (1987). *Family therapy in clinical practice.* New York: Aronson.

Brock, G. W., & Barnard, C. P. (1999). *Procedures in marriage and family therapy* (3rd ed.). Needham Heights, MA: Allyn & Bacon.

Cecchin, G. (1987). Hypothesizing, circularity, and neutrality revisited: An invitation to curiosity. *Family Process, 26,* 405-443.

de Shazer, S. (1985). *Keys to solution in brief therapy.* New York: Norton.

de Shazer, S. (1988). *Clues: Investigating solutions in brief therapy.* New York: Norton.

Duhl, F. J., Kantor, D., & Duhl, B. S. (1973). Learning, space, and action in family therapy: A primer of sculpture. In D. A. Bloch (ed.), *Techniques of family therapy: A primer* (pp. 47-63). New York: Grune & Stratton.

Fisch, R., Weakland, J. H. & Segal, L. (1983). *The tactics of change: Doing therapy briefly.* Jossey-Bass: San Francisco.

Fishman, H. C. (1988). *Treating troubled adolescents: A family therapy approach.* New York: Basic Books.

Haley, J. (1987). *Problem-solving therapy* (2nd ed.). San Francisco: Jossey-Bass.

Lukas, S. (1993). *Where to start and what to ask: An assessment handbook*. New York: Norton.

Minuchin, S. (1974). *Families & family therapy*. Cambridge, MA: Harvard.

Minuchin S., & Fishman, H. C. (1981). *Family therapy techniques*. Cambridge, MA: Harvard.

Patterson, J., Williams, L., Grauf-Grounds, C., & Chamow, L. (1998). *Essential skills in family therapy: From the first interview to termination*. New York: Guilford.

Piaget, J. (1930). *The child's conception of the world*. New York: Harcourt, Brace, & World.

Piaget, J. (1950). *The psychology of intelligence*. New York: International Universities Press.

Pinsof, W. M., & Wynne, L. C. (1995). The efficacy of marital and family therapy: An empirical overview, conclusions, and recommendations. *Journal of Marital and Family Therapy, 21,* 585-613.

Selvini Palazzoli, M., Boscolo, L., Cecchin, G., & Prata, G. (1980). Hypothesizing-circularity-neutrality: Three guidelines for the conductor of the session. *Family Process, 19,* 3-12.

Shadish, W. R., Ragsdale, K., Glaser, R. R., & Montgomery, M. (1995). The efficacy and effectiveness of marital and family therapy: A perspective from metea-analysis. *Journal of Marital and Family Therapy, 21,* 345-360.

Tomm, K. (1987a). Interventive interviewing: Part I. Strategizing as a forth guideline for the therapist. *Family Process, 26,* 3-13.

Tomm, K. (1987b). Interventive interviewing: Part II. Reflexive questioning as a means to enable self-healing. *Family Process, 26,* 167-183.

Tomm, K. (1988). Interventive interviewing: Part III. Intending to ask lineal, circular, strategic, or reflexive questions. *Family Process, 27,* 1-15.

Trepper, T. S., & Barrett, M. J. (1989). *Systemic treatment of incest: A therapeutic handbook*. New York: Brunner/Mazel.

Watzlawick, P., Weakland, J. H., & Fisch, R. (1974). *Change: Principles of problem formation and problem resolution*. New York: Norton.

Whitaker, C. (1989). *Midnight musings of a family therapist*. New York: Norton.

Worden, M. (1994). *Family therapy basics*. New York: Wadsworth.

4

"A Problem Well Stated Is a Problem Half Solved."

A. Peter MacLean

> "A problem well stated is a problem half solved."
>
> Charles Kettering (1876–1958)
> American inventor and engineer

Summary
This chapter is based on the thesis that a comprehensive clinical assessment is an essential first step in the collaborative effort between clinician and client to help solve the problems brought to therapy by the client. A very important engineering concept, the free body diagram, is introduced to illustrate the need to consider *all* the micro and macro influences that impact on a person's mental health. Consequently, it is argued that a proper clinical assessment must incorporate the bio-psycho-social-cultural model of human nature. A close look at clinical assessment is taken and includes defining assessment, and examining "what" and "how" to assess. Three models of assessment in marriage are considered, and several other aspects of the assessment process are presented such as ethics, stages of change, writing an assessment report, and providing feedback to the client.

The great physicist Albert Einstein was once asked what he would do if he was informed that the world would be destroyed in exactly one hour. Einstein was reported to have thought carefully and then responded that he would spend the first 55 minutes collecting as much information as possible to understand the situation, and the last five minutes actually trying to resolve it. This story and the above Kettering insight – a problem well stated is a problem half solved – capture the essence of assessment in clinical work. In the same way that humans habitually need to practice the maxim, think before you act, clinicians need to carry out a comprehensive assessment before proceeding to therapy.

This chapter is organized into four sections. In the first part, the concept of assessment is discussed and several definitions are proposed. Four phases of clinical assessment are described. The second section looks at the question, "What to assess?," and suggests that the bio-psycho-social-cultural model of human nature is necessary to adequately answer it. It is argued that all of these influences on human behavior need to be addressed directly in assessment or, at a minimum, require sensitive recognition of their presence. The third part considers the question, "How to assess?" The four pillars of assessment are presented, and norm-referenced tests, interviews, observations, and informal assessment are discussed as techniques for learning more about the client's problem. Attention is then turned towards assessment in marriage, and two models are presented. The final section discusses assessment as a fundamentally ethical issue, stages of change, writing assessment reports, and giving feedback to the client.

Defining Assessment

The field of mental health has long been dominated by the medical model. Medicine has traditionally espoused the need for the classification of medical problems – namely, diagnosis – prior to treating. An initial interview by a psychiatrist typically will end with a psychiatric diagnosis – a label that defines a patient according to the *Diagnostic and Statistical Manual of Mental Disorders* (DSM-IV-TR; 2000) in North America or the *International Classification of Diseases*, Clinical Modification (ICD-9-CM; 1992) in Europe and other parts of the world. Although it is acknowledged that accurately identifying a disorder before beginning treatment is valuable in providing health services, this simple categorization of disorders fails to recognize the complexity of human nature that is necessary to adequately understand a client's presenting issues and, furthermore risks giving an individual a psychiatric label with potentially harmful effects to his/her self concept. For example, a psychiatric diagnosis misses the less obvious and often important differences among individuals who have been classified into a particular category, e.g., broader macro influences such as culture and gender, the less obvious situational determinants and correlates of a problem, the specific strengths an individual may bring to therapy, and so forth.

In contrast, the *assessment* of mental health problems is much broader in scope, an approach that recognizes the complex nature of issues that a client (considered in this chapter to be an individual, couple, or family) can bring to the clinic. Assessment has been defined in different ways, but the various definitions reflect the attempt to gain a more comprehensive understanding of the client's world. Brock and Barnard (1999) stated that assessment is "the taking in of information to make informed decisions" (p. 18). Assessment has also been described as "a process of solving problems (answering questions)" (Maloney & Ward, 1976, p. 5). Groth-Marnat (1999) makes the following important points about assessment:

The central role of clinicians conducting assessments should be to answer specific questions and aid in making relevant decisions. To fulfill this role, clinicians must integrate a wide range of data and bring into focus diverse areas of knowledge. Thus, they are not merely administering and scoring tests. ... assessment attempts to evaluate an individual in a problem situation so that the information derived from the assessment can somehow help with the problem. Tests are only one method of gathering data, and the test scores are not end products, but merely means of generating hypotheses. ... assessment, then, places data in a wide perspective, with its main focus being problem solving and decision making. (pp. 3-4)

One view of assessment is that it is an ongoing procedure throughout therapy, and it is only when therapy stops that assessment ceases as well. This view is often held by therapists who favor an informal interview approach to gathering information about a client, and who are less inclined to use formal instruments. Although some authors suggest that assessment is both an initial as well as ongoing activity (e.g., Peterson & Sobell, 1994), it is argued here that this view, although promising in theory, with the many demands of clinical work, in practice can easily become a convenient rationalization for not making the time to carry out a systematic initial assessment. This not uncommon omission can then result in poorly focused therapy and ultimately a disservice to the client.

On the other hand, assessment is more commonly recognized as "the group of procedures used at the outset of therapy to design an initial treatment plan" (Brock & Barnard, 1999, p. 18). This is the approach favored by this writer and reflects Kettering's crucial insight that "a problem well stated is a problem half solved." This perspective is relevant not only for more established problems that are being addressed in a clinical setting, but also in attempting to resolve smaller issues that arise in everyday life. If individuals were less inclined to deny and rationalize the problems they experience in their own lives, then they would likely be more inclined to accept the existence of personal problems and thus a solution could be attempted. In short, problems in life rarely get resolved unless people initially recognize that they exist.

Groth-Marnat (1999) suggests that there are four general phases in clinical assessment: 1) evaluating the referral question, 2) acquiring knowledge relating to the content of the problem, 3) data collection, and 4) interpreting the data. Although these steps are defined as distinct sequential components, they can often take place at the same time and interact with each other. Groth-Marnat emphasizes that during these assessment phases "the clinician should integrate data and serve as an expert on human behavior, rather than merely as an interpreter of test scores" (pp. 30-31).

The first phase, evaluating the referral question, refers to clarifying the initial presenting problem, whether this is a formal request for assessment from a referral agency or a couple requesting help with their marriage. Competent assessment of clinical problems can be limited if the issue is not properly understood, so this initial stage is of critical importance. The second phase of assessment is acquiring knowledge related to the content of the problem. This involves being knowledgeable about the specific type of disorder being presented as well as carefully selecting the tests that will be used to collect information about the problem (e.g., being knowledgeable about a test's reliability and validity). In addition, it is important to be sensitive to whether a test is appropriate or not as a function of differences in clients' ethnicity, age, education level, and so forth.

The third phase, data collection, refers to obtaining information from four general areas: test scores, personal history, behavior observations, and interview data. Whereas tests are a key tool for acquiring information about a problem, a client's case history is of equal importance since it provides a context for both understanding and giving meaning to the test results. Observing the behavior of a client (e.g., negative interactions in a dysfunctional family, a disruptive child in the classroom) and interviewing the parents and/or teachers about the client can also be valuable sources of information. It is important to recognize that competent decision-making and problem solving involves not only utilizing multiple sources of information, but also checking the consistency of the data that is provided across these different methods (i.e., convergent validity).

The fourth and final phase of clinical assessment is interpreting the data. This involves a description of the client's current level of functioning, and information related to etiology, treatment recommendations, and prognosis. Etiological considerations should avoid simplistic explanations and instead need to consider the complexity of background factors. For example, a systems approach would include information obtained from a genogram, and identify key communication patterns such as specific interactional patterns, information feedback loops, and so forth. Recommending treatment options involves developing an effective plan for intervention from the obtained assessment data. This will include developing hypotheses (e.g., informed statements about the client's behavior in a given situation), which will be based on a judicious integration of collected information and clinical experience.

The intake and assessment report is the culmination of the assessment process. A good report is an accurate and clear presentation of the collected information together with the clinician's interpretations, conclusions, and recommendations for treatment.

What to Assess?: The Bio-Psycho-Social-Cultural Model of Human Nature

Of central importance in the preceding discussion of defining assessment are the concepts of complexity in client's presenting problems and the need therefore to develop a comprehensive understanding of the client's world. A very important way to come to understand human nature is systemically, i.e., to recognize the existence of the many forces that influence an individual person (Bronfenbrenner, 1995). A very apt metaphor for conceptualizing these influences is the important engineering concept of a free body diagram. Thus, an individual (or couple, family) is isolated from his/her surroundings by drawing a box diagram around the person (see Figure 1). Next, *all* the forces that influence the person are drawn onto the diagram. In the same way that it would be foolish for an engineer to forget to include all of the forces acting on a finite element of material when designing a bridge, a building, or a car – else it will surely fail! – so it is similarly unwise for the clinician to ignore any of the key influences that are impacting on an individual, couple, or family when trying to understand the client's world (i.e., assessing the problem).

The forces impacting on a person can be positive and therefore will push the person in a positive direction towards happiness and good mental health. Such positive forces would include a strong sense of self, human agency (internal locus of control), high morals, balance in life, healthy supportive friendships. In contrast, these forces can be negative and thus would push a person in a negative direction towards unhappiness and poor mental health: e.g., lack of an integrated identity, insecure attachment style, intergenerational influences such as alcoholism, physical, sexual and/or emotional abuse, dysfunctional family members and "friends" that negatively influence the person, inadequate social skills, and so forth.

These positive and negative influences on a person can be better understood using the bio-psycho-social-cultural model of human nature and can be conceptualized as either

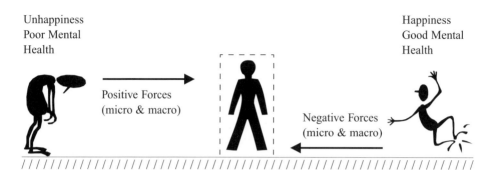

Unhappiness
Poor Mental
Health

Happiness
Good Mental
Health

Positive Forces
(micro & macro)

Negative Forces
(micro & macro)

*Figure 1.*Free body diagram showing positive and negative forces on a client (individual/couple/family). The bio-psycho-social-cultural model is considered essential for understanding human nature, and is conceptualized as being comprised of micro forces (bio and psycho) and macro forces (social and cultural). Any of these four types of forces can exert a positive or negative influence on the client.

micro (i.e., individual – biological and psychological) or macro (i.e., relational – social and cultural) forces. Since clients in therapy are usually experiencing more negative than positive forces – thus pushing them to experience poor mental health – this model will be described initially from the point of view of negative forces. First, *micro or individual influences* that impact the individual can be *biological* in nature. This could include the possibility of genetic predispositions for psychological disorders such as schizophrenia, depression, etc. Similarly, physical health problems can negatively influence an individual's mental health because of pain and/or by reducing motivation and hope for improved health. *Psychological* micro forces that exert a negative influence on the individual can be depicted with the TFB model of functioning, i.e., Thoughts-Feelings-Behavior. It is typically negative affect that motivates a client to seek therapy, but it is very important to recognize the interdependence of thoughts, feelings, and behavior. Thus, feelings can be dramatically improved *indirectly* by modifying specific maladaptive thoughts and behavior (i.e., cognitive-behavior therapy, CBT). Given the powerful influence that changing these factors in therapy can have on improving mental health, it is essential that they be assessed prior to treatment.

Another important psychological micro influence that acts negatively on a client is imbalance. For example, clients often will be nonassertive or aggressive (i.e., not balanced or assertive); have an overdeveloped "parent" or "child" (rather than a balanced "adult" – from the Transactional Analysis model); be too emotional or too rational (and not some form of balance between the two); and/or work obsessively (imbalanced towards "doing" rather than having a balance between "doing" and "being"). These personality characteristics and lifestyles, as well as interpersonal imbalances, are inherently problematic and reflect an ignorance and lack of application of the timeless wisdom in Aristotle's Golden Mean, i.e., find and follow a middle road between the extremes in life. Being alert to imbalance, in its multitude of forms, during the initial assessment is recommended as an important component of understanding the client's world.

Second, *macro or relational influences* that exert a powerful influence on the client are *social* relationships. A major force in this domain is one's family of origin and the intergenerational patterns that can be transmitted through modeling and via operant and

classical conditioning, e.g., authoritarian parenting style, alcoholism, personality characteristics such as aggressiveness, introversion, etc. Another powerful, negative macro force
is unhealthy relationships, e.g., fighting spouses, "friends" who are really pretenders,
acquaintances (often mistaken as friends) who distract you from developing quality, long-
term friendships. Not recognizing and accepting the influence of different gender roles
also exerts an important macro influence on relationships.

The second type of macro force that needs to be considered to better understand
client behavior is the important effect of *culture*. The U.S. and traditional China/Russia
define opposite poles on continua such as individualism-collectivism, capitalism-com-
munism, etc. These cultural differences are powerful influences on the inherent *values* of
each culture, which are subsequently manifested in the *attitudes* and *behaviors* of individuals, couples and families. For example, Buss and a large team of researchers (1990)
surveyed 9,474 adults from 33 countries, on 6 continents and 5 islands, to learn how
culture might influence a person's experience in determining who is desirable as a mate.
Large cultural influences on mate selection were found, with data being depicted on two
dimensions: 1) horizontal axis – whether the culture had traditional values (e.g., China,
India) or Western-industrial (modern) values (e.g., Netherlands, Great Britain); and 2)
vertical axis – the relative importance of education, intelligence and social refinement
(e.g., Columbia, Spain) versus a pleasing disposition (e.g., Indonesia, Estonia) in choosing a mate. Buss and colleagues concluded that mate selection varies dramatically between cultures, and that socialization within a culture is the key factor influencing what
qualities come to be considered attractive in the opposite sex.

It is also very important to recognize that clients come to therapy possessing a variety
of positive qualities (i.e., positive forces pushing them towards greater mental health and
happiness). First, from a biological point of view, someone who has good health, eats a
balanced diet, and exercises regularly may exhibit greater motivation for change than a
person in poor health who eats poorly and does not exercise. Second, psychological factors are powerful influences on mental health. For example, a psychologically-minded
person who has good habits of assertiveness (e.g., readily expresses his/her feelings and
needs in an empathic way; MacLean, 1998) is likely to show more potential for growth
than a passive, aggressive, or, worse, passive-aggressive individual. Similarly, an adult with
a secure attachment style will be comfortable with trust and intimacy, and will often experience higher levels of commitment and relationship satisfaction – very important qualities
that promote mental health. Religious and/or spiritual psychological experiences are also
strengthening for many people (e.g., belief in God, 12-Step programs). Given the common
factors research suggesting that individual characteristics are the number one factor in
therapeutic change (accounting for 40 percent of the outcome variance; Lambert, 1992), it
is clearly very important that these positive biological and psychological micro influences
be identified in assessment. Once recognized, they can then be used by the client and therapist to help counteract the negative forces that have propelled the client into an unhappy
state of mind.

Similarly, there are many positive macro forces that help individuals achieve and
maintain greater quality of life. Third, important social influences such as emotional (and
financial) support from family and friends can be invaluable at times of crisis. Developing greater insight into the differing values of both genders can smooth interactions in
opposite-sex relationships, and generate more understanding and acceptance between
the sexes (e.g., Gray, 1993; Tannen, 1990). The fourth key influence on humans is culture. Since culture is directly related to the development of values in its respective citi-

zens, and since *values strongly influence attitudes and thus behavior*, it is inevitable that some cultural values will be more conducive to higher levels of mental health at certain times. For example, the American work ethic is an important influence in helping to create financial security to meet basic physical needs. On the other hand, too much individualism and an imbalanced lifestyle of "doing" over "being" can harm interpersonal relationships and result in lower levels of individual and relational happiness. In sum, a good initial assessment will literally measure or, at a minimum, develop conscious awareness of these positive influences on a client's mental health. The therapist can then work together with the client to utilize these strengths to develop positive change and growth.

Consistent with the bio-psycho-social-cultural model of human nature, it is the belief of this writer that an adequate assessment must explore, or at least be sensitive to, all of these facets of human functioning. At the individual level, this means examining biological factors such as family history, physical health problems, and pain. Psychologically, it is important to gather information on the thoughts-feelings-behavior and spiritual/religious aspects of individual functioning. At the relational level, an assessment of the quality and quantity of a person's social relationships needs to be carried out. This would include relationships with family members, friends vs. acquaintances, romantic partners, employers, and so forth. The type and frequency of possible negative interactional patterns (e.g., pursue-withdraw) should also be assessed in these relationships. Culture also exerts an important influence on individual and relationship functioning and this needs to be acknowledged in both assessment and treatment. Figures indicate that 50 percent of first marriages in the United States will end in separation or divorce within 20 years, with this figure reaching 67 percent for women who marry under 18 years of age (Bramlett & Mosher, 2001). It is not at all surprising that Americans are often preoccupied with individualism and networking, *and* that the U.S. consistently has the highest or one of the highest divorce rates in the world (Kail & Cavanagh, 2004; Kail, 2001). The often overlooked force of culture on marital relations is further evident in the findings of a very large U.S. national sample (8,383 married couples; Lavee & Olson, 1993). Results revealed that a mere nine percent of American couples were found to be genuinely happily married ("vitalized" couples), whereas the other 91 percent were experiencing reduced happiness and/or were at various levels of marital dissolution. The ramifications of not acknowledging the powerful influence culture exerts on human behavior is stated most clearly by Segall, Lonner, and Berry (1998, p. 1108): "To keep culture peripheral, or, worse, to avoid it altogether lest it challenge one's own view of reality is myopic and a disservice to psychological inquiry."

A valuable contribution to understanding human nature has been given to us by Stephen Covey in his books, *The 7 Habits of Highly Effective People* (1990) and *The 7 Habits of Highly Effective Families* (1997). In his original, remarkably insightful work, Covey argues that in order to achieve effectiveness and thus a high quality of life, people must approach life through an *inside-out approach*: that is, strong personalities are the necessary ingredient for forming strong relationships. Warren (1992) captures this same idea is his observation that "a great marriage requires two healthy people, and the time to get healthy is *before* you get married" (emphasis in original; p. 63). Although acknowledging the relationship between physical health and marital quality, Warren makes it clear that he is not referring to physical (e.g., nutrition and exercise) or even spiritual health, but to the extremely important emotional and mental health of the two people considering marriage. Here again, the important concept of balance is evident: psychological healthiness at the individual level is necessary for relational healthiness to be possible at the couple level. Therefore, determining how effective individuals and families are through their capacity to apply the 7 Habits can also be included as part of a comprehensive assessment.

The very important impact of time also needs to be assessed. Consistent with the major thesis of this chapter, Kail and Cavanaugh (2004) argue strongly that the four life forces (biological, psychological, social and cultural) all operate on humans through the lens of time, i.e., developmental changes occur across the life-span. In other words, a person will often repeatedly experience a particular issue (e.g., a vulnerability) during his/her life. For example, trust (or mistrust) in infancy will develop into progressively more complex forms of trust (or mistrust) over the life-span in relationships with friends and/or a significant other.

Recognizing how the four forces interact and manifest their influence on human development differently across time is essential for understanding human nature in general and a client's problems in particular. For example, developmental aspects of the individual and/or relationship should be considered. This can begin by identifying key early life experiences that may continue to manifest themselves through childhood, adolescence, and adulthood. Intergenerational familial influences also need to be recognized. Since values and attitudes impact behavior, and since values in particular can change as a function of the passage of time, *cohort effects* should also be considered as a potential potent influence on the client, whether this is an individual, couple, or family. It is very important to recognize that the force of time can be either a positive influence on an individual (e.g., adopting the healthy values of an older role model) or a negative influence (e.g., clashing of values between two spouses of different cultural backgrounds or families of origin).

It is recommended that clinicians actually draw a free body diagram of the positive and negative influences acting on a client and identify which of these are of primary or secondary importance. This visual depiction of the many micro and macro forces impinging on a client has the capacity to clarify a client's issues, to identify weaknesses that need minimizing and strengths that need maximizing, and to guide therapeutic efforts toward sustained improvement in mental health.

How to Assess: The Four Pillars and Assessment in Marriage

A cautionary note at this point seems warranted. The amount of information worthy of inclusion in the assessment procedure may be perceived as daunting to some readers. But it is important to remember that the following discussion is a relatively comprehensive overview of assessment techniques that could be employed with individuals and/or couples. In actual clinical work, a smaller number of specific assessment strategies will need to be selected as a function of the particular client. Specific references on the assessment inventories discussed in this text have been given, but the reader is also referred to assessment handbooks for further information (e.g., Fischer & Corcoran, 1994; Touliatos, Perlmutter, & Straus, 1990). It should also be noted that certain assessment measures can only be administered by clinicians with adequate psychometric training (e.g., Minnesota Multiphasic Personality Inventory-2 [MMPI-2; Hathaway & McKinley, 1940; Watkins, Campbell, Nieberding, & Hallmark, 1995]; Wechsler Adult Intelligence Scale–Revised [WAIS-R; Wechsler, 1955; Wechsler, 1981]), so some referrals to a clinical psychologist or psychometrist may be required. Since relatively few companies actually publish psychometric tests, directly contacting them should provide information about what instruments require specialized training (e.g., The Psychological Corporation, National Computer Systems, Psychological Assessment Resources). Nonetheless, the vast majority of assessment measures are readily available, and accessing them should be relatively easy and inexpensive (or free, if in the literature as they often are) to the clinician who recognizes the value of doing an initial evaluation of a client's problems.

The initial referral information and the first interview will be crucial in helping the therapist to define better the presenting problem and therefore to select specific instruments that properly assess the client's world. In addition to carefully selecting assessment instruments, creating simple computer programs to add up item scores (e.g., in Excel) will make scoring much more efficient. Furthermore, an increasingly common scenario in clinical work is to have clients complete questionnaires right on a computer, which further facilitates the processing of assessment information. Some assessment inventories include computer-generated reports that further simplify interpretation (e.g., MMPI-2; Symptom Checklist-90-R [SCL-90-R; Derogatis, 1983]; Neuroticism-Extraversion-Openness Personality Inventory-Revised [NEO-PI-R; Costa & McCrae, 1992; Piedmont, 1998]). Finally, with time and greater experience, the clinician will better be able to select the procedures that optimally examine the special assessment needs of particular clients.

The Four Pillars of Assessment

Having answered the question of what to assess, the question arises as to how to do an assessment. Assessment begins with a referral, whether self- or other-referred. Someone – the client, a spouse, a parent – has posed a question: Why am I feeling so lousy?; How can we regain our previous marital happiness?; How can we change our adolescent's delinquent behavior? As has been argued throughout this chapter, the starting point for answering such questions is to gather "information to make informed decisions" (Brock & Barnard, 1999, p. 18).

Sattler (1992) has defined "the four pillars of assessment" as a "building blocks" approach to gathering information and using it to build hypotheses, formulations, and relevant recommendations with which to help the client. The first pillar is *norm-referenced tests*, which refers to tests that are administered in a standardized way and that have a norm group with which to compare a client being assessed. These tests can be used to understand better an individual client, or a couple or family. The second pillar is *interviews*. This typically refers to a less-structured, open-ended exploration into a range of topics although structured interviews are also employed on a less frequent basis. The goal here is to gather information from multiple sources (e.g., spouse, close friend, teacher) on all key issues. *Observations* define Sattler's third pillar. This often refers to observing the behavior of persons (usually children and families) in their natural settings (e.g., home, school) to note interactions between the referred client and others (e.g., parents, peers), and/or possible differences in behavior between settings. The fourth pillar of assessment is *informal assessment*. Here, specific information about the presenting problem is sought through supplementary techniques such as unstandardized or nonnormed tests, journaling, logging behavior, and so forth.

Considering Sattler's four pillars of assessment as a foundation for how to perform an assessment, the question still remains as to how one carries out an assessment as a function of who is being assessed. That is, how do assessments vary as a function of whether the client is an individual or a couple or family? Since healthy relationships are comprised of healthy persons (e.g., Covey, 1990; Warren, 1992), it is argued that all assessments will require at least a minimal amount of individual evaluation. In the case of a couple or family, further assessment examining the quality of different relationships will also need to be done.

A comprehensive examination of how to do an assessment is beyond the focus of this chapter, so the reader is referred to Groth-Marnat (1999) for more detailed information on assessing adults and Sattler (1998) for children. An overview from Sattler's (1992) view that assessment is comprised of four fundamental domains will be presented. First, norm-referenced tests on individuals are typically carried out objectively (e.g., paper-and-pencil tests) and, to a lesser extent, projectively (e.g., subjective interpretations of images). Of utmost importance when selecting a norm-referenced test is to determine how well the test allows the clinician to answer the referral question (or address the presenting problem). The clinician's experience, knowledge of relevant literature, and practical concerns such as time and cost are also important when choosing a test. Whereas the Minnesota Multiphasic Personality Inventory-2 (MMPI-2; Watkins et al., 1995) gives valuable information about personality and levels of mood (Axis I of the DSM-IV-TR), the Millon Clinical Multiaxial Inventory (MCMI; Millon, 1977; Millon, 1994) assesses personality disorders (Axis II). Other norm-referenced tests include the Beck Depression Inventory (BDI; Beck, 1996; Beck, Steer, & Garbin, 1988) for depression and the Fear Survey Schedule (FSS; Wolpe & Lang, 1964; Wolpe & Lang, 1977) for anxiety. In addition, adult intellectual functioning can be assessed with the Wechsler Adult Intelligence Scale III (WAIS-III; Wechsler, 1997) and general cognitive functioning with the Mini-Mental Status Examination (MMSE; Folstein, Folstein, & McHugh, 1975; Tombaugh et al., 1996).

Whereas these objective tests often make administration, scoring, and interpretation easier, they can facilitate faking of responses and depend heavily upon the client's self-knowledge. In contrast, projective tests such as the Rorschach (a series of 10 ambiguous inkblot cards; Exner, 1969; Exner, 1993) or the Thematic Apperception Test (TAT; a series of ambiguous pictures; Morgan & Murray, 1935; Morgan, 1995) bypass a person's potential conscious resistance and may allow a more accurate evaluation of a person's underlying unconscious structure of personality.

Sattler's second pillar of assessment is interviewing. The word interview was derived from the French words, *entrevoir*, to have a glimpse of, and *s'entrevoir*, to see each other. These roots reflect a key component of good interviewing, namely, rapport. The essential therapeutic alliance between the client and clinician is made possible through Rogers' (1957) ideas of genuineness, unconditional positive regard, and accurate empathy, which enable the development of respect, mutual confidence, and ultimately a trusting relationship. The main function of an assessment interview is to gather information that may otherwise be unobtainable, such as idiosyncratic qualities of the client, his/her/their reactions to present life circumstances, quality of relationships with family of origin members, and so forth. Interviews are an effective way to acquire details about a client's presenting problem, through asking questions about feelings, cognitions, behavior, and physiological arousal. Knowledge about antecedents and consequences of the problem as well as family history and background information can also be obtained by interviewing the client in addition to people who are familiar with him/her. In addition, a crucial function of the interview is to serve as a check on information collected through testing in order to ascertain its validity and overall meaning. In sum, whereas the goals of interviewing during assessment are to establish genuine rapport and to collect important information to adequately define the problem, later interviewing can act to define specific goals that will be worked on in therapy and to help clients explore deeper emotional aspects of their personal issues.

Traditional approaches to understanding client's problems typically view personality as a manifestation of enduring underlying traits, with problems being an indication of intrapsychic conflicts which need to be diagnosed. In contrast, behavioral assessment (Sattler's third pillar, behavioral assessment) perceives personality constructs as a way to summarize particular behavior patterns, behaviors that are maintained by current situational conditions and which need to be precisely identified. A core feature of behavioral assessment is *functional analysis* (Skinner, 1953). This analysis refers to identifying the situational factors (the stimuli) that precede a particular behavior and the consequences that follow it. Thus, once identified, a maladaptive behavior can be changed in therapy by manipulating the stimuli and/or the reinforcers (i.e., the consequences) of the behavior.

The most common type of behavioral assessment is the behavioral interview. Here, the interviewer obtains information about the *antecedents*, *behaviors*, and *consequences* of the presenting issues (ABC model) by asking about pretreatment levels of frequency, intensity, and duration of the problem. This information is very important because it identifies specific areas that will try to be changed during treatment. Naturalistic observation is also used in behavioral assessment, in which trained staff closely monitor the behaviors of, for example, a family at dinner time, a child in a classroom. Whereas this technique is often expensive in both time and money, another method, self-monitoring, is often used and involves the client observing and recording his/her own behaviors, thoughts, and emotions. A comprehensive type of behavioral assessment, which could incorporate interviewing, self-monitoring and naturalistic observation, is Lazarus's (1989) BASIC ID model: behaviors (B), affect (A), sensation (S), imagery (I), cognition (C), interpersonal relations (I), and use of pharmacological drugs (D).

Behavioral assessment is an important component of the clinician's assessment repertoire. This is largely attributable to the fact that the initial identification of problem behaviors is usually directly related to the changing of these behaviors in treatment. Furthermore, initial baseline behaviors provide a valuable comparison point with which to evaluate the efficacy of the treatment, information, which can be very reinforcing for clients as they strive to change self-defeating behavior and maladaptive habits.

Sattler's fourth and last pillar for carrying out an assessment is referred to as informal assessment. This category provides an opportunity for the clinician to supplement data obtained from the other three pillars with some further domain-specific information. This could include giving informal tests created by the clinician or others about the presenting problem, examining prior records, keeping a journal, and so forth. Taken together, information obtained from these four pillars of assessment should give the clinician a comprehensive picture of the client's problem.

Assessment in Marriage

The previous discussion, although more commonly applied to the evaluation of individuals, is applicable to all types of clients. But there are serious limitations to focusing exclusively on the individual, e.g., successful attempts to change an individual can easily be neutralized because the person is still living in a dysfunctional home environment. Besides difficulties at the individual level, problems also occur at the relational level (e.g., marriage and/or family), and these issues also need to be assessed. Considering the marital relationship, and recognizing the limited scope of this chapter, an overview of assessment in marriage will be presented from three key perspectives: 1) Karney and Bradbury (1995) Vulnerability-Stress-Adaptation model of marriage, 2) Johnson model of Emotion Focused Therapy for Couples (EFT; Johnson & Whiffen, 2003; Johnson, 1996; Greenberg & Johnson, 1988), and 3) Gottman's (1999b) Sound Marital House theory. For further information on assessment in marriage, the reader is referred to the following sources: Gottman (1994), Bradbury and Fincham (1990), and O'Leary (1987).

Vulnerability–Stress–Adaptation Model of Marriage

Based on 115 longitudinal studies, Karney and Bradbury (1995) present a model suggesting that there are three general factors that predict *marital quality* or *marital stability*. The first set of variables involves *adaptive processes*, i.e., how well couples communicate and employ problem-solving skills. The second factor is *stressful events* and refers to how well couples manage acute and chronic stressors like the birth of a child, illness, unemployment, and so forth. The third group of variables is *enduring vulnerabilities*, or stable demographic, historical, personality, or experiential factors that individuals bring to a marriage, e.g., attachment style, parental divorce, addictions, and so forth. Bradbury (1995) strongly emphasizes the importance of assessment in marital therapy and suggests a number of psychometrically sound measures that should be used in assessing the four fundamental domains of marriage.

In the first domain, marital quality and stability, marital quality needs to be assessed using measures in two key areas: 1) commitment and 2) marital satisfaction. Stanley and Markman's (1992) 60-item Commitment Inventory distinguishes between two types of marital commitment – personal dedication (i.e., intrinsic motivation to improved the relationship) and constraint commitment (i.e., remaining in the relationship due to social pressure). Several psychometrically strong measures exist to measure marital satisfaction. For example, the 32-item Dyadic Adjustment Scale (DAS; Spanier, 1976) provides a total score as well as four subscale relational scores on satisfaction, cohesion, consensus, and affectional expression. The 15-item Locke-Wallace Marital Adjustment Test (MAT; 1959) is also commonly used to evaluate marital satisfaction.

Other scales of marital satisfaction focus, not on relationship qualities like the DAS, but on subjective global evaluations of one's marriages. These measures are typically much shorter and easier to administer and score than the DAS. Two examples are Norton's (1983) six-item Quality Marriage Index (QMI) and Fincham and Linfield's (1997) Positive and Negative Quality in Marriage Scale (PANQIMS). The latter instrument is a two-dimensional measure comprised of six items – three positive and three negative appraisals of one's marriage and spouse. Besides having the advantages of being better able to measure the single underlying dimension of marital satisfaction as well as the capacity to compare it across studies, the PANQIMS allows the measurement of four types of marital functioning: two traditional types, happy and distressed, plus two new and to-date largely unrecognized categories of ambivalent and indifferent. A second outcome measure, marital stability, refers to how close a couple may be to divorcing and can be measured with the

Weiss and Cerreto (1980) Marital Status Inventory (MSI). This 14-item instrument presents statements depicting different steps in the divorce process.

The second domain for assessment in the Karney and Bradbury (1995) model is adaptive processes. The first component for assessment here is the important area of presenting complaints. The Areas of Change Questionnaire (ACQ; Weiss, Hops, & Patterson, 1973) presents 34 areas in a marriage where change might be desired. Two scores are generated in each area: 1) a desired change score for one's partner, and 2) a perceived change score for oneself. The ACQ provides valuable information on the content and magnitude of problems spouses are experiencing, in addition to the degree that these complaints are being recognized by the spouse.

The second type of adaptive process that needs evaluation is marital interactions. Having identified specific areas of conflict, it is now of value to identify the interpersonal source of these tensions as well as any abilities each spouse may have for resolving them. The 64-item Marital Coping Inventory (MCI; Bowman, 1990) assesses spousal behavior on several dimensions including conflict, introspective self-blame, positive approach, self-interest, and avoidance. Another self-report measure of marital interaction is the Communication Patterns Questionnaire (CPQ; Christensen, 1987). This scale asks spouses to rate the likelihood of 35 behaviors occurring when disagreements arise, as well as examines demand-withdraw cycles between partners.

More than assessing the marital relationship in terms of each individual's perception of the relationship, the main focus in evaluating marital interactions is on *observing* the dynamic interpersonal exchange. According to Margolin's (1983) interactional model of marital assessment, it is the marital relationship that is the "patient" – rather than either spouse. Predominantly from a research standpoint, observational measurement involves first videotaping and then coding the interaction of a couple as they discuss either a hypothetical conflict or an actual marital difficulty. (Although the videotaping and systematic observational scoring of couples may not be considered feasible to most clinicians, much valuable information can still be obtained by carefully observing interactions during session and/or by analyzing and discussing a particular marital problem with clients that was previously recorded at home.) One observational measurement technique, the Rapid Couples Interaction Scoring System (RCISS; Krokoff, Gottman, & Hass, 1989) allows the coding of the content of alternating speakers (e.g., agree, deny responsibility, mind-reading) and the nonverbal affect of both the speaker and listener (positive, neutral, negative). This data can provide valuable information about how positive and negative behaviors and emotions impact the quality of a couple's interactions.

Based on the observational assessment of marital satisfaction, Gottman (1993, 1994) has proposed a balance view of marriage. That is, it is the relative balance between positivity and negativity in couples' observed marital interactions that is the key factor in predicting whether couples are at risk for marital discord and instability. For example, in a four-year longitudinal study of couple types, Gottman (1993) used observed positive and negative behavior to predict which married relationships were most at risk for distress and potential divorce. Five types of couples were identified: stable or low-risk-for-divorce couples (validating, volatile, and conflict-avoiding) and unstable or high-risk-for-divorce couples (hostile and hostile-detached). It is of interest that research findings using more recently developed satisfaction measures to assess global marital functioning via positive and negative appraisals are consistent with Gottman's perspective about the centrality of positive and negative behavior in determining marital satisfaction and stability. For example, *dissatisfied marriages* on the Positive and Negative Quality in Marriage Scale (PANQIMS; Fincham & Linfield, 1997) are perceived by spouses as having low positive and high negative qualities whereas *indifferent marriages* are evaluated as being low in both positive and negative qualities.

Given the important connection between how people think and how they feel and behave, evaluating the cognitions of distressed spouses is another area that warrants assessment prior to treatment. Cognitive assessment can be divided into two areas. First, distressed spouses will often make inaccurate attributions about their partner's behavior along three dimensions – locus, stability, and globality. The Relationships Attribution Measure (RAM) by Fincham and Bradbury (1992) assesses the causal and responsibility attributions spouses make about events in their marriage. A second type of cognition is unrealistic beliefs about marriage. Eidelson and Epstein (1982) developed the Relationship Belief Inventory (RBI) to evaluate five different types of belief about marital relations.

The third fundamental domain of marriage according to Karney and Bradbury (1995) is enduring vulnerabilities. These are personal characteristics each person brings to the marriage, qualities that are relatively stable over the course of the marriage, e.g., family of origin experiences such as parental separation and divorce, sexual attitudes, level of social adjustment. Personality traits and tendencies are better assessed with norm-referenced tests than with interviews. Since marital discord is often related to personality problems, the MMPI or the MCMI (see earlier description) would be obvious choices for assessing these enduring vulnerabilities. Another personality dimension, neuroticism, is also associated with marital deterioration, which could be measured with the 23-item neuroticism subscale of the Eysenck Personality Questionnaire (EPQ; Eysenck & Eysenck, 1978) or the neuroticism scale of the NEO PI-R (Costa & McCrae, 1992). Another type of enduring vulnerability is attachment style, which is discussed in the next section, Emotion Focused Theory for Couples (EFT).

The fourth and final domain of marriage in Karney and Bradbury's factor model is stressful life events. Although interviews can identify many of these circumstances, a standardized approach is of value in order to capture the broad number of stressful events. For example, the Social Readjustment Rating Scale (SRRS; Holmes & Rahe, 1967) asks respondents to indicate which of 43 events they experienced during the last year. Everyday stressors can also impact on psychological and physical well-being, and these can be measured with the Hassles Scale (HS; Kanner, Coyne, Schaefer, & Lazarus, 1981).

Bradbury (1995) points out that these instruments provide only a common denominator for marital assessment and that other information will also be beneficial in supplementing this assessment data. In particular, Bradbury emphasizes the importance of having a thorough working knowledge of diagnostic references such as the *Diagnostic and Statistical Manual of Mental Disorders* (DSM-IV-TR) and/or the *International Classification of Diseases* (ICD-9-CM). Furthermore, one's ability to carry out competent assessments can often be enhanced by obtaining information about the following areas: depression (e.g., Beck Depression Inventory II [BDI-II]; Beck, 1996; Kendall, Hollon, Beck, Hammen, & Ingram, 1987); alcohol use (e.g., Short Michigan Alcoholism Screening Test [SMAST]; Selzer, Vinokur, & van Rooijen, 1975); sexual satisfaction (e.g., Index of Sexual Satisfaction [ISS]; Hudson, Harrison, & Crosscup, 1981); positive feelings in the relationship (e.g., Positive Feelings Questionnaire [PFQ]; O'Leary, Fincham, & Turkewitz, 1983); the role of religion and spirituality in the relationship (e.g., Fincham, Fernandes, & Humphreys, 1993); and relationship ideologies and philosophies (e.g., Relational Dimensions Instrument [RDI]; Fitzpatrick, 1988).

Emotion Focused Therapy for Couples (EFT)

John Bowlby, the originator of attachment theory (1969, 1973, 1980), described attachment as "the propensity of human beings to make strong affectional bonds to particular others" (Bowlby, 1977, p. 201). Although attachment theory was initially used to examine mother-infant interactions (Ainsworth, 1967, 1968), the study of attachment in adult romantic relationships began in the mid-1980s (e.g., Johnson, 1986; Hazan & Shaver, 1987). Several key tenets of attachment theory are relevant to the functioning of adult romantic relationships:

- seeking and maintaining contact with a significant other is an innate motivating force;
- proximity to a loved one offers a safe haven, which reduces feelings of anxiety and vulnerability, and also helps to create a secure base, from which one can more confidently explore and adaptively respond to his/her environment;
- emotional accessibility and responsiveness are the building blocks of attachment bonds (Johnson, 2003).

In happy marriages these attachment needs are being met, whereas in unhappy marriages these core needs are not being met (MacLean, 2001).

Given the nature of attachment bonds, and the fact that love relationships are more emotionally intense than other adult friendships (Rose & Zand, 2000), it would be remiss to have any serious discussion of adult romantic relationships without including the topic of emotions. In the area of couple therapy, clients are seeking to end repeated interpersonal conflicts and to better manage the painful emotions that accompany such distressing interactions. Johnson (1996) uses attachment theory as a guide to couple therapy in her emotionally focused therapy for couples (EFT), now one of the best-documented and empirically validated models of couple interventions (Johnson & Whiffen, 1999). In EFT, the focus is on:

reshaping a distressed couple's structured, repetitive interaction patterns, and the emotional responses that evoke these patterns and fostering the development of a secure emotional bond (Johnson, 1996, 1999). For example, in the process of therapy a repetitive demand-withdraw pattern that is accompanied by anger and frustration, or a withdraw-withdraw pattern characterized by numbing and polarization, will expand into a more flexible pattern of expressing needs and vulnerabilities and responding to such needs in the partner. As a result, the partners are able to comfort, reassure, and support each other, creating a safe haven, which empowers each of them and maximizes their personal growth and development. So "You are impossible to get close to" followed by "You are too angry. I don't want to get close," may become "I need you to hold me" followed by "I want to comfort you. I feel so good when you turn to me" (Johnson & Whiffen, 1999, pp. 366-367).

The process of EFT involves nine steps that are organized into three therapeutic shifts—cycle de-escalation, changing interactional positions, and consolidation and integration (Johnson, 1996). Although EFT does not strongly distinguish between assessment and treatment, the first two steps in the process of change are generally conceptualized as assessment. Since the therapist is working directly with emotions in EFT, it is of utmost importance that clients feel safe and accepted by the therapist – an atmosphere that greatly enhances the likelihood that they will be open and vulnerable with their innermost feelings and needs. Thus, developing a strong therapeutic alliance is necessary right from the initial meeting. Essential for the development of an effective therapeutic alliance in EFT is the consistent use of key features of Rogers' (1951) client-centered therapy. That is, empathy, warmth and genuineness are considered core qualities of the EFT therapist.

In addition to connecting with both partners (i.e., creating an alliance), Step 1 ("Making Maps") in EFT also includes delineating the couple's conflict issues. This involves identifying the areas about which couples primarily fight, e.g., finances, raising children, work vs. leisure balance, and so forth. Step 2 ("Listening to Music") in EFT assessment requires that the therapist go below these tangible manifestations of relationship distress and identify the deeper, core emotional and attachment themes that inevitably underlie these surface issues. For example, one partner may feel that her attachment needs for emotional closeness, safety, and responsiveness are not being adequately met by her male partner. As a result, *rather than directly communicating* these needs to him, nor her associated primary feelings like sadness, fear and hurt, she will be *indirect* and criticize and belittle him about his imperfections and perceived irresponsibilities around tangible family issues ("Pursuer" position in the negative interactional pattern ["the cycle"]). In response, rather than listening attentively and responding empathically to his partner's concerns – *and* in turn express his underlying feelings (e.g., anger, shame, hurt) and needs (e.g., attachment needs for a safe haven, emotional closeness, consistent messages) – he also will *communicate indirectly* by becoming defensive (e.g., counter-attack) and withdraw emotionally and/or physically from her criticisms and nagging ("Withdrawer" position). This pernicious cycle ("Pursuer-Withdrawer" pattern) is the manifestation of unmet attachment needs and is at the heart of troubled marriages (Johnson & Whiffen, 2003).

Other assessment goals during the first two steps of EFT include: assessing the nature of the problem and the relationship, including their suitability for marital therapy and EFT specifically; assessing each partner's goals and agendas for therapy; assessing for contraindications for the use of EFT (e.g., ongoing violence; a verbally abusive husband who demeans his spouse when she talks about being depressed and suicidal); and creating a therapeutic agreement between the couple and therapist (e.g., a consensus on therapeutic goals and how therapy will proceed). "By the end of the assessment … (the therapist) has a map of the typical interactions that define the attachment between this couple, a clear sense of their positions and patterns. The therapist also begins to have a sense of how these are experienced on an emotional level by each partner. He/she begins to sense the *tone* of the relationship, the music of the dance" (pp. 75-76; Johnson, 1996). Information-gathering and rapport-building in the assessment part of EFT are further enhanced by the following interviewing and therapeutic strategies: reflection (i.e., empathic reflections of each partner's experience of the relationship); validation (i.e., conveying the message that the partners' emotions and responses are legitimate and understandable given the context of their relationship; especially important during the initial sessions); evocative reflections and questions (i.e., accessing how each partner perceives and experiences problems in the relationship and identifying the interactional positions and cycle(s); particularly significant in the early assessment sessions); tracking and reflecting interactions (i.e., identifying specific behavioral sequences that typify the relationship and reflect attachment issues); and reframing (i.e., restating partners' behavior in terms of attachment strategies, e.g., "'Moving away' is your way of standing up for yourself, of protecting yourself, from his 'poking.' Is that right?" (Johnson, 1996; Ivey, 1988))."

EFT assessment can also include the administration of psychometric testing to determine each partner's attachment style, which directly relates to each partner's position in the interaction cycle. For example, a "Pursuer" typically has an anxious attachment style whereas a "Withdrawer" has an avoidant attachment style (e.g., MacLean, 2001; Johnson & Whiffen, 2003), although these styles of relating can exist together (see below). The Experiences in Close Relationships scale (ECR; Brennan, Clark, & Shaver, 1998; Fraley, Waller, & Brennan, 2000) is a two-dimensional, 36-item, four-category measure of adult attachment style that assesses general patterns of closeness and intimacy related to attachment in romantic relationships. Whereas secure attachment style is related to positive marital outcomes, insecure attachments—whether anxious (e.g., hyperactivated attachment, anxious-ambivalent attachment, preoccupied attachment), avoidant (e.g., deactivated attachment, dismissing-avoidant attachment), or both anxious and avoidant (e.g., alternately hyperactivated and deactivated attachment, fearful-avoidant attachment, disorganized attachment, unresolved attachment [with respect to trauma and loss])—are associated with lower levels of marital functioning (e.g., MacLean, 2001; Feeney, 1994, Senchak & Leonard, 1992). With secure attachment, appropriate, context-sensitive attachment system activation and deactivation takes place, whereas in fearful-avoidant or disorganized attachment, there is the collapse of any coherent attachment strategy due to the opposing tendencies to seek and avoid connection (Johnson, 2003).

It is common in EFT to conduct an individual assessment session with each of the partners, usually after the first or second couple session(s). There are several reasons according to Johnson (1996) to include these individual sessions: strengthen the therapeutic alliance with each partner; obtain more information from each partner in a different context (e.g., how each partner interacts without their partner present; seek new information that would be difficult to obtain with the partner present, such as commitment level, extramarital relationships, etc.); and refine the therapist's impression of each partner's underlying feelings and unmet attachment needs that directly influence the negative interactional pattern.

An important part of any assessment process is feedback, namely, communicating back to the client a summary of interview information and questionnaire results. With EFT, there is an important psychoeducational component in which the couple is informed by the therapist about their specific type of negative interactional cycle(s), what events in their lives typically trigger it, and how the cycle is to "blame" for their relationship disharmony (and not his/her partner). Moreover, the couple is made aware that it is essential for them to become more *accessible* (i.e., be *expressive* of one's true self through the authentic communication of primary emotions and attachment needs) and more *responsive* (i.e., be *receptive* to one's partner by listening attentively and responding empathically) in their interactions in order to create a more secure attachment bond and therefore a happier relationship.

Sound Marital House Theory

A second approach to assessment in marriage is delineated in Gottman's (1999a, 2001) Sound Marital House (SMH) theory. Gottman suggests that lasting effects in marital therapy are most likely when interventions are designed with three prongs: in everyday non-conflict contexts, 1) increase positive affect; and, during conflict resolution, 2) reduce negative affect, and 3) increase positive affect. The SMH theory of marriage presents a systematic approach to accomplishing success in these three areas. It integrates behavior, cognition and physiology, and also recognizes the symbolic nature of gridlocked marital conflict and the importance of creating meaning in people's lives.

The SMH theory has seven components: 1) love maps (the basement of the house), 2) fondness and admiration system, 3) the emotional bank account (turning toward vs. turning away), 4) positive sentiment override, 5) conflict and its resolution (solvable and perpetual problems), 6) making dreams and aspirations come true (avoiding marital gridlock), and 7) creating shared meaning (the attic of the house). The term Love Maps refers to the amount of "cognitive room" a spouse (particularly husbands) allocates both to developing their marriage as well as creating a roadmap of the inner psychological world of his/her spouse. The fondness and admiration system is the amount of affection (e.g., touching) and respect that is demonstrated between partners. Happy marriages are those where a culture of appreciation is nurtured and a culture of criticism is discouraged. The emotional bank account in marriage refers to the importance of keeping a large bank account during mundane everyday interactions by maximizing behaviors in which a spouse "turns toward" his/her partner (i.e., is emotionally responsive) and minimizing "turn away" behaviors (i.e., is emotionally distant).

The fourth level of the Sound Marital House is positive sentiment override. A happy marriage is one based on a deep friendship, or "a mutual respect for and enjoyment of each other's company" (Gottman, 1999b, p. 19). Moreover, each spouse knows their partner intimately and proactively tries to meet his or her special needs. Marriages based on friendship experience "positive sentiment override," i.e., positive thoughts and feelings about one's spouse and marriage that are so engrained that they readily displace negative thoughts and feelings that may arise. With respect to resolving conflict, Gottman (1999a) reports that, in fewer than one-third of couples over a four-year period, discussions about problems actually showed potential for being resolved. Remarkably, in more than two-thirds of the cases, couples repeatedly engaged in arguing over "perpetual problems." Whereas resolvable issues could be discussed using four basic skills – softened startup, accepting influence, repair and de-escalation, and compromise – perpetual problems typically would escalate to gridlocked conflict, which then led to either high levels of negative affect (i.e., criticism, defensiveness, contempt, and stonewalling) or lack of affect and emotional disengagement.

Gottman's sixth level is helping to make the dreams and aspirations of one's partner come true. For example, each spouse can provide support and tolerance for the other's aspirations, or the couple can share their dream and work together to make it come true. A sound marriage, then, avoids gridlock, a situation in which neither partner can honor the other's dreams on any level. The seventh and final level of the SMH theory is creating shared symbolic meaning. Gottman argues that meaning in marriage comes from meshing individual life dreams, narratives, myths, and metaphors. The affect a couple experiences is linked to the meaning each person places on things like family rituals, people's roles, goals, and the meaning of central symbols in the marriage or family (e.g., What does "home" mean to us?). In the creation of a marriage and family, a new culture that has never existed before is actively created.

Consistent with the central theme of this chapter, Gottman (1999a) argues that the assessment of a marriage is an essential prerequisite to attempting any form of intervention. Gottman's assessment strategy attempts to find answers to six different questions: 1) Overall, where is each spouse in the marriage?; 2) What is the nature of the marital friendship?; 3) What is the nature of sentiment override? (is it positive or negative?); 4) What is the nature of conflict and its regulation (note regulation, not resolution)?; 5) What is the nature of their life dreams and shared meaning system?; and 6) What potential resistances exist? In the Gottman model, the first meeting is a conjoint session lasting one-and-a-half hours, in which each spouse gives a narrative of their situation and expresses their expectations for therapy. Several assessment instruments are then given to the couple to complete at home. The second session involves two individual sessions that are 45 minutes in length. Each partner is assessed for violence, personal goals, and individual psychopathology in this meeting. An important ground rule of these sessions is that there are no secrets, i.e., whatever is said between the therapist and each spouse can potentially be mentioned to the other spouse. Session three is another conjoint session in which feedback from the assessment instruments and interviews is presented to the couple.

Gottman's first area of assessment is to determine where each spouse is in the marriage. This involves administering the Marital Adjustment Test (Locke & Wallace, 1959; or Dyadic Adjustment Scale, Spanier, 1976) to evaluate marital satisfaction and the Marital Status Inventory (Weiss & Cerreto, 1980) to evaluate potential for divorce. During individual interviews, several aspects of marriage are assessed: commitment to the marriage, hope and expectations for the marriage as well as therapy, a cost-benefit analysis on remaining in versus leaving the marriage, and determining whether there is any male physical abuse and if either partner is currently in an extra-marital affair.

Second, the nature of the marital friendship is evaluated. The Oral History Interview is used to assess the first two levels of the Sound Marital House, Love Maps and the Fondness and Admiration Systems. In particular, the therapist is looking for positive affect, "we-ness," interest in one's partner, and negativity, chaos and disappointment. The overriding type of sentiment is the third area of investigation. Each spouse is evaluated with respect to negative sentiment override (e.g., perceiving neutral statements as hostile attacks) and positive sentiment override (e.g., perceiving irritable statements as important information but not as hostility). The nature of conflict and its regulation are assessed next. Two types of conflict (resolvable and perpetual) are investigated using two separate questionnaires, Solvable Problems Scale and Perpetual Issues Scale.

The fifth area of assessment is to learn about the nature and potential fulfillment of each spouse's life dreams and shared meaning system. This is accomplished primarily through the Oral History Interview and parts of the Meaning Interview. The interviewer is trying to learn about how each person is able to honor his/her partner's life dreams and how the couple attempts to create meaning in their lives as well as their relationship. The final component of the assessment involves identifying resistances to change in therapy. This includes different levels of commitment to the marriage, betrayals (past and present), psychopathology (e.g., drug and alcohol abuse), past trauma, disorders of individuation, conflict in values, a chaotic interpersonal style involving a tendency to be reactive, and so forth.

All couples receiving Gottman's marital therapy receive the following assessment instruments: Locke-Wallace (marital satisfaction), Weiss-Cerreto (divorce potential), Demographics Sheet, the Symptom Checklist-Revised (SCL-90-R; Derogatis, 1983; a 90-item scale measuring individual psychopathology symptoms on nine difference subscales), 17-Areas Scale (Gottman, 1999a; to determine potential problem or strength areas in the marriage, e.g., emotional engagement, sexual satisfaction and intimacy, spiritual connection), Perpetual Issues and Solvable Problems Scales, and Sound Marital House scales (Gottman, 1999a; e.g., 20-item scales measuring love maps, fondness and admiration, sentiment override, the Four Horsemen, shared meaning, and so forth). Based on this comprehensive assessment involving both interviews and questionnaires, the couple is given feedback on this information in the third session. Feedback helps to create a more level "playing field" between the therapist and the couple, an experience in which the couple becomes more knowledgeable about their individual as well as relational strengths and growth areas. Furthermore, this information helps to establish a solid foundation of knowledge in both the therapist and client from which to proceed to a marital intervention. Moreover, providing this personal information recognizes the often considerable abilities of the client to help solve their own problems, and is an important positive step away from the expert therapist-dependent patient approach to therapy.

Other Assessment Considerations

All clinicians have values. Moreover, all clinicians have biases that influence the type of therapy they do, the kinds of clients they see, whether they assess or don't assess a client before therapy, and so forth. A study by Boughner, Hayes, Bubenzer, and West (1994) of members of the American Association of Marital and Family Therapy (AAMFT) found that only one-third of respondents reported using any kind of standardized assessment instrument (given sampling bias, this figure is likely inflated when generalized to the population of AAMFT therapists). Surprisingly, the instruments that were commonly employed by these marital and family therapists were individual measures such as the MMPI-2 or the Myers-Briggs Type Indicator.

It is argued that adequately assessing the problems of a client prior to beginning treatment is at heart an ethical issue. Most codes of ethics (e.g., American Association of Marriage and Family Therapy's *AAMFT Code of Ethics*, 1998; American Psychological Association's *Ethical Principles of Psychologists and Code of Conduct*, 1992) emphasize important ethical concepts like risk management, responsibility for client welfare, informed consent, confidentiality, dual relationships, and so forth. The *Canadian Code of Ethics for Psychologists* (2000), however, in addition to these issues, goes an important step further by proposing four hierarchically ranked principles that need to be recognized and considered when there are conflicting priorities in clinical work: Principle I: Respect for the Dignity of Persons (highest ranking); Principle II: Responsible Caring; Principle III: Integrity in Relationships; and Principle IV: Responsibility to Society (lowest ranking). It is the view of this writer that competent assessment, which greatly increases understanding of a client's problem and thus should improve subsequent treatment, is at heart an ethical responsibility. That is, clinical assessment is an essential exercise that shows genuine respect and responsible caring for the client and, ultimately, places the needs of the client ahead of the therapist's idiosyncratic biases.

Lambert (1992) proposes that four therapeutic factors – extratherapeutic, common factors, expectancy or placebo, and techniques – are the principal elements accounting for client improvement in therapy. These factors are believed to account for different proportions of client change during therapy: 1) extratherapeutic (e.g., intrinsic motivation, social support, financial resources; 40% of change); 2) common elements in therapy, especially the quality of the therapist-client relationship (30%); 3) client's positive or negative expectancies about therapy (e.g., placebo effect; 15%); and 4) the particular therapeutic technique employed (e.g., Cognitive-Behavioral Therapy vs. Interpersonal Therapy vs. Psychodynamic; 15%). Positive change is considered to be primarily the result of client/extratherapeutic factors. Often surprising to researchers and clinicians is that it is not the particular technique employed or the quality of the therapeutic relationship that most accounts for change, but that improvement is primarily determined by qualities of the client that are external to therapy itself (Hubble, Duncan, & Miller, 1999). Given this research-based insight, it seems essential to identify where a client is from the point of view of the process of change, so that therapy will not be attempted with individuals who are not yet ready to alter their lifestyles.

Prochaska (1999) describes six stages in the change process that he argues must be experienced in a linear fashion in order to achieve long-term change: 1) precontemplation (i.e., client is underaware of the need for change), 2) contemplation (i.e., aware one has a problem and is considering change), 3) preparation (i.e., have begun to be committed to change and intend to take action soon), 4) action (i.e., client expends the time and energy to change his/her environment, attitudes, and/or behavior), 5) maintenance (i.e., client works to consolidate changes and prevent relapse), and 6) termination (i.e., therapy is stopped since self-efficacy has been reached). It is noteworthy that the first three stages occur prior to any change or attempts at change. Clearly, if clients are in any of these stages – especially precontemplation and contemplation – they may not be good candidates for therapy at that time.

Determining one's level in the process of change in therapy is clearly beneficial. This information can be acquired by using interview questions, for example. Are you intending to change in the near future?; What changes, if any, are you currently working on? Or they could be included in an initial intake form (Proschaska, Norcross, & Di Clemente, 1994). A formal questionnaire could also be employed to determine a client's stage of change at the beginning of therapy, e.g., the 32-item Stages of Change Scale (SCS; McConnaughy, Prochaska, & Velicer, 1983).

The culmination of the assessment process is the Intake and Assessment Report. This is the communication phase of assessment. Groth-Marnat (1999) suggests that every report should be an integration of old information as well as new information that provides a unique perspective of the client. Old information will include basic demographic data, reason for referral, prior reports and clinical information, and relevant history, whereas new information will include assessment results, clinical observations, summary/conclusions, and treatment recommendations.

Stylistically, the assessment report is a combination of the science (and art) of competent information gathering and the art of persuading the reader that one's assessment of the client's problems are accurate and comprehensive, that the conclusions are practical, and that the recommendations should lead to action during treatment. In communicating one's assessment findings, it is of value to follow several writing guidelines: be clear, concise (yet not overlook important details), coherent and cohesive ("4 Cs of good writing"). Jargon should be avoided. As in all written and spoken communication, remember who your audience is. Write so that an intelligent lay person can understand the report. Avoid gross generalizations by including statements that are specifically relevant to the client. With regard to level of detail, some degree of balance is recommended between presenting general concepts, test results, and examples of behavior.

In sum, the old and new information in an assessment report must be woven together like a tapestry, so that it provides integrated, comprehensive, understandable, and clinically useful data that will guide subsequent therapy.

The final and an integral part of the assessment process is communicating salient findings back to the client. Besides it being the right of the client to receive feedback on questionnaires and forms that he/she may have spent several hours completing, there is growing evidence that assessment feedback can be beneficial therapeutically (e.g., Finn & Tonsager, 1992). Initially, the client is given a rationale for the chosen instruments and any questions are answered. It is important not to get bogged down in details when giving feedback, but instead to focus on several key areas, e.g., stage of change, marital satisfaction, level of depression, key family influences, strengths and growth areas, and so forth. This information should be integrated into the context of the client's life and should employ concrete examples to support the findings. Stylistically, it is important to give feedback in a clear, understandable manner that is free of technical jargon and which matches the client's educational level. There are also a number of computer programs available now that generate simplified reports directed toward the client (e.g., Lewak, Marks, & Nelson, 1990).

Although feedback is usually received positively and can actually be a valuable part of the intervention itself, it is important to gauge any emotional reactions the client may have and to have additional counseling available if necessary. The impact of the feedback on the client should not be underestimated and careful planning of what to say and what not to say is essential. Ideally, feedback should give clients valuable inormatio about thir issues, and open up new options as they begin to problem solve collaboratively with their therapist. When carried out in a caring and tactful way, feedback to the client will contribute to a trusting and egalitarian relationship, and sets the stage for the work that lies ahead in treatment.

Conclusion

This chapter is entitled, "A problem well stated is a problem half solved." Since engineers make lifetime careers out of solving problems, and have been major participants in constructing the world in the process, it is not surprising that Charles Kettering strongly emphasizes the need to clearly understand a problem before trying to solve it. Given that one of the best ways to define a clinician is as "a collaborative problem solver," it is suggested that the competent clinician will recognize the inherent need to adequately assess a client's problem *prior to* any attempts to solve them.

It has been argued that an integral part of all clinical work is assessment, the collection and integration of a wide range of information that will guide subsequent treatment. The important engineering idea of a free body diagram was proposed as a model for organizing the bio-psycho-social-cultural influences on human nature. The largely forgotten factor of culture in clinical therapy and research was suggested as being critically important to understanding the astronomical divorce rate and marital unhappiness that exists in U.S. society today. Since healthy individuals are essential for creating healthy marriages, this fact needs to be recognized and acted upon by evaluating both individual and relationship variables when carrying out a marriage assessment. Sattler's four pillars of assessment were discussed and three important models of individual and marital functioning were presented – Karney and Bradbury's Vulnerability-Stress-Adaptation Model, Johnson's Emotion Focused Therapy for Couples (EFT), and Gottman's Sound Marital House Theory. It was argued that at heart assessment is an ethical issue, and that the discipline required to carry out an initial comprehensive assessment reflects respect and responsible caring for the client, and that ultimately this time investment will result in superior therapy.

The central goal of this chapter has been to help develop in the reader a greater appreciation for the value of clinical assessment. In particular, it is hoped that an auspicious seed has been planted that assessment procedures provide a valuable and efficient tool over and above a clinical interview, and that this awareness will grow into application and, ultimately, will result in the provision of enhanced mental health services.

References

Ainsworth, M. D. S. (1967). *Infancy in Uganda: Infant care and the growth of love.* Baltimore, MD: Johns Hopkins University Press.

Ainsworth, M. D. S. (1968). Object relations, dependency, and attachment: A theoretical review of the infant-mother relationship. *Child Development, 40*, 969–1025.

American Association of Marriage and Family Therapy. (2000). *AAMFT Code of Ethics.* Washington, DC: American Association for Marriage and Family Therapy.

American Psychiatric Association. (2000). *Diagnostic and statistical manual of mental disorders* (4th ed. – Text Revision). Washington, DC: American Psychiatric Association.

American Psychological Association. (1992). Ethical principles of psychologists and code of conduct. *American Psychologist, 47,* 1597–1611.

Beck, A. T. (1996). *Beck Depression Inventory-II.* San Antonio, TX: Harcourt, Brace & Co.

Beck, A. T., Steer, R. A., & Garbin, M. (1988). Psychometric properties of the Beck Depression Inventory: Twenty-five years of evaluation. *Clinical Psychology Review, 8,* 77–100.

Boughner, S. R., Hayes, S. F., Bubenzer, D. L., & West, J. D. (1994). Use of standardized assessment instruments by marital and family therapists: A survey. *Journal of Marital and Family Therapy, 20,* 69–75.

Bowlby, J. (1969). *Attachment and loss: Vol. 1. Attachment.* New York: Basic Books.

Bowlby, J. (1973). *Attachment and loss: Vol. 2. Separation.* New York: Basic Books.

Bowlby, J. (1977). The making and breaking of affectional bonds. *British Journal of Psychiatry, 130,* 201–210.

Bowlby, J. (1980). *Attachment and loss: Vol. 3. Loss, stress, and depression.* New York: Basic Books.

Bowman, M. L. (1990). Coping efforts and marital satisfaction: Measuring marital coping and its correlates. *Journal of Marriage and the Family, 52,* 463-474.

Bradbury, T. N. (1995). Assessing the four fundamental domains of marriage. *Family Relations, 44,* 479–468.

Bradbury, T. N., & Fincham, F. D. (Eds.) (1990). *The psychology of marriage: Basic issues and applications.* New York: Guilford.

Bramlett, M. D., & Mosher, W. D. (2001). First marriage dissolution, divorce, and remarriage: United States. *Advance data from vital and health statistics; no. 323.* Hyattsville, MD: National Center for Health Statistics. Available: www.cdc.gov/nchs/releases/01news/firstmarr.htm

Brennan, K. A., Clark, C. L., & Shaver, P. R. (1998). Self-report measurement of adult attachment: An integrative overview. In J. A. Simpson & W. S. Rholes (Eds.), *Attachment theory and close relationships* (pp. 46–76). New York: Guildford Press.

Brock, G. W., & Barnard, C. P. (1999). *Procedures in marriage and family therapy*. Boston: Allyn and Bacon.

Bronfenbrenner, U. (1995). Developmental ecology through space and time: A future perspective. In P. Moen, G. H. Elder, Jr., & K. Luscher (Eds.), *Examining lives in context: Perspectives on the ecology of human development*. Washington, DC: American Psychological Association.

Buss, D. M., Abbott, M., Angeleitner, A., Asherian, A., Biaggio, A., Blanco Villasenor, A., Bruchon-Schweitzer, M., Chu'u, H.-Y., Czapinski, J., Deraad, B., Ekehammar, B., El Lohamy, N., Fioravanti, M., Georgas, J., Gjerde, P., Guttman, R., Hazan, F., Iwawaki, S., Janakiramaiah, N., Khosroshani, F., Kreitler, S., Lachenicht, L., Lee, M., Liik, K., Little, B., Mika, S., Moadel-Shahid, M., Moane, G., Montero, M., Mundy-Castle, A. C., Niit, T., Nsenduluka, E., Pienkowski, R., Pirttila-Backman, A.-M., Pone de Leon, J., Rousseau, J., Runco, M.A., Safir, M. P., Samuels, C., Sanitioso, R., Serpell, R., Smid, N., Spencer, C., Tadinac, M., Todoreva, E. N., Troland, K., Van Den Brande, L., Van Heck, G., Van Langenhove, & Yang, K.-S. (1990). International preferences in selecting mates: A study of 37 cultures. *Journal of Cross-Cultural Psychology, 21*, 5–47.

Canadian Psychological Association. (2000). *Canadian Code of Ethics for Psychologists* (3rd ed.). Old Chelsea, Quebec: Canadian Psychological Association.

Christensen, A. (1987). Detection of conflict patterns in couples. In K. Hahlweg & M. J. Goldstein (Eds.), *Understanding major mental disorder: The contribution of family interaction research* (pp. 250–265). New York: Family Process.

Costa, P. T., Jr., & McCrae, R. R. (1992). *Revised NEO Personality Inventory (NEO PI-R) and NEO Five-Factor Inventory (NEO-FFI): Professional manual*. Odessa, FL: Psychological Assessment Resources.

Covey, S. R. (1990). *The 7 habits of highly effective people*. New York: Fireside.

Covey, S. R. (1997). *The 7 habits of highly effective families*. New York: Golden Books.

Derogatis, L. R. (1983). *SCL-90-R administration, scoring, and procedures manual-II* (revised edition). Towson, MD: Clinical Psychometric Research.

Eidelson, R. J., & Epstein, N. (1982). Cognition and relationship maladjustment: Development of a measure of dysfunctional relationship beliefs. *Journal of Consulting and Clinical Psychology, 50,* 715–720.

Exner, J. E. (1969). *The Rorschach systems*. New York: Grune & Stratton.

Exner, J. E. (1993). *The Rorschach: A comprehensive system: Vol. 1. Basic foundations* (3rd ed.). New York: Wiley.

Eysenck, H. J., & Eysenck, S. B. G. (1978). *Manual of the Eysenck Personality Questionnaire*. Kent, UK: Hodder and Stroughton.

Feeney, J. A. (1994). Attachment style, communication patterns and satisfaction across the life cycle of marriage. *Personal Relationships, 1,* 333–348.

Fincham, F. D., & Bradbury, T. N. (1992). Assessing attributions in marriage: The Relationship Attribution Measure. *Journal of Personality and Social Psychology, 62,* 457–468.

Fincham, F. D., Fernandes, L. O. L., & Humphreys, K. (1993). *Communicating in relationships: A guide for couples and professionals*. Champaign, IL: Research Press.

Fincham, F. D., & Linfield, K. J. (1997). A new look at marital quality: Can spouses feel positive and negative about their marriage? *Journal of Family Psychology, 11,* 489–502.

Finn, S. E., & Tonsager, M. E. (1992). Therapeutic effects of providing MMPI-2 test feedback to college students awaiting therapy. *Psychological Assessment, 4,* 278–287.

Fischer, J., & Corcoran, K. (Eds.). (1994). *Measures for clinical practice: A sourcebook* (Volumes 1 & 2). New York: Free Press.

Fitzpatrick, M. A. (1988). *Between husbands and wives: Communication in marriage.* Newbury Park, CA: Sage.

Folstein, M. F., Folstein, S. E., & McHugh, P. R. (1975). "Mini-mental state." *Journal of Psychiatric Research, 12,* 189–198.

Fraley, R. C., Waller, N. G., & Brennan, K. A. (2000). An item response theory analysis of self-report measures of adult attachment. *Journal of Personality & Social Psychology, 78*(2), 350–365.

Gottman, J. M. (1993). The roles of conflict engagement, escalation, or avoidance in marital interaction: A longitudinal view of five types of couples. *Journal of Consulting and Clinical Psychology, 61,* 6–15.

Gottman, J. M. (1994). *What predicts divorce? The relationship between marital processes and marital outcomes.* Hillsdale, NJ: Erlbaum.

Gottman, J. M. (1999a). *The marriage clinic: A scientifically based marital therapy.* New York: W. W. Norton & Company.

Gottman, J. M. (1999b). *The seven principles for making marriage work.* New York: Three Rivers Press.

Gottman, J. M. (2001). *Marital therapy: A research-based approach (Clinician's manual).* Seattle, WA: The Gottman Institute. Available: www.gottman.com

Gray, J. (1993). *Men, women and relationships: Making peace with the opposite sex.* New York: MJF Books.

Greenberg, L. S., & Johnson, S. M. (1988). *Emotionally focused therapy for couples.* New York: Guilford Press.

Groth-Marnat, G. (1999). *Handbook of psychological assessment* (3rd ed.). New York: John Wiley & Sons.

Hathaway, S. R., & McKinley, J. C. (1940). A Multiphasic Personality Schedule (Minnesota): I. Construction of the schedule. *Journal of Psychology, 10,* 249–254.

Hazan, C., & Shaver, P. (1987). Conceptualizing romantic love as an attachment process. *Journal of Personality and Social Psychology, 52,* 511–524.

Holmes, T. H., & Rahe, R. H. (1967). The Social Readjustment Rating Scale. *Journal of Psychosomatic Research, 11,* 213–218.

Hubble, M. A., Duncan, B. L., & Miller, S. D. (Eds.). (1999). *The heart and soul of change: What works in therapy.* Washington, DC: American Psychological Association.

Hudson, W. W., Harrison, D. F., & Crosscup, P. C. (1981). A short-form scale to measure sexual discord in dyadic relationships. *Journal of Sex Research, 17,* 157–174.

Ivey, A. E. (1988). *Intentional interviewing and counseling: Facilitating client development* (2nd ed.). Pacific Grove, CA: Brooks/Cole Publishing Company.

Johnson, S. M. (1986). Bonds or bargains: Relationship paradigms and their significance for marital therapy. *Journal of Marital and Family Therapy, 12,* 259–267.

Johnson, S. M. (1996). *The practice of emotionally focused marital therapy: Creating connection.* New York: Brunner/Mazel.

Johnson, S. (1999). Emotionally focused couples therapy: Straight to the heart. In J. Donovan (Ed.). *Short term couple therapy* (pp. 14–42). New York: Guilford Press.

Johnson, S. M. (2003). Introduction to attachment: A therapist's guide to primary relationships and their renewal. In S. M. Johnson & V. E. Whiffen (Eds.). *Attachment processes in couple and family therapy* (pp. 3–17). New York: Guilford Press.

Johnson, S. M., & Whiffen, V. E. (1999). Made to measure: Adapting emotionally focused couple therapy to partners' attachment styles. *Clinical Psychology: Science and Practice, 6,* 336–381.

Johnson, S. M., & Whiffen, V. E. (2003). *Attachment processes in couple and family therapy*. New York: The Guilford Press.

Kail, R. (2001). *Development in children* (2nd ed.). New York: Freeman.

Kail, R. V., & Cavanaugh, J. C. (2004). *Human development: A life-span view* (3rd ed.). Toronto, Canada: Thomson Wadsworth.

Kanner, A. D., Coyne, J. C., Schaefer, C., & Lazarus, R. S. (1981). Comparison of two modes of stress measurement: Daily hassles and uplifts versus major life events. *Journal of Behavioral Medicine, 4,* 1–39.

Karney, B. R., & Bradbury, T. N. (1995). The longitudinal course of marital quality and stability: A review of theory, method, and research. *Psychological Bulletin, 118,* 3–34.

Kendall, P. C., Hollon, S. D., Beck, A. T., Hammen, C. L., & Ingram, R. E. (1987). Issues and recommendations regarding use of the Beck Depression Inventory. *Cognitive Therapy and Research, 11,* 289–299.

Krokoff, L. J., Gottman, J. M., & Hass, S. D. (1989). Validation of a Global Rapid Couples Interaction Scoring System. *Behavioral Assessment, 11,* 65–79.

Lambert, M. J. (1992). Implications of outcome research for psychotherapy integration. In J. C. Norcross & M. R. Goldfried (Eds.), *Handbook of psychotherapy integration* (pp. 94-139). New York: Basic Books.

Lavee, Y., & Olson, D. H. (1993). Seven types of marriage: An empirical typology based on ENRICH. *Journal of Marriage and Family Therapy, 19,* 325–340.

Lazarus, A. A. (1989). *The practice of multi-modal therapy*. Baltimore: Johns Hopkins University Press.

Lewak, R. W., Marks, P. A., & Nelson, G. E. (1990). *Therapist guide to the MMPI and MMPI-2*. Muncie, IN: Accelerated Development.

Locke, H. J., & Wallace, K. M. (1959). Short marital-adjustment and prediction tests: Their reliability and validity. *Marriage and Family Living, 21,* 251–255.

MacLean, A. P. (1998). Assertiveness homework for couples. In L. L. Hecker & S. Deacon (Eds.), *The therapist's notebook: Homework, handouts, and activities* (pp. 87–93). Binghampton, New York: The Haworth Press.

MacLean, A. P. (2001). *Attachment in marriage: Predicting marital satisfaction from partner matching using a three-group typology of adult attachment style*. Unpublished doctoral dissertation, Purdue University, West Lafayette, Indiana.

Maloney, M. P., & Ward, M. P. (1976). *Psychological assessment: A conceptual approach*. New York: Oxford University Press.

Margolin, G. (1983). An interactional model for the behavorial assessment of marital relationships. *Behavioral Assessment, 5(2),* 103–127

McConnaughy, E. A., Prochaska, J. O., & Velicer, W. (1983). Stages of change in psychotherapy: Measurement and sample profiles. *Psychotherapy: Theory, Research, and Practice, 20,* 368–375.

Millon, T. (1977). *Millon Clinical Multiaxial Inventory*. Minneapolis, MN: National Computer Systems.

Millon, T. (1994). *Manual for the MCMI-III*. Mineapolis, MN: National Computer Systems.

Morgan, C. D., & Murray, H. A. (1935). A method for investigating fantasies. *AMA Archives of Neurology and Psychiatry, 34*, 389–406.

Morgan, W. G. (1995). Origin and history of the Thematic Apperception Test Images. *Journal of Personality Assessment, 65*, 237–254.

Norton, R. (1983). Measuring marital quality: A critical look at the dependent variable. *Journal of Marriage and the Family, 45*, 141–151.

O'Leary, K. D. (Ed.). (1987). *Assessment of marital discord*. Hillsdale, NJ: Erlbaum.

O'Leary, K. D., Fincham, F. D., & Turkewitz, H. (1983). Assessment of positive feelings toward spouse. *Journal of Consulting and Clinical Psychology, 51*, 949–951.

Peterson, L, & Sobell, L. C. (1994). Introduction to the state-of-the-art review series: Research contributions to clinical assessment. *Behavior Therapy, 25*, 523–531.

Piedmont, R. L. (1998). Interpreting the NEO PI-R. In R. L. Piedmont (Ed.), *The Revised NEO Personality Inventory: Clinical and Research Applications* (pp. 79–112). New York: Plenum.

Practice Management Information Corporation (1992). *International classification of diseases, clinical modification* (ICD-9-CM) (4th ed., 9th rev.). Los Angeles: Author

Prochaska, J. O. (1999). How do people change, and how can we change to help many more people? In M. A. Hubble, B. L. Duncan, & S. D. Miller, S. D. (Eds.), *The heart and soul of change: What works in therapy* (pp. 227–255). Washington, DC: American Psychological Association Press.

Prochaska, J. O., Norcross, J. C., & DiClemente, C. C. (1994). *Changing for good*. New York: William Morrow.

Rogers, C. R. (1951). *Client-centered therapy*. Boston: Houghton Mifflin.

Rogers, C. (1957). The necessary and sufficient conditions of therapeutic personality change. *Journal of Consulting Psychology, 21*, 95–103.

Rose, S., & Zand, D. (2000). Lesbian dating and courtship from young adulthood to midlife. *Journal of Gay and Lesbian Social Services, 11*, 77–104.

Sattler, J. M. (1992). *Assessment of children* (3rd ed.). San Diego: Author.

Sattler, J. M. (1998). *Clinical and forensic interviewing of children and families: Guidelines for the mental health, education, pediatric and child maltreatment fields*. San Diego: Author.

Segall, M. H., Lonner, W. J., & Berry, J. W. (1998). Cross-cultural psychology as a scholarly discipline: On the flowering of culture in behavioral research. *American Psychologist, 53*(10), 1101–1110.

Selzer, M. L. Vinokur, A., & van Rooijen, L. (1975). A self-administered Short Michigan Alcoholism Screening Test (SMAST). *Journal of Studies of Alcohol, 36*, 117–126.

Senchak, M., & Leonard, K. E. (1992). Attachment styles and marital adjustment among newlywed couples. *Journal of Social and Personal Relationships, 9*, 51–64.

Skinner, B. F. (1953). *Science and human behavior*. New York: MacMillan.

Spanier, G. B. (1976). Measuring dyadic adjustment: New scales for assessing the quality of marriage and similar dyads. *Journal of Marriage and the Family, 38*, 15–28.

Stanley, S. M., & Markman, H. J. (1992). Assessing commitment in personal relationships. *Journal of Marriage and the Family, 54*, 595–608.

Tannen, D. (1990). *You just don't understand: Women and men in conversation*. New York: Ballantine Books.

Tombaugh, T. N., McDowell, I., Kristjansson, B., & Hubley, A. M. (1996). Mini-mental state examination (MMSE) and the Modified MMSE (3MS): Psychometric comparison and normative data. *Psychological Assessment, 8,* 48–59.

Touliatos, J., & Perlmutter, B. F., & Straus, M. A. (Eds.). (1990). *Handbook of family measurement techniques*. Thousand Oaks, CA: Sage Publications.

Warren, N. C. (1992). *Finding the love of your life*. New York: Pocket Books.

Watkins, C. E., Campbell, V. L., Nieberding, R., & Hallmark, R. (1995). Contemporary practice of psychological assessment by clinical psychologists. *Professional Psychology: Research and Practice, 26,* 54–60.

Wechsler, D. (1997). *Manual for the Wechsler Adult Intelligence Scale-III*. San Antonio, TX: Psychological Corporation.

Weiss, R. L., & Cerreto, M. C. (1980). The Marital Status Inventory: Development of a measure of dissolution potential. *American Journal of Family Therapy, 8,* 80–85.

Weiss, R. L., Hops, H., Patterson, G. R. (1973). A framework for conceptualizing marital conflicts, a technology for altering it, some data for evaluating it. In L. A. Hamerlynck, L. C. Handy et al. (Eds.), *Behavioral change: Methodology, concept, and practice*. Champaign, IL: Research Press.

Wolpe, J., & Lang, P. J. (1964). A fear survey schedule for use in behavior therapy. *Behavior Research and Therapy, 2,* 27–30.

Wolpe, J., & Lang, P. J. (1977). *Manual for the Fear Survey Schedule*. San Diego, CA: Educational and Industrial Testing Service.

5

Initial Interview with a Family

Volker Thomas

Summary

The chapter describes the initial assessment and evaluation of the Smith family, who sought family therapy because the parents were unable to manage their 9 year old son's behavior effectively. The case illustration is structured according to the assessment guidelines provided in the previous chapters.

1. Phone Contact

Ms. Smith called asking for her husband and their 9 year old son Ben to come in for family therapy because they were at their "wits end" trying to manage Ben. Ms. Smith reported that Ben had recently hit her when she tried to discipline him for hurting their family cat. On the phone Ms. Smith sounded hopeless, helpless, and desperate. Although Ben was an excellent student and the parents had not received any complaints from school about his behavior, Ms. Smith had phoned the school and had a long conversation with Ben's school counselor. The counselor had not noticed any defiant or oppositional behavior at school, but at Ms. Smith's request referred the family to our family therapy clinic.

Ben's early development was within normal range with no unusual behavior. Ms. Smith stayed home from her job as an elementary teacher to fully concentrate on raising her only son, while Mr. Smith advanced quickly in his career as a systems analyst for a large company. The family had a good income, moved 4 times before Ben started kindergarten. By then he could read and comprehend math on a 3rd grade level. Ms. Smith and Ben had developed an extremely close relationship in which she partially compensated for missing her husband, who was rarely home due to increasing work responsibilities. When Ben entered kindergarten, Ms. Smith looked for part-time employment as a 4th grade teacher, but could not find a job. She became increasingly depressed, while Ben enjoyed the company of other children and excelled in the very individualized full-day kindergarten program.

It was not until Ben entered 2nd grade that Ms. Smith found employment at the same elementary school. The next two years were rather uneventful, until Ms. Smith lost her job, when Ben entered 4th grade. Ms. Smith became severely depressed again, was hospitalized for a short period of time and stabilized with anti-depressive medication. It was at this time that Ben became increasingly difficult to manage at home. He challenged his mom frequently about rules, threw temper tantrums when he did not get his way, and openly complained to his dad about mom's poor parenting skills. Mr. Smith who had been oblivious to his wife's emotional state sided with his son's concerns and grew increasingly critical of his wife's parenting. When he was home he would interfere when Ms. Smith tried to discipline Ben, which, after initial relief would worsen the situation. When Ben also began ignoring his father's disciplining attempts, Mr. Smith withdrew into his work, which left his wife resentful and helpless with their young son. At the same time Ben continued to excel at school with the support of a gifted education program and a supportive teacher who knew Ben's home situation quite well.

Ms. Smith was the oldest of three girls. Her mother, a school teacher, stayed home with the girls until the youngest was 4 years old and attended a pre-school. By that time Ms. Smith was in 4th grade. Her father was an accountant in a small local company, where he maintained his position throughout Ms. Smith's childhood and adolescence. Her mother had a drinking problem through which she masked and self-treated depressive tendencies while she stayed home and raised her three daughters. Ms. Smith remembered taking care of her younger sisters when she would come home from school finding her mother drunk and withdrawn in her bedroom. During her elementary school years Ms. Smith worked very hard to maintain her good standing in school and manage the stress at home. Her mother hid her drinking from her father who colluded in the denial explaining his wife's strange behavior (when she was drunk) as being overwhelmed with three young children. He would willingly pitch in, prepare the evening meal, and take care of the children. Ms. Smith felt guilty for keeping the secret of her mother's alcoholism from her father, yet she needed the relief so that she could get her homework done. When Ms. Smith was 8 years old her mother caused a car accident with her three daughters in the car while driving drunk. Fortunately, nobody was hurt in the accident. However, the accident revealed Ms. Smith's mother's alcohol problem and broke the denial cycle. She underwent inpatient alcohol treatment and managed to maintain her sobriety from then on. As part of her recovery, Ms. Smith's mother sought employment and found a teaching position in her children's elementary school.

After a rather uneventful adolescence, during which Ms. Smith had had a tense relationship with her mother and a rather distant relationship with her father, she left home to go to college, where she met her future husband during her freshman year. The young couple got married after Ms. Smith graduated with a degree in elementary education. She found a teaching job and taught 4th grade for several years. During that time Mr. and Ms. Smith unsuccessfully tried to become pregnant for several years. After two years they sought infertility treatment, because Ms. Smith felt incomplete as a woman and wanted a baby "more than anything in the world," Mr. Smith went along with his wife's wishes. Ms. Smith was diagnosed with low levels of the hormones that are needed to trigger ovulation. She felt guilty that it was her fault that they could not get pregnant. Four years and multiple unsuccessful attempts of in vitro fertilization later, the couple gave up, resigned to the apparent fact that they would not have children of their own. For about two years they explored several adoption possibilities when Ms. Smith became surprisingly pregnant. After a difficult pregnancy that included bed rest for the last eight weeks, Ben was born through Cesarean section. Mr. and Ms. Smith were overjoyed that after so many years of disappointment they finally had a healthy boy whom they named

Benjamin. Ms. Smith immediately quit her teaching job and devoted all her time and energy to raising her son who felt like a miracle to her. While she was attending to her baby son, she could tolerate her husband's frequent absences from the home due to his progressing career.

Mr. Smith was the younger of two children. He had a sister 3 years older. Both his parents were laborers who worked in a local factory. His mother worked the early shift (6:00 AM – 2:00 PM) during his formative up years, while his father switched between the early (6:00 AM – 2:00 PM) and late (2:00 – 10:00 PM) shift for most of his childhood. Mr. Smith remembered times when both of his parents were gone when he woke up in the morning and his paternal grandmother, who lived across the street, was there until he and his sister left for school. When Mr. Smith was 12 years old his dad left the family for a younger woman and moved across the country, where he saw him an average of once a year through his adolescent years. He maintained a close relationship to his dad's mother, who remained the stabilizing factor in his family when his mother was dealing with the loss of her husband. Because his father did not send much money to support his children, Mr. Smith began working when he was 14 years old and maintained several jobs throughout high school. At that time he vowed to himself to go to college and better himself through education so that he could have a better life than his parents. He also told himself that he never would act as irresponsibly as his father and would make a good living for his family and take care of them to the best of his ability.

When he met his future wife in college he was impressed by her sense of responsibility, her smartness, and caring warmth. They dated for four years, working through many insecurities and challenges. What kept them together during those years were their shared values of hard work and a vision for a family that would be different from the ones in which they grew up.

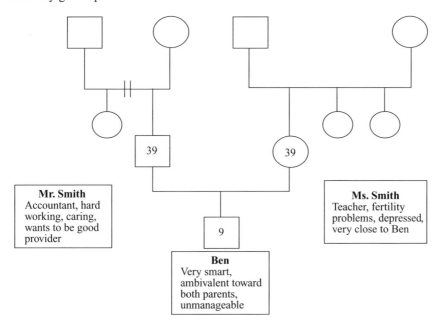

Figure 1: Genogram of the Smith Family

The couple relationship was characterized by a high degree of ambivalence. Based on the genogram the treatment team hypothesized that Ben had developed a central position in the parents' relationship that left him with an inappropriate amount of power in the family. He was triangulated to relieve a high degree of emotional tension between the parents.

2. The First Session

The Smith family appears 15 minutes early and nervously take seats in the waiting room. Ben begins quietly to play with the toys when the therapist David enters the room. David is an experienced family therapist who is married and has three young children. David is trained in both traditional talk therapy and play therapy for children. He greets the three family members and invites them to join him in the therapy room. Before the session the team decided to not have the first session in the play therapy room, because Ms. Smith had expressed some concerns about play as not being "real" therapy. In order to accommodate these concerns David conducted the first session in a regular therapy room without toys with the goal to focus on the parents' concerns and assess Ben's behavior in an environment that felt safer to the parents.

2.1. Beginning Phase and Joining

At the entrance to the therapy room David invites the family to enter and find a place to sit. Ben pushes himself into the room first. He notices a small love seat across from the door, a recliner to the left, and several hard chairs on the right. Without hesitation Ben runs to the recliner, extends the foot rest and reclines the back giggling awkwardly and exclaiming that he is tired and wants to take a nap. The parents look embarrassed and sit down on the love seat next to each other, Ms. Smith on the side next to the recliner. David pulls up one of the hard chairs and notices how Ben looks at his parents triumphantly from his recliner non-verbally checking out their reaction. Ms. Smith nervously, but politely asks Ben to move the back of the recliner and the foot rest up so that everybody can see him. Going back and forth on the recliner several times, Ben finally complies with a smirk on his face that seems to announce moving back whenever he feels like it.

David notices the brief enactment without comment and greets the family members individually. He describes the setting, the purpose of the session, and then invites the family to share with him what brought them to the session. While Mr. and Ms. Smith look at each other, Ben begins to move the foot rest up again and reclines the back stating again that he is tired and needs a nap. Ms. Smith helplessly points at Ben and tells David how difficult it has been to manage Ben's behavior for many months. She proceeds to describe Ben's behavior and her attempts to deal with him. The situation has worsened since Ms. Smith returned from the hospital. She has felt tired and vulnerable, hoping for some cooperation from Ben and support from her husband. While Ms. Smith is talking Ben pretends to sleep in the recliner.

Then David turns to Mr. Smith who has observed Ben without interfering. Mr. Smith reports feeling helpless and being stuck between a rock and a hard place (i.e., his wife and his son). He has tried to be supportive of his wife, but frequently finds himself siding with Ben, when his wife expects too much of their son. Mr. Smith also has felt that his main responsibility is at work so that he can provide for his family and that the crisis at home has negatively affected his work performance.

While Mr. Smith talks about his wife's emotional problems, Ben moves up from his recliner pretending to wake up from a nap. He carefully listens to his dad complaining about his wife. Ben interrupts his Dad, shouting that he should be nicer to mom, because she is tired and depressed. Mr. Smith tries to ignore Ben, looking at his wife in disgust. Ms. Smith reaches over to her son and with an insecure smile tries to caringly touch his head. Ben quickly moves back in his recliner avoiding Mom's contact. The he turns to David telling him that this is the way it has been for a while in the family and that his parents do not know what they are doing. David praises Ben for his wisdom and politely, but firmly asks him to move up and face him so that he can further draw on Ben's wisdom. At the same time David moves up his chair a little closer toward Ben without violating his personal space. After some hesitation Ben complies, sits up in his recliner and faces David. In the ensuing conversation Ben complains about his parents' behavior like a parent complains about his children. He expresses his anger and frustration about having parents who are weak and do not know what they are doing. When David reframes Ben's frustration as caring about his parents he briefly tears up and admits that he is worried about his mom's depression and his dad's absence. Ben has felt pressure to hold the family together for quite some time, and is afraid that everything will fall apart. During this interchange between David and Ben the parents quietly listen crunched in their love seat.

David commends the family for being so open with him and for enacting their problem during the session. Then David asks how the family has tried to solve the problems they have been facing.

2.2. Assessment Phase

Ms. Smith reports that her recent hospitalization for depression was one attempt to tackle the problems they have had with Ben. She and her husband realized that the depression had paralyzed her parenting abilities. Although the hospitalization and the medication treatment brought some relief of Ms. Smith's symptoms she does not feel able to parent her son as she would like. Additionally, the guilt she felt about being a "bad" parent creates a vicious cycle from which she sees no escape.

Mr. Smith has tried his best to "pitch in" at home and relieve his wife of some of the burden dealing with Ben. However, he reports that he feels extremely ambivalent about having more responsibility for Ben. When he observes his wife and Ben he frequently thinks that his wife could "put her foot down" rather than giving in to Ben; or she could just relax a little more and let things go by picking fights with him that are "worth picking." He then secretly finds himself siding with Ben and resenting his wife; which makes it almost impossible for him to support his wife. Additionally, he feels so much pressure from work that he resents the domestic struggles. He expects his wife to handle the home situation better so that he can concentrate on what he considers his primary parental role, that of main financial provider for the family.

Mr. and Ms. Smith have been aware of the parental conflict, and they sought couples counseling prior to Ms. Smith's hospitalization. The counselor referred Ben for play therapy with a colleague and suggested to the parents to relax and wait for the results of the play therapy. While Ben enjoyed the play therapy sessions, and went regularly for about ten sessions, his behavior did not change much at home. At the same time, Ms. Smith felt increasingly more depressed for failing her only child that she withdrew more and more into the depression until she was hospitalized. As they tell their story of failure, both parents express great disappointment, guilt, and shame about not being able to be the parents they would like to be. During the conversation between David and the parents about prior treatment attempts Ben sits up in his recliner and listens attentively.

David has some initial ideas about the family dynamics based on the assessment of the family interactions and the information provided. Both parents feel inadequate in their parenting roles, failing their only child. Ms. Smith had prepared herself personally and professionally to raise a family. Not being able to become pregnant and eventually only having one child shattered her expectation of the kind of family she wanted. Because of her fertility problems she felt responsible failing her and her husband's expectation of her envisioned family life. She tried to compensate for her guilt and shame by focusing all her attention on Ben, not being able to manage him the way she had learned in college. Her inability increased her guilt and shame, which perpetuated an internal vicious cycle that lead her down a path to depression. Not being able to maintain external support through work and other relationships, including her husband, further isolated Ms. Smith and exacerbated her depression. With regard to her family-of-origin, Ms. Smith got caught in her learned pattern of caretaking and deep attachment wounds growing up with an alcoholic mother.

On one side, Ms. Smith was used to being the caretaker of her younger sisters, supporting her mother, and keeping the family together. This pattern made it extremely difficult for her to ask for and accept help from her husband without a sense a failure, letting her family down, and a high degree of guilt and shame. Being the "perfect" parent and primary caretaker of Ben was her only way to succeed. When her longstanding attempts to control these negative feelings failed she became increasingly more depressed and eventually decompensated.

On the other side, Ms. Smith had deep attachment wounds (Johnson & Lee, 2000) because her mother was unable to be a consistent attachment figure due to her alcohol problem and with younger children to care for. These unmet attachment needs made Ms. Smith very vulnerable in meeting her young son's attachment needs and confronted her with her own insecurities. Her insecurities worsened even more when she struggled to become pregnant blaming herself for the fertility problems. Before Ben's birth Ms. Smith's attachment needs had been partially met by her husband's care and love. During Ben's infancy she also met many of her emotional needs through the close relationship with her son. Once her son became older and more independent, and her husband became less available due to his increased absences and work commitments, Ms. Smith could no longer mask her attachment wounds, which fed into the vicious cycle and her depression.

In summary, the harder Ms. Smith tried to be the kind of mother she had envisioned the more she became like her mother, overwhelmed and incompetent, full of guilt and shame, and surrendering her parental authority. Because Ben had no siblings that could take care of him, as she had done with her younger sisters, Ben had to learn to take care of himself and to take on a parenting role.

Mr. Smith developed the sense of failure as a parent when he saw his wife's difficulties interfering with the role as a husband and father he had envisioned for himself. Keeping his family together by being the best provider he could be was his family-of-origin legacy. He never blamed his wife for only having one child. To the contrary, he thought that would make his job as provider easier so that he could be the father to his son he never had in his own father.

On one side, Mr. Smith felt content not to be Ben's primary caretaker and to limit his role in advancing his career for the benefit of his wife and son. This attitude also matched the work ethic of his family-of-origin. During Ben's infancy Mr. Smith was very supportive of his wife's close relationship with her son, although he secretly missed the intimacy he had felt with his wife before they had had Ben. Yet he told himself this was the way it was supposed to be, and he consequently compensated for the loss by investing more time and energy into his job. His professional success further reinforced this decision.

On the other side, Mr. Smith grew increasingly worried as his wife's emotional state worsened and Ben became more and more defiant. Mr. Smith thought that his wife was not "performing up to standard" in her role as mother, which made it more and more difficult to hold up his end of the "marriage bargain." Initially he tried very hard to be supportive of his wife by "pitching in" with Ben's care. Yet the more resentful he became of his wife and the more the domestic issues interfered with his work, the more pressure Mr. Smith felt and he subsequently withdrew. Secretly, he even contemplated divorce and fighting for Ben's custody. Mr. Smith struggled not to become like his father and leave, yet he felt an increasing pressure to give up. His internal compromise was to withdraw into his work, and thus maintain his primary role as provider and to stay out of his "wife's business" of raising Ben.

Initially, David's assessment of the Smith family focused on the parents because he was struck by the spontaneous enactment of the dysfunctional transactional patterns (Minuchin, 1974) of the Smith family symbolized by the seating arrangement during the first session. The parents had relinquished their executive parental power (Minuchin & Fishman, 1981) to their son, who sat in the recliner trying to control his parents' every move. Being able to better understand the parents' dilemma of managing their son, David focused his assessment now on Ben's role in this unfolding family dance (Napier & Whitaker, 1978). David wondered why Ben had continued to perform and behave so well at school while being defiant and misbehaving at home. Ben struck David as a "good kid," who tried as hard as he could to do what he was supposed to do. How was Ben's defiant behavior at home trying to be good? From his assessment of the parents' backgrounds David hypothesized that Ben thought he was supposed to assume power and control in the family when both parents stopped acting as parents as described above. However, as a 9-year-old boy Ben was unable to run a family like adult parents would do. Furthermore, being in charge of the family kept Ben from getting his developmentally appropriate emotional and attachment needs met. Hence, as a compromise he used the power and control the parents had given him by acting out trying to let the parents know that he wanted them to be in charge and help him stop his misbehavior. In other words, Ben limited his defiance to those adults who he needed to have power and did not execute it appropriately. That was the reason why he behaved well at school and with David, who respected him as a 9-year-old boy and treated him accordingly.

David's initial assessment of the Smith family hypothesized that, due to the lack of differentiation and self-confidence (Bowen, 1978), the high degree of stress and anxiety, and the considerable attachment wounds (Johnson & Lee, 2000), the Smith parents had relinquished their parental authority (Ms. Smith by developing worsening depressive symptoms; Mr. Smith by increasingly withdrawing into his work; both by frequently disagreeing and mutually criticizing each other's parenting in front of Ben) to the only son. He tried to comply with the parents by assuming familial power, yet also was attempting to remain true to himself as a 9-year-old child by acting out. David saw the fact that Ben had been able to maintain good behavior and performance at school as a hopeful sign that restructuring the family's interactional pattern (Minuchin, 1974), and that helping the parents to individuate from the transgenerational patterns of their respective families-of-origin would change the parents' parenting and improve Ben's behavior.

2.3. End Phase

After consulting with the treatment team that had observed the initial session from behind the one-way mirror, David returns to the Smith family and the following conversation develops:

David: The team and I are very impressed how each of you cares about the well-being of the family. Mr. Smith, we are particularly impressed of your love and commitment for your wife and your son. You have vowed to yourself that you would not make the same mistakes as your father and be there for your wife and your son by providing for them adequately. You have done an excellent job advancing your career and earning more and more income so that your family can live comfortably. Your devotion to your family, both your wife and your son are second to none.

Mr. Smith (tears up): I appreciate your acknowledgement, but why do I resent my wife so much; why does she express so little appreciation for what I do; and why doesn't Ben listen to me?

David: Those are good questions. Let me come back to them in a moment. Before I do that I would like to compliment you, Ms. Smith for your dedication and love for both your husband and your son. You used the parenting skills you learned as the eldest child in your family, your professional training as elementary school teacher, and all your love and energy to raise your only son, whom you have had after a long battle with infertility. You vowed to yourself that you would be the best mother you could be to this most precious child that you have conceived, carried, and delivered under very difficult circumstances. And you also decided not to have anything, such as alcohol, interfere with your availability to your son; in other words you want to be a better mother to your child than the experience you had with your own mother growing up. Thus, you put your career on hold after Ben's birth and dedicated your life to your son.

Ms. Smith (tears up): Yes, but why has it been so difficult with Ben lately; why have I been so depressed and felt so much guilt and shame as a parent; why does my husband resent me so much; and why doesn't Ben behave the way he used to?

David: These are excellent questions, which are similar to your husband's. Please let me direct a few words to Ben before I answer your questions. Ben, I am particularly impressed how much you love your mom and dad, and how hard you have tried to be a good boy and do what you are supposed to do. You are a very smart boy who knows very well what's going on with your parents. I am wondering how you feel when you see your mom and dad tear up as they just did when I talked to them. I bet you have seen them like that before.

Ben (looking at his parents, shakes his head slightly): Yah!

David: Well, if it's OK with you I will explain to your mom and dad, how you have tried your hardest to be a good boy and son. What do you think?

Ben (looks at David indicating his permission): OK?!

David: Mom and dad, Ben has been trying to be a good boy as a 9 year old knows how to be good. As smart as he is, he has understood that neither of you have been able to run the family the way you were used to in the past. As you know from your own childhoods, when things do not go well, kids get scared and they try to make things better. Ms. Smith, you did that by taking care of your younger sisters when your mom drank. Mr. Smith, you worked very hard to be there for your mom when your dad had left. Well, when Ben sensed that you had difficulty being in charge of the family he got scared and felt pressure to take over for you so that the family would not fall apart.

Ben (starts crying quietly as he listens attentively): Yah.

David: Unfortunately, 7-year-old children are not made and ready to run families quite yet, because they still need their moms and dads to do that for them. As hard as Ben tried, he was facing a terrible dilemma, because he could not take care of his mom and dad and be taken care of at the same time. Thus, he took care of you (i.e., taking charge of the family) by making you take care of him (i.e., acting out, misbehaving, throwing tantrums), hoping that you would understand his dilemma and comfort him. However, you both were so busy trying to be a good mom and dad that you did not realize that Ben was trying to be good as well. Instead you thought he was behaving the way he did because you were "bad" parents, and he was a "bad" boy. Thus, you did what you were used to and what your parents did (although you had vowed never to do that). You, Mr. Smith, withdrew just like your father and left your wife and son alone dealing with their dilemmas. You, Ms. Smith, became increasingly depressed (which had similar consequences as your mother's drinking) and could not parent your child effectively any longer. You, Ben, thought you had not tried hard enough to be a "good" boy and acted out more. Consequently, things turned increasingly more difficult and all three of you felt worse and worse.

Ms. Smith (tears rolling down her cheeks): I guess I didn't know that Ben was trying to be a good boy. It makes me feel terrible to realize that I misunderstood my little boy. Doesn't that confirm that I am a bad Mother?

David: You could see it that way. I would like to suggest a slightly different way of looking at it. Parents are human and struggle at times; and that's OK. Children understand that and don't get scared right away. However, if the parents continue to struggle there is a time when it becomes too difficult for children. Apparently, that's when Ben started to act out.

Mr. Smith: Are you suggesting that my wife and I let it continue too long, and now we have damaged Ben beyond repair?

Ben (continues to listen attentively): Hm.

David: I am very confident that Ben will be fine. He is a smart kid and wants to be a good boy. Am I right, Ben?

Ben (wiping away his tears): Yah, all I want is to be a 9-year-old kid.

Ms. Smith (trying to help Ben blow his nose): Well ...

Ben (pushing her arm away): I can blow my nose by myself (wiping it with his sleeve)!

Ms. Smith (backing off): ... so what can we do to make things better, David?

David: For you, Mr. and Ms. Smith, to regain your confidence that you can parent this smart and perceptive son of yours without losing the inner battle not to become like your parents; and for you Ben, to be OK with being a 9 year old boy like at school and doing all the things you enjoy, while respecting your mom and dad. In order to get to this point I suggest that I have a session just with Ben and a session just with mom and dad. Then we will meet again as a family and decide together how to proceed. How does that sound Mr. and Ms. Smith?

Ms. Smith (with a tentative smile): If you say so, let's give it a try.

Mr. Smith (thoughtfully): Why not.
David: Ben what do you think? Do you want to meet with me in a couple of days in our play room, we have pretty cool toys?
Ben (with a smiling smirk): If you say so, sir!
David: Great, let's schedule the two sessions. Thanks for coming in today and for being so open and caring about your family.

From the parents' reactions David concludes that they have gained some hope that the difficulties they have been experiencing may be resolvable. They eagerly schedule two more sessions, one for Ben and one for them. Then they ask to schedule a third session for the whole family as David had suggested. Meanwhile Ben arises from the recliner walks up to David smiling. David raises his right hand and asks: "Give me five"! Ben strikes David hand exclaiming: "See you in a couple of days". David has the impression that Ben has connected with him.

3. The Second Session – Play Session with Ben

A few days later Ms. Smith brings Ben in for the scheduled play therapy session. Initially, David was a little concerned that Ben would engage his parents in a power struggle about the session, which is quite common especially for pre-adolescent boys to be reluctant to attend sessions involving play that they consider "childish". Thus, it is a positive sign that the family shows up on time and Ben appears excited about the session.

After briefly checking in with Ms. Smith, David takes Ben into the play therapy room, while Ms. Smith stays in the waiting room. David's plan calls for a non-directive play session with the goal to further assess the family dynamics from Ben's perspective. The play therapy room is equipped with several stations that feature different toys. When Ben enters the room he notices a large wooden doll house with a box of people and animals of different races and ethnicities to the right of the entrance. Next he sees a large wooden box with dress up clothes that compliment several hats and helmets hanging from a plastic chain attached to the wall above the box. In the corner across from the entrance on a small table is an assortment of art supplies, including paints, colored crayons, markers, and different sizes of paper. Next to the art table stands a box with an assortment of hand puppets. Finally, in the other corner is a large sand tray next to shelves with hundreds of small objects.

David explains that Ben may play with any of the toys in the room. The only rule he must follow is not to throw or break objects or hit David. If Ben violates the rule David will give him a warning. After the 3rd warning they will have to terminate the play session. David tells Ben that they have 30 minutes to play and invites him to begin.

To David's surprise Ben goes right to the doll house and carefully explores the three stories of the wooden structure that stands about four feet tall. He rearranges most of the furniture making it look like "my house." Then he opens the plastic box with the dolls and carefully selects two adult and two child dolls. He places the "mom and dad dolls" in the bedroom and a "baby girl doll" in a cradle next to the parents' bed on the second floor. A "boy doll" walks up the stairs, passes the parents' bedroom toward his room on the third floor, where he plays on a computer for awhile. As he is playing Ben explains that this is his family, mom and dad, he and his baby sister. After a while the Ben doll gets up from the computer walks downstairs to the kitchen, looking for a knife. When he realizes that this doll house doe not have knives, he climbs back up the stairs, tiptoes into the bedroom where mom, dad, and baby sister are sleeping. Quietly he takes the baby out of her cradle and carries her downstairs explaining that she will not wake up. In the kitchen he carefully wraps her in a tissue and leaves the house. Carrying his wrapped baby sister in his arms he looks for the garbage can. When he can't find one he picks a spot and designates it as the dump. He carefully deposits his baby sister in the dump covering her with a piece of paper that Ben has picked up from the arts table. Then he looks at David exclaiming: "Now she's dead!"

David acknowledges Ben calmly stating: "You want me to know that your baby sister is dead." Then David takes the boy doll back into the house walks up the stairs to the parents' bedroom, removes the cradle, and wakes them up. He orders the parents to get up and fix him something to eat. The parents comply. All three go downstairs in the kitchen and both parent dolls busy themselves fixing something to eat from the Ben doll. He has many demands and none of the food is good enough. None of them mention the missing baby doll. Suddenly Ben turns to David and says: "That's it, I'm done!" David is puzzled as to what happened during the role play and asks Ben about the baby girl doll. Ben explains: "Mom and dad sent me to my room; they loved the baby sister more than me; so I killed her and dumped her in the garbage; now I have mom and dad to myself again."

David thanks Ben for his play noticing two aspects: (1) In terms of content, David wonders about the significance of the "baby sister," Ben "killing" her very "gently," and why nobody acknowledged her absence; instead Ben ordered his parents around who "willingly" complied. (2) In terms of process, Ben played very calmly and quietly, not once challenging any rules about the play time by him at the beginning of the session. David decides to share the information of the play session with the parents and asks for Ben's permission as they walk back to the waiting room to meet Ms. Smith. Ben looks at David briefly and says with the same smirk on his face as he had sitting in the recliner during the first family session: "Sure, you can tell 'em!" As they reunite with Ms. Smith Ben smiles at his mom, "That was fun; we can go home now." Mom smiles back apprehensively and turns to David. He affirms the two of them looking at Ms. Smith: "Ben had a good time in the play room and gave me permission to share with you and your husband what he played. I suggest that we talk about Ben's play when you, your husband, and I meet later this week. Please give my regards to your husband. – Ben, you did a great job today, give my five!" Ben smiled hitting David's hand rather softly. Then David shook Ms. Smith's hand as she and Ben left the waiting room. As they walked down the hallway Ben turned around and smiled at David with the now familiar smirk.

4. The Third Session with the Parents

Two days later David met with Mr. and Ms. Smith. They reported that after the play session Ben had been quite pleasant, until he threw a temper tantrum when the parents got ready to leave for their session. Ben insisted on coming along and having another play session with David. When the parents stood their ground and wanted to leave him with a babysitter as planned, Ben became very angry, screamed and yelled, and tried to hit Ms. Smith. Eventually the parents, along with the babysitter, calmed Ben down enough so they could leave for their session with David.

At the beginning of the session David compliments the parents for responding "as a team" when Ben became upset before they left. Both parents confirm that they talked after the first session and agreed that it would be important for them to work together and not undermine each other in dealing with Ben. Then David shares his observations from the play session. While listening to the story Ben played out in the doll house, both parents appear shocked and embarrassed especially when Ben dumped the "baby girl" in the garbage. Ms. Smith tears up as she did in the first session and admits that she has had a secret fantasy of having another baby. Because she grew up with two sisters she would love to have a daughter. But because of her fertility problems she has given up on ever having another baby. However, she knows that she "will never feel complete as a mother and woman" without having a daughter. Then she adds that in some awkward way Ben reminds her of this flaw day in and day out. She has fought these thoughts and associated feelings for years, but they seem to be catching up with her whenever she feels bad about herself. David commends Ms. Smith for her openness in talking about these painful and shameful issues.

Mr. Smith follows his wife's story attentively in awe. He has been totally unaware of her fantasies and becomes increasingly withdrawn. When David turns his attention toward Mr. Smith he avoids eye contact, obviously feeling uncomfortable about the situation. After some hesitation he turns to his wife and shares with her that he also has had fantasies about having a daughter, but that he has not dared to openly talk about them because he did not want to hurt his wife's feelings and bring up the fertility problem. The couple spontaneously embrace in a moment of soft tenderness while David sits back witnessing this connecting moment between two partners who have been disconnected in guilt and shame for several years. The ensuing therapeutic conversation focuses on the pain over the infertility that has made it so difficult for them to be open and honest with each other.

David talks about Ben's wisdom who has sensed the issue for quite some time and played out the "solution" during his doll house play. The parents realize that "killing" the baby girl doll suggested to let go of their fantasies and enjoy what they have, a very smart and sensitive son who loves his parents very much. David also helps them to see that their secrecy and disconnection paralyzed them and gave Ben the executive power in the family. This dysfunctional interactional pattern has been closely associated with Ms. Smith's depression and Mr. Smith's withdrawal into his work. For Mr. and Ms. Smith the puzzle pieces of their family problems begin to fall into place. Now they understand why the previous play therapy was not helpful for Ben. They have to do some work around their expectations (e.g., secret fantasies) of each other as partners and parents and release Ben from the delegated position of power. David is very moved by the couple's realizations and confirms their significance for a better family life and an easier management of Ben. However, David also points out to Mr. and Ms. Smith that they will have to work some to convince Ben that he can give the executive power back to them, that they can handle their grief over the loss of the "baby girl", and that this family is not going to fall apart.

Mr. and Ms. Smith feel some relief from the session and express hope that they will be able to work things out with Ben and between the two of them. A final assessment session is scheduled for the entire family for the following week in David's office.

5. The Fourth Session with the Entire Family

The family arrives at the clinic office in time. When David greets them in the waiting room, Ben avoids making eye contact with David, keeping busy with a hand held computer game. The parents smile at the therapist while getting up and following him down the hall to the therapy room. Somewhat reluctantly Ben comes along still playing his game. Entering the therapy room the parents sit down on the love seat as in the first session. To the parents' surprise Ben walks passed the recliner to one of the hard chairs, sits down on the floor in front of it and places his elbows on the seat to support his arms still playing the computer game.

David: Welcome back! Before we talk about the three sessions we've had so far and develop a treatment plan, I would like to extend a special welcome back to you, Ben. Your parents told me when I met with them the other day that you wanted to come in with them for another play session. Sorry it didn't work out that day, but we may have some more play sessions in the future (as he is talking David walks up to Ben, sits down on the floor next to him and looks at the computer game). What are you playing? Looks like you are good at this!

Ben (pretending to ignore David continues with his game): It's just another game.

David (getting up and taking a place on the chair next to Ben): Well, if you want to keep playing, that's fine with me, if it's also OK with your parents. Meanwhile I will talk with them. You are welcome to join in any time you're ready, OK?

Ben (shakes his head slightly in agreement and continues his game):

David turns to the parents and points out the differences in Ben's behavior compared to the first session when he engaged the parents in a power struggle about the recliner. Ben is still somewhat reluctant to participate in the session and continues to quietly play his video game. The parents agree, reporting that Ben has been much more compliant and respectful at home for the last few days. They do not know how the change has come about but are very pleased.

David: Did you talk with Ben about our play session and the baby sister?

Ben (puts down his computer game and looks at his mother)

Ms. Smith: We thought we would talk about it here. Well, Benjamin, when we met with David he told us about your doll house play, during which the little boy took his little baby sister, wrapped her and dumped her in the garbage. It seemed like you were the little boy getting rid of his sister.

Ben (getting up from the floor, looking at David upset): What did you tell them?

David (calmly moving closer to Ben putting his hand on Ben's shoulder): Remember, you gave me permission to tell your parents about our play session. I told them what a brave and wise boy you are. You knew what your mom and dad had been thinking about for a long time. In your play you helped them see what they could not face; the fact that they will not have another child and that you won't be a big brother.

Mr. Smith (with tears in his eyes): You see Ben, mom and I have always thought that if we had another child, like a baby girl, we would be better parents and a happier family. As you know it's been difficult for us to have babies. So we were so grateful and fortunate to have you. Unfortunately, some times we took you for granted because we wanted another baby so badly.

Ms. Smith (holding her husband's hand): And we forgot some times how much we love you. In your play you showed us that it is time for dad and you and I to be a happy family, and not to wait any longer for a baby we will never have.

Ben (getting up from his chair and walking over to his parents): So, you aren't mad because I killed the baby; you don't think I am bad because I got rid of the baby?

David: No Ben, it's OK to pretend while playing; that does not make you a bad boy. You helped your mom and dad to see something they had known but not talked about.

You have freed them to be your parents again, so that you can be the 9-year-old boy you want to be.

As the family embraces in a hug David sat back and lets them take their time to reconnect in an way they have not been able to do for a long time. The dysfunctional interactional pattern has been successfully interrupted creating space for a new pattern to emerge.

David: I'm glad you have figured out what has made your family life so difficult lately. Now it is time to talk about how you can be a happy family in the future and deal with the challenges that a smart and perceptive 9-year-old boy like you, Ben, poses to such loving and caring parents like you, Mr. and Ms. Smith. Being effective parents is a hard job that requires team work, and being a 9-year-old boy is also a hard job that needs consistent parents. Because you enjoyed our play session so much I suggest that we have a few more of those. Parallel I would like to offer the parents some more sessions to talk more about how to parent a 9-year-old in the context of the families in which you grew up. Finally, we'll have a few family sessions and tie things up. The whole process should not take more than 10–12 sessions. What do you think?

All family members agreed to the plan and the therapy progressed smoothly. After some initial temptations to retain the power his parents had delegated to him, Ben learned how to deal with inevitable daily frustrations in developmentally appropriate ways, express his needs openly, and act like the 9-year-old boy he wanted to be and could be outside the family setting. Mr. and Ms. Smith had to fully grieve the loss of their fantasies that were closely associated with their fertility issues. As Ms. Smith learned to accept her reproductive limitations she grew more self-confident as a mother and dealt more effectively with her tendency to get depressed. She eventually found a full-time job as a teacher in which she directed some of her fantasies of having more children. The job also enabled her to be home for Ben after school. Mr. Smith became more appreciative and supportive of his wife's parenting, which released him from the bind between resenting his wife and withdrawing into work. He quickly began to enjoy his work more again and paradoxically found himself wanting to spend more time at home with his wife and Ben.

References

Bowen, M. (1978). *Family therapy in clinical practice.* New York: Jason Aronson.

Johnson, S. M., & Lee, A.C. (2000). Emotionally focused family therapy: Restructuring attachment. In C. E. Bailey (Ed.), *Children in therapy: Using the family as a resource* (pp. 112–133). New York: W.W. Norton.

Minuchin, S. (1974). *Families and family therapy.* Cambridge, MA: Harvard University Press.

Minuchin, S., & Fishman, H. C. (1981). *Family therapy techniques.* Cambridge, MA: Harvard University Press.

Napier, A. Y., & Whitaker, C. A. (1978). *The family crucible.* New York: Harper & Row.

6

The Context of Family Assessment

Dieter Benninghoven, Sabine Krebeck, & Uta Bohlen

Summary
This chapter examines the context of family assessment and family therapy. A distinction is made between the context of the institution and that of the referral system. A further point of discussion is the influence of larger systems on family assessment. In each case, an analysis is made of the possible objective realities that the therapist and families may be confronted with, which expectations, assumptions, hypotheses etc. these realities may give rise to and how therapists can deal with them.

Introduction

In order to understand the meaning and implications of context, the reader is requested to complete the following task:

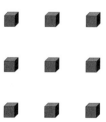

Figure 1.

Join all nine points together using a maximum of four straight lines. The four lines must all meet up with one another, and the task must be completed without once lifting the pencil from the paper. Have fun! You will find the solution at the end of this chapter.

The most common difficulty people experience when tackling this kind of task is that they focus all their attention on the square containing the nine points. They do not leave the context of the problem behind them. Only after several unsuccessful attempts, if they have not already given up, will they start to extend their visual angle and look for a solution outside of the square. In order to solve the problem, however, one must leave the given environment and take a look at the wider context of the system within which the problem lies.

Working with families shows that family therapy is, to a large extent, influenced by the circumstances surrounding it. As shown in the above task, if a therapy is to be successful, the implications of the broader context in which it lies must be taken into consideration.

For family therapists, with their training of thinking in complex networks of relationships, it was a natural step to take a further look at the interconnections between various types of therapeutic undertakings. This led them to the question of which larger systems may exert an influence on the familial or the therapeutic system. In other words – if one reflects on how family members may influence the behavior of the IP, it is logical to follow on by considering what influences may come from outside of the family. Three contextual areas are relevant in family assessment:

– The context of the institution, the influence of the institution in which assessment and therapy take place,
– The context of referral, i.e., the influence of the support system that recommended or prescribed therapy for the family, and
– The influence of other, larger systems in which the family is embedded and in which they have certain roles and tasks to fulfill.

In all three areas, families and therapists make previous assumptions on the influence of these factors, at least on an unconscious level. This chapter shows how each of the three areas affects the assessment process.

We will examine the objective contexts therapists and families are confronted with, the possible expectations, fears, dangers, and resources families and therapists associate with these realities, the questions therapists can ask to clarify the effectiveness of these factors and how such thoughts can, in turn, result in changes in the context.

The Structure of the Institution

The following section provides a detailed description of the implications of the various contexts in which family therapy takes place, the questions this entails for therapists and how working with families in a particular institution reflects back on the institution itself.

In order to comprehend this interactive process, the basic principles governing the functioning and organization of family systems can also be applied to systems involved in the area of mental health. In these systems we also find various levels which can – according to how complex they are – be classified along the lines of a hierarchy. Here, the word hierarchy is used to indicate that the complexity of the levels increases in a hierarchical sense from the individual to the system as a whole.

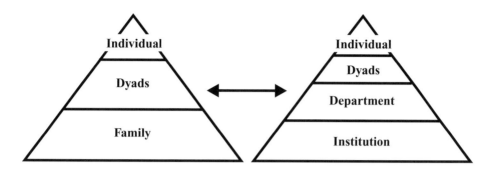

Figure 2. The levels of the family and the institution

On the individual level a series of single persons interact with one another. These single persons join up with others to form dyads. For example, colleagues act as co-therapists and treat families together, or two employees meet up on weekends to play tennis. Above the levels of the individual and the dyad we find any number of organizational subsystems, according to the size of the institution.

The parallelism between the systems of family and institution are illustrated in Figure 2. From a systems perspective it is true for institutions, just as for families, that it is not enough to look at the whole system (the institution) and/or parts of the whole (the individual colleagues); the interaction between the parts must also be examined. There are also interfaces between the levels.

Thus, if the interaction between family and institution is to be defined, it is not enough to examine isolated interaction in the therapy room. The following additional steps must be taken:

- The interaction of the various levels *within* the systems family and institution must be observed;
- The interaction of the various levels *between* the systems representing family and institution must be defined;
- And finally, it must be taken into consideration that interactions between the levels within one system also influence the levels of the other system.

In the following sections, a closer look is taken at interactions within the institution where family therapy takes place.

The Level of the Individual

On the individual level the following factors are important: the gender of colleagues, their marital status (single / in a relationship / married / children), their occupational category, their level of income, their working experience, which therapeutic school of thought they belong to, and what ambitions the employees have with regard to their working environment. Related to this are questions concerning the competence of the individual employees. Here, a distinction must be made between formal and informal competence.

For example, it is important who hires new employees, who is responsible for the distribution of funds, who makes the final decisions on assigning cases, who is consulted
when these decisions are made and who is not. Often, *rituals* provide information on the
informal competence of the individual. Who has the largest room, the newest, fastest
computer, who has a master key for the whole building, but also who is in charge of the
coffee kitty, who organizes the staff outing, who decides which pictures are hung on the
walls?

The Level of Dyads

On the level of dyads the most important aspect is which team members form partnerships for co-therapy. It can be interesting to ask whether the co-therapists belong to the
same school of family therapy, whether their gender differs, whether they have the same
professional qualifications, what positions they occupy in the formal and informal hierarchy, etc.

The Level of Subsystems

The various professional groups that make up an institution form separate subsystems
consisting of e.g., social workers, psychologists, and physicians. Other subgroups are
formed on the basis of members of the management team, academics, and colleagues
who practice therapy.

Affiliation to one or another of the groups often decides on which staff meetings a
colleague is expected or allowed to attend. This infers a certain level of co-determination
and the authority to make decisions.

Subsystems can also be defined by the participation in leisure activities. Alongside
these more informal subsystems, formally established subsystems such as trade unions
also exist.

The Level of the System as a Whole

On the level of the institution there are a series of variables that can play an important
role. For example the name of the institution is important, also the type of funding and
the underlying assignment this implies. Can family therapy be reimbursed through the
health insurance system or do families have to pay for treatment themselves? Does the
institution offer therapy or counseling? Is there a general consensus within the organization that accepts family therapy as a method of treatment, or are competitive/complemen-
tary forms of therapy available? (see Gester, 1988 for a detailed summary).

Three Steps in the Assessment of the Institutional Context

Assessment within the framework of family therapy treatment does not only entail the
therapists' assessment of the family system. Families also form hypotheses on the institution they have turned to for help – i.e., families assess the organization where the therapy

takes place. Even though the assumptions arising from this assessment are not explicit, they do have an implicit effect (Simon & Weber, 1987). It is advisable to bear the following three steps in mind during the assessment process:

- Before a family takes steps towards seeking external help from an organization, the employees of the organization should consider which expectations or fears their institution might arouse on the part of the family.
- In the phase where hypotheses are formed, following initial contact, therapists should reflect on which specific expectations this particular family could have towards the institution.
- Therapists should check their hypotheses concerning the expectations of the family during therapy sessions.

The Various Types of Institution

In the case of *family therapy within in-patient setting*, the definition of an individual patient displaying symptoms is supported by the institutional setting. An individual family member is receiving intensive individual treatment. Families may understand the invitation to take part in a consultation as a good opportunity for a detailed, informative discussion. They expect to find out, at last, what is actually wrong with the ailing family member. Quite often, therapists are expected to provide support. Another danger may be the expectation that the patient's long-awaited retribution towards the family may take place during the consultation, in the presence of an objective witness – the therapist (Reich & Rüger, 1994). The question concerning the family's and IP's expectations of therapy is extremely important in in-patient psychotherapy.

This is also basically true of family therapy within in-patient settings such as *psychiatric hospitals* (Moser & Margreiter, 2001). Here the additional connotation associated with psychiatric hospitals must be taken into consideration. Does the family feel that, by participating in psychiatric therapy, it will have to accept the label of *madness* from the IP? Or is the aim of family therapy in the psychiatric unit to make the IP more compliant towards taking medication? Here – as in other areas – the most important aspect is that the special conditions of the context of the *psychiatric unit* must be taken into consideration.

In *family therapy in an organization whose aims include social control over its clients,* or at least where this cannot be excluded, i.e., counseling centers or the child protective services, therapists should always be aware of the special context. Here, social control means that treatment is carried out at the request or under the orders of a third party (Gester, 1988). A family that is in danger of its children being taken away enters family therapy under completely different circumstances than a family who wishes to make changes of its own free will (Russinger & Wagner, 1999).

Finally, we consider *the context of family therapy in private practice*. One special aspect here is that there is usually no possibility of co-operation with other therapists. This can lead to problems – for example, in a situation where a couple is expected to discuss sexual problems with a single therapist, representing a single gender. Also, families usually have to pay for the treatment they receive in a private practice themselves. This leads to a different context than in therapy that is provided free of charge.

Hypotheses must be drawn concerning the families' expectations towards the institution; however the process does not stop here. These hypotheses must then be checked in discussions during therapy. The following list of possible questions serves as a guide.

- What did you expect/fear when you decided to seek the help of this institution?
- What did you expect/fear when you received our letter?
- What did you expect/fear when you read the sign on our door?
- What would have to happen for you to drop out of treatment in this institution?
- What would be different for you if you had sought help somewhere else?
- Are there themes that you would be more likely to talk about if the video cameras were switched off?
- Who would bear the cost if you had to pay for family therapy out of pocket?
- Which family member's health insurance would pay for the treatment, if this were possible?
- What difference would it make if the interviews took place with a psychiatrist, psychologist, psychotherapist, etc.?
- What would be different if I were a man/woman?
- If this treatment were unsuccessful, would you blame the therapist, the team of therapists or the institution as a whole?

Finally, we must point out the implications for institutions of working with families. In the 1980s, many discussions were held on this topic, based on family therapy within psychiatric units (e.g., Ludewig & Villiez, 1984; Moser & Margreiter, 2001; Rotthaus, 1984; Schweitzer, 1984). This implies that working with families changes the institution within which therapy takes place, when we consider that the experiences of the pioneers of family therapy (e.g., Haley, 1975 or Selvini-Palazzoli, 1983) within psychiatric clinics are reported to have been extremely frustrating.

The first family therapists' euphoric view of family therapy as the ideal treatment for all psychological and psychosomatic problems has not been confirmed. Today, family therapy within institutions is usually seen as a useful additional form of treatment, although it is considered preferential to all other kinds of treatment as far as certain disorders are concerned. Nonetheless, thanks to its empirically documented successes, family therapy has become an essential integral part of treatment in mental health care.

The Context of Referral

The basic conditions also include the context of referral. There are various ways in which a family can come to receive family therapy – their family physician can prescribe it, a CPS worker can order or enforce it, etc. The kind of referral, or the significance of the form of the referral for the family, has a considerable influence on the motivations, expectations, and aims of the family during treatment.

It is not possible to discuss the complete range of possible forms of referral here. A few examples are used to describe important aspects during the assessment process that must be recognized by family therapists. These include the role of the person who refers the family for therapy, the reasons he or she gives for the referral and how this is seen by the family, and finally the relationship between the referring person and the family therapist.

The Role of the Referring Person in the Family System

When a member of a family first calls to make an appointment, he or she is asked who has recommended family therapy. On the basis of this information, the family therapists form hypotheses concerning the possible role of the referring person within the family. When the family attends the first interview, these hypotheses can be checked and any necessary corrections made.

For example, the initiative may stem from the family's physician, whose role is normally to provide basic health care. Generally this will be someone the family members like and trust, a person they rely on and who has possibly advised them to seek the help of a family-counseling center.

In a case where family therapy is carried out as a part of the inpatient therapy of one of the members of a family (see above), the referral is made within the hospital. The hospital can take on several roles for the family, depending on how the other family members experience the inpatient treatment of the patient. They will attend interviews with certain ideas, wishes, and fears – for example with the need to defend themselves or make accusations, combined with the wish to talk or be given information.

A completely different situation arises when the referral takes the form of a court order. The light in which the referring person is seen by the members of a family varies according to the court or official procedure – for example as a controlling social force, as someone who enforces punishment or as a referee. Difficulties arise in family interviews due to the fact that the family has no real aim of its own.

The referring person could also be an individual therapist treating one of the members of the family. He or she may have differing functions for different family members. The therapist's client may view him as a crucial source of support, while the rest of the family experience him or her as an unsettling or even threatening influence.

The quality of the relationship between the referring person and the family should then be examined more closely. If the referral has been made by the family physician, for example, we should ask if the relationship with the family is neutral and indifferent or close and intense. If the person who has recommended treatment has unconsciously taken on a role that maintains family homeostasis through long or intense relationships with one or more of the family members, the family will obey his or her wishes and go to therapy sessions together so as not to lose the physician as a member of the family. They want to please him or her and display their goodwill towards the doctor. After the "successful" failure of family interviews, they return to the referring person and continue to live as before. For family assessment this means that the game between the referring clinician and the family must be brought to a close by means of therapeutic intervention before a new therapeutic working alliance can be formed and new goals developed. Only then can family therapy begin (Selvini-Palazzoli et al., 1981).

– Which family member has the closest relationship with the referring family physician, who has the least close relationship?
– How would the relationship between the family physician and the family be affected if the symptom were to disappear? In this case, who would be pleased, who would be afraid?

Thus it becomes clear that not only the role of the referring person influences assessment and the therapeutic process, but also vice-versa family interviews can change the function of the referring person. If the game between the family and the referring person is ended, as shown above, he may lose his importance for the whole family.

Reasons for Referral

As well as the relationship between the referring person and the family, the reasons he or she gives the family for his referral, or how the family reacts to these reasons, are also significant.

For example, if family therapy is initiated by the individual therapist treating one of the family members, the family therapist may well draw the conclusion that the individual therapist suspects there is an association between his client's specific problem and interactions within the family. This hypothesis must be checked, i.e., verified or rejected, in the initial interview. The individual therapist may also view family therapy as a more detailed form of assessment or as a useful additional procedure. Possibly the referral is simply an expression of his or her own helplessness in dealing with the client. In discussions with the family, the family therapist tries to find out the significance of the referral for the individual family members – one of the family members may share the referring person's opinion and is interested in taking part in family interviews, whereas the rest of the family considers the procedure to be unnecessary.

The family member whose individual therapist makes the referral to family therapy may experience this as a form of betrayal or rejection; on the other hand he or she may see the referral as a form of constructive support.

- Why did your therapist send you to a family-counseling center?
- In what way does your therapist believe the problem to be connected with the family?
- Which members of the family think your therapist is right, who disagrees?

In family therapy practice it is common for the family, or some members of the family, to already have several attempts at therapy behind them. Thus, in the first interview on the telephone, it is important to ask which therapists/institutions have already been consulted.

For example, if the family therapist receives the information that several attempts at therapy have already failed, he or she must find out whether the referring person, other helpers, and the family see family therapy as a last chance, associated with great hopes and expectations, or whether it is viewed as another duty to be performed, so that "no stone has been left unturned".

- How do you think family interviews could help you, when you have already tried so many different things?
- What would have to happen in the interviews for you to break up the treatment?

On the other hand, family interviews can have an effect on the reasons for referral, or rather the way in which these are perceived by the family. For example, in a case where family interviews have merely been prescribed to provide an individual therapist with a thorough assessment of one member of a family, the whole family could find them so helpful that they ask for a further referral to family therapy.

Relationship Patterns Between the Referring Person and the Family Therapist

The relationship between the referring person and the family therapist, or between the two institutions they belong to, is also significant for the context of referral. This relationship has an influence on the attitude and motivation of the therapists themselves and their importance for the family. Both aspects must be taken into consideration in the assessment process; the latter of the two must be discussed with the family.

For example, if the referring person is important for the family therapist, whether for private or for career reasons, this will have consequences for the diagnostic and therapeutic situation. The therapist may wish to produce a particularly successful family therapy, so that the therapist becomes more interested in changes within the family than the family itself. This situation may also arise if there is a competitive relationship between the referring person and the family therapist. If the member of the family who is receiving individual therapy detects, or merely imagines, an element of competition between the two therapists, the family members may feel drawn into conflicts of loyalty or feel afraid of losing the individual therapist if helpful family interviews take place. In any case it should be borne in mind that the success or failure of family therapy undoubtedly influences the relationship between the referring person and the family therapist.

The connotations of the relationship between the referring person and the family therapist should be discussed with the family. Such factors as whether the individual therapist who refers his client to family therapy has a co-operative relationship with the family therapist, whether he or she considers family interviews to be compatible and helpful in combination with the continuing individual therapy or thinks more highly of his own methods, will have an obvious or hidden influence on the acceptance of the family members.

- What does your individual therapist think of our family interviews?
- What would have to happen in the interviews for her to consider them useful?
- What chances do you think your individual therapist gives to changes being introduced as a result of family interviews?

Other Support Systems / Larger Systems

The influence of other larger systems in which the family is embedded and within which the family, or individual family members, take on certain roles and duties, is an important aspect of the external context of family therapy and assessment.

Experiences made by families or individual family members in their interaction with and within these systems are significant for the current therapy situation. Their motivation, expectations and behavior are considerably influenced by these experiences.

- Which other systems are important for the family or the individual family members?
- Which roles and tasks do the family or members of the family have within these systems?
- Which contradictory expectations and difficulties for family therapy arise from these obligations and in which corresponding expectations and possibilities for co-operation might they result?

- How do other systems affect the self-image of the family or members of the family and their coping patterns?
- What effect does working with a family have on its dealings with other systems?

Which Other systems May Be Significant?

School, for example, plays a considerable role in the life of a child, who spends almost half of its waking life there. For children, teachers are figures of authority who bear part of the responsibility for their upbringing. Relations with fellow students play a major part in the formation of social behavior. A child can strive towards being as successful as possible, as a student, making friends with other children in class or being liked by teachers.

Parents often go to work. They may work for public authorities or private companies, as part of the management structure or in a more dependent position further down the hierarchy. They may be popular with their colleagues or have problems with their boss, they may be aiming to go up the career ladder or be close to retirement age.

If medical problems exist, families may be receiving treatment from hospitals, clinics, rehabilitation centers, specialists, GPs or healers. If members of the family are handicapped or chronically ill, they may receive additional care from health care providers, who take some of the pressure off the family. On the other hand they may become unwelcome members of the family because they are there so often. In the case of psychosocial problems the family may seek the help of social psychiatric services such as counseling centers (e.g., marriage, drug or educational counseling), psychiatric practices or psychotherapists. Public offices such as the social welfare office take care of low-income families; the youth welfare office is responsible for families with foster children. Children's homes take over the care of children whose parents are no longer in a position to look after them. Families with children who have become young offenders will come into contact with juvenile detention centers or probation officers. Families may receive support from these systems; on the other hand they may also feel patronized by them and suffer from a loss of autonomy.

In the case of divorce, the courts play a considerable role in deciding who retains custody of the children.

This list of instances is by no means complete – its purpose is simply to touch upon the various kinds of other systems families may come into contact with. In the life of a family these systems may have a specific significance for the genesis, maintenance or reinforcement of problems, and their solutions within family therapy.

The significance of the participation of other systems is particularly relevant as far as so-called multi-problem families are concerned. Such families are often dependent on many various support systems at the same time.

The following example is used to illustrate the situation such a family may find itself in. A family therapist invited all persons involved in the outside support of a family consisting of three people to attend a family interview. The family was confronted with almost four times as many helpers as there were members of the family.

The importance of the role of other systems for families is also illustrated by Imber-Black (1994), who uses a whole series of examples to show the interconnections between families and larger systems.

- If you could turn to a single helper for advice, which person would you be most likely to choose?
- Would the problem continue to exist if you did not have commitments towards school/work etc.?

Contradictory Expectations and Obstacles

Implicit Contradictory Assignments

Problems can arise when expectations differ from a successful outcome of therapy. For example, a boy plays clown during lessons at school. The therapist could diagnose his behavior as socially unacceptable and proceed to work on trying to make the boy stop playing around. However the therapist can only achieve this if he bears in mind the fact that the boy relies on his position as the comedian of the class to gain acceptance from his peers; it also ensures that he receives attention from teachers, who have to admonish him continually. If the therapist forces him to give up his role, the boy will automatically be drawn into a conflict between contradictory assignments from the two systems. If he stops clowning around he loses his position in the class, and gains the therapist's approval. If he does not give up his role as clown, he will retain the acceptance of his fellow students but fail to gain the therapist's approval. In order to solve this conflict, the therapist could suggest alternative ways in which the boy could satisfy his need for approval. The boy's teacher, or a school psychologist who may have been consulted, probably view the problem in an isolated way. They may see it as disruptive for the classroom situation or as an expression of the child's lack of integration in the social structure of the class, without considering the boy's situation at home. However, the boy could be behaving in this way at school because he is not able to play and act in a normal way for his age at home, as his parents forbid boisterous behavior.

In family interviews, a mother complains that her husband neglects their children. The man is employed by a company, where he works overtime every evening, and sometimes also on weekends. When he comes home he is tired, appears absent-minded and is not interested in family life. At first glance, the man might well be evaluated as a bad father and husband. However, the man's behavior is easier to understand when it becomes clear that he is under huge pressure at work; there is a strong climate of competition between colleagues within the company and the boss demands one hundred percent commitment from his employees. The man, fearing for his career, sacrifices more time for his job than he would like to. In this case, the incompatible demands of being a successful working man and a loving father result in a conflict for the man and also for his family.

A family that is faced with the threat of its children being put into foster care is sent to family interviews by the youth welfare office. The youth welfare office expects therapy sessions to take place weekly. The assignment the youth welfare office gives to the family therapist is to assess the functional ability of the family and to give indications for the children to be taken away from the parents, should this be considered necessary. The expectations and wishes of the family, however, revolve around allowing others as little insight into their affairs as possible, so that they can stay together. For this reason, the family attends interviews at irregular intervals, and it is unusual for all the family members to turn up at the same time. If interviews are centered around the family's fear of their children being taken away the family may remain silent, saying nothing at all about any problems that may exist for fear of these being grounds for the youth welfare office to put the children into foster care.

If the family members have experienced previous disappointments with therapists, failed attempts at therapy or at seeking help from other support systems in dealing with problems, this can also result in negative expectations towards the current therapy situation. Family therapy is placed on a list of experiences of failure.

The above examples clearly indicate how a family's expectations towards family therapy are influenced by the views of other systems on the assignment and aims of family therapy, and how the influence of other systems can become an obstacle for solving problems within therapy.

Explicit Contradictory Interventions

As shown above, problems in family therapy can arise as a result of unspoken, unconscious beliefs and expectations. However explicitly formulated, differing, possibly even contradictory interventions or recommendations given to a family by support systems are equally harmful.

A family comes to family interviews because the daughter wets the bed. She also wets herself at school. As the problem has begun to disturb classes, the daughter's teacher has consulted the school psychologist, who recommends inpatient treatment for the child. The family therapist may not have been informed of the advice given by the school psychologist. The family therapist may consider treatment in a hospital too extreme and suggest trying family interviews first. Now the family is faced with a conflict. Whose advice should they take? The family would like to show loyalty to both support systems, but this is not possible in the given circumstances. This conflict could, for example, cause the family to break off family interviews. If the therapist is not able to determine the cause of the conflict, this decision will remain a mystery to him or her.

The following example shows how differences between the assignments of the family and another support system can lead to conflicts in the family therapy situation, rather than different assignments given by two separate support systems.

A family whose children have been in the care of foster parents is about to be reunited. The youth welfare office prescribes weekly interviews with a family therapist. The family attends the first interview, where they state that they only wish to come in every four weeks in future, because they do not see what there is to talk about every week. The family therapist is confronted with two completely incompatible assignments.

As seen in the above examples, contradictory assignments are most likely to occur if the co-ordination or co-operation between systems is unsatisfactory or non-existent. Therapists have no notion of the roles played by other helpers, or these are not taken seriously due to lack of time or interest. Resentment towards other institutions and helpers, and also professional jealousy, often lead to therapists and institutions disregarding one another and thus working against each other in a completely ineffective way.

Corresponding Expectations and Possibilities for Co-operation

However, it is possible for several support systems to work with a family and achieve a working situation based on constructive and efficient co-operation. A family is more likely to embark upon a new therapy with positive expectations if they have been helped by other people in the past, e.g., if one of the family members has already completed a successful therapy.

It is helpful if the various helpers communicate with one another and make agreements, thus avoiding contradictory recommendations or superfluous activities (Seckinger, 2001).

In the case of the family interviews arranged by the youth welfare office, for example, it could prove helpful for the family therapist to invite the youth welfare office to a family interview in order to clarify the situation.

It is important for the conflict to be brought out into the open, so that the terms of existing contracts can be re-negotiated. The family therapist could act as a mediator between the two parties, helping them to find new compromises.

In the case of the boy who plays the clown at school, it would also be useful for the family therapist to co-operate with the teacher and the school psychologist. The family and the teacher could work together to define the difficult behavior at school and at home and decide what the aims of therapy could be, bearing in mind the needs of the boy, the parents, and the teacher.

- Which persons outside of the family could be against/for changes that might take place as a result of family therapy?
- Who would be most likely to offer you support in introducing changes?
- Who is most likely to hinder you in your efforts to encourage changes?

Self-Images and Coping Patterns within the Family

The self-images and coping patterns within a family can be characterized by various mechanisms. There could be a family tradition of attitudes towards helpers over the generations.

For example, a family taking part in family therapy reports that both parents have recently completed successful individual therapies. This has proved extremely helpful for both parties. However, partnership problems have now arisen and the partners both wish to tackle these together in family interviews. Both families of origin have always taken advantage of professional help to solve problems.

This could have resulted in the following pattern – *We need constant help from outside, we cannot cope without support.* Once one problem is solved, a new one immediately takes its place, and a new helper must be found.

In other families the following rule may exist – *Family affairs have nothing to do with other people.* A family that has adopted such a rule will basically refuse all help from outside and will always see it as interference. It will have a hostile or unfriendly attitude towards the therapist.

The following example illustrates differing coping patterns within families. A boy has begun to display aggressive behavior towards other people and objects, both at school and at home. The family reacts in an extremely relaxed, calm way. Their reaction could indicate that they believe their son's aggression is nothing serious. Children behave aggressively at a certain age; he will grow out of it. Possibly other boys in the families of origin have displayed rather aggressive behavior. In another family, however, the mother has been following discussions in the press and on television about violence and aggression among children and young people, and is extremely worried about her son. She has read that aggressive young people must receive therapy and believes that the family will never be able to solve this problem on its own.

As discussed above, the positive or negative experiences of families as far as therapy or help from outside are concerned can also influence the family's feeling of competence or powerlessness in the therapy situation.

- How would you have coped with the problem you are faced with now five or ten years ago?
- What would you do if you felt that family therapy was not helpful for you at this point in time?
- Is there a family on television or in a novel that you would compare your family with?

Implications for Other Systems

Finally it must be pointed out that family therapy has an effect on the interactions of the family or its individual members within other systems. In the case of the father who had no time for his children as he was under such pressure at work, family therapy sessions could result in the man attempting to make clearer boundaries between his working life and his private life. One possible solution would be to set aside special times for his children. This would probably entail cutting down the amount of time he spends at work. He would no longer be able to work overtime every day; he would be late with some of the tasks his boss gives him, some of his work he may not manage to complete at all. The director of the company and the other employees would notice that the man was putting in less effort. He may no longer be considered reliable. Some of his tasks would be given to other employees, he may be looked over for promotion or even lose his job.

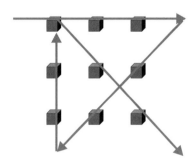

Figure 3.

Concluding Remarks

The definition of context in the assessment process provides not only the therapist but also the family with an important source of orientation at the outset of therapy. Without speaking of the actual problem, it provides an opportunity of looking at the therapy situation from a metaperspective and reflecting on the relationships at hand. This can be a good starting point for the development of a successful therapy especially in cases where a therapeutic process has reached a dead end, when there seems to be no chance of further progress, when therapy seems doomed to failure because of difficult patterns or conflicts. This situation can be compared with the task that was presented at the beginning of this chapter. The problem-solver has already drawn a multitude of lines in an attempt to join the nine points together, and begins to despair of ever finding a solution – he has reached the point where there is the greatest danger of giving up. The only solution is to take a look at the context in which the problem is set. In the same way, a clear definition of the broader context of family therapy, incorporating information on experiences with other systems and related expectations and attitudes, which may have been neglected up to this point, may provide the new impulses required to help the therapy on its way.

References

Gester, P. (1988). Von der nutzlosen Notwendigkeit einer Systemanalyse. *Kontext, 15,* 93–102.

Haley, J. (1975). Why a mental health clinic should avoid family therapy. *Journal of Marital and Family Counselling, 1,* 3–13.

Imber-Black, E. (1994). *Familien und größere Systeme: im Gestrüpp der Institutionen.* Heidelberg, Germany: Carl-Auer-Syteme.

Ludewig, K., & von Villiez, T. (1984). Warum systemische Therapueten Systeme wie die Psychiatrie nicht vermeiden sollten. *Zeitschrift für systemische Therapie, 2*(1), 29–38.

Moser, C., & Margreiter, J. (2001). Systemische Praxis in der Akutpsychiatrie – Das Haller Modell. *Familiendynamik, 26,* 2, 135–151.

Reich, G., & Rüger, U. (1994). Die Einbeziehung der Familie in die stationäre Psychotherapie. *Nervenarzt, 65,* 313–322.

Rotthaus, W. (1984). Das Jammern über die Institution als Alibi. *Zeitschrift für systemische Therapie, 2*(1), 39–40.

Russinger, U., & Wagner, E. (1999). Gewalt-Zwang-System. Systemisch-konstruktivistische Perspektive in der Jugendhilfe. *Zeitschrift für systemische Therapie, 17*(3), 144–156.

Schweitzer, J. (1984). Zu den Grenzen der Koevolution von Psychiatrie und Systemischer Therapie. *Zeitschrift für systemische Therapie, 2*(1), 47–50.

Seckinger, M. (2001). Kooperation – eine voraussetzungsvolle Strategie in der psychosozialen Praxis. *Praxis der Kinderpsychologie und Kinderpsychiatrie, 4*(1) 279–292.

Selvini-Palazzoli, M. (1983). Über die Familientherapie hinaus. *Familiendynamik, 8,* 166–181.

Selvini-Palazzoli, M., Boscolo, L., Checchin, G., & Prata, G. (1981). The problem of the referring person. *Journal of Marital and Family Therapy, 6,* 3–9.

Simon, F. B., & Weber, G. (1987). Vom Navigieren beim Driften – Die Bedeutung des Kontextes der Therapie. *Familiendynamik, 12*(4), 355–362.

7

The Family's Social World

Silvia Echevarria-Doan, Martha Marquez, & Diane Estrada

Summary

Implicit in the assessment of a family's social world is the family's ecology or culture. As such a culturally responsive framework is proposed in this chapter when client-families are assessed in therapy. This framework embraces cultural diversity and is contextual and systemic in nature. It also recognizes the effects that the therapist's and the client's culture has on therapy. Assumptions upon which this framework is based and methods used are illustrated by utilizing acutal case examples.

Introduction and Goals of the Chapter

Encountering clients for the first time presents us with a number of choices. Usually the nature of this encounter is more social at first as client and therapist gain familiarity with each other and clients get more acquainted with their surroundings, our presence, and our style of interaction with them. In essence, as we are both sizing up the situation, one can say it is here that we begin our assessment process concerning who we are dealing with and how we will work together. Beyond the social nature of our initial contact with clients, we generally move into some form of inquiry, usually informed by a certain frame of reference that guides our line of questioning. For instance, if you were to encounter the following client-families for the first time, what might some of the assumptions, practices, and guiding theories be that would direct your line of questioning with these clients?

Mari is a 29 year-old Polish/Italian-American Presbyterian female who is currently studying architectural design. Joshua is her 22-year old Irish/Russian-American boyfriend who has dropped out in his senior year of college "to support the family". The couple presents with difficulty in meeting each other's expectations. Mari complains that Joshua needs to "grow up" and learn to be more supportive. Joshua states Mari is constantly irritable in their interactions and he struggles finding ways to be supportive.

Roger, a 43 year-old African American attorney and his two teenage daughters, Shawna and Zari, come to therapy seeking help with the youngest daughters' acting out behavior in school. Jesse, Roger's wife, died 1 year ago after a long battle with cancer. Jesse was of Jamaican descent. Roger reports that Zari has been associating with "troublemakers" and is not following house rules. Zari states that she is simply hanging out with her friends and that Roger does not trust her judgment.

Rebeca, a 40 year-old Chicana/Sioux Indian female is seeking therapy for her two sons, Mario (age 16) and Carlos (age 13). Rebeca's ex-husband is Latino/Irish/German. Both the children and Rebecca identify themselves as "Hispanic/Chicanos". Rebeca has been divorced for 2 years and is concerned about her youngest son's "silence". The boys' father has remarried and Rebeca is particularly concerned about her sons' relationship with their father. Ever since Rebeca attempted to collect child support from him he started to threaten her for custody of the children.

How might you proceed with your assessment of each of these client systems? Would you follow a similar (or a different) format in your assessment of each of them? If so, what might you emphasize differently or consider more significant (or important) in each case as you arrive at a better understanding of these client-families and their reason for seeking therapy? Given some of the cultural variables that have been cited, would you find yourself making use of this information in some way? Had culturally oriented information not been provided, would your assessment of these clients include a way of arriving at that type of information? Do your current methods of client assessment include ways of considering the client's multicultural context as part of their larger system? Or, do you inquire about a client's cultural/ethnic/racial identities when you work with certain clients only? Finally, we ask that you consider the consequences of your responses to each of these questions.

These are some of the important questions we have considered in writing this chapter. Our answers to some of these questions are presented as we discuss our views pertaining to the client-family's social world, a central part of our assessment process. We believe a client's social world is made up of various multicultural dimensions that clients identify with (e.g., ethnicity, class, age, gender, race, religion, and sexual orientation, among others). Our methods of assessment emphasizing these dimensions will be explained as we introduce the "framework for embracing cultural diversity" (Echevarria-Doan & Marquez, in press; Rafuls & Marquez, 1997) that guides our work with clients. This framework has a great deal to do with the therapist's own cultural awareness of self and others.

As Latinas, it is difficult not to think in cultural terms because we live in a world which combines at least two cultures – the culture we came from and historically share with our families, and that which we immigrated to and have grown to identify with (in a number of different ways). This bicultural/multicultural existence requires us to deal with a constant interplay of being Latina on one hand and American on another depending on the context that defines the moment. It is what Shorris (1992) refers to in his book *Latinos* as the "in-between," when one is not totally Latino and not totally American. Identifying with either one or both has a great deal to do with who one interacts with, where the interaction takes place, the language used throughout the interaction, among other variables. It is a constant foreground/background experience, which is performative, fluid, and emergent (McGoldrick, 1998) depending on defining points of cultural intersections wherein specific parts of our cultural selves are strengthened over others (Laird, 1998). Thus, our cultural awareness of self and our awareness of others in relation to who we are is something we have practiced most of our lives.

Much of our influence toward culturally based assessment has a great deal to do with our personal sense of self (i.e., who we are and where we come from). In this chapter we will present the assumptions, standards, and methods that are associated with our assessment of clients in family therapy. Initially, we will provide some guiding definitions of culture along with some historical accounts of theorists and clinicians that have influenced our thinking and practice. Most notably, these influences will represent the major assumptions and concepts which have led us to our use of the framework for embracing cultural diversity (Echevarria-Doan & Marquez, in press; Rafuls & Marquez, 1997) developed by the second author. This framework is contextual and systemic in nature and recognizes the effects that the therapist and client's culture has on therapy. It is based upon the belief that therapists need to continually address their own individual issues toward diversity as part of their work with clients if they are to be culturally competent practitioners. We will also expand upon the case examples we introduced earlier by applying some of the principles and practices of the framework for embracing cultural diversity and a concluding summary of the chapter will also be provided.

Defining Culture

A family's social world encompasses multiple dimensions that are commonly associated with a family's ecology or culture. An ecological or cultural view of a client's relational context is quite useful when assessing a client system. We believe that family therapy assessment from a culturally based perspective has a great deal to do with how expansive or restricted one's definition of culture is. Assessment for those with a broader definition of culture may guide them to apply general standards of practice that lead to inquiry about cultural identity regardless of a client's identity, background, or cultural affiliation. Assessment for those who adhere to a more narrowly defined view of culture might limit their inquiry about ethnicity, cultural dimensions, or one's social world to clients whose cultural differences are more noticeable. This latter view constitutes the more common assumption that culturally based inquiry (e.g., regarding ethnicity, class, gender, race, and sexuality) need only happen with clients whose specific cultural categories are more salient.

McGoldrick (1998) asserts that culture is not measurable, generalizable, static, nor can it be defined. She describes culture as performative, improvisational, fluid, and emergent. By that she means that we are culturally different depending on our context and thus, who we are changes from moment to moment. She refers to cultural intersections which combine different parts of our cultural selves such as ethnicity, gender, social class, and other narratives related to our ecological context. The categorizations that make up our cultural selves are not considered stable, fixed, nor do they stand-alone. Instead, some of its forms and meanings may become more salient over others depending on our cultural context. For instance, our Hispanic/Latina sense of self is experienced very differently with our families as we share in traditional holiday rituals in contrast to professional circumstances where we might lecture about said experiences. In this broader view which asserts that culture is contextually based, one may argue that we all experience culture regardless of skin color, gender, physical features, etc. So, the question is, do we ask about a client's culture only when he/she is considered to be "different," "non-white," or "minority," or should we ask about culture regardless?

We must clarify here that we are aware of the fact that in many cases one's salient features (e.g., skin color, hair, language, etc.) are what others see first and foremost. In these cases it is difficult to ignore culture based on difference and not have that part of us enter into our interaction with others (whether or not it is acknowledged). For those who experience this, it is difficult not to have aspects of culture, race, and ethnicity brought up whether they want that or not. Thus, it is important to note that regardless of context, some of these categories (which are not as changeable or fluid as the others) can be much more salient throughout one's lived experience than it is for those of a more dominant or mainstream group. Our premise is that culture is a part of everyone's experience and therefore requires us to include it in our assessment of all clients, not just a selected few.

Falicov (1998) underscores the multidimensionality of culture by defining it as:

[those] sets of shared world views, meanings, and adaptive behaviors derived from simultaneous membership and participation in a variety of contexts such as language; rural, urban, or suburban setting; race, ethnicity, and socioeconomic status; age, gender, religion, nationality; employment, education and occupation, political ideology, [and] stage of acculturation. (p.14)

She goes on to explain that a family's culture is defined by a combination of multiple contexts and partial perspectives that are a part of the cultural subgroups that we belong to. A multidimensional perspective of culture challenges us to adopt a pluralistic identity that is not static and can evolve (as we do within each of the given dimensions that construct our world). In essence this dispels the myth of cultural purity that is often attributed to white culture, as though whites do not juggle numerous dimensions of gender, class, migration, education, geographic location, religion, or sexual orientation in their daily existence.

Our orientation toward assessment is ecologically nested, culturally based, and utilized with each of our clients regardless of their family identity. Our views and practice are informed by a number of historically significant developments in family therapy that we will outline in the following section.

Historical Development and Major Proponents Associated with Multiculturally Based Assessment in Family Therapy

In 1982, Harry Aponte referred to McGoldrick, Pearce, and Giordano's *Ethnicity and Family Therapy* as a "leap ahead for the field of psychotherapy," considering it "both a professional stance and a political act by the editors who [assumed] the position that ethnic difference [was] to be considered an active dynamic in the treatment of families (McGoldrick, Pearce, & Giordano, 1982). Aponte further assumed that after reading this ground breaking contribution to our field it would be difficult for therapists to assess, treat, and communicate with families without being culturally sensitive to client families' as well as our own family roots. Two decades later, we are not so sure that his forecast held its ground as is evident with ongoing recommendations for the need to be inclusive of culture in one's thinking and practice.

A revised edition of McGoldrick, Pearce, and Giordano (1982) appeared in 1986 with an even more expansive base of ethnically defined families specific to over forty nationalities. And of course, most recently there is McGoldrick's (1998) *Re-Visioning Family Therapy*, wherein a plea is made for us to reform our views and "vision" in family therapy to be more inclusive of the often invisible organizing principles of culture, class, race, gender, and sexual orientation in our work. Besides McGoldrick's contributions, we have been influenced by others like Sluzki (1979) who addressed the impact of migration on families, Saba, Karrer, and Hardy (1989) who wrote about minority families' experiences in family therapy, and Karrer (1989) who specifically addressed cultural interactions between therapists and minority families. We have also been influenced by Waldegrave's (1990) politically and culturally-embedded practice of "just therapy," Breunlin, Schwartz, and MacKune-Karrer's (1992) transcending model of meta-frameworks, and of course Celia Falicov's work, which we discussed previously (Falicov, 1998, 1995, 1988a, 1988b).

Those who have addressed the importance of race and class issues have also influenced our multiculturally embedded assessment process because of the direct impact that race and class can have on family life. With the exception of Minuchin's work in the 1960s, it was not until the 1990s that race entered into family therapy's consciousness (Minuchin, Montalvo, Guerney, Rosman, & Schumer, 1967). Many of the contributions in this area in the late 80s and early 90s were spearheaded by Nancy Boyd-Franklin (1989), Ken Hardy (1993, 1995), and Elaine Pinderhughes (1989). As with ethnicity and culture, family therapists still contend with the impact of racism in their clients' lives and the biases that underlie many of their conceptions of family health and pathology. Similarly in terms of class, Kliman (1998) refers to the "psychic constraints of class" which if addressed, can help families locate their difficulties within their economic system or lack of resources rather than in themselves and their family. She states, "[e]xploring the role of class in family life is an exercise in social justice" (p. 54). Given these orientations that have informed us regarding the importance of ethnicity, race, class, and cultural context, we will describe the framework of embracing cultural diversity, which guides our assessment process with all clients.

The Framework for Embracing Cultural Diversity: Major Assumptions and Concepts

This framework provides a method of teaching therapists how to be more culturally aware, sensitive, and accepting towards their clients. Ideally, therapists begin the process long before seeing clients and continue the process throughout their development as therapists. This framework embraces the idea that awareness is a life-long endeavor that is dynamic and multidimensional. Assumptions underlying this framework are:
(1) Families and their situations are all systemic and contextual in nature. That is, families bring with them a number of interconnected variables that occur within different dimensions of lived experience. All of these variables affect their pre-

senting problem. From an individual perspective, clients experience internal and biologically influenced processes that they may struggle with that also affect the family. Individuals are also affected by their interpersonal relationships with others in their lives, thus the influence of family on their interal processes.

(2) Neglecting to incorporate contextual variables in a working hypothesis in therapy can be disrespectful and potentially dangerous. Focusing primarily on the problem or a solution could devalue the life experiences in a family by assuming that all families with a particular presenting problem are similar. It might also subtly convey that families should all assimilate to the host culture and adopt its values.

(3) The therapist's culture becomes part of the family's system as they are affected by the therapist and the therapist is affected by the family. Thus the therapist's own life experiences have an impact on the assumptions that underlie the questions, the direction of therapy, and the change process. (Karrer, 1989). Because of this assumption, the framework focuses heavily on the self-of-the-therapist and ways in which therapist can increase and embrace cultural awareness for themselves, and as a result, their clients.

(4) All cultural experiences should be validated within the context of uniqueness and strengths. As McGoldrick (1982) asserted, "there is a common tendency for human beings to fear, and therefore reject, that which they can't understand" (p.4) Clinically, this leads to labeling that which is different as wrong or bad thus, families from different cultural influences could easily be pathologized. Resource-oriented research and practice (Rafuls, 1994, Echevarria-Doan, 2001) has found that resource-based language in therapy has a positive influence on how client-families perceive themselves and how therapists viewed their ability to change. Thus an overarching theme of strength is also included in this framework.

Tenet 1: Consider a Larger Multidimensional Definition of Culture

As discussed earlier, so often the term culture is narrowly defined to include only race or ethnicity. What we have discovered through such fields as anthropology, archeology, and ethnography is that what constitutes an individual's culture is much broader and can include multiple variables. Combine this concept of the individual's culture with that of the family and the meaning of culture becomes wonderfully complex. Below is a partial list of factors that should be considered when developing an idea of the family's cultural identity.

Shared historical contexts
Political status
Immigration for purposes of political asylum
Immigration for purposes of saving family and self
Leaving behind valued elements
Similar dialects/languages
Similar attire
Interpersonal space
Beliefs about gender and power
Shared values regarding marginalization and oppression

Shared experiences: disasters/climate
Social class
Appearance: skin color/shades, eye shape/color, height
Similar habits
Similar life styles
Levels and value of education
Religious practices
Spiritual orientation

The multidimensional nature of culture is evident with the various combinations of these factors that can be influencing individuals at different life stages and at different times. Combine this idea again with the notion that families are composed of several individuals whose cultural factors may be combined similarly or not. For example, the factors that are most influential for a pre-adolescent may be related more towards appearance and issues of fitting in a culture as opposed to an adult who may be more concerned with social class and issues of marginalization. For the entire family then, all of these issues are a part of the family's cultural context.

Tenet 2: Interact with Others and Examine Similarities and Differences

Immersion into the life of others who are culturally different than oneself is an optimal method for learning about life experiences. Attempting to embrace emotionally what others have experienced will assist in sensitizing and appreciating their perspective. This is not a passive but active concept. Therapists do not have to wait for the culturally different client for this to take place. All around us there are opportunities to learn about other cultures: art festivals, museums, concerts, books, movies, neighbors, community centers, organizations, historical readings etc. We can make a concentrated effort to increase our own repertoire of friends and acquaintances to include those from different cultures.

In addition, we can make deliberate attempts to dialogue about meaningful cultural issues and examine our differences and similarities. This can help reduce our fears of the unfamiliar, help us to learn to talk comfortably about cultural issues, and help to dispel stereotypes we may have developed. A probable side effect could be the discomfort that results from an awareness of the often painful struggles that others have experienced due their differences and also a discomfort at our own realization of our flawed biases and assumptions. Often we must dwell in discomfort and examine its nature in order to move forward, a thread that is present in all aspects of this framework.

Tenet 3: Accept and Celebrate a Personal Journey Towards Self-awareness

In conjunction with embracing the cultural differences in others, therapists must examine their own cultural identity both past and present. We can begin by considering the factors addressed in tenet one from our own life experience perspective. Interviewing family members from different generations can illuminate for us intergenerational customs and beliefs that may still be present in our lives. For example, we are often unaware as to the roots of our own upbringing until we examine further back in our family's history.

Furthermore we should examine our own biases and assumptions regarding different cultural factors such as race, gender, ethnicity, family constellation, and more. Many of us do not readily admit that we are biased in thinking that two parent families are healthier than one-parent families; however this kind of bias can guide our thinking in therapy. Likewise, our assumptions regarding certain cultural factors can also affect our therapy. Many assume that all Hispanic parents are conservative and old-fashioned. This can be in part accurate; however, this can also serve to narrow our vision as therapists. Identifying and addressing these biases and assumptions is a necessary step towards cultural self-awareness. A further examination into the roots of these biases and assumptions can help us deconstruct our own experiences and develop a fuller understanding of them.

Finally, we can request critical feedback from others regarding their perceptions of our biases and assumptions. The purpose would be to genuinely learn about ourselves through the lenses of those close to us. In order for this exercise to be meaningful, it would require a true level of honesty, disclosure and of acceptance on our part as exemplified in Halvey's (1998) "genogram with an attitude" and some of the exercises proposed in Echevarria-Doan & Marquez (in press). Our openness would be essential and discomfort could arise during these experiences; however, the benefits would far outweigh the risks.

Overarching Tenet 4: Examine Individual Personal Experiences with Difference

This tenet ties together the previous three tenets in a manner that is recursive in nature. While considering a larger multidimensional definition of culture, interacting with others and examining similarities and differences, and accepting and embracing a personal journey towards self-awareness, therapists need to examine how they are influenced by their own individual personal experiences with cultural factors. What personal experience do we have where we felt prejudice from someone? On what grounds were we marginalized? Religion, appearance, language? How did we feel? How has that experience influenced our lives today? How has that experience influenced how we feel towards that group or individual that made us feel marginalized? The answers to these questions can broaden our vision of culture and can help us realize the roots of our biases and assumptions. We can learn about the lens through which we see others as well as ourselves. It is vital that we accept our own place along this journey towards cultural identity formation.

Consider also the effects on therapy if we learn about cultural differences solely through our own personal experiences. For many, these experiences are broad and can indeed contribute to the understanding and progress of therapy. However, for others, relying on their own life experiences may be too narrow a base to draw from. We may still be healing from the wounds left by past experiences with prejudice, discrimination, marginalization, or oppression and be unaware of their residual presence in our thinking. We may very well unintentionally project our sentiments on to those we work with in therapy. Learning from our own painful experiences can serve to assist others in our work.

Description of Our Assessment Process

The Therapist's Self-Assessment

Consistent with the framework for embracing cultural diversity, an assessment of a client's social world must begin with the assessment of the therapist's own social world. The same questions we ask of our client's and the same exploration we embrace for our clients we should first engage in for ourselves. Beginning with this step sensitizes therapists to the complexities of a client family's culture and gives us a basis from which to begin to assess the potential multidimensional interactions with clients.

We believe that the process of therapy itself is influenced by our own personal values and world-views. Thus, we recommend that therapists first explore their own cultural and social world by reflecting on the factors listed previously that would be taken into account when developing ideas about the family's cultural identity. Prior to meeting with clients for the first time, cultural aspects of our selves are potentially evident. Simply through our name, clients might be able to ascertain our gender and/or our ethnicity, which may influence how our clients perceive us. Therapists might consider how their gender and/or ethnicity have impacted other interactions in the past. In addition, our agency or office location can potentially reveal some aspects of our socio-economic level or social class or at least the economic surroundings we choose to locate our practice in.

As we meet with clients we continue to reveal more of ourselves culturally through our physical surroundings. What adorns our offices, what reading material we select, and what we choose to wear add to the socio-economic clues of lives, whether intentional or not. In addition, our own physical appearance may or may not tell others about our race or ethnicity. Our skin color, our attire, our size can all be revealing. Society also decides what we consider attractive and what we do not. And since human interaction is often influenced by attraction, we can assess our own attractiveness and how it has affected our lives both in the past and in the present. Much of this is culturally related since different cultures have their own norms of what is considered attractive.

Other contextual issues that may be physically evident include our age, sometimes our physical ability, our health, our educational background, and occasionally our religious or spiritual practices. Since our theory of therapy and the process of therapy itself are influenced by our own personal values and world-view, it is important that we examine events that have contributed to their formation. Some of our ideas have developed because of socio-political events, environmental issues, and many of the previously mentioned issues. For many, surviving disaster or political persecution has hardened them or made them more sensitive to others. Some might have residual feelings of resentment and pain. Also, living in an environment or culture where political unrest is often accompanied by violence or threats of violence can have a long-lasting impact. We also know that surviving disaster can make us more resilient as we balance the remaining memories.

All of these issues can potentially influence us to expect our clients to respond as we have responded and to be at the same place we are in terms of healing. We should constantly remind ourselves that there are multiple healthy ways of responding to situations. We also may impose our own vision of events, which can be inaccurate and lead to further expectations.

Scenario #1 – Mari & Joshua

You may recall our opening description of Mari and Joshua as a young couple who held disparate expectations of one another (particularly as they pertained to Joshua). In this case, Jennie, their therapist, was a married Irish/Japanese woman who was aware that her own beliefs about a husband and wife's role in marriage were heavily based on her own life experiences and family history. In supervision she found it helpful to discuss how her gender, religion, and culture were impacting her work with Mari and Joshua. This was especially useful because Jennie found herself becoming frustrated with Mari's demands that Joshua "grow up" given that Joshua was "sacrificing" his schooling to "support the family". In her case, Jennie examined her beliefs around gender as they compared with those held by Mari and Joshua, while also acknowledging how these beliefs impacted the couple's relationship and their expectations of each other. Jennie later recognized that part of her frustration with Mari was that she too was raised with the belief that a "good man" is a "good provider" and that while education is important, a woman's family comes first above all else. These beliefs were conflictual with Jennie's beliefs around the importance of "choice" for clients. Her own frustrations with her own conflictual beliefs were impacting her view and meaning making of her work with these clients.

By constructing a cultural genogram (Hardy & Lazloffy, 1995) with the couple it also became obvious that their beliefs about marital roles and responsibilities were also influenced by other contextual factors like religion, ethnicity, family legacies, and cross-cultural beliefs and values. Cultural genograms can be good assessment tools to help clients tell their cultural stories in a larger visual context. Questions regarding the larger family's influence on relationships can be visually portrayed and family patterns better understood. For example, during the cultural genogram construction, Jennie asked Mari how the females in her family of origin experience support from the males in the family. A pattern of emotional disconnection and financial dependence became evident in her familial gendered context. Mari had seen many of the women in her family become depressed and isolated from their male counterparts. Mari had decided that she would go to school and have a successful career and be financially independent in order not to suffer the same fate as her older female members. Joshua was aware of the importance of having a successful career for Mari and had decided to quit school in order to "help her" achieve her dream. In this process, he had inadvertently recreated the pattern that Mari was hoping to avoid.

Jennie proceeded to ask Joshua the same question for his family of origin. How do males show support for other family members? In his family, males were "good providers". It was through this process that males exhibited their love and commitment to their female partners. The more concerned Mari became, the harder Joshua worked in order to provide for her. It was what he knew best. Covering the impact that culture had in their case softened a good deal of the blame and animosity previously noted when the couple first came in. Thus, allowing them to negotiate new rules and establish new meanings regarding these particular aspects of their relationship.

Other less obvious influential contextual issues in a therapist's life include our sexual orientation and our own lived experiences. Whether or not we choose to reveal these issues to our clients does not diminish their influence on our lives. Our sexual orientation may have led us to experience marginalization of some kind or inclusion, which can help us be more sensitive or hinder our sensitivity. An awareness of this can at the very least prepare us for our clients' similar scenarios or their similar feelings as they experience marginalization and inclusion as well. Our lived experiences can include our lives with our families of origin and the complex interactions involved with multigenerational influences.

Assessment of the Therapeutic System

An analysis of the therapeutic system in which we are involved with our clients is vital to the understanding of our role and ultimately the clients' dynamics in the therapeutic system. A systems perspective has taught us that much of the dynamics that occur on one level of interaction is occurring on other levels as well. For instance, one of the systemic influences that need to be considered is the client's funding source (i.e., third party payment through insurance, client self-pay, government grants, local and state grants, private contributors or others). Contrary to what many fantasize, the funding source influences how we view our situation and potentially how we work with our client families. We may feel pressure to complete therapy early, to guide our work towards a particular outcome, to give a particular diagnosis, or to report to various people with power concerning rather delicate information.

Other systemic influences include the health of the system we work in. We ought to assess if those in power are abusing their power in some form that influences our work. Our ability to influence our system, or the amount of voice we feel we have as therapists, contributes to our personal sense of strength and importance. This, in turn, will impact our work with our clients. If we are in a position of power in our work environment, aside from the position as a therapist, it is important to assess our ideas of management and collaboration. We can often translate those ideas to the therapy room as well.

Often, we might also be witnesses to office politics that infringe on a healthy work environment. There could be physical conditions that influence the therapy as well, both positively and negatively

Upon Meeting the Client Family: The Therapist's Continued Self-Assessment

Once we have met the entire family system we will be working with, it is important to assess our own assumptions, biases, and experiences about the social and cultural world of the family. This process is also continuous for several reasons. First, it may take several sessions before we have the opportunity to meet the entire family system we will be working with. Second, we may only know of influential members through their description by the attending family members. Third, important social and cultural clues may not be mentioned in the first few sessions. Fourth, many other clues are not only not mentioned initially but also may not be superficially noticeable. Relying on a family's phenotype as the sole clue to their cultural background leads to incomplete assumptions and potential errors.

With the information we obtain from the first meeting with clients, we can begin to explore what our reactions are. Is the client family of a race, gender, ethnic, or economic background that we have feelings or preconceived ideas about? These feelings and ideas need not be categorized as positive or negative to be influential in the therapy process. Perhaps we may assume that Asian-American individuals are good with mathematics, for example. Although a seemingly benign idea, it is still regarded as an assumption that has the potential of being inaccurate or at least guiding our thinking. Some assumptions might also be helpful in understanding our clients' situation. In this same example, we might be able to appreciate an Asian-American family's struggle if one child earned a low grade in mathematics. Regardless of the outcome, knowing our assumptions about contextual issues that our clients bring has an effect on our thinking and thus, on our therapy with clients.

Of paramount importance is our assessment of our biases of our clients. We should ask ourselves if we have any judgments about our clients already based on what we have learned about them in the first session. Again, these cultural issues may be primarily the superficial or physical issues nevertheless we may have some significant biases. Some of our biases may have been generated from our society's influences, our own family's influences or teachings, or from our own lived experiences. Considering the previous example, we may have a personal family history involving political persecution from an Asian country. This might have an initial impact on our feelings about our client.

Assessment of the Client Family

An assessment of our client families begins with our first encounter and continues throughout therapy as we collect, confirm, and integrate the cultural and social clues we are given by clients. We can incorporate formal methods of assessment as through intake forms or general therapy forms, or we can choose to assess more informally.

Inquiry is an inherent part of assessment that is substantively informed by the questions we pose and often based on perspective, theory, research, personal life experience, beliefs, and practice preferences. The kinds of questions we ask clients are generated from the framework we have described. Our goal in assessment is to ask relevant questions that address the client's concerns/problems/ issues and also facilitate a culturally responsive process for them. In order to do this we must address the client's larger social context. Some of these questions might have clients consider whether they are concerned about their socioeconomic status, gender, race, ethnicity, education, religion/spirituality, sexual orientation, age, or physical and emotional abilities as part of their presenting problems; Or, whether any of these aspects of their lives have any bearing or influence on the situation that brings them into therapy

The telephone contact

If the therapist is able to engage in the first telephone contact with clients, we can begin our assessment by noticing any speech-related issues. Although potentially inaccurate, this information can help us start on the path of gathering data. We can notice any foreign accents, dialects, speech mannerisms, or disfluencies. These clues might shed some light on health or ability issues, acculturation issues, issues related to geographical origins. This can also be partially accomplished if we listen to a recorded message from our clients. All of these data, would need to be confirmed upon meeting with the client family.

We can also gather data for our cultural assessment during that first phone contact by listening specifically for certain clues. Clients usually discuss briefly their concern that is bringing them to call for help. They also occasionally mention what may seem like superfluous information. As clients talk, we must keep an open ear for mention of minute details that may reveal some ideas such as their views about couplehood, child rearing, appropriate behavior, and many more issues that may be related to their culture or life experiences. All of the above information can be written down for us to use during therapy. Keeping a list of the data that we have gathered, and constantly updating it as we confirm or eliminate information, helps us in the assessment process.

Written assessment

Therapists generally ask clients to read and fill out a variety of forms and paperwork prior to entering therapy. Included in the information forms, we can ask questions that will expand our understanding of our client's culture. A statement on our form declaring our desire to understand and include cultural issues in therapy might help clients understand why such information is being requested. For example, "It is my hope to behave as respectfully as possible with all my clients and to learn about each client's uniqueness, thus I am asking for information about your cultural background that will help me achieve that goal. Participation from as many family members as possible answering these questions is extremely beneficial." Such a statement will help clients understand much about the therapist's thinking and also help clients feel less threatened about potential marginalization if that is what they have experienced in their lives.

Questions about a client's social world can range from general, "Please describe your family's cultural background", to specific such as "Describe your ethnicity, race, religious/ spiritual background ...." More specifically, therapists may want to consider asking clients how some cultural issues currently relate to the situation that brings them to therapy. "Are there any economic issues in your life that relate to the issue that brings you to therapy now?" It is important that therapists keep in mind that families are composed of multiple members thus ample space for responses is needed. We should also encourage responses from other family members throughout the written assessment, which could include background information from extended family members that still influence our clients.

Given our expanded definition of culture, therapists should also consider asking about issues clients may not traditionally associate with culture. For example, many may not see the relevance of health issues or issues related to ability although they may have profound influences on a family. Clients may not have considered issues related to power and gender imbalances in relationships. Issues such as these might need to be worded with language that is readily understandable by most people. For example, "Are there issues in the family that are related to or exist because of the fact that you are a man or a woman? As an example, does someone in your family feel that they have an unfair share of household chores or wage earning?" Other issues not necessarily considered cultural issues are experiences with environmental or natural disaster. We could ask, "Has anyone in the family experienced some extraordinary event that has impacted their lives such as war, a hurricane, or famine?"

Finally, any assessment that occurs in writing must be constantly modified as we receive information from clients about appropriateness of certain questions. Clients are often our best teachers especially with issues of wording. Our openness to modification will also demonstrate our thinking and will improve future assessments. We should also include an open-ended question about other information we may not have asked about which clients consider important for our therapeutic work together. This question can be designed to include any issue that was not covered by us during our interviews with clients.

As we continue to assess for our client's social world, we need to confirm our understanding of the written portion of our assessment. This is an evolving process, since a therapist's primary goal in the first session is to listen carefully to the clients. Thus confirmation and further assessment must be intertwined with the therapy process.

Sessions with Clients

As therapists meet with clients for the first time, it is important that therapists refrain from the temptation to collect superficial information and accept the data without confirmation. Human interaction is based much on the subjective thinking of those involved. Such subjectivity has the potential of leading to erroneous conclusions. In addition, in the first session clients may not feel as comfortable revealing extensive information. They may be nervous or hesitant while protecting their vulnerability and building trust in their relationship with their therapist. These issues may color the cultural issues therapists are assessing for.

Assessment of the client's social and cultural world during therapy consists of observation and conversation. Therapists look at the clients and their physical clues just as discussed with the self-assessment of therapists. Issues such as skin color, gender, and dress are important observable clues. Therapists can also observe the interactions of the clients for ideas of how that family interrelates according to their own cultural rules and norms. Power dynamics and gender issues may also be noticeable during sessions and catalogued as further information as yet to be confirmed.

Scenario # 2 – Roger, Shawna, and Zari

The second family introduced earlier in the chapter was seen by Annie, a 24-year old, White, female therapist, of Irish/German descent. Annie was concerned about her ability to be effective with Roger and his two daughters, Shawna, and Zari. She was specifically concerned that her age would be a problem in her ability to build rapport with this family. As the youngest in her family, she often felt that she hardly had a voice in matters and with the age disparity between her and the father in this case, she was somewhat intimidated by his presence and incredulous nature. It was helpful for Annie to discuss the interrelatedness of age and power issues she experienced in this case. Furthermore, she had to consider how other issues associated with appearance (i.e., gender and race) impacted the work she did in therapy. Rather than simply focusing on differences, she simply needed to be aware that these factors could influence their interactions with each other. In the following transcript Annie found that her discussion with the family about gender and ethnic distinctions among them brought up how much Zari and Shawna missed their Jamaican mother who had recently passed away. Through Jesse they had established a strong Jamaican identity that Roger was not particularly acknowledging. Besides this, some obvious issues related to the family's grief were also addressed.

Annie: Roger, how have you and the girls talked about their role as females in this family?

Roger: What do you mean? I am the father they are the children. That's everybody's role.

Annie: How has your job as a parent changed since Jesse passed away?

Roger: There are more things to keep track of. I have to work twice as hard to make things run smooth at home? That's why I need Zari to stop her running around with these people and stay at home where I can keep an eye on her.

Annie: Zari, how have things changed at home since your mom passed away?

Zari: Everything is different.

Annie: How?

Zari: I do not know. It just is ... Mom did things differently than Dad ... I miss her.

Annie: Shawna, do you know what your sister is talking about?

Shawna: Yeah. Mom had her own way of doing things.

Annie: Hmm ... I wonder if you and Zari reminisce about those times. Would you mind sharing those times here in session?

Shawna: (with understood hesitation at first) No, I guess not.

Zari and Shawna shared stories of their mom's singing and dancing and cooking. All of these activities had a Jamaican flavor to them. This cultural connection had been lost, along with their mother's life.

Annie: Roger, do you remember this also?

Roger: Yes, I do.

Annie: It sounds like you miss that cultural connection too.

Roger: Yes. I do plan to take the girls to Jamaica to visit their grandmother in the summer.

Annie: Sounds wonderful. In the meantime, I wonder how Zari and Shawna attempt to stay connected with the Jamaican part of their culture?

Zari: I hang out with my Jamaican friends, but dad does not like them.

Roger: I do not like them because one of them got into trouble with the cops. Not because they are Jamaican.

Annie: So, you are concerned about Zari and her safety and do not want for her to get into trouble. How do you see your job as a Dad? As the male head of the family?

Roger: It is my job to protect them. Besides, Shawna does not hang out with those kids and she misses the cultural connection too.

Annie: Sounds like you are curious about how Shawna has dealt with this loss. I wonder if you can ask her about it?

Roger: Well ... Shawna ... how do you?

Shawna: I don't. I miss her. I cry most of the time.

Annie: Roger, how do you deal with it?

Roger: (silence) ... I work.

Annie: Maybe we can spend some time talking about how all of you grieve and what do you hold to be important at this time. How does religion or spirituality influence your view of death?

Throughout her work with this family, Annie engaged in several conversations about her own spiritual beliefs about death, her connection to Shawna and Zari as a female, and her connection to Roger as the "responsible one" who was also ethnically different from Shawna, Zari, and Jesse.

Therapists are often hesitant to ask clients directly about cultural information for fear of offending clients. Such discomfort can be openly discussed with our clients, and indeed the path has been paved if there is a portion of the assessment in the written forms. By asking clients directly about cultural and social issues we are modeling for them an openness to talk about these issues as well as an openness to tackle potential discomfort or embarrassment. We can help offer language for clients to use while discussing cultural issues and they in turn can help us modify and learn more appropriate terminology for their specific culture. Often many cultural issues are extremely obvious and if the therapist does not address the issue, then they are modeling avoidance or insensitivity. The clients may also feel that the therapist is incapable of working with their particular issue or that the therapist is judgmental or biased.

Scenario #3 – Rebeca, Mario, and Carlos

Julia, a 32-year old Latina therapist, worked with Rebeca, Mario, and Carlos over a period of three months. Rebeca presented as a very angry and disillusioned woman. She was irate with the center and its request for the father's permission for the children to be seen in therapy. She reported several attempts to get services for her sons which resulted in being given the "run-around". Her anger towards her husband was also very evident. Anger was a factor of great concern to Julia, since her Venezuelan upper class family upbringing did not approve of public displays of anger.

In supervision, Julia discussed her experience of social class and how it might impact the process of therapy as she worked with this single working class mother of two. Questions about Julia's experience as a Latina of Venezuelan nationality in contrast to the experience of a Hispanic/Chicana family were also raised. Other questions she considered were: How might their ethnic backgrounds be alike and different? How might the cultural meaning making of Latina and Hispanic interact in the therapy process? How would issues of acculturation be examined? How did acculturation impact interactions among members of this family? How did acculturation influence the belief system of the therapy team in their work with this family? How did Julia's migration experience inform her work with families? How did this family's migration history impact their lives and their view of the world? And finally, how did the family's broader cultural experiences influence Carlos' "silence" (one of the mother's primary concerns in therapy)?

Questions like these that Julia asked of herself and her clients invite dialogues about one's larger social context. Our socialization has inhibited our ability to see the impact of these larger social contexts on our everyday lives. However, we have been urged not to ignore the power of exploring these larger contexts for our selves and our clients. A culturally responsive therapist is willing to engage in these conversations in order to more fully understand our clients' social world. This has allowed us and our clients to understand and experience different ways of viewing the problem, quite often the key to successful therapy.

Summary and Conclusions

We have discussed assessment of a family's social world within a very broad definition of culture as it pertains to the framework for embracing cultural diversity. The core of this framework addresses the therapist's own awareness of cultural identity as it pertains to self and others. Several steps delineating this culturally based method of assessment have been described and illustrated with case scenarios. Some thoughts about constraints and obstacles that get in the way of this form of assessment have also been discussed.

As systems therapists, we must assess cultural issues with all of our clients and those who are important in their lives by taking into account the cultural background and influencing issues of the whole client system. There may be cultural issues from generations back in a family or from a work environment that is affecting the client family currently. As discussed in the framework for embracing cultural diversity, the cultural issues must be considered within their multidimensional view. It is not sufficient to simply know the client family's ethnic background or political inclinations. We also need to assess how other cultural issues interact such as gender or religious beliefs. In addition, each family member's cultural context must be intertwined with the others in their family to attempt to grasp the multidimensional view of the client's social world. As imagined, the process is continuous, perhaps even without a definitive end.

References

Boyd-Franklin, N. (1989). *Black families in therapy: A multisystems approach.* New York: Guilford Press.

Breunlin, D., Schwartz, R., & MacKune-Karrer, B. (1992). *Metaframeworks: Transcending the models of family therapy.* San Francisco: Jossey-Bass, Inc.

Echevarria-Doan, S. (2001). Resource-based reflective consultation: Accessing client resources through interviews and dialogue. *Journal of Marital and Family Therapy, 27,* 201–212.

Echevarria-Doan, S., & Marquez, M. G. (in press). Counseling Cuban American families using the Framework for Embracing Cultural Diversity. In C. Lee (Ed.), *Multicultural issues in counseling: New approaches to diversity* (3rd ed.), Alexandria, VA: American Counseling Association.

Falicov, C. J. (1998). *Latino families in therapy: A guide to multicultural practice.* New York: Guilford Press.

Falicov, C. J. (1995). Training to think culturally: A multidimensional comparative framework, *Family Process, 34,* 373–388.

Falicov, C. J. (1988a). *Family transitions: Continuity and change over the life cycle.* New York: Guilford Press.

Falicov, C. J. (1988b). Learning to think culturally in family therapy training. In H. Liddle, D. Bruenlin, & D. Schwartz (Eds.), *Handbook of family therapy training and supervision.* New York: Guilford Press.

Halevy, J. (1998). Genogram with an attitude. *Journal of Marital and Family Therapy, 24,* 233–242.

Hardy, K. V., & Laszloffy, T. A. (1995). The cultural genogram: Key to training culturally competent therapists. *Journal of Marital and Family Therapy, 21,* 227–237.

Hardy, K. V. (1993). War of the worlds. *Family Therapy Networker, 17,* 50–57.

Karrer, B. M. (1989). The sound of two hands clapping: Cultural interactions of the minority family and the therapist. In G. W. Saba, B. M. Karrer, & K. V. Hardy (Eds.), *Minorities and family therapy.* New York: Haworth Press.

Kliman, J. (1998). Social class as a relationship: Implications for family therapy. In M. McGoldrick (Ed.), *Revisioning family therapy: Race, culture, and gender in clinical practice.* New York: Guilford Press, pp. 50–61.

Laird, J. (1998). Theorizing culture: Narrative ideas and practice principles. In M.

McGoldrick (Ed.), *Revisioning family therapy: Race, culture, and gender in clinical practice* (pp. 20–30). New York: Guilford Press.

McGoldrick, M. (1998). *Revisioning family therapy: Race, culture, and gender in clinical practice.* New York: Guilford Press.

McGoldrick, M. (1982). Ethnicity and family therapy: An overview. In M. McGoldrick, J. K. Pearce, & J. Giordano (Eds.) *Ethnicity and Family Therapy.* New York: Guilford Press, pp. 3–30.

McGoldrick, M., Pearce, J. K., & Giordano, J. (1982). *Ethnicity and Family Therapy.* New York: Guilford Press.

Minuchin, S., Montalvo, B., Guerney, B., Rosman, B., & Schumer, F. (1967). *Families of the slums.* New York: Basic Books.

Pinderhughes, E. (1989). *Understanding race, ethnicity, and power: The key to efficacy in clinical practice.* New York: Free Press

Rafuls, S. E. (1994). Qualitative resource-based consultation: Resource-generative inquiry and reflective dialogue with four Latin American families and their therapists. (Doctoral Dissertation, Purdue University, 1994). *Dissertation Abstracts International, 56–02,* p.0716.

Rafuls, S. E., & Marquez, M.G. (1997). La Familia Fernandez: Counseling Cuban Americans. In C. C. Lee (Ed.), *Multicultural issues in counseling: New approaches to diversity.* (pp.269–294) (2nd ed.). Alexandria, VA: American Counseling Association.

Saba, G. W., Karrer, B. M., & Hardy, K. V. (Eds.) (1989). *Minorities and family therapy.* New York: The Haworth Press.

Shorris, E. (1992). *Latinos: A biography of the people.* New York: Norton.

Sluzki, C. E. (1979). Migration and family conflict. *Family Process, 18*(4), 379–390.

Waldegrave, C. (1990). Just therapy. *Dulwich Centre Newsletter, 1,* 5–46.

8

The Multigenerational Perspective of Family Assessment

Günter Reich, Manfred Cierpka, & Almuth Massing

Summary
The development of the multigenerational perspective is outlined; socio-historical and unconscious aspects of family histories and related processes are described. The clinical manifestations of these processes and the significance of the various generations for one another are examined.

Introduction

The multigenerational perspective comprises three dimensions:
- the psychoanalytic theory of the unconscious conflict and its intrafamiliar tradition, along with aspects of self and object relationship psychology,
- the perspective of systems theory, particularly second-order cybernetics,
- and the socio-historical dimension of family life and experience.

The family system may be seen not only on a contemporary, horizontal level but also as a vertical, historical system with a spiral development.

Here we assume that the past, especially the unconscious, conflict-ridden, unfinished past, is present in contemporary events and exerts a considerable influence on experience and behavioral patterns.

Consequently, "disorders and conflicts in the child generation often result from conflicts between parents and grandparents or partners and their parents. This arises through multiple intrafamilial transference processes. We also assume that the same basic conflicts are repeated in families over the generations, i.e., that 'intrafamilial repetition compulsion' exists" (Massing et al., 1999, p. 21). The fewer breaks there are in this continuity over the generations, the more this repetitive tendency gains in strength. Psychological disorders arise when families, under the influence of repressed conflicts and resulting repetitive fantasies, experience and behavior patterns, are no longer able to come to terms with contemporary changes in an alloplastic and autoplastic way. Consequently, they cease to mature at certain points in their development.

Symptoms and problems within the family may be understood as attempts to solve conflicts. Such conflict-solving attempts are the best possible means at the family's disposal, taking the given external circumstances and internal coping abilities into account. They are compromises born of conflicting intrafamilial and intrapsychic tendencies. They are multiply determined and fulfill multiple functions. Of central importance here is the *psychic reality* (Freud, 1917) of the system as a whole and that of its individual constituents, preconscious and unconscious relationship fantasies and interpretative patterns.

Traumatic experiences within the family are often the starting point for the development of rigid, dysfunctional conflict-solving attempts, relationship patterns, and interpretations of external and internal reality. Of interest to psychoanalytic family therapists are not the objective facts, but how these are processed and interpreted. Here, the respective individual version of events is important, along with the collective patterns it results in.

The introduction of the dimension of contemporary history throws light on the interaction between the macro and micro-social processes influencing individual family members. The multigenerational perspective sees families as entangled in historic events, socioeconomic changes and the changing values, ideals and ideologies of the prevailing subcultural reference group rather than simply as an independent, autonomous system responsible for its own destiny. This view of the extended social context also serves to qualify and correct normative clinical assessments.

Historical Development

The multigenerational perspective has been developing since the 1950s, resulting from an association between psychodynamic and system theoretical views in the treatment of severe psychic disorders in children, adolescents and young adults (psychosis, anorexia) and in the treatment of severe partnership conflicts. Psychoanalytically oriented object relationship psychological researchers such as Winnicott (1969) concentrated primarily on the early interaction between mother and child and its repetition in adult life. Carrying on from here, Dicks (1967) developed the collusion concept, which was further expanded upon by Willi (1975) (see Massing et al., 1999).

Furthermore, the above-mentioned family therapy researchers, along with others such as Gregory Bateson and the Palo-Alto group around him (Bateson et al., 1969) showed that problematic relationships not only influenced early childhood but, in severe disorders, continued up to adulthood (e.g., Lidz and Fleck, 1965).

In the 1950s, Mendell and Fischer (1956, 1958) described similarities in the basic conflicts and behavior in a family with depressive identified patient over three generations. Even before this, the psychiatrist Hill (see Bowen 1960a) stated that, in schizophrenic psychoses, a decreasing degree of individuation and interpersonal boundaries could be observed over three generations.

This hypothesis was systematized and extended by Bowen to become a theory of multigenerational emotional processes (see Kerr and Bowen, 1988). This school of family therapy stresses the importance of the genogram, which is today used by family therapists from all schools as a standard assessment instrument (see Guerin & Pendagast 1976; McGoldrick & Gerson, 1998; and the notes on this section). This multigenerational perspective was developed still further, particularly by Framo (1982, 1992) relating to conflicts and crises in relationships between partners and Boszormenyi-Nagy and Spark (1973/1981) and Boszormenyi-Nagy and Krasner (1986) relating to the ethic-existential dimension of relationships, particularly the dynamics of loyalty, merit and legacy over the course of generations.

Empirical Findings on Continuity over the Generations

Many studies in the area of developmental psychology have quantitatively proved the existence and effects of continuity over the generations. In attachment research, repetitions in relationship patterns over several generations and their reappearance in contemporary partner and parent-child interactions were observed (Benoît & Parker, 1994; Mikulincer & Florian, 1999, Ricks, 1985, Zimmermann et al., 1995). This is also observed in the tradition of divorce (Pope & Mueller, 1976), in the development of attitudes towards bringing up children (Schneewind, 1999), in processes of destructive parentification (Jurkovic, 1998), in the experience of violence (Cierpka, 1999, Rosen, 1998) and in single parent families (Cierpka et al., 1992). Specific methods of quantification (e.g., the PAFS-Q, Personal Authority in the Family System Questionnaire, by Bray et al., 1984; see Schneewind et al., 1989) were developed to investigate the key concepts of multigenerational family therapy. Here, the construct of personal authority has a central mediating position between the levels of the individual and the family (Vierzigmann, 1995). The studies based on Bowlby's (1973/1975) attachment theory have extreme relevance for the practice of family therapy. They reveal predictable continuity between the adaptive behavior of the mother and her parents up to attachment between mother and child in the following generation (Grossmann et al., 1988; Stroufe & Fleeson, 1985, Zimmermann et al., 1995) and repetitions in insecure attachment behavior over generations (see also the detailed literature review by Emde, 1988a, 1988b and Fonagy, 2001).

Painful emotions concerning a mother's own experiences as a small child can influence the attachment process with her children. The circumstances surrounding this are discussed in research on the effect of breaks in these patterns over the generations (Grossmann et al., 1988, Main et al., 1985; Sroufe & Fleeson 1985) – if there is continuity in the difficult and painful attachment patterns, the mothers are more likely to deny their unfavorable early mothering and idealize their own parents. They express no anger. In cases where this pattern is changed over the generations, mothers do not idealize their parents and do not deny the painful emotions that belong to their relationship with them. Mothers who have generally more positive experiences in their later relationships than their own mothers are able to describe the unfavorable circumstances of their own early mother-child relationship and express the painful emotions it evokes. According to Sroufe and Fleeson (1985), a third relationship is generally responsible for a break in this continuity (see also Tress, 1986). Either an emotionally attainable alternative parent was available during childhood or another emotionally stabilizing relationship was formed, e.g., to a psychotherapist. New experiences in adolescence, support in a new social environment, supportive marriage partners and their families are also major factors leading to a break in the continuity of unfavorable mothering behavior over the generations (see also Ricks, 1985, Zimmermann et al., 1995).

These results are highly important for psychotherapy, as they show that the cycle of neurotic repetitions can be broken if painful, denied emotions are worked through within the context of new relationships. Multigenerational family therapy can build the basis for new experience and a new start in behavioral patterns by working on denied conflicts and emotions.

The Dimensions of the Multigenerational Perspective

Socio-historical Influences on the Family

Of course it is not possible, here, to provide a complete list of all the socio-historical aspects that can influence the development of families. However, some basic examples are given below.

The Third Reich – from the point of view of the perpetrators as well as the victims – often throws its shadow on the development of families, for example in the form of continuing, preconsciously transferred Nazi values and related ideologies. This can even result in disorders in the child generation (see also Massing, 1991, 1994; Massing and Beushausen, 1986).

For example, the son of a family was threatening to commit suicide. He was suffering from the effects of an early infantile paralysis with one-sided paresis. Because of the suicide threats, the mother was subject to feelings of guilt and self-accusation. The father developed complex idealizations involving competitive sports. Both parents tabooed or mystified the infantile paralysis. The unconscious motto was: "our son is not handicapped." In a family therapy session with the mother, her father and a sister, a family secret was spoken about for the first time – the grandmother of the identified patient had been put to death during the Third Reich for being mentally handicapped. The grandfather still believed the reasoning behind the laws of that time concerning hereditary diseases i.e., that "unworthy" life is congenital. In the multigenerational session between the father and his mother, who was over 80 years old, her merciless delegations based on her continuing Nazi ideals became a topic of discussion. Although her own husband had been killed in the war, she still believed in the motto "better to die like a hero than to live like a coward." The symptoms of her grandchild, who felt like a cripple both mentally and physically, were an expression of the ideals of the grandparent generation. These had been passed on by the middle generation in complicated transformation processes, especially guilt and idealization.

Other long-term influences are wartime experiences, particularly the death of relatives, expulsion and flight. An example from more recent times is the German reunification, which has brought not only new opportunities but also a loss of security, familiar bonds and orientation and has forced people to completely change all their accustomed ways of life. Family therapists have been and are still confronted with these processes. For example, an increase in the number of cases of bulimic eating disorders in the generation of the children has been observed in Eastern Germany. These often mirror the loss of orientation caused by role reversals within the family since the reunification (see Cierpka et al., 1994; Ratzke, 1994).

As well as the change in the role of the woman, which is experienced as an open or underlying conflict in many partnerships, external circumstances also lead to problems in coming to terms with a changed role or role reversal.

Until well into the last century, material security and traditional affiliations to certain groups and social strata played a central role in partnerships and family relations. Now, on the other hand, the wish for happiness, security and confirmation is generally directed at family relationships, at the partner or children, who are overburdened as a "haven in a heartless world" (Lasch, 1977). The wishes for happiness directed at the children stand at complete odds with environmental threats and the normative compulsion for the child to develop in a satisfactory way.

For example, a mother visits a breast-feeding course with her baby to seek guidance in giving her child the "right" kind of care through breast-feeding. At the same time, she has her breast milk checked regularly for harmful substances.

Parallel to these processes, an increased density in the relationship between the generations can be observed. Simply due to the increase in life expectancy, more and more grandparents are able to experience the birth and childhood of their grandchildren (see Lauterbach, 1994). The huge number of possibilities for identification within our society implies a variety of affiliations between the generations (see Lüscher, 1993).

Assessment Questions

- To which socio-cultural milieu does the family belong? Which past and present processes of change does this imply?
- What changes have taken place – in the nuclear family and in the grandparents' generation?
- How have political changes or migration affected the lives of the last three generations?
- Were family members involved in these events? If so, how?
- Which values, ideals and role requirements does this background suggest?
- Which values, ideals and role requirements are associated with the socio-cultural background of the family and the changes it has undergone?

The Family Feeling – A Link Between the Generations

All groups that live together as family units develop a family feeling to provide a balance between the individuals' wishes and the family system's need for maintenance and cohesion.

The individual development of the family feeling goes hand in hand with an inner picture of the *family as a whole*. This picture serves the purpose (mainly on an unconscious level) of imagining one's own family at a later point in time. The realization of one's own lifestyle also forms a framework that enables the next generation to develop biologically and psychologically (including the individual development of the *family feeling*).

The development of the inner concept of family is based on the identification with a psychosocial compromise experienced by the child within the network of family relationships. We assume that the child does not only identify with the basic dyadic and triadic object relationships, but also with the family as a whole.

Identification with the primary persons of reference and family allows an active construction of *family representations* to take place. From these the *family identity* is formed in a further, superordinate endopsychic structure. This intrapsychic structure gives the ego access to a specific ability – the idea of and the feeling for a family.

An individual's development of family representations implies an internalized identification with the family, going beyond dyadic and triadic patterns. "Identifications in dyadic relationships and within the family contribute to the development of these family representations, as long as they have been gained *in association with the internalization of functions of the forming, maintenance and reorganization of the 'family as a whole'*" (Cierpka, 1992, p.85) There is a clear connection between the concepts of family representation, family identity, and family feeling. The development of a family feeling is coherent with the endopsychic structuring of family representations and family identity (see also Sperling, 1988).

By establishing these ideas on the psychosocial configuration family and the feelings associated with it, the child acquires the ability to form social relationships within her or his own family and in larger groups, first in day care and then at school. Family identity also incorporates a future perspective that allows the child – and later the adult – to form ideas about a family of its own.

As to the identification processes, we assume a concept of active assimilation. The child is born into a family, but must assimilate the family concept little by little. As they grow up, children demand that their parents change in order to meet the challenges of the various stages of development and to take on appropriate roles. The child does not simply identify with the functions and processes in the family. It contributes to the development of these functions.

Clinically the concept of the family feeling is helpful, as patients present their internal image of the family during treatment. Sometimes it is strongly linked with life plans, expectations from the family and corresponding disappointments.

The family images of patients who are suffering under the strain of separation or divorce from their partners usually include at least two aspects (Cierpka, 1999a). On the one hand patients describe a nostalgic, harmonious utopian family, on the other hand they paint a picture of a family of origin (and usually the present family) torn by inner conflicts. As children these patients did not experience their parents as a couple, either in a partnership or in a sexual sense. Often they were drawn back and forth in a conflict of loyalty between their parents, or they were forced to take sides with one of them. These relationship patterns evidently result in considerable internal conflicts, and later to restraint in their experience and relationships with their own partners and families (see also Massing et al., 1999; Reich, 1991).

Assessment Questions

- Do the family members describe the nuclear family as a whole unit as well as in terms of individuals, dyads and triads?
- Does the family therapist gain the impression of an internal image of the family as

a whole or rather as consisting of individuals, dyads and triads?
- How could the complete picture be described?
- Do the children and the adults describe themselves as belonging to both parents and their families of origin or mainly or exclusively to one side?
- How are ruptures in the family feeling dealt with?

Trauma, Fantasy, Defense

Severe psychiatric disorders always seem to result from traumata in the family system. Often, these traumatizing events have taken place in the previous generation, who were not able to deal with them at the time.

In general, these traumata – for example severe illnesses, frequent deaths, loss of property or employment, loss of cultural orientation and social valence, forced migration, violence, sexual abuse – are emotionally far more serious than the family members involved can admit or allow themselves to perceive under the prevailing circumstances.

Feelings of fear, shame and guilt, and binding loyalties are the basic motives of defense. They are intended to protect the identity and integrity of the system inwardly and outwardly, against the real or imagined judgment of the outside world. Families or family members sometimes see themselves as the perpetrators of blows for which, upon closer examination, they have little or no responsibility. On the other hand, the actions of family members can be projected onto the outside world, thus completely denying the family's involvement.

Defense processes are organized interpersonally within families in typical interaction sequences, where patterns such as displacement, isolation, denial, reaction formation, identification with the aggressor, and reversal into the opposite as described in psychoanalysis take place. Along with the global denial of whole segments of experience within the family, the latter patterns are those observed most frequently in familiar defense mechanisms.

Consequently a reversal of roles and affects takes place. Pride takes the place of humiliation, being put to shame and devalued results in the judgment, condemnation, denunciation, and exposing of others. The defense patterns and resultant attitudes and family ideologies are carried on from one generation to the next.

The defense against traumata and the conflicts it infers leads to the compulsive repetition of destructive patterns in the family history. These generally take place at critical points in the family's life cycle development, when the system is under a particular level of strain (see Andolfi, 1982; Bronfenbrenner, 1979; Carter and McGoldrick, 1980; Reich, 2003).

Assessment Questions

- Which traumata have played a part in the development of the family?
- Which emotions, e.g., fear, feelings of guilt or shame, have developed as a result of these traumata?
- How did the family cope, how is it coping with the emotions evoked by the traumatic experiences?
- What patterns of defense against painful emotions and conflicts can be observed?

- What family fantasies are called to mind?
- Are repetitions of destructive patterns linked with traumatization?

Identification, Counteridentification and the Return of the Repressed

Transactional patterns from the past are mainly traditionalized in the family's values, rules and ideal formations (the superego and the ego ideal) and in internalized object relationships. This happens via processes of identification. Children identify with the idealized parent and grandparent figures, by whose imaginary or real strength they feel protected and guided. They also identify with them as aggressors. Both patterns play an important part in the formation of the superego (Freud, 1923, 1928, 1933).

Identification and counteridentification with the family's lifestyle, which is some-times more difficult to define, is of particular significance. It is reflected not only in values and views but also in taste, daily, weekly, and yearly rhythms, special rituals (for example on festive occasions) and especially in basal "atmospheric" characteristics such as a sense of smell, temperature, or basic emotional moods. The development of such lifestyles is closely linked with the central relationships formed in childhood. They enter the interaction field of the individual via these relationships, where they then become internalized and strongly libidinised. They form crystallization points of mutual obliga-tion in the multigenerational network of relationships and provide a sense of security and belonging (Boszormenyi-Nagy & Spark, 1973/1981; see also Dicks, 1967; Massing et al., 1999).

Children identify unconsciously with their parents' and grandparents' guilt, without being aware of the source of the guilty feelings. This "borrowed guilt" (Freud, 1923) can be accompanied by borrowed shame (see Massing et al., 1999; Wurmser, 1990). This means that children can be ashamed for their family because their parents or grandpar-ents have done something shameful or have been humiliated. This kind of continuity over the generations can create the impression that shame is contagious (Hilgers, in press). Stierlin (1974b) refers to cycles of guilt and shame which, used in defense against one another, can influence lives over generations.

Identification with the position of the victim seems to be particularly shameful and humiliating for individuals and families alike. Families or family members often deny their own identity as victim and defend against it by identifying with the aggressor, which is more in keeping with the ego ideal and easier on their sense of self-esteem.

Family myths (see below) can be used to support the defense of the family's unbear-able self-perception via a reversal into the opposite. They also provide an image of family values and relationship configurations for identification processes.

Counteridentification is a common mechanism used to come to terms with the family of origin, to gain distance from it, and move away from its traditional patterns. This implies the adoption of values, ideals, and lifestyles that are antithetical to those found within one's family. Detachment attempts during adolescence often result in counteridentification; however it is not uncommonly found in earlier stages of develop-ment. When, for example, children notice that positive areas are already "occupied" by siblings, they will often seek out other (seemingly) opposite domains. Thus the musical child's younger sibling is good at sports, the child who is a good at languages is comple-mented by a little scientist, the well-behaved child's counterpart is a rowdy, etc. Another example of counteridentification is an antithetical choice of partner – often a person seeks the opposite of her or his own family in a partner or even in the partner's family (see below).

In many families, as in larger social systems, the "swing of a pendulum" can be observed in identifications over the generations. The same characteristics that the parents rejected in their own parents, the things they were desperate to get away from, reappear in their children, possibly in a milder form.

The tensions that occur because of the "return of the repressed" (Freud, 1937) can be constructive; they can lead to a synthesis between tradition and new ideas and thus to more tolerance towards various ways of living. However, within rigid family systems, counteridentification also tends to be rigid. The values, lifestyles or aims in bringing up children, although different to that of the previous generation, are adhered to with the same measure of superego stringency practiced by the parents, as defined by a symmetrical relationship structure. However, this also means that a basic emotional identification with the family of origin remains. Repressed elements return in exactly the same form as before, or they break out in an unexpected crisis, e.g., when consciously non-violent parents hit their children in a sudden attack of anger, despite all their good intentions.

Assessment Questions

- Which identification paths seem to exist from the family of origin through the parents to the child generation?
- Do the conscious lifestyle and the conscious orientation adopted by the parents express more identification or more counteridentification with the families of origin?
- Which denied identifications can we assume the parents and the children to harbor? How do these manifest themselves?
- Can repetitions of constructive patterns and pattern changes be observed as well as unconscious repetitions of destructive patterns?

Loyalty, Merit, and Legacy

The (family's) historical events and traumata and how they are dealt with, combined with identifications within the family system, form the "psychic heritage" of the family, the legacy from which the duties and obligations of the individual family members are drawn; in the same way the legacy itself is also dependent upon these duties and obligations. Here the existential, ethical dimension of family relationships introduced by Boszormenyi-Nagy and Spark (1973/1981) is touched upon. This is the unconscious crux point, the unconscious center of transactions, where everything runs together. This legacy and the bonds of loyalty it implies give the individual family members a sense of purpose and direction. They incorporate developments over the generations and make a considerable contribution to the formation of the family feeling (see above).

Boszormenyi-Nagy and Spark (1973/1981) and Boszormenyi-Nagy and Krasner (1986) assume that a kind of bookkeeping, a ledger of merits, exists within families, where the merits and debts of family members in terms of what they have done or should do for one another are measured up. The balance of give and take must be constantly regained according to changing external circumstances and norms and developments in the lifecycle.

The need for justice in human relationships is seen as a basic motivating force, with all the power of an instinct. A violation of relational justice is perceived as a justification for destructive or autodestructive behavior and withdrawal from social responsibility and rules, e.g., resentment or narcissistic views and behavior (see Wurmser, 1993).

This means that parents are under obligation to their children because of their very existence, their helplessness and dependency, just as children are under obligation to their parents because of the fact of being born and cared for. They can fulfill this obligation by bringing up children themselves. Parents can deny the obligation towards their children by neglecting them or overburdening them with unresolved conflicts. The legacy passed on in this way can become impossible to fulfill.

A constant imbalance in the reciprocity of give and take gravely endangers trust in relationships. Boszormenyi-Nagy and Krasner (1986) see this as the major cause for all disorders in human existence. For example, the need for belongingness is exploited when narcissistic, material, or sexual needs are satisfied under the flagship of "higher values", resulting in relational corruption. This ambiguity and the mistrust it causes can be observed in all seriously disturbed families.

In the ethical-existential perspective of relationships, individuation is seen as the "capacity for balancing old and new loyalty commitments" (Boszormenyi-Nagy and Spark 1973/1981, p. 78), e.g., in partnerships and the creation of a new family unit.

Assessment Questions

- In which areas can a stable balance of give and take between the generations be observed, where is the balance disturbed?
- Are patterns of open or hidden exploitation visible or probable between or within the generations?
- How may these be connected with destructive or self-destructive behavior patterns?
- Can destructive or self-destructive relational and behavioral patterns be seen as an attempt to harmonize conflicting demands for loyalty and/or the need for individuation?

Clinical Manifestations of Multigenerational Processes

In clinical assessment the above-mentioned multigenerational processes can be revealed with the help of several phenomena as described below.

Related Individuation

Related individuation is a perspective defined by Stierlin (1978, 1989, Stierlin et al., 1985) in the dynamics of family relationships to define the ability for self-differentiation and self-detachment. This concept has been adopted by many family therapists under various perspectives based on research and treatment (e.g., the "collective cognitive chaos," Wynne & Singer, 1965; the "consensus sensitivity," Reiss, 1971b; the "intersubjective fusion," Boszormenyi-Nagy, 1965). It was especially developed from the multigenerational point of view by Bowen and his colleagues (Bowen, 1978; Guerin & Pendagast, 1976; Kerr & Bowen, 1988; McGoldrick & Gerson, 1985).

Starting out from the premise that couples generally marry with a similar level of differentiation, Bowen describes (e.g., Bowen, 1978; Kerr & Bowen, 1988) how anxiety, which arises during the various developmental stages of the family, can be moderated or bound by marital conflicts, dysfunction of the parents and the involvement of the children. This is a considerable factor in defining what level of individuation is possible for a child. If conflicts between parents and grandparents or partners cannot be resolved, children become constantly involved in triangular relationships over the generations, for example, with the transference of patterns of blame and self-blame (see Kerr & Bowen, 1988; McGoldrick & Gerson, 1998).

Related individuation can lapse into isolation and fusion. It is considerably affected by binding and expulsion (Stierlin, 1972). Binding often holds children (and parents) within the clutches of the family community – separation is viewed as a danger to the system and is linked with feelings of guilt ("separation guilt", Modell, 1988). Stierlin (1972, 1978) describes binding on a level of emotional experience and the gratification of instinctual drives (id level; e.g., through regressive overprotection, overstimulation with sexual and aggressive stimuli), on a level of cognitive and perceptive functions etc. (ego level; reality testing, defense mechanisms), and through obligations, demands of ideals and of conscience (superego level; e.g., feelings of guilt and shame).

If a too high priority is given to the binding mode, the emotional relationship is "overcathected"; in the rejection mode it is "undercathected," the child is considered unimportant and emotionally neglected. Not feeling important for others can cause the individuals concerned to drift aimlessly through life, longing for ties but shrinking away from them in fear and mistrust, or to become independent at a very early stage, overvaluing autonomy and treating others neglectfully.

Assessment Questions

- Does the emotional relationship between the family members appear to be strong or weak?
- Of which family members is this particularly true?
- On which levels are the ties between the respective parent and child generations particularly strong:
  - the level of emotional experience and the gratification of instincts (id)?
  - the level of thought, reality testing, and defense (ego)?
  - the level of conscience, norms, and ideals (superego)?

Delegation and Parentification

The theory of delegation, introduced by Stierlin (1974a, 1978), describes how individual family members are drawn into a system of "missions" over the generations. Missions can be transferred in processes of attribution on a conscious, preconscious, or unconscious level. They can refer to any level of the psychic structure, to the id, ego, and superego. A mission that has not been successfully carried out in the history of the family is delegated on to the next generation (Stierlin, 1974a, 1978), which continues to work on it either in the close proximity of the family of origin or in the role of an outcast. Parents' fantasies about "their child" can begin to take effect before or during conception. Grandparents can also wish for grandchildren with certain attributes and abilities and begin to fantasize about them long before their conception can even be thought about.

Fantasies also arise during pregnancy and while thinking about how to name the child; these are then enacted when interaction begins after birth. Such attributions, identifications, and projections vary in their degree of rigidity. Cramer (1994b) showed that they can cause massive disorders in the interaction between parents and children and abnormalities in children even in the first year of childhood. These fixed, unconscious fantasies are usually rooted in conflicts or malfunctions in the relationship between the mother or both parents and their parents, i.e., they involve at least three generations.

Delegations can "get off the track" if they overestimate or distort the abilities of the child, if assignments are too rigid and if conflicting or irreconcilable assignments exist – for example, when parents are at odds with one another and each demands that the child takes their side, or if they have completely conflicting ideas about the child's future career. Split loyalties can also occur when the family's values conflict with those of the society as a whole, as children have the need to identify not only with their parents or a single parent but also with the extended family and their social environment.

A special form of delegation is parentification (Boszormenyi-Nagy & Spark, 1973), a form of role reversal in which children take over the function of parent or partner. Up to a certain degree, this process is normal and reasonable, and in keeping with a child's social needs and the dialectic antithesis of alternating subject and object roles. Boszormenyi-Nagy and Spark (1973/1981) describe the following forms of parentification:

- Manifest caretaking roles, where for example a child takes over the function of holding its parents' marriage together or a partner is expected to provide the parental care he or she did not receive as a child.
- Sacrificial roles, where individuals give up their own development, sacrificing body and soul for the sake of others.
- Neutral roles, such as the "healthy sibling," where the individual's own suffering is repressed or consciously concealed.

Assessment Questions

- Which missions appear to have been given to the children by the parents/grandparents, and to the parents by the grandparents?
- How are these missions communicated (openly formulated, concealed, or indirect)?
- How conscious are the individuals involved of these assignments?
- Are parents or children parentified in these processes? In what way?
- Are split loyalties being caused by conflicting delegations?
- What unconscious or conscious demands do the delegates have as a result of these assignments?

Avoidance of Mourning

Every stage of development implies loss as well as gain, the growth of relationships, in many ways, goes hand in hand with death and dying.

As in psychoanalysis, multigenerational family therapy gives great importance to the ability to mourn. It promotes and allows room for emotional growth, emotional differentiation, and, connected with this, related individuation and the internal possibility and readiness to enter into new relationships following e.g., a great loss (see Boszormenyi-Nagy & Spark, 1973/1981; Boszormenyi-Nagy & Krasner, 1986; Paul & Paul, 1977; Paul, 1978).

Reactions involving mourning are often defended against,
- if the losses for the family members are too painful and sudden;
- if they occur at the same time as other unpleasant events, so that there is not enough time and capacity available to process them emotionally;
- if they are connected with conflicts of loyalty, e.g., for children involved in divorce conflicts; (see Reich, 1991, 1994c); or
- if they are connected with feelings of guilt and shame.

The defense against mourning can result in family members blocking out their loss; emotions in general can become obstructed. Central areas of the individual's self are put into "deep freeze"; the ability to function within relationships becomes numbed – "relationship stagnation" takes place (Boszormenyi-Nagy & Spark, 1973/1981; Boszormenyi-Nagy & Krasner, 1986). The internal availability of the family members for new relationships or for changes within existing relationships is restricted. Success and progress in other areas, especially where performance is involved, can reinforce the defense. This has also been described as a collective pattern (Mitscherlich & Mitscherlich, 1967).

Unprocessed grief can also result in adults continuing to crave parental care, for example from their partner or children. There is a compulsion to try to bring the lost "back to life," although this is impossible (see Reich, 1988b). There is a danger of symbiotic, fusioned, or undifferentiated family relationships formed in an attempt to avoid the repetition of traumatic loss. Separation difficulties in children and young adults may arise as a result. Distance from the family can imply danger and death, unbearable loss and consequently separation guilt.

Children can become parentified if they are conceived following the death of a sibling or another family member, if this loss is not appropriately processed. They are unknowingly seen as a substitute for the deceased person. The parents' deep depression can be passed on to the child, although neither side is aware of this emotional contagion.

Unprocessed grief can lead to family secrets being harbored in connection with a death, accompanied by feelings of menace. In some families this can produce symptoms of severe depression, masochism, or self-destruction, even in the next but one generation (see Boszormenyi-Nagy & Spark 1973/1981; Massing et al. 1999). Breaks in relationships are often a further sign of unprocessed mourning, indicating an avoidance of the integration of the ambivalent feelings associated with grief.

Assessment Questions

- Are there incidences of death and other losses in the family history?
- How were these processed? To what extent can the family members admit to their grief and other feelings connected with the loss?
- How openly can the family members speak about the loss and the feelings it evokes?
- Do unprocessed losses appear to be holding back the development of the family and its members (e.g., symbiotic relationship patterns, emotional numbness, or self-destructive repetitions)?

Family Myths

Family myths are stories told by families about themselves as a whole unit, a subgroup or individual members. They are over-determined, take on defense functions (internally), protection functions (externally), and, at the same time, serve the purpose of securing the integrity of the group, giving individual members the feeling of having a place within the context of the clan and its history (see Ferreira, 1963; Reich, 2001; Sperling, 1988; Stierlin, 1973).

Myths communicate the self-images (Sperling, 1988), norms, ideals, and values of the family that largely constitute the "we-feeling," the family feeling (see above) ("We Millers have never had an easy time of it," "Us Smiths don't like to appear to be too successful – other people get jealous," "Although we've got on well, we're still simple, honest people at heart", etc.).

Myths often obscure the existence of events and circumstances, outwardly or inwardly. This can be comforting, but on the other hand it can have negative, sometimes disastrous consequences in that family members or the whole group are held back in a certain position or at a certain point of their development.

Myths regulate the feeling of self and self-esteem, and particularly family loyalty. They dictate, directly or indirectly, what one ought to be like in order to be "part of." Myths pass on identification patterns and delegations. Myths meet the child's elementary need to define itself within a broader context. "Tell me about the olden days" is not only a request for parents or grandparents to tell adventure stories from times gone by; it also expresses a desire to learn about one's own prehistory and to define oneself. Thus, myths provide identity.

Stierlin (1973) distinguishes between three kinds of myths:
- Myths of harmony, in which internal conflicts are denied and ascribed to the influences of the outside world.
- Myths of forgiveness and atonement, where accounts of merit and guilt are drawn up or falsified, for example, by giving someone else the blame for the family's bad luck.
- Rescue myths, where members of the family are given the role of a healer or even of a savior.

Assessment Questions

- Which stories do the family members tell about the nuclear family and the families of origin?
- What is the theme of these stories (harmony, conciliation, salvation, or other themes)?
- Which functions do these stories have for the family?

Family Secrets

Secrets serve the purpose of withholding certain information from certain people or keeping it between people in a certain way. Family secrets do not usually concern feelings and thoughts but events, for example, the fact that a family member has served a prison sentence, deaths, abortions, alcohol abuse, incest, illnesses, extramarital affairs, and children resulting from these, (see Karpel, 1980; Pincus & Dare, 1980; Massing et al., 1999; Reich, 2001).

Karpel (1980) approaches this topic in a systematic way, thus providing the most reliable information up to date. He describes the following levels:

- Individual secrets – here there is a barrier between the holder of the secret and all other family members.
- Internal family secrets – at least two members of the family keep a secret from at least one other family member. This creates subsystems within the family, the "secret-holders" and the "unaware." A further complication can arise when the secret-holders are not aware that others know, resulting in a further secret.
- Shared family secrets – all members of the family know something that the outside world is not allowed to know about.

Secrets can deeply influence the emotional climate of families, although the source of this influence may not be registered. In this way, a feeling of menace can arise.

Most importantly, the existence of secrets has a huge significance for the dynamics of loyalty within families, particularly when one of the parents or the grandparents let children in on a secret involving the other parent. This can lead to split loyalties (Boszormenyi-Nagy & Spark, 1973/1981) with feelings of guilt and shame that can tear at the integrity of the subject. Shared family secrets can also lead to split loyalty in children, who need a sense of belongingness and loyalty towards their social environment as well as towards their family.

Secrets cause people to feel more powerful, especially towards the uninformed ("I know something you don't know"). They can also imply an increase in power over the individual involved in the secret, which can be taken as far as atmospheric or actual blackmail. Secrets create alliances and barriers between single family members, family subsystems, and the family and the outside world. In extreme cases, secrets can render it impossible for families to form anything but superficial relationships with the outside world.

The distinction between family secrets and the private sphere is dependent upon the context and is governed by the family subculture and the extended sociocultural surroundings. In very close-knit families, members can feel guilty if they keep so much as a thought or a feeling to themselves. The practice of revealing everything usually has negative consequences.

The evaluation of the question "privacy vs. secrecy" in family assessment is mainly dependent on the consequences for the uninformed – is power at stake in the keeping of the secret? Is trust damaged or destroyed? Can feelings of humiliation and shame be expected? Does the secret create a fearful atmosphere? Are perceptions and feelings invalidated? These are some of the questions that should be asked not only by the person in charge of the secret but also by therapists, in order to take on a position of accountability with discretion if they suspect the existence of a secret during assessment or treatment (Karpel, 1980; see also Framo, 1992). The initiation of therapists in the "secret milieu" can lead them into considerable ethical and practical difficulties. Karpel (1980) describes reparative and preventive strategies, which, however, do not guarantee protection for the therapy.

Assessment Questions

- Are there indications of events in the family history that are kept secret, e.g., atmospherically, scenically, through family myths or gaps in the genogram (see chapter on genograms)?

- Could this be an individual, internal, or shared family secret?
- What power constellations and loyalty problems could it result in?
- What are the family's views on privacy?

The Importance of Different Generations in Family Diagnostics

The Middle Generation: The Conflicts of the Couple within the Family System

Family therapies are usually initiated by parents with one or more children who are suffering from certain symptoms, or by couples where one or both are suffering from symptoms or conflicts within the relationship. The middle generation is the activation point for entering into treatment. The forming of partnerships (through marriage or otherwise) is a prerequisite for the development of a family consisting of three generations. For this reason we have chosen to begin with this level.

In family dynamics, the relationship between two partners is not only an encounter between two individuals with their internalized object relationships, but also the meeting of two family systems (see Reich, 1993). The choice of a partner always represents a conflicting attempt at individuation for both parties (see Reich, 1993).

In forming the new relationship, both are searching for the satisfaction of unfulfilled wishes, the management of unresolved conflicts and the compensation of deficits. Together, they hope to change and improve the relationship patterns they have experienced up until that point, especially within the family of origin. This is usually the main priority – but alongside it, or beneath it, but always closely connected with it, there is a strong tendency towards repetition, towards the re-enacting of the very same conflicts and relationship patterns experienced in the family of origin, the conflicts the couple intended to rid themselves of. In this way, any choice of partner is rooted in ambivalence.

When serious, lasting conflicts exist within a partnership, ambivalence seems to dominate. Because of strong ties with the patterns from the families of origin, the ambivalence cannot be used productively to promote further development (see Reich, 1988). Often, partners with similar experiences of relationship patterns and conflicts in significant areas of their families of origin find their way to one another, although their methods of coping with these can differ completely (see Dicks, 1967; Framo, 1982; Kerr & Bowen, 1988; Napier, 1971; Reich, 1993).

The feeling of togetherness that results from a common background of experience, often comprising unresolved conflicts, is a resource that the couple can draw upon for communication and the optimization of innovative potential (see Dicks, 1967; Napier, 1971; Reich, 1993; Welter-Enderlin, 1992). However, if the unresolved conflicts from both biographies affect too many areas of the couple's life together, or if they are too far-reaching and intense, they can lead to a recourse to familiar, unproductive relationship patterns that only serve to reinforce the conflicts (see Dicks, 1967; Reich, 1993; Willi, 1975). There is also a tendency to promote similarities between the partner and former persons of reference, to maneuver the partner into relationship patterns that resemble familiar patterns from the past.

In this way, the choice of partner is followed by the changing of the partner to comply with internalized object relationships. This is particularly true in the case of the antithetical choice of partner that opposes the internal prototype of former persons of reference.

From the point of view of family dynamics, early childhood is of less importance for the formation of couple relationships than adolescent individuation (see Reich, 1993). If adolescence cannot be successfully used as a "second chance" (Eissler, 1966) in the life of an individual to come to terms with unresolved pre-oedipal and oedipal conflicts and accompanying fixations, thus modifying family ties, lifestyles, and values, the choice of partner is taken as the "third chance" to delegate unresolved problems to the partner, the relationship, the children, or the parents-in-law.

Through the formation of a partnership and the development of their own relationship patterns and rules, the partners attempt to leave childhood relationships behind. Here a transfer of loyalty from the family of origin to the new relationship and the new nuclear family is required, i.e., more importance must be given to the partner and children and their new life together than to parents, siblings, and other relatives and persons of reference. The more rigid the loyalty system of the original families, the harder it is to form an intimate relationship with others.

In order to build a new, self-contained family unit, it is also necessary to amalgamate the values and lifestyles of the families of origin and their specific subcultures (Sperling, 1979). Family styles are closely connected with the basic vital sense and the dynamics of loyalty, which means that any marital conflicts arising in this area are particularly serious.

The two sets of in-laws and their relationships with one another have important, sometimes reparative functions for the development of the nuclear family. The couple's relationship, representing the union of two family systems with their ledgers of debts and merits, becomes the "nodal point in a loyalty fabric" (Boszormenyi-Nagy & Spark, 1973/1981, p. 46). This relationship offers the families of origin the chance to achieve a new balance of merit. The two families can act as mutual balancing systems; the unresolved conflicts in one family can be solved with the help of the other, for example by projecting them onto the other family (Boszormenyi-Nagy & Spark, 1973/1981; Boszormenyi-Nagy & Krasner, 1986; Framo, 1982, 1992; Reich, 1993).

Partners may hope to receive what they lacked in the family of origin from their parents-in-law and new family. Disappointments in this "second chance family" (Lager, 1977) can result in crises in the relationship. Open or concealed rejection on the part of parents-in-law is often the source of continual conflicts or leads to a distance between the partners that is difficult to bridge (Friedman, 1980; Reich, 1993; Sperling & Sperling, 1976). In the next generation, this may result in conflicts of loyalty and delegation, as children generally feel an affiliation to both the family systems from which they originate.

In serious conflicts between two partners and marriage crises, several of the following factors are usually present on the level of family dynamics:

- The conflicts are repetitions of conflict patterns from the parent-child relationships of both partners, the deepest internalized relationship prototype there is.
- They are repetitions of conflict patterns in the marriages of the parents of both partners, the deepest internalized model for a partnership.
- The transfer of loyalty from the family of origin to the partnership and the forming of a new, self-contained family unit has not taken place, or not to a sufficient degree.
- Due to strong disagreements between the two sets of in-laws, it has not been possible to blend the two different family styles together to form a new individual lifestyle.

- The families of origin reject one another or the new daughter / son -in-law, either openly or covertly, so that the partners experience a constant conflict of loyalties if they think highly of the new in-laws or partner.
- The families of origin interfere in the couple's relationship, or are drawn into it, so that the development of a new, self-contained unit or independent individual development is rendered impossible.

A serious crisis in a relationship usually occurs at a developmental stage involving a change in the familiar norms and rules for the relationship. This reminds the partners of unresolved problems in the families of origin, allowing a "return of the repressed" to occur (Freud, 1937). The longer a relationship continues, the greater the chance of repetitions.

The vertical dimension and the importance of the families of origin for each other are often disregarded in assessment, which mainly concentrates on the horizontal dynamics of the relationship. As Framo (1977) claims, "If you are treating a couple and you do not specifically ask them what is going on in the relationships with their parents, brothers, sisters, aunts, uncles, and in-laws, they usually do not tell you" (p. 237). The significance of the multigenerational system can only be discovered by exploring it in depth.

Assessment Questions

- How successful was the individuation of partners from their families of origin in adolescence?
- To what extent are wishes for change and individuation delegated to the partner, the new nuclear family or the partner's family?
- To what extent are they expected to make up for past disappointments or unresolved conflicts?
- Has a transfer of loyalty from the families of origin to the partner and children taken place?
- Has the nuclear family become a new, self-contained family unit with its own lifestyle, or is it still largely influenced by one or both families of origin?
- How much shared lifestyle and experience do the partners bring into the new relationship? To what extent does this provide them with a basis for communication and the solving of conflicts?
- Do the two families of origin, the partners and the in-laws show mutual respect, or do they reject one another?
- How do the partners deal with rejection on the part of the families of origin and the in-laws?

Children in Family Assessment

The Significance of Children

Family therapists assume that infants are not asocial beings, as was believed for a long time; and this assumption is confirmed by sound empirical results from research programs on infants and young children (e.g., Stern, 1985). In their own way they take on a caring function in the family right from the beginning. If this is exploited by parents who are too involved in their own conflicts, they can develop "narcissistic entitlements", destructive and self-destructive experience and behavior patterns (Boszormenyi-Nagy & Krasner, 1986).

Not only social circumstances influence children but also the emotional representation of the parents and their own narcissistic entitlements in the form of delegations.

Abraham stresses the importance of naming children (1982), and this theory is often proven to be correct. Children may be named after relatives, according to certain traditions, after a person whose death the family cannot get over. Whether a child is named after a character in a novel or according to the current fashion, certain fantasies and wishes connected with the name are passed on, on a conscious or an unconscious level; certain expectations are directed at the child.

The Role of the Child Within the Family

Symptoms developed by a child are a manifold expression of a general disorder in the family system. As such, they can be understood as a signal and "metaphorical expression" (Madanes, 1981) of insufficient flexible coping potential in the family as a whole.

One-sided changes in a child inevitably lead to irritations in the family system. These can provide the necessary impulse for developmental processes in the family system to take place. On the other hand, they can result in the manifestation of symptoms by other children or the parents.

In this way, the unhealthy child may be seen not only as a victim (Hoffmann, 1982), but also as part of a balancing act within the family. It is not the weakest link, but in some ways the strongest – by means of its symptoms it clearly publicizes the fact that there is something wrong, something unhealthy, in the system as a whole.

A child's symptoms are also an expression of its loyalty to the family; the child puts aside its individual growth in favor of the interests of the group. This perspective is important for the role of the siblings and their relationship to one another, particularly as far as the question of "healthy" and "unhealthy" children is concerned (see below). For these reasons, the terms "designated patient," "index patient," or "symptom carrier" are often preferred to be used in family therapy.

Sibling Subsystem: "Healthy" and "Unhealthy" Siblings

The relationship between brothers and sisters is often the most important following that between a child and its parents. Even in preverbal interaction, siblings develop a subsystem with its own boundaries and culture, in which each child has its individual feelings for brothers and sisters. This is quite separate from the social relationships outside of the family, including peer relationships (Hartmann, 1993).

The important learning and emotional experiences made in this subsystem do not include the hierarchical parental dimension and thus take place on a horizontal level (Cierpka, 2001). Strong feelings of love and hate, far too dangerous to be displayed openly to parents, can be tried out together and against one another. Brothers and sisters learn to win, to lose, to play, and to fight with one another, are forced to come to terms with feelings of envy and guilt. The siblings know who stands where, who is on which parent's side. They can protect each other against the parents or against threats from the outside world. They can learn to get along with someone they do not always like, for long periods of time (Reich et al. 2002). Brothers and sisters do not primarily evaluate one another's' differing characteristics in terms of "unhealthy," "conspicuous," and "healthy," as Kniskern pointed out (1981). In therapy, siblings are often strongly inclined to protect one another against pathological definitions.

If the importance of the sibling subsystem is ignored and therapists choose to treat only the parents and identified patient, they run the risk of reinforcing the family's belief that there is only one patient. Parents wish to retain the illusion that the other children are normal and that they are good parents (Zilbach et al. 1972). However, one-sided settings can lead to differences becoming established between the siblings and the subsystem becoming weakened. The "strange" child not only feels more left out; it can also develop a diffuse feeling of shame for being different and somehow wrong.

Moreover it is wrong to assume that children, especially small children, are spared by being kept out of family therapy sessions – the family reality they are exposed to at home is generally far more extreme than the situation in the consulting room.

When considering the question of "healthy" and "unhealthy" siblings, an important aspect is the assignment of roles as an aspect of unconscious repressed parental motives (see above). Framo (1965) pointed out that identified patients often grew up under completely different family circumstances than their brothers and sisters.

Of course, "healthy" brothers and sisters generally appear better socially adapted than the "unhealthy" ones. However, upon taking a closer look, it is not unusual to discover that they also suffer from disorders, even serious personality disorders or psychotic tendencies (Lidz et al., 1963). For example, a small patient complained that she suffered from asthma and felt unhappy. She was envious of her brothers and sisters who were healthy. However, both of her siblings were in medical treatment for manifest psychosomatic symptoms. They thought of themselves as "normal," as though their illnesses were nothing. "Healthy" siblings can appear to be more stable than they are; the identified patient functions as a warning (Framo, 1965, p. 220).

On the other hand, the brothers and sisters can feel neglected because the parents give so much attention to the unhealthy child. If the symptoms of the identified patient improve and other brothers and sisters or one of the parents become ill, this indicates that the dynamic conflict potential in the family system is still at work. Following a diagnostic assessment of the dynamics of the system and how it could be processed, individual therapies such as child therapies can be carried out in a more selective way, with less resistance from the family.

It is not unusual to find that, during the course of assessment and therapy, the child moves out of the focus in treatment as a complex, disturbed relationship between the parents is uncovered. If the focus shifts to the couple, it is advisable to invite the original families of both partners, including their own brothers and sisters, as an aid to assessment using the multigenerational perspective.

Assessment Questions

- What assignments have been given to the children by the parents and grandparents, for example via their name?
- What position do the children hold in the maintenance of intrafamilial balance?
- What patterns of behavior can be observed within the sibling subsystem?
- Is there a dichotomy between "healthy" and "unhealthy" children?

– In what way does this consolidate existing dysfunctional relationship patterns in the family?

The Grandparent Generation in Family Assessment

The socio-historical orientation of the multigenerational perspective implies the active participation of the grandparent generation in the assessment and therapeutic process.

Grandparents are invited
- as living witnesses of historical events,
- as representatives of traditionalized attitudes regarding the social norms and values that have determined family life and continue to influence it,
- as "guardians" of family history, providing a deeply rooted feeling of family identity and belongingness on the level of binding and loyalty,
- as those who are able to provide information on aging, ailments, parting, and death,
- as the material and immaterial supporters of the parent and children generations in many forms of family life, e.g., single parent families.

The first task in family assessment is to discover which aspect is the most important. In general, the role of grandparents in all the categories mentioned above is becoming more important, simply because of increased life expectancy.

The Significance of Grandparents for Family History

The fact that grandparents are invited to family sessions indicates that they have a lasting real or projected dominant significance for the family. This emerges far more clearly here than by examining family relationships using the classical method of family reconstruction. Resistance phenomena in the middle generation, sometimes expressed in terms of concern for the ageing parents, can cover up unprocessed aggressive wishes and accompanying fear, or feelings of guilt and shame (Sperling & Sperling, 1976; Sperling et al., 1982; Reich, 1982, 1984).

The greatest advantage of a multigenerational session is that it allows a reconstruction of the past to be made with the help of the actual people who witnessed these historical events. Often, parents and grandchildren are completely unaware of the events that have determined their experience via the family climate and manifold transference processes, as these lie so far back in the past or have never been spoken about.

The idea of involving grandparents does not mean that memories and fantasies should be brought up for discussion like "excavational finds" (Freud, 1914a) or "historical truths" (Loch, 1976). Rather, a collective attempt should be made to investigate how the family adheres to the orientation, values, and ideologies of the grandparents.

A problem of intrafamilial ault relationships that is sometimes difficult to overcome is that the younger generation does not recognize the development and related attitude changes of the older generation. This means that they adhere to loyalties that are impossible to fulfill and pass mistakes on. (Massing et al., 1999, p. 90).

In the multigenerational family therapy sessions the stagnating modes of processing, rigid loyalties, parentification or delegation patterns between parents and grandparents can be quickly recognized, as an indication of further work to be done within the therapy.

The outcome is important from the point of view of assessment; either a more flexible dialogue between the generations is achieved, or at least a clearer boundary between the generations in open dialogue. This can encourage the middle generation's claims for reparation to be brought into perspective or rigid loyalty commitments to be revised.

The Grandparents as Aging People

The grandparents should also be given the opportunity to describe the developmental stages they have experienced throughout life. Both sides now have the chance to listen to one another, and this can provide an impulse for the old people to look back and take stock of their lives in a more satisfactory way.

The presence of the old people is a reminder of the proximity of growing old, physical disability, parting, dying, and death. Certain phenomena, which have perhaps been ignored or idealized by the middle generation, can be reintegrated into family experience. Illness, dying, and death can be valuable as specific information about life. This information comprises real experience and obligations of loyalty.

Old age is a complex borderline experience; familiar, routine ways of dealing with problems fail. Growing older drives people to search for links between the past and the future. Aging persons call their life-long efforts to achieve conformity into question, although they are under no obligation to do so. The ageing process can destabilize the whole sense of identity.

The extrovert ego may make way for a more inwardly oriented ego, focusing on the ageing and infirm body. According to Améry (1979), self-knowledge vs. self- alienation is one of the basic experiences of old age, although differences can be observed between men and women. For women, attributes such as beauty and femininity are firmly linked together in the collective consciousness, whereas men are more concerned with performance and resilience. Complaints connected with old age and illnesses can be experienced as defects.

This phenomenon, criticized as the deficit model by Lehr (1978), stands in the way of a gradual reconciliation with a new phase of life that at first appears to be alien. The reconciliation can find its expression in sensuality, for example, in tenderness and sexuality between old people. If sexual desire declines or is weakened by illness, tenderness and empathy with the partner can become more important.

The Grandparents as Supporters

The material support and help of the grandparents, e.g., in looking after the children, is often vital for the parent and grandchild generations. Single parent families in particular frequently rely upon this support (see Reich & Bauers, 1988; Cierpka et al., 1992). Grandparents also represent a soothing and secure constant element in the lives of the children, especially in times of external change or when faced with their parents' separation. These aspects may be observed in all social strata. They often represent an invaluable resource for families.

This form of mutual dependency can become problematic if grandparents harbor expectations in return for their help, or if the grandparents interfere and take on a too active role in conflicts, for example, in the case of divorce, by perpetuating one-sided accusations of guilt against one parent via the grandchildren. If single parents rely upon their parents to look after the children, they can begin to feel dependent or morally obliged towards them, and thus avoid necessary confrontations.

Grandparents can also stir up jealous conflicts between brothers and sisters in the middle generation via the grandchildren, by showing obvious favoritism in terms of material gifts or attention.

For example, during a multigenerational session, a grandfather stirred up a quarrel between the grandchildren, then stated, "You're just like my brothers and sisters." He, who had been underprivileged as a child, identified with a particular grandchild, whom he placed in a privileged position. Now he secretly enjoyed the grandchildren's rivalry.

Assessment Questions

- What links exist between the nuclear family and the parents' families of origin? How is contact initiated, and how often?
- Is contact evenly distributed, or one-sided in favor of a certain side of the family?
- Is contact sought equally from the grandparents and the nuclear family, or more frequently from one side? Is the contact stronger between children and grandchildren than between parents and grandparents, the other way round, or equally strong?
- What role do the grandchildren, parents, and children play for one another in a material sense (care, financial support, childcare)? What role do the grandparents play in the relationships and conflicts of the nuclear family?
- Are past conflicts and images of the grandparents formed in former stages of the life cycle projected onto the grandparents by the parents? Are the children involved in this?
- What questions could the grandparents wish to ask the family therapist and the nuclear family? Which specific problems do the grandparents have or can be assumed to have?
- In which areas could the involvement of the grandparents in the assessment process throw light on family conflicts and their resolution and on resources?
- To what extent could family assessment (and family therapy) be of use to the grandparents with their specific questions and problems?

References

Abraham, K. (1982). *Über die determinierende Kraft des Namens. Gesammelte Schriften, Bd I* [On the determining power of names. Collected writings, Vol. 1]. Frankfurt: Fischer. (Original work published 1912).

Améry, J. (1979). *Über das Altern. Revolte und Resignation* [On aging: Revolt and resignation] (5th ed.). Stuttgart: Klett-Cotta.

Andolfi, M. (1982). *Familientherapie. Das systemische Modell und seine Anwendung* [Family therapy: The systemic model and its application]. Freiburg i.B: Lambertus.

Bateson, G., Jackson, D. D., Laing, R., Lidz, T., Wynne, L. et al. (1969) *Schizophrenie und Familie* [Schizophrenia and the family]. Frankfurt: Suhrkamp,.

Bateson, G., Jackson, D. D., Haley, J., & Weakland, J. (1956). Toward a theory of schizophrenia. *Behavioral Science, 1*, 251–264.

Benoit, D., & Parker, K. C. H. (1994). Stability and transmission of attachment across three generations. *Child Development, 65*, 1444–1456.

Boszormenyi-Nagy, I. (1965). Eine Theorie der Beziehungen. Erfahrung und Transaktion. In J. Boszormenyi-Nagy & L. Framo (1975), *Familientherapie. Theorie und Praxis* (pp. 51–109). Reinbek: Rowohlt.

Boszormenyi-Nagy, I., & Krasner, B. R. (1986). *Between give and take: A clinical guide to contextual therapy.* New York: Brunner/Mazel.

Boszormenyi-Nagy, I., & Spark, G. (1973) *Invisible Loyalties.* Harper & Row, New York.

Bowen, M. (1960). A family concept of schizophrenia. In D. D. Jackson (Ed.), *The etiology of schizophrenia.* New York: Basic Books.

Bowen, M. (1960). The family as the unit of study and treatment. *American Journal of Orthopsychiatry, 31*, 40–60.

Bowen, M. (1978). *Family therapy in clinical pratice.* New York: Jason Aronson.

Bowlby, J. (1975). *Attachment and loss* (Vol. 1). München: Kindler.

Bray, J. H., Williamson, D. S., & Malone, P. E. (1984). Personal authority in the family system: Development of a questionnaire to measure personal authority in intergenerational family process. *Journal of Marital and Family Therapy, 10*, 167–178.

Bronfenbrenner, U. (1979). *The ecology of human development.* Harvard University Press, Cambridge, MA.

Carter, E. A., & McGoldrick, M. (1980). The family life cycle: A framework for family therapy. New York: Gardner

Cierpka, A., Frevert, G., & Cierpka, M. (1992). "Männer schmutzen nur!" – Eine Untersuchung über alleinerzeihende Mütter in einem Mutter-Kind-Programm [Men only make a mess! – A study of single mothers in a mother-child program]. *Praxis der Kinderpsychologie und Kinderpsychiatrie, 41*, 168–175.

Cierpka, M. (1992). Zur Entwicklung des Familiengefühls. *Forum der Psychoanalyse, 8*, 32–46.

Cierpka, M., Ratzke, K., Reich, G., Armbrecht, B., Franke, A., Scholz, M., & Plöttner, G. (1994). Familien in Ost- und Westdeutschland. *Familiendynamik, 19*, 295–307.

Cierpka, M. (1999a). Das geschiedene Familiengefühl in Scheidungsfamilien. In A. Schlösser & K. Höhfeld (Eds.), *Trennungen* (pp. 85–100). Gießen: Psychosozial Verlag.

Cierpka, M. (1999b) (Ed.). *Kinder mit aggressivem Verhalten* [Children with aggressive behavior]. Göttingen: Hogrefe.

Cierpka, M. (2001). Geschwisterbeziehungen aus familientherapeutischer Perspektive – Unterstützung, Bindung, Rivalität und Neid [Sibling relationships from a family therapy perspective – Support, attachment, rivalry, and envy]. *Praxis der Kinderpsychologie und Kinderpsychiatrie, 50*, 440–453.

Cramer, B. (1994). Die früheste Bindung [The earliest attachment]. In P. Bucheim, M. Cierpka, T. Seifert (Eds.), *Neue Lebensformen – Zeitkrankheiten und Psychotherapie* (pp. 256–263). Berlin: Springer.

Dicks, H. V. (1967). *Marital tensions.* London: Routledge & Kegan Paul.

Eissler, K. R. (1966). Bemerkungen zur Technik der psychoanalytische Behandlung Pubertierender nebst einigen Bemerkungen zum Problem der Perversion [Remarks on the techniques of psychoanalytical treatment of pubescents with comments on the problem of perversion]. *Psyche, 20,* 837–892.

Ferreira, A. J. (1966). Familienmythen [Family myths]. In P. Watzlawick & J. Weakland (Eds.) *Interaktion* (pp. 85–94). Bern: Huber.

Fonagy, P. (2001). *Attachment theory and psychoanalysis.* New York: Other Press.

Framo, J. L. (1965). Beweggründe und Techniken der intensiven Familientherapie [Motivations and techniques of intensive family therapy]. In I. Boszormenyi-Nagy, J. L. Framo (Ed.) (1975) *Familientherapie* (Vol. 1, pp. 169–243). Reinbek: Rowohlt.

Framo, J. L. (1977). In-laws and out-laws. A marital case of kinship confusion. In J. L. Framo (1982), *Explorations in marital and family therapy* (pp. 225–238). New York: Springer.

Framo, J. L. (1982). *Explorations in marital and family therapy.* New York: Springer.

Framo, J. L. (1992). *Family-of-origin-therapy: An intergenerational approach.* New York: Brunner/Mazel.

Freud, S. (1914). Erinnern, Wiederholen, Durcharbeiten [Remembering, repeating and working through] (pp. 126–136). *Gesammelte Werke*, Vol. 10. Frankfurt: Fisher.

Freud, S. (1917). Vorlesungen zur Einführung in die Psychoanalyse [New introductory lectures on psycho-analysis]. *Gesammelte Werke*, Vol. 11. Frankfurt: Fisher.

Freud, S. (1923). Das Ich und das Es (pp. 235–289) [The ego and the id]. *Gesammelte Werke*, Vol. 13. Frankfurt: Fisher.

Freud, S. (1928–1933). Neue Folgen der Vorlesungen zur Einführung in die Psychoanalyse [New introductory lectures on psycho-analysis]. *Gesammelte Werke*, Vol. 15. Frankfurt: Fisher.

Freud, S. (1937). Der Mann Moses und die monotheistische Religion [Moses and monotheism]. *Gesammelte Werke*, Vol. 15. Frankfurt: Fisher.

Friedman, L. J. (1980). Integrating psychoanalytic object-relations understanding with family systems intervention in couples therapy. In J. K. Pearce & L. J. Friedman (Eds.), *Family Therapy* (pp. 63–79). New York: Grune & Stratton.

Grossmann, K., Premmer-Bombik, E., Rudolph, J., Grossmann, K. E. (1988). Maternal attachment representations as related to patterns of infant-mother attachment and maternal care during the first year. In R. Hinde & J. Stevenson-Hinde (Eds.), *Relationships within families: Mutual influences*. Oxford: Clarendon Press.

Guerin, P. J., & Pendagast, E. G. (1976). Evaluation of family system and genogramm. In P. J. Guerin (Ed.), *Family therapy* (pp. 450–464). New York: Gardner Press.

Hartmann, K. (1993). *Die Geschwisterbeziehung* [The sibling relationship]. Göttingen: Hogrefe.

Hilgers, M. (in press). Zur Bedeutung von Schamaffekten bei der Behandlung schwerer Störungen [The significance of shame effects in the treatment of severe disorders]. *Psychotherapeut*.

Hoffmann, L. (1982). *Grundlagen der Familientherapie* [Basic priniciples of family therapy]. Hamburg: Isko-Press, Vopel.

Jurkovic, G. J. (1998). Destructive parentification in families. In L. L'Abate (Ed.), *Family psychopathology: The relational roots of dysfunctional behavior* (pp. 237–255). New York: Guilford Press

Karpel, M. A. (1980). Family secrets. *Family Process, 19,* 295–306.

Kerr, M. E., & Bowen, M. (1988). *Family evaluation: An approach based on Bowen theory.* New York: WW Norton & Company.

Kniskern, D. P. (1981). Including children in marital and family therapy. In A. S. Gurmann (Ed.), *Questions and answers in family therapy.* New York: Brunner, Mazel.

Lager, E. (1977). Parents-in-law: Failure and divorce in a second chance family. *Journal of Mariage and Family Counseling, 3,* 19–23.

Lasch, C. H. (1977). *Geborgenheit. Die Bedrohung der Familie in der modernen Welt* [Belonging: The threat of the family in the modern world]. München: Steinhausen.

Lauterbach, W. (1994). *Lebenserwartung, Lebensverläufe und Generationenfolgen in Familien oder: Wie lange kennen sich familiale Generationen?* [Life expectations, life courses, and generational consequences or how long do familial generations know each other?]. University of Konstanz, Social Science Faculty.

Lehr, U. (1978). Kontinuität und Diskontinuität im Lebenslauf [Continuity and discontinuity in life course]. In L. Rosemayr, *Die menschlichen Lebensalter* (pp. 228–141). München: Beck.

Lidz, Th., Fleck, S., Alanen, Y. O., & Cornelison, A. (1963). Schizophrenic patients and their siblings. *Psychiatry, 26,* 1–18.

Lidz, Th., & Fleck, S. (1965). *Die Familienumwelt des Schizophrenen* [The family environment of schizophrenics]. Stuttgart: Klett-Cotta.

Loch, W. (1976). *Psychoanalyse und Wahrheit* [Psychoanalysis and truth]. *Psyche, 30,* 865–989.

Lüscher, K. (1993). Generationenbeziehungen: Neue Zugänge zu einem alten Thema [Generational relationships: New approaches to an old theme]. In K. Lüscher & F. Schultheis (Eds.), *Geneartionenbeziehungen in "postmodernen" Gesellschaften. Analysen zum Verhältnis von Individuum, Familie, Staat und Gesellschaft* (pp. 17–50). Konstanz: Universitätsverlag Konstanz.

Madanes, C. (1981). Beschützen, Paradox und So-tun-als-ob [Protection, paradox and to act-as-if]. *Familiendynamik, 3,* 208–224.

Main, M., Kaplan, N. & Cassidy, J. (1985). Security in infancy, childhood and adulthood: A move to the level of representation. In I. Bretherton & E. Waters (Eds.), *Growing points in attachement theory and research* (pp. 66–104). Monographs of the Society for Research in Child Development, 50, Serial No. 209.

Massing, A. (1991). Reinszenierung nationalsozialistischer Weltbilder im psychotherapeutischen Prozeb [Restaging national socialistic world views in psychotherapeutic process]. *Forum Psychoanal, 7,* 20–30.

Massing, A. (1994). Zukunft braucht Herkunft [The future needs origin]. *Kontext, 25,* 100–114.

Massing, A., & Beushausen, U. (1986). "Bis ins dritte und vierte Glied": Auswirkungen des Nationalsozialismus in der Familie ["Into the third and fourth generations": The effects of national socialism in the family.] *Psychosozial, 28,* 27–42.

Massing, A., Reich, G., & Sperling, E. (1999). *Die Mehrgenerationen-Familientherapie* [Multiple generational family therapy] (4th rev. ed). Göttingen: Vandenhoeck & Ruprecht..

McGoldrick, M., & Gerson, R. (1985). *Genograms in family assessment.* New York: WW Norton & Company.

Mendell, D., & Fischer, S. (1956). An approach to neurotic behaviour in terms of a three generational family model. *Journal of Nervous Mental Disorders, 123,* 171–180.

Mendell, D., & Fischer, S. (1958). A multi-generational approach of treatment of psychopathology. *Journal of Nervous Mental Disorders, 126,* 523–529.

Mikulincer, M., & Florian, V. (1999). The association between parental reports of attachment style and family dynamics, and offspring's report of adult attachment style. *Family Process, 38,* 243–257.

Mitscherlich, A., & Mitscherlich, M. (1967). *Die Unfähigkeit zu trauern* [The inability to grieve] (13th ed.). München: Piper.

Modell, A. H. (1988). Psychoanalysis in a new context. Madison: CT: International Universities Press.

Napier, A. Y. (1971). The marriage of families: Cross-generational complementarity. *Family Process, 10,* 373–395.

Paul, N. L. (1978). Die Notwendigkeit zu trauern [The necessity of grieving]. *Familiendynamik, 3,* 224–259.

Paul, N. L., & Paul, B. B. (1977). *Puzzle einer Ehe* [The puzzle of a marriage]. Stuttgart: Klett-Cotta.

Pincus, L., & Dare, C. (1980). *Geheimnisse in der Familie* [Secrets in the family]. Gütersloh: Gütersloher Verlagshaus.

Pope, H, & Mueller, C. H. W. (1976). The intergenerational transmission of marital instability. Comparisons by race and sex. *Journal of Social Issues, 32,* 49–66.

Ratzke, K. (1995). *Zur Analyse soziokultureller Bedingungen der Geschlechtsrollenannahme am Beispiel gestörten Essverhaltens* [The analysis of the sociocultural conditions of gender role assumption with the example of disturbed eating behavior]. Göttingen: Cuvillier Verlag.

Reich, G. (1982). Tabus und Ängste des Therapeuten im Umgang mit der eigenen Familie [Taboos and fears of therapists in their contact with their own families]. *Zeitschrift für Psychosomatische Medizin und Psychoanalyse, 28,* 393–406.

Reich, G. (1984). Der Einfluß der Herkunftsfamilie auf die Tätigkeit von Therapeuten und Beratern [The influence of the family of origin on the ability of therapists and advisors]. *Praxis der Kinderpsychologie und Kinderpsychiatrie, 33,* 61–69.

Reich, G. (1993). Partnerwahl und Ehekrisen [Partner choice and marriage crises] (4th ed.). Heidelberg: Asanger.

Reich, G. (1991). Kinder in Scheidungskonflikten [Children in divorce conflcits]. In H. Krabbe (Ed.), *Scheidung ohne Richter. Neue Lösungen für Trennungskonflikte* (3rd ed., pp. 59–85). Reinbek: Rowohlt.

Reich, G. (1994). Familiendynamik und therapeutische Strategien bei Scheidungskonflikten. *Psychotherapeut, 39,* 251–258.

Reich, G. (2001). "Das hat es bei uns nie gegeben!" Familiengeheimnisse und Familienmythen [That never happened with us!]. *Kontext, 32,* 5–19.

Reich G., Killius U., & Yamini, A. (2002): Geschwisterbeziehungen als eigenständiger Erfahrungsraum im familiären Kontext [Sibling relationships as an autonomous realm of interpersonal experience in the family]. *Kontext, 33,* 99–109.

Reich, G. (2003). Familien- und Paarbeziehungen bei Persönlichkeitsstörungen – Aspekte der Dynamik und Therapie [Family and couple relationships in personality disorders – Aspects of the dynamics and therapy]. *Persönlichkeitsstörungen, 7,* 72–83.

Reich, G., & Bauers, B. (1988). Nachscheidungskonflikte – eine Herausforderung an Beratung und Therapie [Post divorce conflicts – A challenge for counseling and therapy]. *Praxis der Kinderpsychologie und Kinderpsychiatrie, 37,* 346–355.

Reiss, D. (1971b). Varieties of consensual experience I. A theory for relating family interaction to individual thinking. *Family Process, 10,* 1–27.

Ricks, M. H. (1985). The social transmission of parental behavior. Attachment across generations. In I. Bretherton, & B. Waters (Eds.), Growing points in attachment theory and research. *Child Development, 50,* 233–278.

Rosen, K. H. (1998). The family roots of aggression and violence: A life span perspective. In L. L'Abate (Ed.), *Family psychopathology. The relational roots of dysfunctional behavior* (pp. 333–357). New York: Guilford Press.

Schneewind, K. A. (1999). *Familienpsychologie* (2nd. Ed.). Stuttgart: Kohlhammer.

Schneewind, K. A., Backmund, V., Sierwald, W., & Vierzigmann, G. (1989). *Dokumentationsband der psychologischen Teilstudie des Verbundprojekts "Optionen der Lebensgestaltung junger Ehen und Kinderwunsch"* [Documentation volume of the psychological project of the main project "Options of life structure of young couples and the wish for a child]. Ludwig-Maximilian University, Institute for Psychology, München.

Sperling, E. (1979). Familientherapie unter Berücksichtigung des Dreigenerationen-Problems [Family therapy with consideration of the three generation problems]. *Zeitschrift für Psychotherapie und medizinische Psychologie, 29,* 207–213.

Sperling, E. (1988). Familienselbstbilder [Family self images]. *Praxis der Kinderpsychologie Kinderpsychiatrie, 37,* 226–231.

Sperling, E., Massing, A., Reich, G., Georgi, H., & Wöbbe-Mönks, E. (1982). *Die Mehrgenerationenfamilientherapie* [Multiple generational family therapy]. Göttingen: Vandenhoeck & Ruprecht.

Sperling, E., & Sperling, U. (1976). Die Einbeziehung der Großeltern in die Familientherapie [The inclusion of grandparents in family therapy]. In H. E. Richter, H. Strotzka, & J. Willi (Eds.), *Familie und seelische Krankheit* (pp. 196–215). Reinbek: Rowohlt.

Sperling, M. (1955). Psychosis and psychosomatic illness. *International Journal of Psychoanalysis, 36* (4-5), 320–7.

Sroufe, L. A., & Fleeson, J. (1985). Attachment and the construction of relationships. In W. Hartrup W, & Z. Rubin (Eds.), *The nature and development of relationships.* Hillsdale, NJ: Erlbaum.

Stern, D. N. (1985). *The interpersonal world of the infant. A view from psychoanalysis and developmental psychology.* New York: Basic Books.

Stierlin, H. (1972). *Separating parents and adolescents.* New York: Quadrangle Press.

Stierlin, H. (1973). Gruppenphantasien und Familienmythen. Theoretische und therapeutische Aspekte [Group phantasies and family myths: Theoretical and therapeutic apsects]. In Stierlin, H. (Ed.), *Von der Psychoanalyse zur Familientherapie* (pp. 150–163). Stuttgart: Klett.

Stierlin, H. (1974a) Eltern und Kinder. *Das Drama von Trennung und Versöhnung im Jugendalter* (pp. 44–80) [Parents and children: The drama of separation and reconcilliation]. Frankfurt: Suhrkamp.

Stierlin, H. (1974b) Scham- und Schuldgefühl in der Familienbeziehung. Theoretische und klinische Aspekte [Shame and guilt feelings in family relationships]. In Stierlin, H. (Ed.), *Von der Psychoanalyse zur Familientherapie* (pp. 182–203). Stuttgart: Klett.

Stierlin, H. (1978). *Delegation und Familie* [Delegation and the family]. Frankfurt: Suhrkamp.

Stierlin, H. (1989). *Individuation und Familie* [Individuation and the family]. Frankfurt: Suhrkamp.

Stierlin, H., Rücker-Embden, I., Wetzel, N., & Wirsching, M. (1985). *Das erste Familiengespräch* (3rd ed.) [The first family interview]. Klett, Stuttgart

Tress, W. (1986). *Das Rätsel der seelischen Gesundheit. Traumatische Kindheit und früher Schutz gegen psychogene Störungen* [The puzzle of mental health: Traumatic childhood and the early protection against psychogenic disorders]. Göttingen: Vandenhoeck & Ruprecht.

Vierzigmann, G. (1995). Persönliche Autorität im Familiensystem: ein Bindeglied zwischen individueller und familiärer Ebene [Personal authority in the family system: A link between the individual and familial levels]. *System Familie, 8,* 31–41.

Visher, E. B., & Visher, J. S. (1979). *Stepfamilies: A guide to working with stepparents and stepchildren.* New York: Brunner/Mazel Publishers.

Welter-Enderlin, R. (1992). *Paare – Leidenschaft und lange Weile. Frauen und Männer in zeiten des Übergangs* [Couples – Passion and boredom: Women and men in times of transition]. München: Piper.

Willi, J. (1981). *Die Zweierbeziehung* [The couple relationship]. Hamburg: Rowohlt.

Winnicott, D. W. (1969). *Kind, Familie und Umwelt* [Child, family and enivronment]. München: Reinhardt.

Wurmser, L. (1990). *Die Maske der Scham. Die Psychoanalyse von Schamkonflikten und Schamaffekten* [The mask of shame: The psychoanalysis of shame conflicts and shame affects]. Berlin: Springer.

Wurmser, L. (1993). *Das Rätsel des Masochismus. Psychoanalytische Untersuchung von Über-Ich-Konflikten und Masochismus* [The puzzle of masochism: A psychoanalytical investigation of superego conflicts and masochism]. Berlin: Springer.

Wynne, L. C., & Singer, M. (1965). *Denkstörung und Familienbeziehung bei Schizophrenen. Teil 14* [Thought disorders and family relationships in schizophrenics. Part 14]. *Psyche, 19,* 82–160.

Zilbach, J. J., Bergel, E., & Gass, C. (1972). Die Rolle des Kleinkindes bei der Familientherapie [The role of the small child in family therapy]. In C. J. Sager, H. Singer, H. S. Kaplan, *Handbuch der Ehe-, Familien und Gruppentherapie.* Vol. 2, (pp. 468–487). München: Kindler.

Zimmerman, P., Spangler, G., Schieche, M., & Becker-Stoll, F. (1995). Bindung im Lebenslauf. Determinanten, Kontinuität, Konsequenzen und zukünftige Perspektiven [Attachment on the course of life: Determinants, continuity, consequences and future perspectives]. In G. Spangler & P. Zimmermann (Eds.), *Die Bindungstheorie. Grundlagen, Forschung und Anwendung* (pp. 331–332). Stuttgart: Klett-Cotta.

9

The Family Life Cycle and the Genogram

Tina Timm and Adrian Blow

Summary
Genograms are a useful tool in the assessment of individuals, couples, and families. This chapter first gives a historical and theoretical background on the use of genograms. It continues by covering specifics about how to use genograms effectively in assessment, including the logistics of how long it should take, who to include, and what information to collect. The chapter illustrates how the genogram, as a powerful process tool, is used to uncover information, including belief systems and emotions, that will help the therapist to make sense of the presenting problem. Different types of genograms with a specific topic focus are discussed. The Appendix includes a detailed list of genogram assessment questions that can be used in the actual clinical interview.

Introduction and Goals of the Chapter

A genogram is a diagram that depicts important information about a family over several generations. Genograms provide an excellent way for therapists to collect information about a family, particularly during the initial assessment phase of therapy, but also throughout therapy. This information helps the therapist and client/s to understand the development of the presenting problem; to understand its meaning in a context; and to formulate hypotheses on how to proceed in treatment. It is an efficient way to assess and hypothesize about the connection between life cycle events, transgenerational patterns, and the presenting problem. It may provide crucial clues for both the therapist and client as to how to proceed in the subsequent sessions.

A genogram uses symbols, lines, and brief narrative to depict key information about a family and its history. Genograms are tangible and graphic representations of everything from a simple family structure to complex family patterns. The genogram offers many benefits to the standard assessment. First, the genogram can provide, at a glance, a historical map of key life changes in the family and an overview of important contextual, social, economic, and political events. Second, the genogram can be an effective means of alliance building with a client or family. It is a way to get to know the family in a way that is typically non-threatening. The genogram interview can be a way of engaging the whole family early in treatment. The process of collecting genogram information builds rapport while quickly highlighting important assessment information. By collecting the information in a collaborative, structured way, it allows people to give factual information with a minimum amount of defensiveness. Third, the genogram also helps to reframe the presenting problem as a systemic issue. Family members may come to see the multiple influences on the family and specific individuals within the family. Families are able to view their problems with both a current and historical perspective. Significant events within the family life cycle are also clearly displayed, helping family members see possible connections between events. Fourth, where detailed narrative text in the chart may get ignored, the genogram is an easy reference point to orient the therapist or supervisor when reviewing a particular case. Fifth, the information compiled about a family can be referenced throughout treatment, and if need be, changed. Because the genogram is a dynamic, ongoing tool it provides many benefits to the therapist with regards to ongoing assessment throughout treatment. Finally, at a professional level, a genogram provides a much-needed common language among marriage and family therapists.

In short, a genogram can record comprehensive demographic information, map the emotional system of a family, hypothesize about how past events may be influencing current issues, and develop strategies for intervention. Clearly the genogram is a powerful assessment tool that all marriage and family training should include in their work.

The main goal of this chapter is to give a broad overview of how to use genograms in the assessment of individuals, couples and families. Upon reading this chapter, the reader should know what a genogram is, the history of genogram usage, research related to the genogram, what theories are important related to genograms, what information to collect, how to analyze genogram information, specific types of genograms, how to use genograms in therapist training, and how technology has influenced genograms.

The Historical Use of the Genogram

The process of diagramming a family has been called a variety of names over the years including family tree and family genealogy. However the genogram differs in that it is not just a collection of information. The genogram provides a therapeutic focus when family information is organized in a way that helps to make sense of the presenting problem. The genogram adds a much deeper level of understanding about the family.

The genogram has been written about for over 20 years. The Bowen school of family therapy is most often associated with and given credit for its popularization, but the genogram is used much more widely in the field of marriage and family therapy than that would imply. Because of its universal usefulness, it has become an assessment tool that is used across theoretical orientations, not just with Bowen theory or other transgenerational theories.

While theories related to transgenerational family therapy date back to the 1950s (Nichols & Schwartz, 2004) it wasn't until the early 1980s that a standardized, systematic way of recording historical family data was developed (McGoldrick, Gerson, & Shellenberger, 1999). Historically, one of the biggest difficulties faced by proponents of the genogram was the lack of an agreed upon, uniform way of depicting information that was collected. There was little consistency in what symbols were used, how relationships were depicted, and what information was gathered. Without this standardization, the usefulness of the genogram was significantly reduced and communication between therapists hindered. If one clinician could not understand a genogram that was completed by another, the information would remain confusing, potentially be useless and open to subjective interpretations.

In the early 1980s, a committee was convened in order to agree on a standardized format for the genogram. This committee was organized by the North American Primary Care Research Group and included key people such as Murray Bowen, Jack Froom, and Jack Medalie (McGoldrick et al., 1999). Monica McGoldrick and Randy Gerson were instrumental in promoting the standardized use of genograms in the field of marriage and family therapy through their book *Genograms in Family Assessment* (McGoldrick & Gerson, 1985). Now more than ever, marriage and family therapists and other disciplines can communicate genogram information to each other in a common language.

Consistently, genograms have focused on the nuclear and extended family over three generations. However, the information collected about these generations has varied greatly. Even though genogram language is becoming more standardized, the genogram is ever evolving and there is no one right way to do them. Being creative and adaptive are valued in the process. In recent years, the genogram has been used to look at both specific issues in families and specific populations. This will be discussed in more detail later in the chapter.

Research On the Genogram

Despite the widespread use of genograms in marriage and family therapy, there has been limited empirical research on the clinical use of the genogram. Most of the research that has been completed is in the field of family medicine investigating how genogram information is related to health assessment and outcomes (Haas-Cunningham, 1994; Rogers & Holloway, 1990; Rogers & Rohrbaugh, 1991; Rogers, 1994). To date, there has only been one reliability study specifically in the field of marriage and family therapy (Coupland, Serovich, & Glenn, 1995). This study found that key persons and symbols for key persons were accurately recorded by students, but other information, such as unnamed persons, occupations, relationship descriptors, medical issues, personal issues, descriptive phrases, and other significant symbols, were only recorded moderately accurately.

This lack of research is puzzling. Given the wealth of current and historical information that can be collected and advancements in technology, there is much potential for studying families and family process through the use of genograms. More research is clearly needed in this area (McGoldrick et al, 1999).

Theoretical Underpinnings of Genogram Work

Genograms have been valued because of their utility in tracing the history of a particular family back into previous generations. Many theories of MFT use genograms to assess the history of a family. However, history has not been viewed the same way by all theories of family therapy (Blow & Sprenkle, 2001). Different MFT theories privilege history in different ways. Traditionally, in MFT, Bowen theory has been the major theory connected to genograms usage. However, not all MFT practitioners adhere to Bowen and his ideas. Despite this, genogram usage is still quite common among MFT practitioners although different practitioners use it in different ways and to a different level of depth depending upon their theoretical orientation.

This chapter will focus on Bowen theory as well as other theories of MFT and how they specifically use genograms in assessment. What we find is that the emphasis of information gathering and the goals of treatment are different, but many operate with the same assumptions and focus on the importance of life cycle events.

Major Assumptions of Genograms

There are several major assumptions underlying genogram construction. First, is the understanding that families are inextricably interconnected both within the family and with the larger systems around them (McGoldrick et al., 1999). Family members and the problems they present with do not occur in a vacuum. Second, is the assumption that history is important and that the past significantly influences the present in some way. Third, it is assumed that unresolved life cycle events and the resulting family patterns may organize family systems and are the system's adaptation to its context at that moment in time. These patterns may repeat themselves in subsequent transitions or in subsequent generations. Fourth, the presenting problem of the individual or family can be alleviated or changed through the use of this historical information. This last assumption is very important because the goal of treatment is always to provide this relief. The information itself is meaningless if it does not help the family in some way.

The Family Life Cycle

The family life cycle is a very important component of the genogram. The work of Monica McGoldrick and Betty Carter in particular (Carter & McGoldrick, 1999) focus on the importance of life cycle events in the function of the family. They view the family life cycle as having a large impact on human development and believe that problems are best conceptualized and treated "within a multigenerational context of family connections that pattern our lives" (p. 1). With regards to the treatment of symptoms and difficulties in people's lives, they state:

From a family life cycle perspective, symptoms and dysfunction are examined within a systemic context and in relation to what the culture considers to be "normal" functioning over time. From this perspective, therapeutic interventions aim at helping to reestablish the family's developmental momentum so that it can proceed forward to foster the uniqueness of each member's development. (p. 1).

They believe that family life has become much more complex over the years and that many "normal" life cycle events can no longer be taken for granted. All life cycle transitions are seen to have different meanings for particular families and are always modified by the specific lenses of culture and gender held by families.

One definition of family is, a group of people who share a history and a future with each other and move together through time as a unique system (Carter & McGoldrick, 1999). In today's aging society this may include up to five generations. Carter and McGoldrick (1999) promote the notion that all families have normative as well as idiosyncratic life cycle phases to negotiate through life. These phases represent transitions that affect all members of a family. They also represent a set of tasks, principles and challenges that family members need to successfully negotiate in order to move on developmentally. These family life cycle stages include normal events faced by most families such as leaving home, birth or adoption of children, raising children and adolescents, launching children, and death. The life cycle events also include idiosyncratic life cycle events that occur in many families. These are transitions such as divorce, remarriage, single parent families, same sex parenting, and the like. Regarding these many life cycle events, Carter and McGoldrick (1999) state that key family relationship changes are more likely to occur at some times than at others. They are especially likely at points of life cycle transition. Symptoms tend to cluster around such transitions in the family life cycle, when family members face the task of reorganizing their relations with one another in order to go on to the next phase

Particularly important in assessing the family life cycle are vertical and horizontal stressors (Carter & McGoldrick, 1999). Vertical stressors include those events and themes that are handed down through generations such as genetics, temperament, family attitudes, myths, taboos, historical events and the like. They are given and cannot be changed. However, the way individuals interpret these events and deal with them *can* be changed. Horizontal stressors include events in the life of an individual and family that unfold over time due to normative developmental events in a family (puberty, leaving home) and idiosyncratic events (divorce, remarriage). Horizontal stressors further include both predictable events (marriage, child birth, death) and unpredictable events (loss of job, war, untimely death) (Carter & McGoldrick, 1999).

From a life cycle perspective, the genogram is extremely useful in recording how these significant events occur over time. It may also reveal "stuck points" where families have not fully negotiated a life cycle event or intergenerational patterns where life cycle themes are repeating themselves unconsciously (McGoldrick, 1999).

Bowen Theory

Differentiation of Self and Fusion

Using biological terminology, Bowen (1978) came up with the terms differentiation of self and fusion to describe what people need to change in their interactions with each other. In biology, two cells that are fused are interconnected in such a way that they can almost be viewed as one cell. The two cells need to go through a process of differentiation so that they become two distinct cells. In a relationship, fusion occurs when individuals lose their selves in relation to significant others. This occurs often because the individual is essentially afraid that the significant person will abandon them or receive some kind of emotional punishment from that person if they don't maintain this level of closeness.

Differentiation involves engaging family members in non-reactive ways. Bowen (1978) refers to this as the ability to separate intellectual functioning from emotional reactivity and not be pulled into the emotionally reactive forces of a family. Schnarch (1997) refers to differentiation the "ability to maintain your sense of self when you are emotionally and/or physically close to others — especially as they become increasingly important to you" (p. 56). Differentiation is the ability to stay connected to significant other people without being emotionally consumed by them. He states:

> Well-differentiated people can agree without feeling like they're "losing themselves," and can disagree without feeling alienated and embittered. They can stay connected with people who disagree with them and still "know who they are." They don't have to leave the situation to hold onto their sense of self. (p. 56).

According to Bowen, if one is successful in differentiating oneself from one's family, one can be more differentiated in all subsequent relationships. McGoldrick and Carter (2001, p. 285) summarize this nicely when they state, "grounding oneself emotionally and learning to connect emotionally by developing a personal relationship with every member of one's family are, indeed, the 'blueprints' for all subsequent emotional connection." An example of this process would be a woman who desires to have a professional career but is married to a man who wishes her to be a stay-at-home-mom. Her venturing out into the workplace would come at the risk of punishment from her husband, including possible emotional and physical abuse. She might legitimately fear the loss of intimacy in the marriage, her husband leaving, or the harmful effects of a tense marriage on her children. The emotional toll of entering the workforce might be too high for her and so she may put her career aspirations aside. Her self-identity in this example is intricately linked to the identity that her husband would like for her to have; they are fused. In order for her to differentiate from her husband, she would need to get in touch with her needs for professional and financial autonomy and follow her own ambitions. She would need to be able to tolerate the emotional anxiety that would come with making this decision while not disengaging from her husband. McGoldrick and Carter (2001) aptly define this process as:

> The extent to which individuals are able to think, plan, know, and follow their own values and self-directed life course, while being emotionally present with others, rather than living reactively to the cues of those close to them. They do not have to spend their life energy keeping themselves emotionally walled off, or maneuvering in relationships to obtain control or emotional comfort...In their personal relationships they can relate warmly and openly without needing to focus on others or on activities or impersonal things in order to find common ground. (p. 284)

Triangles

A triangle as a stabilizing factor in relationships in which there is a high degree of emotional intensity (Bowen, 1978). When there is tension between two people, they will regularly pull in a third person in order to diffuse the anxiety. An example of this process is where a child is pulled into the conflictual relationship of his or her parents. This child will then serve as a stabilizing factor in the relationship and will become a critical component of the relationship. However, this is not a healthy position for a child to be in and he or she can be psychologically affected if the intensity is too great. A major goal of Bowen theory is to break triangles through getting people to communicate directly to each other in non-reactive ways and helping the third person to stay out of the process. Genograms are ideal ways to powerfully depict triangles in families throughout generations.

Intergenerational Transmission Process

Family members influence each other in circular ways (Bowen, 1978). Events that occur or issues that are unresolved in one generation can impact and even unknowingly repeat themselves in subsequent generations. The history of the family can organize interactions and behavior in the present. For example, there may be a family secret that cannot be talked about within a family because of the emotional intensity associated with talking about it. The overt and covert rules of the family passed down through the generations are that this topic is to be avoided and is not safe to talk about. The goal of Bowen theory is to interrupt this intergenerational flow of emotional patterning by helping individuals to change their predictable input and emotional reactions to significant family members (Bowen, 1978). In this case, a family member would begin to talk openly about the family secret despite the pressure not to. This may "interrupt the previous flow of interactions in the system [and in so doing] other family members will be jarred out of their own unthinking responses" (McGoldrick & Carter, 2001, p. 283).

Emotional Cut-Offs

The concept of distancing and emotional cut-offs is another important Bowenian concept (Bowen, 1978). Many times cut-offs come about in a family system when the pull towards fusion becomes too great and an individual cuts off in order to manage the need for independence. A young woman with anorexia presented for therapy with her family. Her mother had extremely high expectations for her in terms of how she should look physically as well as how much she should achieve academically and financially. She was involved in her daughter's life in invasive ways and her daughter felt she had little to say over decisions about her own life. She felt smothered by her mother much of the time, but also felt as if she could not tell her mother her true feelings or make her own decisions for fear that her mother would abandon her. In therapy, the young woman talked about how she viewed her two options. The first option was to completely lose her self and her own needs and subscribe to her mother's expectations of beauty and success. The other option was to break away from her mother completely, a process she was sure would result in an emotional and perhaps even a physical cut-off. This was intensified by the knowledge that her own mother had been cut off by her mother when she married against her wishes. There was a historical precedence of a cut off in the face of disagreement. Both extreme options indicate an unhealthy emotional connection and the eating disorder was unlikely to subside if she followed either option. The goal of treatment was to help her to separate from her mother without cutting off from her and without her mother abandoning her. Genograms often reveal themes of cut offs in the family process. The threat of cut-off is a very powerful manipulative force in the family that helps to keep members "in line".

Bowenian Theory in Practice: Coaching

Bowen theory is focused on helping individuals to change themselves in relation to their own families (Bowen, 1978). In this change process, the therapist acts in the role of a coach who meets with clients in order to help them to differentiate from the emotional forces of their families. McGoldrick and Carter (2001) refer to the basic idea of differentiation from ones family as a process in which:

If you can change the part you play in your family and hold it despite the family's reaction while keeping in emotional contact with family members, you maximize the likelihood (not a guarantee!) that they will eventually change to accommodate your change…The ideal of family systems work is to develop a person-to-person relationship with each living person in your extended family. (p. 291)

This coaching process involves five phases (McGoldrick & Carter, 2001). These five phases are a) *engagement and system mapping* where the therapeutic relationship is built and the genogram completed; b) *planning* which involves learning about the system and the client's role in it; c) *reentry* which consists of reentering one's family with the goal of developing genuine and emotionally engaged relationships with each member of one's family; d) *the main work* which involves definite changes on the part of the client in order to change maladaptive family patterns based on family themes from the past; e) *follow through* which includes additional consultation with clients in order to help them if they are stuck or if they see potential crises in the future. In this chapter we will focus on the first two phases of the process, which focus on assessment.

The therapist (coach) and client use the genogram together to help the client reconnect with his or her family of origin in a different way. In the first step of coaching, engagement and system mapping, constructing a genogram is essential (McGoldrick & Carter, 2001). During this stage, the therapist connects with clients and helps them to see their problems in systemic ways. Through a process of circular questioning (Tomm, 1984; 1987) a genogram is constructed in a way that helps the client to see his or her problem within the context of his or her family over three or more generations. During this process, the therapist is able to comment, reflect, and possibly draw tentative conclusions about the meaning and significance of family events and patterns. It is extremely useful to do a timeline along with the genogram that maps out the time sequence of significant events and their impact on life cycle development. McGoldrick and Carter (2001) recommend that during this time, the therapist "set a calm, matter-of-fact tone to help defuse the intensity of emotion that is aroused by a current crisis or by opening up anxiety-producing material" (p. 288). The genogram process also is an ideal arena in which to educate clients about important concepts such as triangles, boundaries, and differentiation of self. Depending on the presenting issues, many of these will sound very familiar to the client.

During the second phase of treatment, known as the planning phase, an individual learns more about the system and his or her role in it. This phase may be revisited many times in order to update information as it is revealed or as it changes. During this phase, gaps in the genogram are filled in through "research" into the family history. In this phase, the client gets a deeper understanding of how the emotional system of the family operates. This sets the stage for the real work of coaching where the client engages his or her family in new ways. The genogram is continually referred to throughout this process.

Contextual Theory

Contextual therapy is based upon the work of Boszormenyi-Nagy, and focuses on the roots of relational damage in families and how this damage affects the family as a whole (Boszormenyi-Nagy & Krasner, 1986; Boszormenyi-Nagy & Spark, 1984). The genogram is used to identify the family legacies and loyalties that frequently manifest themselves in "destructive entitlement." The goal of contextual therapy is the healing of damaged relationships through commitment and trust. Contextual therapy is based on four dimensions. They are objectifiable facts, individual psychology, family or systemic transactions, and relational ethics.

Objectifiable facts

These include things in the life of an individual such as genetic inheritance, physical health, historical events, and events that occur in the life cycle. They are events that are specific and objective.

Individual psychology

This includes the way in which an individual subjectively integrates various life experiences. According to Hargrave (1994), individual psychology produces subjective influences on relationships as individuals strive for recognition, love, power, and pleasure and are motivated by aggression, mastery, or ambivalence.

Family transactions

These are the interactional patterns of relationships that are communicated between family members. These define power alignments, structure, and belief systems within families.

Relational ethics

These deal with the subjective balance of justice, trustworthiness, loyalty, merit, and entitlement between those who are in relation to each other. Ideally, individuals engage in relationships that include a balanced give and take between relational entitlements (what one is entitled to receive from the relationship) and obligations (what one is obligated to give to relationships). With regard to destructive entitlement in relationships, Hargrave (1994, p. 25) states:

> When there is a consistent or severe imbalance in this relational give-and-take, individuals feel that they either have been cheated by or have over-benefited from relationships. Instead of there being a balance that builds trustworthiness in a relationship, trust is drained and the members of the relationship feel that their just entitlement is threatened...[and] the relationship becomes an unstable arena.

In the contextual therapy approach, the genogram is utilized to help family members understand how relational damage came about. Past life cycle occurrences, events, patterns of interaction, and transmission are all investigated. Current behavior may be linked to past generations in the family. This is an excellent way to increase understanding of the problematic issue as well as create empathy for its origin.

Postmodern Theories

Postmodern therapies such as narrative therapy and solution-focused therapy look at history in families but not in the same way as traditional MFT theories. Postmodern therapies see genograms, as used in the past, as a tool used to identify what is wrong with clients and their families. These therapists believe that genograms have tended to overfocus on pathology and dysfunctional patterns (Bertolino & O' Hanlon, 2002; 1996). Kuehl (1995) came up with the idea of using a solution-oriented genogram with clients. Through this approach, instead of focusing on pathology and dysfunction, therapists use the genogram as a tool to investigate exceptions to problems and previous solutions to types of problems that exist in family backgrounds. The shift in focus of postmodern therapies is to the resilient qualities of families and family members that have enabled members of families to stand up to adversity. Bertolino and O' Hanlon state that:

> This way therapists learn about the influence of problems over clients and families, and clients' and families' influence over problems. Exploring clients' historical and familial roots can be particularly useful when clients feel or think that their problems are a result of their families. We investigate contextual influences in the same way that we would search for exceptions and solutions with problematic stories. (2002, p. 189)

It is clear that while postmodern therapies look at history, it is viewed in a different light to that of Bowen. For them, the genogram is a useful tool to actually focus on exceptions to the problem.

Using the Genogram in Assessment

Unfortunately, it is beyond the scope of this chapter to teach the reader all of the intricacies of genogram diagramming. The reader is referred to the excellent work of McGoldrick and Gerson (1985) for this information. The goal of this chapter is rather to illustrate the usefulness of the genogram in the assessment process.

Improperly used, the genogram can serve as a deterrent and distraction to the process of therapy. It can stand between an effective alliance between the therapist and client, detract from the presenting problem, or render therapy sessions boring by collecting meaningless historical data. Properly used, the genogram has the ability to powerfully connect the presenting problem to the family system and its transgenerational context. It has the ability to change the meanings of problems within the family system, as well as raise important emotional reactions that provide clues to stuck points that exist within the family system.

We believe that successful genogram interviewing should use a postmodern perspective. The process should be both collaborative and transparent. This is not an assessment technique that the therapist does *to* the family; rather it is one done *with* the family. The information gathered reflects the constructionistic nature of family communication because meaning is created during the process. Meanings are particularly rich when all family members share information about the family history. All family members present are active participants in the process and it is believed that everyone present in the room has important information to contribute.

One of the biggest fears that families have when they begin treatment is that they are "screwed up" or that the therapist knows things about them that they are not telling. The genogram allows the clinician to be transparent with the family by not only having them involved in the process, but by making the information available to them as well. To do this, clinicians can draw the genogram as it is being completed so that the whole family can see it as it develops. This can be done using a large piece of paper, a grease board, or a portable chalkboard. There are also a number of computer programs that create genograms if the therapy room has this technology. Families are typically interested in the diagram and become more involved in the process as they watch it grow. Since the genogram should be included in the case file after completion, doing it on paper has some advantages because the clinician doesn't have to copy the information from the temporary media after the session. It is also suggested to offer the family a copy of the genogram. For some, this is the first time they have seen their family depicted in this way and they are quite pleased to have this information compiled in such a concise, readable way. Also, it can be helpful to have the family take the genogram home and review it in order to correct any information that may inaccurately recorded and/or add information that they did not know off the top of their head in session.

We believe that there are several important points to consider when using the genogram in assessment.

Timing

As in all therapy, the timing of therapeutic interventions is critical to their success. We strongly believe that the timing of genogram usage should occur within the building of a strong therapeutic alliance, in the context of the presenting problem (initially), and as a smooth and natural part of the therapy process. We begin gathering genogram information from the first phone call made by the client, but do not allow it to get in the way of connecting with the client/s.

How Long Should it Take

The length of time needed to complete a genogram varies greatly depending on how much information is collected. A basic diagram showing who is in the family may only take 10 minutes, while a comprehensive genogram assessment may take multiple sessions. We believe that the time taken to do a genogram varies from family to family depending on the presenting problem, the needs of the family, and the information that is revealed. For example, when a genogram reveals extensive family secrets such as sexual abuse, we will normally spend much more time than if it reveals limited information.

Just as assessment is an ongoing process, so is the construction of the genogram. It can be used throughout the family therapy. Clients should be told that they can add or change information as they remember, as it becomes available to them, or as they feel comfortable sharing more intimate details. Some information will come in the form of, "I'm not sure this is important, but ..." This is an introduction that typically leads to very relevant information about the presenting problem. Families have information that they previously didn't think was relevant but through the process of therapy they realize its importance.

Who to Include

While genogram information can be collected from an individual, it is preferable to have as many members of the family as possible. This allows for increased thoroughness and reliability because some members of the family will know information that others will not. It also provides the richness of multiple stories and perspectives, and because "the whole is greater than the sum of its parts," the therapist is also able to notice family interactions, emotions, and other important process issues. However, when only one person is present the genogram is still very useful. Murray Bowen was a big proponent that family therapy can be done with only one person in the room (Kerr & Bowen, 1988; McGoldrick & Carter, 2001).

Information to Collect

Genograms are used differently in therapy depending on the theoretical orientation of the therapist. However, there are also some similarities in the information collected by all therapists. The information collected on the genogram can be as extensive or brief as the assessment requires. In general, the information can be divided into five sections, the diagram itself, basic information about each person, relationships between members, historical timeline, and additional relevant information.

The Diagram

The diagrammatical structure of a genogram typically provides data on three genera-tions. However, sometimes therapists choose to only look at one or two, depending on the need. It details the gender of each person (square for male, circle for female), sibling order (chronological from left to right), and the status of legal relationships (solid line for marriage, dotted line for living together, one slash mark for separation, two slash marks for divorce). The identified patient (IP) can easily be found (denoted by a double circle or double square). Further, a circle (or circles) can be drawn around the family members that currently live together in the same dwelling. Significant others in the life of the family should also be included (fictive kin, non-related caregivers, etc.). They can be placed on the side of the genogram, using the same format as above, with a brief explanation of who they are.

Some family diagrams are simple and straightforward. Others may have multiple marriages, separations, divorces, and remarriages resulting in a complex genogram that may include biological, step, and half siblings all within the same family. Using standard-ized genogram formatting has helped these genograms to be much more consistent.

Basic Genogram Information

Basic genogram information includes information on each person such as name, age, date of birth, place of birth, occupation, education, religion, ethnic background (migra-tion dates if appropriate), geographic location, dates of marriages, separations, and divorce, and for members who are deceased, the date and cause of death. However, this is the most basic of information. The diagram becomes more and more clinically useful as systemic information is added. See Appendix B for a detailed list of possible information to include on the genogram.

Relationships Between People

Genograms are also used to collect information about relationships between people, characteristics or roles people play in the family, and clues to important triangles that exist in the family. Lines are drawn from one person to another and relationships can be depicted as close (one solid line), very close/enmeshed (three solid lines), conflictual (jagged line), enmeshed and conflictual (three solid lines with a jagged line over the top), distant (dotted or dashed line), or cut-off (a solid line with an open gap in the middle). Intergenerational patterns of relationships can seem quite obvious once this information is recorded.

Relationships are the part of the genogram that are most likely to change over time. Families may struggle with what to put on the genogram when the relationship has been different over the years. When the relationship change is significant, it is important to note both on the genogram. For example, if there was a cut-off at one point and now there is not, note how long or during what years the cut-off occurred as well as the current relationship. Asking questions about what originally caused the cut-off and how it was resolved will typically reveal very interesting information about how the family deals with crises.

Historical Timeline

The historical timeline outlines important dates or critical events that have affected the life of the family (Stanton, 1992). These are particularly related to horizontal stressors in families (Carter & McGoldrick, 1999). The timeline shows the events, changes and transitions that have occurred in the family's life cycle. They can be developmental (e.g., marriage, children leaving the family), unpredictable (e.g., untimely death, development of a chronic illness, unemployment, affairs) or historical (e.g., natural disasters, war, economic depression). It is often particularly helpful to view the history of the presenting problem within the context of family events over time. For example, a client with an eating disorder can record on the timeline significant family events as well as the manifestations of the eating disorder over time (when it was worse, when it improved, when it first started, when relapse occurred, etc.).

Additional Relevant Information

Other information can be added as appropriate to the specific individual or family. This information may include vertical stressors (Carter & McGoldrick, 1999) at the individual level (e.g., genetic makeup, disabilities), immediate family (e.g., violence, sexual abuse, addictions, depression), extended family (e.g., family patterns, myths, triangles, secrets, legacies), community (e.g., lack of social connection) or the larger society (e.g., racism, sexism, homophobia, poverty, etc.). See appendix B for a complete list of information to consider.

Locating Key Information

Collecting all of the information discussed above may seem overwhelming. However, depending on the presenting problem, or the specific goals of treatment, the information will be more or less focused. The genogram is merely a skeleton on its own. It is the therapist's responsibility to put meat on the skeleton's bones by finding the relevant timeline events and additional information that is key to the presenting problem.

The important question is how to figure out what information is important and what information is interesting but irrelevant. First and foremost, we privilege information on a genogram that is seen to be important to the specific client or family. We regularly ask our clients, "What information is most significant to you?" or "What information on this genogram is the most difficult for you to talk about?" There may be many pockets of note-worthy information that the therapist may consider important, but the family will typically lead you to the one that holds the most intensity for them at that time.

We believe that through a postmodern lens, the viewpoints of the client are most significant. However, on occasion, information that is not significant to a client may in fact be very important. When a topic on the genogram is met with resistance, it may be important to explore further. Resistance may occur because of denial, the emotional intensity attached to the issue, or even fear. We have learned that this information is best processed slowly and with the utmost respect for the client. Intensity is useful but not if it is too much, too fast. We believe that hunches, intuition, and therapeutic experience are essential and may lead to important areas or connections. Knowing that the questions we ask as therapists shape the direction and focus of therapy, we must be mindful of our power in this situation. Sometimes we miss key information because we are taking it in the wrong direction or we have failed to ask the right questions.

Nisbett and Wilson's (1977) work warns us that peoples' reports about their experiences often reflect their personal theories of attribution (what's *supposed to be*) rather than accurate observation (what *is*). In many families it is not uncommon to hear that everyone is the family is "close" to one another. Therefore, it is useful to ask for descriptions rather than conclusions (Nichols & Schwartz, 2004). Instead of asking "Do you have a good relationship with your parents?" which is a leading question and puts pressure on clients to say yes because they are *supposed* to have a good relationship with their parents, ask more specific questions. For example, "Where do your parents live?" "How often do you see them? Call them? E-mail them?" "Do you feel you can talk to your mom about anything?" "Are there any topics that are off limits?"

Process Issues

Beck (1987) argued for the genogram to be used as a process instrument. He argues that the genogram should not be constructed in an "affective vacuum" (p. 343) but rather with an eye for process and emotion. In Bowen theory it is expected that the therapist stays as calm and as neutral as possible and not to overreact to or accentuate pieces of information over other information on the genogram (McGoldrick & Carter, 2001). Beck (1987) recommends that from a process perspective, clinicians attend to family member's non verbal responses to information revealed; that clinicians intervene with regards to emotions in the moment in the here-and-now; that the therapist attend at all times to the mood, affect, and posturing of the client as the genogram information is discussed. The therapist should ideally skillfully move back and forth between the data collection process and the affective component of the material gathered.

Wachtel (1982) sees the genogram as an excellent tool to get at emotions in families. She believes that genograms are particularly helpful in getting emotionally closed off clients with rigid views to see their problems through an alternate lens. Through empathy and expanding stories, emotional issues can rise to the surface.

There are four areas of genogram information that the therapist should take particular note of because they can help focus the treatment by identifying key information.

Issues that Raise High Levels of Affect

On many occasions when collecting genogram information, clients will become emotional. Sometimes, strong emotions will well up without warning when a specific event is discussed. We believe that these issues may represent unresolved issues that may be integrally linked to the presenting problem. In doing genogram work, we continually monitor body language, affect, and tone of voice. If we notice a change in these areas, we will ask about them. This is part of our view that the genogram should be used as an instrument that intervenes at a process level in the family rather than a content level. Because of its information gathering purpose, it is all too easy to overfocus on content issues. We need to be sensitive to what is going on emotionally with clients. For example, in working with a male client his eyes teared up briefly as he talked about his father dropping out of college early in order to take care of his terminally ill father. After probing and exploring, it turned out, this was very significant to in the client's current dissatisfaction with work and feelings of being unappreciated by his own immediate family.

Issues that raise inappropriate affect

At times in the genogram process, inappropriate affect will come up in talking about certain family issues. For example, a client may laugh when discussing a traumatic or negative event in the family. This may be a clue that something is unresolved. There may be a long history of negating emotions in the family.

Areas that Create Defensiveness or Avoidance on the Part of the Client

Clients may want to avoid certain issues in their lives and "not want to go there." These areas are often laden with emotional intensity that may have to do with family secrets, shameful events, or issues that they want to "keep in the past." These areas often hold the key to the current presenting problem. An example would be the client who was sexually abused as a child and says, "It's no big deal," "I've already dealt with that," or "There's nothing I can do to change it now, so why talk about it."

Missing or Unknown Information

It is very interesting to note what information is missing or unknown on the genogram. Sometimes the information that is not there says more than the information that is. This is not information that the family doesn't want to talk about, as described above, it is information that just isn't available for some reason. For example, some families know every last detail and date about one side of the family and virtually know nothing about the other. Why might this be? It is also common for there to be a "black sheep" in each generation that the family knows very little about. Sometimes this is a result of that person's attempt at a "geographical cure," meaning that they moved far away from the family in hopes that the miles between them would somehow heal them. This typically does not work and in some cases actually increases the emotional intensity. Bowen (1978) explains that two sure signs of emotional cutoff are denial of the importance of the family and an exaggerated façade of independence.

At times this missing information will prompt family members to begin asking questions and doing historical research on the family. Individuals can learn more information by speaking to relatives, consulting a family tree, looking up media records, and finding genealogical records.

Analyzing Genogram Information

The overall goal of constructing a genogram is not merely to have information; it is to do something based on what is learned from that information. The most useful way of doing this is to analyze the genogram for themes and patterns over the generations that may currently be influencing the family or individual family members. The fact of the matter is that most families tend to repeat themes from the past. Things that have happened in previous generations have an uncanny way of showing up again. Some people think this is a coincidence. But, in transgenerational family therapy it is known as a theme or pattern and this information is vital to making changes in the present.

You will want to evaluate where individuals and the family are in the life cycle. As families move through these stages they must reorganize in order to move to the next phase. If this adjustment, or reorganization doesn't happen successfully, the family may get stuck. In addition to noting what stage the family is currently in, questions should be asked about how they have successfully negotiated change in the past.

McGoldrick et al. (1999) suggest looking for cross-generational patterns in five areas. 1) Patterns of functioning. Are there things about how this family functions that you see in previous generation also? These patterns could be adaptive (creativity, resilience, strengths) or maladaptive (battering, child abuse, alcoholism, suicide, etc.). They can include repetitive symptoms, or relationships. 2) Patterns of relationships. Repeated triangles, coalitions, cut-offs, patterns of conflict, over- and under-functioning are central to genogram interpretation. For example, a family might have a pattern of forming relational triangles with mother and a child. 3) Patterns related to position of family. People in similar positions as a previous generation member tend to repeat the same patterns. For example, the only son of a man who spent time in prison during his twenties may pattern himself after his father and end up going to prison during his twenties. Or a person may remarry and form a similar family constellation to the one he or she grew up in. This factor may influence relationships with other in the same repetitive pattern. 4) Coincidences of dates. For example, the death of one family member or anniversary of this death occurring at the same time as symptom onset in another, or the age at symptom onset coinciding with the age of problem development in another family member. If a client's mother died suddenly when she was 45, when the client approaches or reaches that age, symptoms of anxiety could appear due to her unconscious fear that she too may die at that age. 5) The impact of change and untimely life cycle transitions. Look for changes in functioning and relationships that correspond with critical family life events and untimely life cycle transitions, such as births, marriages, or deaths that occur "off schedule". A teenage pregnancy has a significant impact on the family relationships as the family moves to accommodate it. Some families do better than others with these transitions.

Genograms With a Specific Focus

Genograms can be used in a broad way as described above, or in more specific, focused ways. Depending on the presenting problem, or characteristics of the clients, using one of the following specific genograms may be advised (DeMaria, Weeks, & Hof, 1999). See Appendix A for specific questions to ask for these types of genograms.

The Sexual Genogram

The sexual genogram (Berman & Hof, 1987; Hof & Berman, 1986) is used to focus on intergenerational issues related specifically to sexuality. This is particularly useful when the presenting problem is sexual in nature. Powerful messages about sexuality are passed down through the generations and have significant influences on future generations.

Genograms That Focus on Culture

As the names imply, the cultural genogram (Hardy & Laszloffy, 1995) or culturagrams (Congress, 1994) explore intergenerational issues related to culture. These can be used in the training of marriage and family therapists to increase awareness of their own cultural issues and how those might affect their work as a therapist. With clients they can help to understand the impact of culture on the family, become more empathic with regard to cultural differences, and empower culturally diverse clients and their families.

The Gendergram

Gendergrams (White & Tyson-Rawson, 1995) are an assessment tool used for examining the influence of gender within couples and families. Gender roles and family patterns of gender stereotypes have a huge impact on relationships from generation to generation. Looking at the genogram with this lens can help couples and families to understand more clearly how gender issues are affecting their relationships.

The Spiritual Genogram

Frame (2000) created the spiritual genogram to use with individuals and families. Through the spiritual genogram, a multigenerational map of family members' religious and spiritual affiliations, events and conflicts is created. The goal of the spiritual genogram is to help clients make sense of their family's religious and spiritual heritage and investigate how these issues impact individuals, couples, and families in the present. Important rituals, events, break aways, and the like related to religious life are recorded.

The Genogram as a Projective Technique

According to Wachtel (1982) and Kaslow (1995), the genogram can also be used as an effective projective technique. Wachtel sees the genogram as a map to the unconscious with information remembered and revealed by the client reflective of core internal conflicts. She states that to use the genogram in this way, clinicians must

> … listen carefully to what might otherwise be thought of as little more than "incidental" information; almost everything that is said is looked at as potentially revealing of some central theme for the individual and the current family system. The stories have both a latent and a manifest meaning. (p. 340).

In using the genogram projectively, the therapist needs to listen carefully to the words and phrases used and both the positive and negative emotional weight of these words. This helps the therapist to learn about clients' values and red flags that could not otherwise have been disclosed consciously. Further, unconscious disclosures can reveal important solutions as to how an individual would like to change in the future.

Color-Coded Genograms

Lewis (1989) adapted the genogram to incorporate color. Colors are assigned by the client to signify different issues or emotions in the family. The assigning of color and the discussion of the rationale for choosing a particular color can be a revealing part of the therapeutic process.

Play Therapy Techniques with Genograms

Family sculpting, popularized by Satir (1967), has family members act out various roles in the family to explore themes and patterns. Photographs and videos can be used to reveal family stories and feelings about past experiences (Kaslow & Friedman, 1977). Art therapy and drawing can encourage the family to use symbolic imagery to express issues and emotions (Kwiatkowska, 1978).

Other Types of Genograms

In addition to Friedman, Rohrbaugh, and Krakauer's (1988) time-line genogram, there are genograms to explore the "functional" family (Watts-Jones, 1998), ones to look at attachment (Friesen & Manitt, 1991), genogrids to depict the networks of lesbian families (Burke & Faber, 1997), genograms to facilitate career decisions (Moon, Coleman, McCollum, Nelson, & Jensen-Scott, 1993), genograms with children (Fink, Kramer, Weaver, & Anderson, 1993) genograms to illustrate the placement of children in the child welfare system (McMillen & Groze, 1994), and ones to work with the elderly (Ingersoll-Dayton & Arndt, 1990). The possibilities to adapt the genogram are endless.

The Training of Therapists

Teaching students of marriage and family therapy how to complete genograms is very important and widely used in training programs. The classic genogram assignment for therapists is described by Guerin and Fogarty (1972). In focusing on their own genogram and family of origin, therapists can experience first hand what it is like to compile the information and then look at the meaning of the information (Titelman, 1992). Typically, supervisors or instructors have their supervisees/students draw and examine their genograms in small group settings. In using genogram information in doing self-of-the-therapist work, Timm and Blow (1999) state that too often self-of-the-therapist work has overly focused on deficits and not looked at the ways in which painful life events or family dynamics have shaped the resources and competencies of the therapist. The genogram assignment is particularly useful in helping therapists work through issues from their own families that might impede their effectiveness as a therapist as well as identifying issues that help them to be more effective as therapists. In a safe group setting it is helpful for the therapist to hear reflections from the group about both of these areas.

A double-genogram can also be effectively used in supervision. Braverman (1997) suggests that supervisees make two genograms – one of the client family and one of their own family. The therapist then identifies similarities between the two genograms, and the subsequent strengths and blockages that arise out of these similarities.

The Use of Technology

Until the late 1990s, genograms were primarily drawn by hand. This could be quite a time-consuming process as the clinician worked to fit all the information on the genogram and put it in the proper format. Just a few new pieces of information would change the spacing of all the information and timely redraws would be necessary to keep the information in a readable format.

Fortunately, computer software has been developed to provide ease in the physical construction of the genogram (Gerson & Shellenberger, 1999a, 1999b; WonderWare, 1998). These programs easily format the genogram as it is created and as information is added. This substantially increases readability and eliminates time consuming redrawing. The software also allows the therapist to create databases of information. Information can then be compiled, sorted, printed, etc. Furthermore, this information can be used to analyze the genogram. An individual family can be analyzed for themes and patterns or multiple families can be scanned for similar issues or family constellations. And all of this can be done in a short period of time. The ability to do this has many implications for assessment as well as research.

Just as the more sophisticated statistical programs have moved research to higher levels of efficiency, accuracy, and complexity, the use of genogram computer technology creates a more realistic opportunity for large-scale genogram research. If the thousands of genograms that were produced by clinicians every year were a part of a computer database (minus identifying information) it would allow for a wealth of complex, systemic information.

Family genealogy programs are also available (Broderbund, 1998; Palladium Interactive, Inc., 1998). They are not for family assessment per se, but rather to record demographic information, family history, and family stories. These programs even have the capacity to incorporate family pictures and videos as part of the computer records. Furthermore, the Internet allows for access to information that previously would have taken years to collect or would have been impossible to find. There are web sites that focus on genealogies and include large databases on family histories. Investigating family genealogy has become increasingly popular and individuals looking for information or specific people or families have turned to the web with great success. We predict that these web sites will become increasingly popular in the decades to come and family history will be recorded more and more.

Conclusion

Genograms are an important and powerful tool in the assessment of individuals, couples, and families. The information that is collected provides clues into the history of the presenting problem as well as a roadmap to intervention.

The exciting thing about genograms is that they are still evolving. Much is still to be learned about the powerful ways they can be used both for clinical work and for research. We have only just begun to scratch the surface of their potential.

References

Beck, R. L. (1987). The genogram as process. *The American Journal of Family Therapy, 15,* 343–351.

Berman, E. M., & Hof, L. (1987). The sexual genogram – Assessing family-of-origin factors in the treatment of sexual dysfunction. In G. R. Weeks & L. Hof (Eds.), *Integrating sex and marital therapy: A clinical guide.* New York, NY: Brunner/Mazel.

Bertolino, B., & O' Hanlon, B (2002). *Collaborative, competency-based counseling and therapy.* Boston, MA: Allyn & Bacon.

Blow, A. J., & Sprenkle, D. S. (2001). Common factors across theories of marriage and family therapy: A modified Delphi study. *Journal of Marital and Family Therapy, 27,* 385–401.

Bowen, M. (1978). *Family therapy in clinical practice.* Northvale: Jason Aronson.

Boszormenyi-Nagy, I., & Krasner, B. R. (1986). *Between give & take: A clinical guide to contextual therapy.* New York: Brunner/Mazel.

Boszormenyi-Nagy, I., & Spark, G. (1984). *Invisible loyalties.* New York: Brunner/Mazel.

Braverman, S. (1997). The use of genograms in supervision. In T. Todd & C. Storm

(Eds.), *The complete systemic supervisor: Context, philosophy, and pragmatics* (pp. 156–172). Boston: Allyn and Bacon.

Broderbund Software, Inc. (1998). Family Tree Maker, Deluxe edition III (Computer software). Novato, CA: Authors.

Burke, J. L., & Faber, P. (1997). A genogrid for couples. *Journal of Gay and Lesbian Social Services, 7*(1), 13–22.

Carter, B., & McGoldrick, M. (1999). *The expanded family life cycle: Individual, family and social perspectives.* In B. Carter & M. McGoldrick (Eds.), *The expanded family life cycle: Individual, family, and social perspectives* (3rd ed.) (pp. 1–26). Boston: Allyn and Bacon.

Congress, E. P. (1994). The use of culturagrams to assess and empower culturally diverse families. *Families in Society: The Journal of Contemporary Human Services*, 531–539.

Coupland, S. K., Serovich, J., & Glenn, J. E. (1995). Reliability in constructing genograms: A study among marriage and family therapy doctoral students. *Journal of Marital and Family Therapy, 21,* 51–263.

DeMaria, R., Weeks, G., & Hof, L. (1999). *Focused genograms: Intergenerational assessment of individuals, couples, and families.* Philadelphia, PA: Brunner/Mazel.

Fink, A. H., Kramer, L., Weaver, L. L., & Anderson, J. (1993). More on genograms: Modifications to a model. *Journal of Child and Adolescent Group Therapy, 3,* 203–206.

Frame, M. W. (2000). The spiritual genogram in family therapy. *Journal of Marital and Family Therapy, 26*(2), 211–216.

Friedman, H., Rohrbaugh, M., & Krakauer, S. (1988). The timeline genogram: Highlighting temporal aspects of family relationships. *Family Process, 27,* 293–304.

Friesen, P., & Manitt, J. (1991). Nursing the remarried family in a palliative care setting. *Journal of Palliative Care, 6*(4), 32–39.

Gerson, R., & Shellenberger, S. (1999a). The Genogram-Maker Plus for Windows and Macintosh (Computer software). Macon, GA: Humanware.

Gerson, R., & Shellenberger, S. (1999b). The AutoGenogram for Windows and Macintosh (Computer software). Macon, GA: Humanware.

Guerin, P., & Fogarty, T. (1972). Study your own family. In A. Ferber, M. Mendelsohn, & A. Napier (Eds.), *The book of family therapy* (pp. 445–467). New York: Science House.

Haas-Cunningham, S. M. (1994). *The genogram as a predictor of families at risk for physical illness* (Doctoral dissertation, Syracuse University, 1993). Dissertation Abstracts International, 54(9-b), 4590.

Hardy, K. V., & Laszloffy, T. A. (1995). The cultural genogram: Key to training culturally competent family therapists. *Journal of Marital and Family Therapy, 21,* 227–237.

Hargrave, T. D. (1994). *Families & forgiveness: Healing wounds in the intergenerational family.* New York: Burnner/Mazel.

Hof L., & Berman, E. (1986). The sexual genogram. *Journal of Marital and Family Therapy, 12*(1), 39–47.

Ingersoll-Dayton, B., & Arndt, B. (1990). Uses of the genogram with the elderly and their families. *Journal of Gerontological Social Work, 15*(1–2), 105–120.

Kaslow, F. (1995). *Projective Genogramming.* Sarasota, FL: Professional Resource Press.

Kaslow, F., & Friedman, J. (1977). Utilization of family photos and movies in family therapy. *Journal of Marriage and Family Counseling, 3,* 19–25.

Kerr, M. E., & Bowen, M. (1988). *Family evaluation: An approach based on Bowen theory*. New York: Norton.

Kuehl, B. P. (1995). The solution-oriented genogram: A collaborative approach. *Journal of Marital and Family Therapy, 21,* 239–250.

Kuehl, B. P. (1996). The use of genograms with solution-based and narrative therapies. *The Family Journal: Counseling and Therapy for Couples and Families, 4*(1), 5–11.

Kwiatkowska, H. Y. (1978). *Family therapy and evaluation through art*. Springfield, IL: Thomas.

Lewis, K. G. (1989). The use of color-coded genograms in family therapy. *Journal of Marital and Family Therapy, 15,* 169–176.

Marlin, E. (1989). *Genograms: The new tool for exploring the personality, career, and love patterns you inherit.* Chicago, IL: Contemporary Books, Inc.

McGoldrick, M. (1999). History, genograms, and the family life cycle: Freud in context. In B. Carter & M. McGoldrick (Eds.), *The expanded family life cycle: Individual, family, and social perspectives* (3rd ed.) (pp. 47–68). Boston: Allyn and Bacon.

McGoldrick, M., & Carter, B. (2001). Advances in coaching: Family therapy with one person. *Journal of Marital and Family Therapy, 27,* 281–300.

McGoldrick, M., & Gerson, R. (1985). *Genograms in family assessment*. New York: W. W. Norton & Company, Inc.

McGoldrick, M., Gerson, R., & Shellenberger, S. (1999). *Genograms: Assessment and intervention* (2nd ed.). NY: W. W. Norton & Company, Inc.

McMillen, J. C., & Groze, V. (1994). Using placement genograms in child welfare practice. *Child Welfare, 73,* 307–318.

Moon, S. M., Coleman, V. D., McCollum, E. E., Nelson, T. S., & Jensen-Scott, R. L. (1993). Using the genogram to facilitate career decisions: A case study. *Journal of Family Psychology, 4,* 45–56.

Nichols, M. P. & Schwartz, R. C. (2004). *Family therapy: Concepts and methods* (5th Ed.). Needham Heights, MA: Allyn & Bacon.

Nisbett, R. E., & Wilson, T. D. (1977). The halo effect: Evidence for unconscious alteration of judgments. *Journal of Personality and Social Psychology, 35,* 250–256.

Palladium Interactive, Inc. (1998). Ultimate Family Tree Deluxe (version 2.0) (Computer software). Spencer, IN: Authors.

Rita, E. S. & Adejanju, M. G. (1993). The genogram: Plotting the roots of academic success. *Family Therapy, 20/1,* 17–28.

Roberts, J. (1991). *AFTA diversity packet*. Unpublished materials.

Rogers, J. C. (1994). Can physicians use family genogram information to identify patients at risk of anxiety or depression? *Archives of Family Medicine, 3,* 1093–1098.

Rogers, J. C., & Holloway, R. (1990). Completion rate and reliability of the self-administered genogram (SAGE). *Family Practice, 7,* 149–151.

Rogers, J. C., & Rohrbaugh, M. (1991). The SAGE-PAGE trial: Do family genograms make a difference? *Journal of the American Board of Family Practice, 4,* 319–326.

Satir, V. (1967). *Conjoint family therapy*. Palo Alto, CA: Science & Behavior Books.

Schnarch, D. (1997). *Passionate marriage*. New York: Norton.

Stanton, M. D. (1992). The time line and the "Why now?" question: A technique and rationale for therapy, training, organizational consultation and research. *Journal of Marital and Family Therapy, 18,* 331–343.

Timm, T. M., & Blow, A. J. (1999). Self-of-the-therapist work: A balance between remov-ing restraints and identifying resources. *Contemporary Family Therapy, 21,* 331–351.

Titelman, P. (1992). The therapist's own family. In P. Titelman (Ed.) *The therapist's own family: Toward the differentiation of self* (pp. 3–42). Northvale: Jason Aronson.

Tomm, D. (1984). One perspective on the Milan systemic approach: Part II. Description of session format, theory and practice. *Journal of Marital and Family Therapy, 10,* 253–271.

Tomm, K. (1987). Interventive interviewing: I. Strategizing as a fourth guideline for the therapist. *Family Process, 26,* 3–13.

Wachtel, E. F. (1982). The family psyche over three generations: The genogram revisited. *Journal of Marital and Family Therapy, 8,* 334–343.

Watts-Jones, D. (1998). Towards an African-American genogram. *Family Process, 36,* 373–383.

White, M. B., & Tyson-Rawson, K. J. (1995). Assessing the dynamics of gender in couples and families: The gendergram. *Family Relations, 44,* 253–260.

WonderWare, Inc. (1998). Relativity (Computer software). Silver Spring, MD: Author.

APPENDIX A

Genogram Interview Questions

General (Adapted from McGoldrick, Gerson, & Shellenberger, 1999)

- Who lives in the household?
- How is each person related?
- Where do other family members live?
- How long have the two of you been together?
- Do you have any children in this relationship? With previous relationships?
- How many times have you been married?
- How many siblings do you have? Where are you in the birth order?

Presenting Problem (Adapted from McGoldrick et al., 1999)

- Which family members know about the problem?
- How does each view it? And how has each of them responded?
- Has anyone in the family ever had similar problems?
- What solutions were attempted by whom in those situations?
- When did the problem begin? Who noticed it first? Who is most concerned about the problem? Who the least?
- Were family relationships different before the problem began? What other problems existed?
- Does the family see the problem as having changed? In what ways? For better or worse?
- What will happen in the family if the problem continues? If is goes away?
- What does the future look like? What changes do family members imagine are possible in the future?

Current Family Situation (Adapted from McGoldrick et al., 1999)

- What has been happening recently in your family?
- Have there been any recent changes in the family (e.g., people coming or leaving, illnesses, job problems)?

Specific People (Adapted from McGoldrick et al., 1999)

- Let's begin with your mother's family. Your mother was which one of how many children?
- What is her name?
- When and where was she born?
- Is she alive? If not, when did she die? What was the cause of her death?
- If alive, where is she now?
- What does she do?
- Is she retired? When did this happen?
- When and how did your mother meet your father? Did they marry? If so, when?

- Had she been married before? If so, when? Did she have children by that marriage? Did they separate or divorce or did the spouse die? If so, when was that? What was the cause?
- What is the name of (your brother, sister, aunt, etc.)?
- How old are they?
- What is their highest level of education? If currently in school, what grade or year in college, major? Etc.
- Are they currently employed? If so, in what profession?
- What are their current religious practices?
- Where do they currently live?

Relationships (Adapted from McGoldrick et al., 1999)

- Are there any family members who do not speak to each other or who have ever had a period of not speaking? Are there any who were/are in serious conflict?
- Are there any family members who are extremely close?
- Who helps out when help is needed? In whom do family members confide?
- All couples have some sort of marital difficulties. What sorts of problems and conflicts have you encountered? What about your parents' and siblings' marriages?
- How do you each get along with each child? Have any family members had particular problems dealing with their children?

Informal Kinships (Adapted from McGoldrick et al., 1999)

- To whom could you turn if in need of financial, emotional, physical, and spiritual help?
- What roles have outside people played in your family?
- What is your relationship to your community?
- Who outside the family has been important in your life?
- Did you ever have a nanny or caretaker or babysitter to whom you felt attached? What become of her or him?
- Has anyone else ever lived with your family? When? Where are they now?
- What has been your family's experience with doctors and other helping professionals or agencies?

Roles (Adapted from McGoldrick et al., 1999)

- Has any family member been focused on as the caretaker? The problematic one? The "sick" one? The "bad" one? The "mad" one?
- Who is the family is seen as the strong one? The weak one? The dominant one? The submissive one?
- Who in the family is seen as the successful one? The failure?
- Who is seen as warm? As cold? As caring? As distant?

Secrets (Adapted from DeMaria, Weeks, & Hof, 1999)

- What were the taboo subjects in your family of origin?
- How did you know that such subjects were taboo? Did a family member explicitly

tell you or did you simply know implicitly? What happened if anyone tried to raise taboo subjects?
- What were the "rules" regarding privacy in your family? How have they influenced you and your family?
- Did a family member ever make a secret with you that excluded other family members? What was this experience like for you? What was the secret?
- Did you ever make a secret with a family member that excluded other family members? What was this experience like for you? What was the secret?
- Did your family keep secrets from extended family? How did these affect relationships?
- Did your family keep secrets from the outside world? What was that experience like for you?
- How do you think your family's cultural and religious backgrounds affected their beliefs regarding secret keeping?
- Were there secrets that men kept or secrets that women kept?
- Were there secrets in your family that were eventually disclosed? How did relationships shift? What was the impact on individual functioning and identity?

Marital Patterns, Divorce, and Extramarital Affairs (Adapted from DeMaria et al., 1999)

- What are the patterns of marriage and divorce in the famiy system? f there are divorces, what are the known circumstances about the divorces?
- What types of marriages are there in the family system? Have family members participated in premarital counseling or marital therapy?
- What are the patterns of sexual infidelity in the family system? Are there reconciliations? Were any children born of these liaisons? Are there secrets about infidelity?
- What kinds of stresses have resulted for the family if there has been a divorce or affair?
- How have parents worked out custody and visitation?

Spiritual (Adapted from Frame, 2000)

- When you were growing up, what role, if any, did religion/spirituality play in your life? What role does it play now?
- What specific religious/spiritual beliefs do you consider most important for you now? How are those beliefs a source of connection or conflict between you and other family members?
- What religious/spiritual rituals did you participate in as a child or adolescent? How important were they in your family of origin? Which ones do you still engage in? Which ones have you let go? What new rituals have you adopted as an adult? How do these rituals connect to your religious/spiritual belief system?
- What did/does your religious/spiritual tradition say about gender? About ethnicity? About sexual orientation? How have these beliefs affected you and your extended family?
- Was it acceptable for family members to seek a different spiritual or religious path? Who in the family would be supportive? Who would not be supportive and why?

- How do you think religion/spirituality has been a source of strength and coping for your family?
- How do you think it has interfered in family relationships?
- What patterns of behavior and relationship resulting from religion/spirituality emerge for you as you study your genogram? How are you currently maintaining or diverting from those patterns?
- How does your religious/spiritual history connect with your current distress or with the problem you presented for therapy? What new insights or solutions may occur to you based on the discoveries made through the genogram?

Critical Life Events (Adapted from McGoldrick et al., 1999)

- How did other family members react when a particular family member was born? Who attended the christening ceremony or bris? Who was named after whom and who "should have been"?
- How did the family react when a particular family member died? Who took it the hardest? The easiest? Who attended the funeral? What was the effect when the will was read? Who wasn't there? Who "should have been"?
- When and why did the family migrate to this country? How did they cope with the multiple losses of migration? How many generations of the family have lived in the US? What was the context into which they came and how did they fit into it? How did the initial generations manage the adaptation to these new circumstances? How did they survive? Which members of the immigrant generation learned the language?
- What gender constraints have the women and men in the family experienced?
- What cultural prejudices have family members experienced?

Serious Problems (Adapted from McGoldrick et al., 1999)

- Has anyone in the family had a serious medical or psychological problem? Been depressed? Had anxieties? Fears? Lost control? Has there been physical or sexual abuse?
- Are there any other problems that worry you? When did that problem begin? Did you seek help for it? If so, when? What happened? What is the status of that problem now?

Work (Adapted from McGoldrick et al., 1999)

- Have there been any recent job changes? Unemployment? Do you like your job? Who else works in your family? Do they like their work?

Finances (Adapted from McGoldrick et al., 1999)

- How much income does each member generate? Does this create any imbalance in family relationships? How does the economic situation compare with that of your relatives?
- Is there any expected inheritance? Are there family members who are expected to need financial help or caretaking at some time?

- Are there any extraordinary expenses? Outstanding debts? What is the level of credit card debt?
- Who controls the money? How are spending decisions made? Are these patterns different from the ways money was handled in the families of origin?

Drugs and Alcohol (Adapted from McGoldrick et al., 1999 and DeMaria et al., 1999)

- Do any family members use medication? What kind and for what? Who prescribed it? What is the family's relationship with that physician?
- Do you think any members drink too much or have a drug problem? Has anyone else ever thought so? What drugs? When? What has the family attempted to do about it? Has anyone ever participated in Alcoholics Anonymous (AA) or Narcotics Anonymous (NA)?
- How does the person's behavior change under the influence of the drug? How does the behavior of others change when a member is drug involved?
- What kinds of other addictions exist in the family (e.g., gambling, shopping, food, etc.)?

Trouble with the Law (Adapted from McGoldrick et al., 1999)

- Have any family members ever been arrested? For what? When? What was the result? What is that person's legal status now?
- Has anyone ever lost his or her driver's license?

Physical or Sexual Abuse (Adapted from McGoldrick et al., 1999)

- Have you ever felt intimidated in your family? Have you or others ever been hit? Has anyone in your family ever been threatened with being hit? Have you ever threatened anyone else in your family or hit them?
- Have you or any other family members ever been sexually molested or touched inappropriately by a member of your family or someone outside your family? By whom?

Gay and Lesbian (Adapted from McGoldrick et al., 1999)

- Who was the first person you told about your sexual orientation?
- To whom on your genogram are you out?
- To whom would you most like to come out?
- Who would be especially easy or difficult to come out to?

Solution Based/Narrative (Adapted from Kuehl, 1996)

- How have you prevented the problem from completely taking over your life?
- How else can you convince the problem it is not welcome?
- How did you stop the (presenting behavior)?
- How did those around you respond to this change?
- What else is different?

- Two-weeks ago, did you think you would be reporting this kind of success?
- As these changes continue, how different do you think things will be in another two weeks?
- What does this tell you about yourself?
- What does this tell those around you about yourself?
- What does this tell you about each of them?
- What will be different for you when things improve?
- What will be different for your children and grandchildren?
- How will you contribute to these changes?
- What is helping your family improve each generation?
- What are you doing to add to this pattern?
- As these changes continue, how will you (your children) benefit one week (month, year, generation) from now?

Sexual Genogram (Hof & Berman, 1986)

- What are the overt/covert messages in this family regarding sexuality/intimacy?
- What are the overt/covert messages in this family regarding masculinity/femininity?
- Who said/did what? Who was conspicuously silent/absent in the area of sexuality/intimacy?
- Who was the most open sexually? Intimately? In what ways?
- How was sexuality/intimacy encouraged? Discouraged? Controlled? Within a generation? Between generations?
- What questions have you had regarding sexuality/intimacy in your "family tree" that you have been reluctant to ask? Who might have the answers? How could you discover the answers?
- What were the "secrets" in your family regarding sexuality/intimacy (e.g., incest, unwanted pregnancies, extramarital affairs, etc.)?
- What do the other "players on the stage" have to say regarding the above questions? How did these issues, events, and experiences impact upon him/her? Within a generation? Between generations? With whom have you talked about this? With whom would you like to talk about this? How could you do it?
- How does your partner perceive your family tree/genogram regarding the aforementioned issues? How do you perceive his/hers?
- How would you change this genogram (including who and what) to meet what you wish would have occurred regarding messages and experiences of sexuality/intimacy?

Cultural Genogram (Adapted from Hardy & Laszloffy, 1995)

- What were the migration patterns of the group?
- If other than Native American, under what conditions did your family (or their descendants) enter the United States (immigrant, political refugee, slave, etc.)?
- What were/are the group's experiences with oppression? What were/are the markers of oppression?
- What issues divide members within the same group? What are the sources of intragroup conflict?

- Describe the relationship between the group's identity and your national ancestry (if the group is defined in terms of nationality, please skip this question).
- What significance does race, skin color, and hair play within the group?
- What is/are the dominant religions(s) of the group? What role does religion and spirituality play in the everyday lives of members of the group?
- What role does regionality and geography play in the group?
- How are gender roles defined within the group? How is sexual orientation regarded?
- What prejudices or stereotypes does this group have about itself? Do other groups have about this group? Does this group have about other groups?
- What role (if any) do names play in the group? Are there rules, mores, or rituals governing the assignment of names?
- How is social class defined in the group?
- What occupational roles are valued and devalued by the group?
- What is the relationship between age and the values of the group?
- How is family defined in the group?
- How does this group view outsiders in general and mental health professionals specifically?
- How have the organizing principles of this group shaped your family and its members? What effect have they had on you"?
- What are the ways in which pride/shame issues of each group are manifested in your family system?
- If more than one group comprises your culture of origin, how were the differences negotiated in your family? What were the intergenerational consequences? How has this impacted you personally?

Culturagram – recent immigration (Adapted from Congress, 1994)

- What brought you to the United States? Why did you decide to leave (country of origin)?
- How long have you lived in the United States? In this community?
- Do you have a visa? A green card?
- How old were you when you came to the United States?
- What language do you speak at home? In the community?
- What clubs/groups do you belong to?
- When you are sick what do you do? Where and to whom do you turn for help?
- What kinds of family parties do you have? What holidays do you celebrate? How do you celebrate?
- What particular events have been stressful for your family?
- Do you believe everyone should have a high school/college education?
- What role do you think women should play in the family? Men? Children?

Gendergram (Adapted from White & Tyson-Rawson, 1995)

- What are your significant memories of (key person)?
- How did this person influence how you felt about yourself as a female or male? What did you learn about being a man or woman from this person?
- What did you learn from this person about how women/men interacted with other

women/men? What did you learn from this person about how women/men interacted with men/women?

- As an adult looking back on these relationships, in what ways have these persons had a lasting influence on how you view yourself as a woman or man?
- How did changes in your physical appearance, whether due to maturation, accidents, or illness, influence how you felt about yourself as a man or woman?
- What did you learn about your sexuality during this time period? How did you learn it?
- In what ways did what you learn impact your definition of yourself as a woman or man?
- What spiritual/religious influences were important to you at this time and how do you think they have informed your feelings about yourself as a man or woman?
- Describe the emotional climate of your family of origin.
- How was affection expressed? Between women? Between men? Between women and men? Between adults/parents and children?
- How was conflict handled?
- Did men and women express the same emotions differently?
- How secure did you feel when you were at home?
- How was conformity to your family's gender norms rewarded? How was nonconformity punished?
- What did men/women do in your family? At home? At work? In the community? For recreation? As caregivers? As disciplinarians? In relationships with others?
- What were your family's criteria for a successful man? A successful woman?
- What were your peer group's gender norms or rules and how was conformity to them rewarded? How was nonconformity punished?
- Were there any conflicts between the gender norms or rules of your family and those of your peer group? If so, how did you handle them?
- What did you learn at school/work about the roles of men and women?
- During your childhood, how would you have described the ideal female? The ideal male?
- Do you remember any things from television or other media that influenced your ideas about being a man or woman?
- What gender-related roles do you notice yourself playing at this stage of your life?
- What patterns do you see in gender issues at this stage of your life?
- Are there repetitive themes in your relationships?
- Which of these roles, patterns, and themes do you want to enhance and continue?
- Which of these roles, patterns, and themes do you want to work to change?

Career/Academic Genogram (Adapted from Moon et al., 1993; Rita & Adejanju, 1993)

- What are the multi-generational themes concerning education? Careers? Work values? Work ethics? Gender roles? The importance of money?
- What were the family rules about the "acceptable" range of employment possibilities? Geographic location?
- What were the overt/covert messages in your family regarding education and academic success?

- Who was the most encouraging/discouraging in terms of academic striving and in what ways?
- How was academic achievement encouraged? Discouraged? Controlled? Within a generation? Between generations?
- What questions have you been reluctant to ask regarding academic success in your family tree? Who might have the answers? How would you discover those answers?
- What were the "rules," "secrets," "myths" in your family regarding success (e.g., dangers, cut-off from family)?
- What do the other "players on stage" have to say regarding these questions? How did these issues, events, and experiences impact upon you? Within a generation? Between generations? With whom have you talked about this? With whom would you like to talk about this? How would you do it?
- How would you change this genogram (including who and what) to meet your wishes regarding academic striving and success?
- How did decisions get made about education? Career?
- Has anyone in the family ever broken out of the career that was dictated to them?
- Are people allowed to change careers?
- What has been the influence of larger social changes or historical events on family members' career choices?
- Are there emotionally charges issues in the family related to loyalty issues? Aborted dreams? Achievement expectations?
- What impact has culture or ethnicity played in career decision making?
- What were the messages about leisure time? How many roles were family members expected to carry?

Socioeconomic Status (Adapted from Roberts, 1991)

- What did your parents teach you about social class? With what class did your parents identify themselves?
- How did this fit or not fit with what they modeled for you by their behavior, where they lived, who they associated with, and so forth?
- What opportunities do you think your parents felt they had to shift social class? Would your parents agree or disagree with your perception?
- How important was social class to them and to your siblings in the neighborhood in which you grew up?
- Do you think your family was more or less concerned about social class than other families?
- How might things have been different in your family if different economic possibilities had been available?
- Do different members of your family belong to different social classes? Have members of your family changed class (up or down) due to marriage, making or losing money, illness, or bad luck?
- When you were growing up, what messages did peers pass on about social class?
- What ideas about social class do you want to pass on to the next generation? How are these the same or different from what your parents taught you?
- What meanings do you think people ascribe to social class in our society?

- Where do you see yourself in relationship to these kinds of assumptions?
- Think back to when you first visited, lived in, worked in a neighborhood of a different social class. How did you think about social class differently/act differently, after that?

APPENDIX 2: Family Patterns to Consider (Adapted from Marlin, 1989)

Affairs
Alcohol Abuse
Anxieties
Attitudes
Behavior
Birth Order
Career Choices
Catastrophes
Coincidences
Conflicts
Deaths
Dependency
Depression
Disease
Divorce
Drugs
Eating Disorders
Empathy
Entertainment
Escapes
Fears
Finances
Fun
Functioning
Illness
Incest
Inconsistencies
Indecision
In-law Trouble
Insensitivity
Intermarriage
Intimacy
Intrigue
Jail
Jealousy
Legal problems

Marriages
Martyrs
Mediators
Medical history
Migration
Military Service
Money
Mysteries
Myths
Nicknames
Occupations
Parent-child Relationships
Perfectionism
Politics
Power
Pressure
Public service
Religion
Remarriage
Rescuing
Resilience
Roles
Secrets
Separations
Sickness
Single Parents
Suicide
Temperaments
Tension
Traditions
Tragedy
Trauma
Triangles
Trouble
Violence
Work

10

Assessment of Parenting Styles and Behavior

C. Everett Bailey

Summary
This article provides an overview of the measurements found in the scholarly literature that can be uses to assess parenting styles and behaviors. It addresses the historical development of parenting measures as major assumptions and concepts. It reviews instruments which can be used to assess parental support, control, structure,
and parenting styles. In addition, it presents questions that clinicians can use to assess
parent's supportive behavior, control, and the structure they provide. The medium of
family play therapy is introduced, which allows therapists to observe parent-child
interaction and dynamics. The chapter concludes with a case example that illustrates
the use of family therapy with a family and how it can aid therapists in assessing
parenting styles and behaviors.

In his seminal article outlining the determinants of parenting, Belsky (1984) describes
children's healthy socioemotional and cognitive development as being promoted by attentive, warm, stimulating, responsive, and nonrestrictive caregiving. Parents that are
sensitively attuned to children's capabilities and developmental tasks promote children's
emotional security, behavioral independence, social competence, and intellectual achievement. Sensitive parents are psychologically healthy adults who are able to accurately
appraise the perspective of others, empathize with others, and adopt a nurturant orientation. Parents who have an internal locus of control, high levels of interpersonal trust, and
an active coping style exhibit more warmth, acceptance, helpfulness, and low levels of
disapproval when interacting with their children. Whereas, depressed mothers are more
disruptive, hostile, and rejecting in their interaction, which undermines children's functioning.

Several family scholars have documented the determinants of child outcomes. The
variables affecting child outcomes range from the child's individual factors (i.e., biological, genetic, psychological), family and other social support (i.e., parents marriage, siblings, extended family, peers) and the larger society (i.e., government, financial, community) (Belsky, 1984; Cummings, Davies, & Campbell, 2000). However, there is over-

whelming evidence to suggest that parenting "occupies a central role in any understanding of the normal and abnormal development of children" (Cummings et al., 2000, p. 157).

Parenting behaviors have a significant impact on children and their development. The effects of parenting styles and behavior on children's social competence, emotional development, academic performance, behavioral compliance, and prosocial behavior are well documented (Bornstein, 1995; Maccoby & Martin, 1983; Rollins & Thomas, 1979). As a result there is an abundance of research on how to intervene with parents. A key aspect of such research on understanding parental behaviors and styles and their impact on child functioning, is assessing the parent behaviors and styles. A key to effectively understand and intervene with parents is having scientifically sound instruments to assess parenting behavior. The purpose of this chapter is to provide an overview of measurements currently found in the scholarly literature and to identify ways to clinically assess parenting styles and behavior.

Historical Development of Parenting Measures

In 1899, Charles Sears developed one of the first surveys on parenthood. He developed an instrument to assess adults' attitudes toward the punishment of children (Holden, 2001). The prevailing view at the time by most scholars was that parental attitudes determined parental behavior, which in turn affected child outcomes. As a result most of the early parenting instruments were designed to measure parental attitudes (Holden, 2001). It was not until the 1930s that researchers developed a variety of measures to assess a wide range of parenting variables. Starting in the 1930s, scholars also recognized the importance of gathering data on children's perceptions of their parents and began to develop measures of how children viewed parental attitudes, beliefs, and behavior. In all, 204 parenthood instruments were developed from the time period of 1936 to 1974. The majority of these instruments focused on parental social cognition and behavior. The typical survey at this time asked parents to state whether they agreed or disagreed with a list of statements about children. Instruments assessed a variety of parental attitudes toward discipline, overprotection, use of fear, sex roles, independence, etc. Other instruments developed during this time period, measured the parent-child relationships. These measures were designed to assess parent-child interactions, the quality of the parent-child relationship, the level of parent involvement with the child, and parent-child decision-making (Holden, 2001). Most of these instruments utilized the method of observations as opposed to the self-report measures used to collect data about parental attitudes. Instruments were also developed to examine the overall quality of the home environment and the parents' marital relations. As the development of measurements has improved only 18 of the 204 instruments developed during this time period are still used today (Holden, 2001).

There are several trends that characterize the parenting instruments that have been developed since 1974. As our understanding of the complexities of parenting has evolved, our instruments have become more sophisticated and measured a broader number of variables. Dix and Gershoff (2001) describe five trends in measuring parenting over the last three decades. The first trend is the importance of assessing parent's situation specific and moment-to-moment cognitions. The second trend is the significance of measuring the context in which parent-child interaction takes place. The third trend is to acknowledge the bi-directional aspect of the parent-child relationship. The fourth trend is recognizing the importance of motivation and emotions in the parenting process. Finally, the fifth trend is viewing the family as a system and the importance of looking at family factors outside the mother-child relationship, such as marital and sibling relationships.

Since 1975, 128 parenting instruments have been developed or used. They cover six general areas:

(1) Parental social cognition and behavior
(2) Parent-child relationships
(3) Home environment
(4) Parental cooperation/transition to parenthood,
(5) Parental self-perceptions, and
(6) Child self-perceptions

The largest category of instruments assesses parental behavior as reported by both parents and children. Instruments measure such parental behaviors as punishment, strictness, permissiveness, acceptance, involvement, responsiveness, restrictiveness, intrusiveness, supervision, and monitoring. Instruments that measure relationship quality most often assess the parent-child attachment relationship as well as support, intimacy, warmth vs. rejection, parental involvement and overall relationship quality. One of the most notable trends in the assessment of parent-child relationships is a shift from using observational methods to reliance on children's reports. This is largely a result of the growing acceptance of the notion that the child's perceptions of parental actions may largely account for their impact on child outcomes. Dix and Gershoff (2001) report that compared to the 1980s twice as many instruments on the quality of the parent-child relationship were developed during the 1990s and that two-thirds of them relied on reports from children. Even with this emphasis on child reports, nine new observational instruments were developed to measure the parent-child relationship in the last decade. Most of them were designed to assess specific dimensions of interaction including: parent-child communication, parental responsiveness, and the overall quality of interaction.

Major Assumptions and Concepts

Parenting assessment instruments focus on a variety of different parenting variables including parental attitudes, child-rearing practices, behavioral intentions, parents' beliefs, attributions, perceptions, parent-child interactions, quality of parent-child relationship, parental involvement, interparent cooperation, parental self-perceptions (i.e., self-esteem, satisfaction, anxiety, stress, anger), and child self-perceptions (Dix & Gershoff, 2001). For the purposes of this chapter, the focus will be on those instruments that measure parental behavior and parenting style.

The parenting research literature identifies parental support and control as being two parental behaviors that significantly impact child outcomes (Maccoby & Martin, 1983; Rollins & Thomas, 1979). According to the parenting literature, three parenting behaviors further define the support variable: nurturance, sensitivity to the child's input, and a nonrestrictive attitude. Research on parenting behavior has found that all of these dimensions are positively correlated with children's competence, self-reliance, and compliance

(Slater & Power, 1987). Nurturance relates to the emotional relationship the parent has with the child and the parent's ability to be warm, encouraging, and affectionate with the child. Sensitivity to the child's input refers to the parent's openness to the child's thoughts, feelings, and desires. It reflects the parent's flexibility and willingness to consider what the child wants when making a decision. A nonsrestrictive attitude is the parent's willingness to allow the child to take risks, be expressive, to have different experiences, and perhaps to experience failure. Such an attitude enables the child to make choices and learn from them in a supportive, encouraging environment so that the negative consequences are not too overwhelming.

The parenting research also divides parental control into three dimensions: type of control strategy, amount of control, and maturity demands. These variables have been shown to consistently correlate with children's adjustment (Slater & Power, 1987). The types of parental control range from being rigid and using coercive methods, which are negatively related to children's outcomes, to being flexible and using inductive methods, which are positively related. The amount of control seems to have a curvilinear relationship with children's adjustment. Research has shown that both low amounts (permissiveness) and high amounts (authoritarian) of parental control are related to children's maladjustment. The effect of the amount of parental control on children's adjustment is related to the amount of parental support, involvement, and acceptance (authoritative) (Slater & Power, 1987). Maturity demands is the amount of expectations that parents have for children depending on their stage of development. The appropriate amount of demands on children is related to children's compliance, self-efficacy, and self-confidence (Slater & Power, 1987).

A third parenting construct that does not fit into the categories of parental support and control is parental structure. This construct can also be broken down further into three dimensions: parental involvement, parental consistency, and parental organization. Parental involvement is the degree that parents are actively a part of their children's lives. Parental consistency or predictability helps children to trust their world and their environment. Parental organization is the parent's ability to bring order to the child's world and is reported to predict child adjustment. Development research has shown that providing structure for children is critical for their optimal development. "Predictable, involved parents who create a relatively organized environment for their children may be providing needed external structure until the children are developmentally prepared to internally provide structure themselves" (Slater & Power, p. 200, 1987).

Parenting Measures

The Handbook of Family Measurement Techniques (Touliatos, Perlmutter, & Straus, 2001) catalogues the numerous parenting instruments identified in the parenting literature. Details about these instruments and their availability can be found in the Handbook itself. However, for the purposes of this paper, the instruments related to measuring parenting behavior and parenting styles are listed below with a reference and a brief description of the variables measured by the instrument. Based on the parenting variables identified in the literature, those instruments that assess parenting dimensions related to parental support (i.e., nurturance, sensitivity to child's input, nonrestrictive attitude), parental control (i.e., type of control, amount of control, maturity demands) and parental structure (i.e., parental involvement, consistency, organization) will be identified.

Instruments

Parent Behavior Checklist (Platz, Pupp, & Fox, 1994)

The PBC assesses nurturing, type of parental control, and parents' maturity demands on children. It is a 100-item survey which measures parents' self-report on three subscales 1) expectations, 2) discipline, and 3) nurturing. The 50-item expectations scale measures parents' expectations of their children's development and ability to meet developmental milestones. The 30-item discipline scale assesses parents' responses to children's misbehavior. The nurturing subscale includes 20 items that assess parent's behavior that promote children's psychological growth. The scale is reported has having good reliability and validity with alphas of .97, .91, and .82 and test-retest correlations of .98, .87, and .81.

The Parenting Style Questionnaire (Bowers, Smith, & Binney, 1994)

The PSQ measures nurturance, parents' nonrestrictive attitude, type of parental control, and the amount of parental control. It is a 30-item questionnaire combined with a Q-sort procedure. The instrument measures children's perception of their parent's parenting style. It has five subscales which ask children to report their parents' warmth, punitiveness, overprotection, accurate monitoring, and neglect. Test-retest reliability ranges from .45 to .91 and alphas range from .58 to .87.

Parental Support Inventory (Barber & Thomas, 1986)

The PSI is designed to assess the amount of support children and adolescents experience from their parents. It is a 20-item questionnaire which asks children and adolescents about the amount of general support, physical affection, companionship, and sustained contact they receive from their mother and father. Chronbach's alpha is reported to range from .85 to .90 for fathers, and .79 to .87 for mothers.

Parent-Child Relations and Parental Monitoring (Fuligni & Eccles, 1993)

The PCRPM assesses parents' nonrestrictive attitude, and amount of parental control. It is an 11-item scale which asks preteens and young adolescents to report their perceptions of parental strictness, the degree parents involve them in decision-making, and parental monitoring of activities outside the home. The authors report alphas for the subscales to be .62, .60, and .69.

Weinberger Parenting Inventory (Parent and Child version) (Feldman & Weinberger, 1994)

The WPC is a 49-item questionnaire that assesses parent's nonrestrictive attitude, type of parental control, and parental consistency. It measures children's, adolescent's and parent's perceptions of the parents' behavior including subscales on parental permissiveness, harshness, inconsistency, child-centeredness, and psychological intrusiveness. All subscales have alphas above .70.

Alabama Parenting Questionnaire (Frick, 1998)

The APQ is a 42-item questionnaire that measures type of parental control, amount of parental control, and parental involvement. It assesses children and parents' perception of parenting strategies. It includes six subscales: dimensions of involvement, positive parenting, monitoring/supervision, consistency, and discipline practices. Alphas for each of the subscales range from .45 to .93.

Parenting Practices Scale (Strayhorn & Weidman, 1988)

The PPS is a 34-item survey used to assess type of parental control, amount of parental control, and parent's maturity demands on children. The questionnaire is administered to parents who report their responses and practices regarding their preschool children's behavior to assess if the parents have age-appropriate expectations. In addition, items assess parents ability to identify positive behavior in their child, enforce commands, avoid ineffective discipline strategies, and be consistent in meeting the child's needs. Alpha for the scale was .78 with a test-retest correlation of .79.

Parenting Styles

Baumrind (1967) developed the notion of parenting styles based on the construct of parental control and parental support. Baumrind identified three different parenting styles along these dimensions. Authoritative parenting style is high in control and high in support. Authoritative parents balance control with warmth. They establish clear explicit expectations and limits regarding their children's behavior. At the same time they have fair realistic maturity demands and are responsive to their children's feelings and needs. When disciplining their children authoritative parents offer choices and use reasoning and persuasion. They have a "give and take" philosophy that respects the child's independence and autonomy. They are also flexible and seek to establish a "goodness of fit" with the child's personality and developmental needs. Authoritarian parenting style is high in control and low in support. Parents who exhibit this parenting style use physical, emotional, and psychological means to coerce their child to comply. They frequently spank, yell, criticize, or threaten in order to force their child to behave. Psychologically they may show little interest in what the child is saying or invalidate what the child is saying. Authoritarian parents may treat the child in a condescending or patronizing way often demeaning the child by putting him/her down. They also use guilt induction or love withdrawal as means to control the child. Permissive parenting style is low in control and high in support. Permissive parents believe children will flourish in development if allowed to explore life with few parental demands or restrictions. They avoid using authority and set few limits.

Assessment of Parenting Styles

Parenting Styles and Dimensions Questionnaire (Robinson, Mandleco, Olsen, & Hart, 1995)

The PSDQ is a 62-item self-report questionnaire developed to measure parenting styles (i.e., authoritative, authoritarian, and permissive). The scale consist of subscales on warmth and involvement, reasoning/induction, democratic participation, good-natured/easygoing, verbal hostility, corporal punishment, directiveness, lack of follow-through, ignoring misbehavior, and confidence. Alphas for the three parenting styles were .91 (authoritative), .86 (authoritarian), and .75 (permissive).

Parenting Style and Parental Involvement (Paulson & Sputa, 1996)

The PSPI is a 37-item self-report questionnaire. Both adolescents and parents report on parental demandingness, responsiveness, and parental involvement. Adolescents can complete the survey for both their mother and father. Alphas for the subscales range from .68 to .86.

Methodological Issues

In their review of parenting measures and research, Holden (2001) and Dix and Gershoff (2001) both express several methodological concerns. The first is an over reliance on self-report measures. About 90% of the parenting instruments are based on parent or child self-reports (Dix & Gershoff, 2001). Self-report can be a legitimate method of collecting data especially when researchers are trying to assess parent's or children's perceptions, beliefs, and attributions. However, there are many research questions related to actual parental behavior and parent-child interactions where observational methods are preferred and self-reports would be less than adequate. Some research shows very modest relations between self-report and observed behavior. Furthermore, self-reports rely on the individual's memory to recall the occurrence and frequency of certain behaviors in the past. And as is often the case, people recall and report information selectively. So although parents may actually believe that they behave in a certain way, in fact their perception may be quite different from their actual behavior. As a result there is a need to develop more observational parenting measures since only 10% or 16 instruments rely on observation.

Reliability and Validity

Another concern is the lack of reliability and validity reported for most of the parenting instruments. Holden (2001) reports that only 8% of the parenting surveys reported both test-retest reliability and internal consistency. In addition, no reliability data were provided for over a third of the instruments. For those surveys that did report reliability data only a few attained a high level of reliability (i.e., test-retest correlations or alpha coeffecients above .90) with many of them reporting marginal acceptable levels (.60 to

.70). With regard to validity, only 25% of the surveys are supported with validity data (Holden, 2001). The major limitation concerns the lack of research that shows the relationship between self-report data and actual behavior.

Limitations of Samples, Culture, Gender

In most cases, research using the various parenting assessments has failed to report information about the samples used to collect the data. With the increased realization of the influence that culture and gender has on parenting practices, it is important to assess the appropriateness of utilizing parenting instruments with different cultures and socioeconomic groups. In addition, continued reliance on data collected from mothers, rather than fathers, creates a bias in our understanding of the parenting process. It will be important to evaluate the effectiveness of using specific parenting instruments, designed by and tested on white, middle-class samples, with families from other cultures and backgrounds.

Need of Multiple Methods of Data Collection

One of the main critiques of the parenting assessment methods is that they rely primarily on self-report, single-informant measures. As a result what we know about parenting is based more on parental perceptions of what they think is happening more than what is actually happening. The main recommendation is that researchers develop and utilize multiple and diverse methods of measuring the same construct in order to avoid the limitations of relying on just one method.

Clinical Assessments

To help clinicians assess parental behaviors, some therapists have developed guidelines to use in a clinical interview. The following questions have been adapted to assess parental behaviors from Resnikoff (1981):

(1) What is the outward appearance of the family? How far apart do children sit from their parents? Who sits next to whom? Who stays closest to the therapist?
(2) What is the cognitive functioning in the family? Are two messages being communicated between parents and children when only one message is intended? Who gives and who receives various communications?
(3) What repetitive, nonproductive sequences do you notice?
(4) What is the basic feeling state between parents and children, and who carries it?
(5) What parental roles reinforce children's resistance, and what are the most prevalent parental defenses?
(6) What subsystems are operative in this family?
(7) Who carries the power in the family?
(8) How are parents and children differentiated from each other, and what are the subgroup boundaries?
(9) Are the parents aware of which part of the life cycle the family is experiencing, and are the parents problem-solving methods appropriate to that state of the life cycle?

Bagarozzi (1986) offers the following guidelines in clinically assessing parenting behavior.

Structural Considerations

(1) To what degree have parents been able to develop a parental coalition enabling them to set goals, solve problems, negotiate conflicts, handle crises, and complete individual and family developmental tasks?

(2) To what degree do intergenerational ties exist? To what degree do these ties constitute a problem for a successfully functioning parent-child relationship?

(3) To what degree has each parent achieved separation-individuation (autonomy) from his or her parents and significant others in his or her family of origin?

(4) To what degree have children achieved age-appropriate levels of separation-individuation (autonomy) in the family?

(5) To what degree have generational boundaries been developed in the family (e.g., between parental subsystems and children subsystems)?

(6) To what degree have the parents successfully developed clear and definite personal system (ego) boundaries?

(7) What types of communication-relational patterns exist between parents and the parent-child dyads (e.g., complementary, symmetrical, parallel, pseudo-complementary)?

(8) To what degree is the coparental relationship or parent-child dyads restricted by a predominant communication-relational pattern?

(9) To what degree do parental and children subsystems use positive feedback?

(10) To what degree do parental and children subsystems use negative feedback?

(11) To what degree is the parental and family system open to input from outside the system?

(12) What type of authority or power structure exists between parents and the parent-child dyad? To what degree does this structure prevent constructive goal setting, problem solving, conflict negotiation, and crisis resolution?

(13) To what degree have the parents and children been able to negotiate mutually acceptable patterns of separateness (distance) and connectedness (closeness)?

(14) Is there a recognizable hierarchy between the parents and children? To what degree is this hierarchy flexible? To what degree does this hierarchy prevent the family from setting goals, solving problems, negotiating conflict, resolving crises, and meeting individual and family developmental tasks?

Process Considerations

(1) To what extent have parents and children been able to devise and agree upon rules for sharing, for exchange, and for distributive justice in the family?

(2) To what degree are parents and children successfully resolving their individual developmental tasks at this time in their lives?

(3) To what degree are parents and children successfully resolving current family developmental tasks?

(4) To what extent are parents emotionally supportive of each other? To what extent are parents supportive of their children? To what extent are children supportive of their parents and their siblings?

(5) To what extent are parents capable of being intimate (physically, emotionally, intellectually, and psychologically)?

(6) To what extent are parents and children appropriately intimate with each other (physically, emotionally, intellectually, and psychologically)?

(7) To what degree have both parents and children together developed successful goal setting, problem solving, conflict negotiation, and crisis management strategies?

(8) To what extent are problem solving, goal setting, conflict negotiation, and crises resolution in the family impaired by unresolved issues of transference between parents and children?

(9) To what extent are problem solving, goal setting, conflict negotiation, and crises resolution impaired by unresolved issues of projective identification between parents and children?

(10) To what degree are parents and children involved in unconscious collusion that prevents them from successfully setting goals, solving problems, negotiating conflict, and overcoming crises?

(11) To what degree do parents and children use functional communication skills?

(12) To what degree is scapegoating used between parents and children?

(13) To what extent do redundant, cyclical interactional patterns prevent parents and the children from setting goals, solving problems, negotiating conflict, overcoming crises, and achieving family developmental tasks?

(14) To what extent do family rituals stand in the way of successful goal setting, problem solving, conflict negotiation, and crises resolution?

(15) What are the recurrent themes in the family? To what extent do these themes symbolize or represent unresolved parent-child conflicts?

(16) To what degree do parents enact roles that are more appropriately filled by children?

(17) To what degree do children enact roles that are more appropriately filled by parents?

(18) To what degree do parents serve as appropriate sex role models?

(19) What are the parents' socialization patterns? Do these patterns differ substantially from this family's particular subcultural, ethnic, and religious group? Do these patterns differ substantially from the general patterns of society?

(20) What are the parent's and children's defensive process?

(21) Are there cross-generational alliances in the family system? What are the predominant triangular patterns in the family?

(22) What are the central rules in the family that stand in the way of successful goal setting, problem solving, conflict negotiation, crisis resolution, and achievement of individual and family developmental tasks?

Multidimensional Assessment of Parenting

Slater and Power (1987) break parenting down into three dimensions: support, control, and structure. These different parenting variables can be observed and assessed clinically in a family therapy session. Parenting support, which consists of the parent's nurturing attitude, their sensitivity to the child's input, and the parent's nonrestrictive attitude toward the child. Clinicians can observe the parent's nurturing attitude by noticing how much warmth and affection the parents exhibit toward their children during a session.

Questions to Assess Parent's Supportive Behavior

The following questions might be helpful to consider when assessing parent's supportive behavior:

- Are the parent's nurturing and affectionate with their children?
- Do they talk to their children with kindness and respect?
- Do the parents point out the child's positive behaviors and attributes?
- Do the parents verbally express their affection to the child?
- Do they express their appreciation for the child's positive actions?
- Do they demonstrate physical affection for the child?
- Do they talk to the child in a condescending tone or a respectful tone?
- Are they open to their child's input?
- Do they listen with the intent to understand their child's perspective, feelings, experience?
- Do they show a willingness to include the child in decisions affecting the child and the family? Are the parents flexible, open to new ideas, and willing to change parenting decisions based on their child's feedback?
- Do they allow the child freedom to express his or her ideas, feelings, wants, and desires without challenging, dismissing or disagreeing with them?
- Do the parents allow the child to make their own decisions on age appropriate issues?
- Is the parent supportive of the child's initiative to try new things and let them fail?
- Does the parent encourage the child to try new experiences and to obtain new information?

Questions to Assess Parental Control

These questions will assess the type of control strategy, the amount of control, and the maturity demands placed on the child.

- Do the parents use inductive methods of control or do they discipline using fear, coercion, threats, punishment, or love withdrawal?
- Do they use reasoning to explain to the child appropriate and inappropriate behavior?
- Do parents ask the child how his/her behavior affects others?
- Do parents ask questions that foster children's development of conscience and awareness of their own emotions?
- Do they utilize a variety of control strategies such as let situations go, take away a privilege, reason with the child, send them to their room?
- Are they rigid or flexible in their control?
- Do parents accept responsibility for their behavior instead of blaming the child?
- Are the parent's defensive about their parenting?
- Do the parents often criticize the child?
- Do the parents have realistic and developmentally appropriate expectations of the child's behavior?
- Do they have reasonable age-appropriate demands on the child's responsibilities in the home? Does the parent interact with the child in a way that demonstrates their understanding of the child's developmental stage?

- Is the parent patient with the child if they are struggling with a developmental task?
- Do the parents set age-appropriate limits and expectations for their child?

Questions to Assess Structure Developed by Parents

The following questions assess the structure the parents provide their children.
- Are the parents involved in the child's life without being intrusive?
- Are the parents aware of where the child is and who they are with?
- Are they supportive of the child's activities?
- Are they consistent and predictable in their parenting behavior?
- Do the parent's provide organization to their child's schedule and daily activities?
- Are their established routines to the child's day and week?
- Are their clear and age appropriate expectations of the child's responsibilities?

Family Play Therapy

The above questions can be used by a therapist to assess parenting during a family session. One of the challenges of conducting a family session is to engage children in the process. In order to assess parenting in a clinical setting it is necessary to observe parents and children interacting. One of the best ways to facilitate parent-child interaction is to have them engage in family play therapy. Family play therapy consists of a variety of different activities that involves both parents and children in a common activity which allows clinicians to observe parents interacting with their children and assess parenting behaviors. Using play in family therapy engages family members in a common, pleasurable task that decreases family member's defensiveness and resistance. By observing the family's interaction during family play therapy, therapists are provided a broad spectrum of diagnostic information about parenting behaviors and parent-child interactions. During these family play sessions, therapists have the opportunity to observe parent's ability to communication. Clinicians can determine if parents send clear messages and are congruent with their verbal and non-verbal cues. Therapists can watch parent-children dynamics during family play therapy to determine the boundaries between the parental and child subsystem and whether parents and children are enmeshed or disengaged. In addition, family structure can be observed to identify appropriate hierarchy in the family system and whether children are parentified and parents have abdicated their parental role. The degree of flexibility and rigidity in the parent's thinking, expectations, affect and involvement can be assessed. The degree of family cohesion can also be assessed by observing how open or closed the family system is. Finally, clinicians can observe the degree of emotional connectedness between the parents and children.

Family play therapy also allows for the observations of the parents' and children's ability and willingness to organize around a task. It can reveal whether the parents' leadership style is democratic or authoritarian and their use of power and delegation within the family. Family interaction around a common task can also show the parents' capability to help family members to negotiate and reach consensus. In addition, family interaction can expose any cross-generational alliances or triangulation within the family system. The family play therapy will also show the level of affective and physical contact and whether family members find the contact rewarding.

Gil (1994, 2000) has developed several activities that clinicians could use to assess parenting behavior in a clinical setting. Such activities include family puppet interview, family art drawing, mutual story telling, family play genogram, building a family aquarium, playing the Thinking, Feeling, Doing game developed by Richard Gardner, doing a family collage, etc.

The family puppet interview is an activity that engages the whole family. It consists of each family member choosing a puppet. The family is asked to use the puppets to create an original story that has a beginning, middle and the end. Once the family has created and practiced their story, they act it out for the therapist. At the end of the story the therapist asks the puppets questions related to the process, feelings, actions, and relationships while staying in the metaphor of the story. During the play and the post-production questions the therapist can observe the parents interaction with the children and the roles they take on in the play.

Another activity is the family play genogram. This activity is an extension of using the traditional genogram. In this activity each family member is asked to pick a figurine, object, or cut out a picture that represents each member of the family. Next, they pick out a figure that depicts the relationships between every member of the family. Again the therapist pays attention to the process and the parent-child interaction. In addition this activity can help the therapist assess the parenting behavior from the children's perspective.

A third activity is the family aquarium. This activity involves the entire family and requires them to create a fish representing them and place it in an aquarium with the other family members' fish. Each person is to draw and cut out a fish and decorate it using sequins, glitter, markers, yarn, crayons, etc. Then the family members are asked to place (glue) their fish onto a poster board (an aquarium) in a way that represents their relationships within the family. The family then works together to decorate the aquarium.

The purpose of these activities is to engage both parents and children in the therapeutic process and allow the therapist to observe parent-child interaction. In addition these activities can be therapeutic and diagnostic by revealing the parent-child and marital dynamics.

Case Example: The Stanley Family

Brittany, 12 years old, had been diagnosed with oppositional defiance disorder and was referred for family therapy. Brittany was a very vivacious girl who had good grades in school and was involved with several extra-curricular activities in school. However, recently she had quit playing volleyball and tennis and her grades were deteriorating. Brittany would often stay up late at night and then not be able to get up in the morning and would miss the bus. As a result, she had a chronic tardiness problem at school that was becoming more of a concern. The parents would vacillate between rescuing her and implementing tough love with Brittany. During one incident Brittany missed the bus and demanded that her father, David, drive her to school. Her father refused and told her to walk or ride her bike. Brittany refused so her father called the police to come and take her to school. The precipitating event that brought Brittany and her family into therapy was when Brittany went over to her friend's house and refused to come home. Brittany's Mom,

Kathy, went and picked Brittany up and drove her straight to a for-profit psychiatric clinic in the community and had her admitted. Brittany was released two weeks later and referred to family therapy. Brittany, Kathy, and David were also participating in individual outpatient therapy. After a couple of initial sessions with Kathy, David, and Brittany, I invited the whole family, which included Brittany's older brother Kenny, age 15 and her younger sister, Tammy, age 10 in for a family therapy session. In the first couple of family therapy sessions I had the family members do a collage that described their family. The collages were very diagnostic of the family and revealed some of the issues the family was dealing with. Their collages revealed the contempt that the children felt toward their mother and how disconnected they felt from their father. It also revealed that Brittany was clearly the leader of the family and spoke most openly about the problems in the family. In the next family session, I had the family play the Talking, Feeling, Doing game. In this board game the players land on spaces where they have to pick a card that asks them to describe a thought, a feeling, or action related to a given scenario.

As the parents and children interacted during this activity, the family's dynamics revealed several dimensions of the parent's behavior. First, it was clear that Brittany and her older brother Kenny were aligned and at the top of the family hierarchy. Mom and Dad had abdicated much of their parental responsibilities allowing Brittany and Kenny to control the game. Brittany would instruct other family members on how the game should be played. Several times she would tell a family member that his/her turn was over and would take the dice away and hand it to another family member, telling him/her to roll the dice. Brittany was also the one that enforced the rules of the game. Most efforts by Kathy to provide structure to the game were superceded by Brittany's contradictions and insistence that it be done a certain way. During one instance, Kenny did not want to answer a question and when Kathy coaxed him to give some kind of response Brittany contended that he did not have to respond. Kathy gave a few examples of how Kenny might respond to the question but quickly acquiesced when Brittany took the dice, handed them to another player and told them to go. In contrast to Brittany, Kenny did not attempt to control the game as much, but instead was allied with Brittany against her parents and younger sister in expressing his disdain and contempt, particularly towards Kathy. For example, one time after Kathy gave one of her responses, both Kenny and Brittany remarked that her answer was lame and that she should not be given a chip for answering it. Both Kenny and Brittany, through verbal and nonverbal communication would be critical of their mother's behavior and how she did not know how to play the game. They would also be demeaning and put down the Kathy's and Tammy's responses as well as contradict Kathy's statements on how the game should be played. It was clear that Brittany was in charge as she would tell the other family members, especially Kathy, what to do and when to do it. Even when the game was ending, it was Brittany who dictated to her parents and siblings that it was time to go and they had to leave even though the session was not quite over.

During most of the game David was very passive and disengaged. During one of the David's first turns, he read the question in a very softly spoken matter of fact voice, briefly responded and then sat back in his chair. None of the other family members were even aware that he had taken his turn. David was completely ignored and he seemed to be comfortable with that role. He was withdrawn from the game with only an occasional brief comment on the games procedure or anther family member's responses that usually was ignored. I also observed that the family members gave very little support to each other. Their comments were often derogatory, critical, and argumentative that either discounted or contradicted the responses of other family members. The parents did not address the disrespectful remarks, and what was especially noteworthy is that David did not seem at all concerned about the negative remarks that Brittany and Kenny directed at Kathy.

About half way through the session, I asked the family to stop playing the game so that I could share with them a few observations. I pointed out a few strengths of the family including the fact that they were all willing to participate and were thoughtful with their answers and they enjoyed spending time together. I then pointed out that many of the comments that they made to each other during the game were intrusive and disrespectful. For example, while a family member was thinking out loud about his/her response to a question, Kathy and Brittany would often interject a response that would suggest that the person's response was not acceptable. At other times a family member would either verbally or nonverbally mock someone's response. I also pointed out that family members rarely listened without interrupting, or shared positive or supportive comments with each other. I gave the family some examples of some supportive comments that would validate the person's feelings and experience (e.g., that would be hard, tell me more, how did you feel about that, I did not know that you felt/thought that way, I did not know that happened) without contradicting him/her. I then asked the family if they would continue playing the game and to pay attention to their responses to each other and try to decrease the derogatory, critical comments and replace them with more supportive statements. As the family returned to the game, they seemed to be more aware of their interactions and caught themselves responding critically, and even shared a positive comment or two. The next week I met with the parents alone to address more specifically some issues related to their parenting behaviors. During the next few sessions I met with both David and Kathy to address issues related to parental support, control, and structure.

The first issue that I addressed with David and Kathy was the hierarchy in the family system. Based on my observations of the family dynamics the sibling subsystem, namely Brittany and Kenny, were structurally above the parental subsystem. I talked about the need for David and Kathy to be in charge of the family and not Kenny and Brittany. One thing that needed to occur to facilitate such a shift in the family system was that David needed to be actively involved in parenting the children. This would entail his participation in establishing and enforcing family rules and decisions. He needed to be positively involved with parenting the children not just when a situation had escalated to the point that Kathy could not handle it, but also before a situation got out of control. It was important for him to be aware of where the children were and what they were doing and to not abdicate his parental role to Kathy or to Brittany and Kenny. In order for this to happen, though there were some important changes that needed to take place within the marital subsystem. I pointed out that to support this change in the parental subsystem Kathy needed to make room for David's parenting, encouraging his involvement, even expecting it while not criticizing or dictating the way he was involved. It was critical that Kathy and David be in agreement and be able support each other in their parenting decisions. In order to be more supportive they both needed to avoid blaming each other, and focus on what they could do now instead of whose fault it was.

Another area that I focused on in the sessions with David and Kathy was increasing the amount of parental support they provided their children. One of the issues that the family identified as a goal for therapy was to be able to treat each other with more respect. We discussed the need for Kathy and David to develop an environment of respect in the family. It was important that Kathy and David set the tone in the family by talking respectfully to each other and to the children. After all if David did not show respect to

Kathy (and vice versa) then how could they expect the children to respect her. I also stressed that they should expect the children to talk respectfully to them as parents. This was especially a concern regarding how disrespectful and condescending Brittany and Kenny were towards Kathy. I encouraged David that it would send a significant message to the children that disrespectful language was not permissible. He should set and enforce a limit, in a non-threatening or non-violent way, when he heard the children talk to Kathy disrespectfully by telling the children it was not acceptable for them to talk to her that way. In addition, in order to establish more respect among family members it was important to earn the children's respect by treating them with respect and supporting them. We talked about ways that the parents could put "money in the bank" with the children and be more supportive. We discussed ways to build trust and respect with their children by being more responsive, listening to them without judging, criticizing, or contradicting, telling them something they are doing right, expressing appreciation or complimenting them, engaging in positive or fun interaction, encouraging them, or spending time alone with each child. I felt it was especially important for David to spend one-on-one time with each child, and particularly Brittany, since he was very disengaged from them and needed to have positive interaction with each of them rather than having most of his interactions be disciplining them.

We also discussed how to effectively establish parental control during these sessions. One of the areas we explored was how to respond to the children when they are expected to do something. I pointed out that the parents should set age-appropriate limits on the children's behavior, activities, and expectations. In addition, I stressed that during the process of setting limits and establishing expectations for the children it was critical to allow the children input into the decision making, especially since they were adolescents, and to be responsive to their children's feelings and ideas. They should also be willing to negotiate the timing and accomplishment of their children's responsibilities (i.e., work around the house, use of the phone and computer, etc.) given certain age-appropriate parameters. Furthermore, I encouraged them to avoid demands, ultimatums, threats, and confrontation with children that could escalate the situation into physical confrontation or calling the police.

In addition to noting the changes Kathy and David needed to make in order to improve their parenting behavior, I also identified the strengths they exhibited as parents. I shared with them that as parents they exhibited a lot of care and concern for their family and were committed to improve their family relationships. As individuals and as a couple they had overcome a lot of negative behaviors including the abuse and neglect they experienced during childhood, their substance use, and the domestic violence that occurred in their marriage. They were aware of the negative legacy of their own family-of-origin and had a strong desire to not pass that legacy on to their own children. They both had a lot of insights on how to deal with family problems and were willing to acquire new information and the necessary professional support that would help them make their desired changes. Furthermore, they had a strong religious faith that they could rely on and gain strength from during challenging times. Like supportive parenting, therapy that acknowledges parental strengths provides the needed support and hope that parents need to be the type of parent's they want to be. In addition to pointing out their strengths, I also highlighted the progress they were making over the course of therapy. I complimented David as he became more engaged in parenting the children. I also emphasized several instances where they were working more effectively as a team on parenting issues. I acknowledged Kathy's change as she became more complimentary of David and less blaming towards him. Furthermore, I underlined how Kathy decreased the negative and hope-less thoughts she often had about herself, David, and her family. At the beginning of therapy she would often remark that their marriage/family was hopeless and they were "screwed up." As therapy progressed those thoughts and expressions became less ex-treme and frequent and were replaced with more balanced and hopeful statements such as "at times things are better" and "we just need to keep working at it." As a result of stressing the strengths and progress they were making, they were both more open to considering and changing ineffective parenting behaviors.

Conclusion

The assessment of parenting behaviors has improved significantly over the past century. There are a variety of assessment instruments that collect data on a wide range of parenting behaviors from both the parent's and children's perspective. In addition several observa-tional instruments have been developed to augment our ability to more accurately assess parental behavior. However, the instruments developed to measure parental behavior are not without their methodological problems including insufficient or no reliability or va-lidity data as well as not being culturally and gender sensitive. As a result, it is important to assess parenting behaviors both through the use of self-report instruments, observa-tion, and clinical assessments.

Often times it is the child that is identified as the "sick one" in the family. But often their symptoms are related to problems residing within the family system and particularly within the parental/marital subsystem. This is not to say that the child does not play a role in family problems but he/she does not have the power or primary responsibility for changing family interactions. Although therapy can help children process their emotions, self-regulate, and teach them effective coping skills, the primary focus of therapy needs to be on changing parental behaviors in order to improve the parent-child relationship.

Since the goal of family therapy is to improve the quality of parent-child interactions it is necessary to observe parents and children interacting in order to assess parenting behavior. Family play therapy can be an effective technique to engage both parents and children in a therapy session and allow for a clinical assessment. Clinical assessments should evaluate the parent's supportive behavior, use of control, and their ability to pro-vide structure in the child's life. It is believed that as clinicians can effectively assess parenting styles and behavior they can develop treatment plans that can ameliorate par-ent-child relationships and ultimately child outcomes.

References

Bagarozzi, D. A. (1986). Some issues to consider in the assessment of marital/family functioning. *American Journal of Family Therapy*, *14*, 84–86.

Barber, B. K., & Thomas, D. L. (1986). Multiple dimensions of parental supportive be-havior: The case for physical affection. *Journal of Marriage and the Family*, 48, 783–794.

Baumrind, D. (1967). Child care practices anteceding three patterns of preschool behav-ior. *Genetic Psychology Monographs, 75 (1),* 43–88

Belsky, J. (1984). The determinants of parenting: A process model. *Child Development*, *55*, 83–96.

Bornstein, M. H. (Ed.). (1995). *Handbook of parenting*. Mahwah, NJ: Lawrence Erlbaum.

Bowers, L., Smith, P. K., & Binney, V. (1994). Perceived family relationships of bullies, victims, and bully/victims in middle childhood. *Journal of Personal and Social Relationships*, 11, 215–232.

Cummings, E. M., Davies, P., & Campbell, B. (2000). *Developmental psychopathology*. New York: Guilford.

Dix, T., & Gershoff, E. T. (2001) Measuring parent-child relations. In J. Touliatos, B. F. Perlmutter & Straus, M. A. (eds.), *Handbook of family measurement techniques* (pp. 125-142). Thousand Oaks, CA: Sage Publications, Inc.

Feldman, S. S., & Weinberger, D. A. (1994). Self-restraint as a mediator of family influences on delinquent behavior: A longitudinal study. *Child Development*, 65, 195–211.

Frick, P. J. (1998). *Conduct disorders and severe antisocial behavior*. New York: Plenum.

Fuligni, A. J., & Eccles, J. S. (1993). Perceived parent-child relationships and early adolescents' orientation toward peers. *Developmental Psychology*, 29, 622–632.

Gil, E. (1994). *Play in family therapy*. New York: Guilford.

Gil, E., & Sobol, B. (2000). Engaging families in therapeutic play. In C. E. Bailey (ed.), *Children in Therapy: Using the family as a resource*. New York: W. W. Norton.

Holden, G. W. (2001). Parenthood. In J. Touliatos, B. F. Perlmutter & Straus, M. A. (eds.), *Handbook of family measurement techniques* (pp. 137–149). Thousand Oaks, CA: Sage Publications, Inc.

Maccoby, E. E., & Martin, J. (1983). Socialization in the context of the family: Parent-child interaction. In E. M. Hetherington (Ed.) & P. H. Mussen (Series Ed.). *Handbook of child psychology: Vol. 4. Socialization, personality, and social development* (pp. 1–101). New York: John Wiley.

Paulson, S. E., & Sputa, C. L. (1996). Patterns of parenting during adolescence: Perceptions of adolescents and parents. *Adolescence*, 31, 369–381.

Platz, D. L., Pupp, R. P., & Fox, R. A. (1994). Raising young children: Parental perceptions. *Psychological Reports*, 74, 643–646.

Resnikoff, R. O. (1981). Teaching family therapy: Ten key questions for understanding the family as patient. *Journal of Marital and Family Therapy*, 7, 135–142.

Robinson, C. C., Mandleco, B., Olsen, S. F., & Hart, C. H. (1995). Authoritative, authoritarian, and permissive parenting practices: Development of a new measure. *Psychological Reports*, 77, 819–830.

Rollins, B. C., & Thomas, D. L. (1979). Parental support, power, and control techniques in the socialization of children. In W. R. Burr, R. Hill, F. I. Nye, & I. L. Reiss (Eds.), *Contemporary theories about the family: Research-based theories* (pp. 317–364). New York: The Free Press.

Slater, M. A., & Power, T. G. (1987). Multidimensional assessment of parenting in single-parent families. In J. P. Vincent (Ed.), *Advances in family intervention, assessment, and theory* (Vol. 4, pp. 197–229). Greenwich, CT: JAI Press Inc.

Strayhorn, J. M., & Weidman, C. S. (1988). A parent practices scale and its relation to parent and child mental health. *Journal of the American Academy of Child and Adolescent Psychiatry*, 27, 613–618.

Touliatos, J., Perlmutter, B. F., & Straus, M. A. (Eds.) (2001). *Handbook of family measurement techniques*. Thousand Oaks, CA: Sage Publications, Inc.

11

Systemic Assessment

Douglas H. Sprenkle

Summary
The purpose of this chapter will be to explicate the systemic perspective to assessment. First, the author will delimit how the term *systemic* is used in this chapter, since the term is sometimes used as a general term for any family therapy perspective. Next, the author will trace the historical development of the more specific systemic perspective described in this chapter. The heart of the chapter will focus on specific interventions that the clinician, who employs this approach, can use to assess families. Since assessment and treatment are virtually identical in this model, the model will also serve as a template for intervention. A major focus will be to help the reader learn the art of asking good clinical questions, specifically the kinds called *circular* and *reflexive* questions that encourage family members both to view their issues differently and to open space for them to resolve their issues. A case illustration will be utilized to make these interventions more concrete and user friendly. One of the author's major goals is that the reader will be able to implement many of these question asking techniques, which can be used regardless of the reader's theoretical orientation. The research evidence in support of this perspective will also be described. The chapter will close with the section on strengths and limitations of the approach and suggestions for future research.

Delimiting the Term Systemic

The term systemic, as employed in this chapter, refers to a specific way of conducting interviews, centered on the art of asking questions, that was originally developed by theorists/clinician/researchers at the Center for the Study of the Family in Milan, Italy in the 1970s (Selvini Palazzoli, Boscolo, Cecchin, & Prata, 1978), and was subsequently modified in directions to be described below. It is an approach which centers on the belief that carefully crafted questions are at the heart of the assessment process. Furthermore, they can stimulate family members to view their problems very differently and subsequently generate their own solutions to their difficulties. The historical evolution of this approach will be described in the next section.

This more technical use of the term systemic needs to be distinguished from the more general use of the word. The vast majority of marriage and family therapists would consider themselves to have a systemic orientation or to be systems theorists. In this more general sense, a systemic perspective refers to a way of thinking about human behavior. Marriage and family therapy arose, in part, because the founders of the field thought it important to move beyond individual personalities to the patterns that connect people. They believed that human behavior was organized by the interpersonal context in which it occurs. If a family member is "troubled," marriage and family therapists typically focus on the ecology of relationships in which the person and her/his problems is embedded. While MFTs have historically, as well as currently, disagreed regarding the extent to which the internal life of the individual also needs to be addressed in therapy, they are unified in the belief that there is a complex web of interpersonal forces that surrounds human difficulties, and that these should be a major focus of attention.

Currently, there is a small group of theorists, influenced by the philosophy of social constructionism, that rejects the terms systems and systemic, not because they reject the interpersonal view but because they believe that these terms represent an inappropriate metaphor for family interaction (De Shazer, 1991; White & Epston, 1990; Freedman & Combs, 1998). Specifically, they believe that placing an emphasis on systems reifies a particular form of family structure and they prefer family metaphors which emphasize that family interaction is more organized around "meaning"(such as personal or family narratives) than around structure. This view, has, in turn, been criticized for not giving enough attention to interactional dynamics among family members (Minuchin, 1998). However, some defenders of this anti-systemic view argue that their issue is more to do with the best way to describe an ecological perspective than a rejection of that perspective (Freedman & Combs, 1998). Whatever the merits of this debate, again, the vast majority of marriage and family therapists would assert that they have a systemic perspective in the general sense described in the previous paragraph.

Historical Development

In the more narrow sense of the term, the systemic perspective refers to the work of the Milan associates and their professional progeny. Under the leadership of the late dynamic Mara Selvini Palazzoli, a group of four Italian psychiatrists took the family therapy world by storm in the late 1970s when they published *Paradox and Counterparadox* (Selvini Palazzoli et al., 1978). This book was a compendium of dazzling theories and interventions based on their interpretations and adaptations of the ideas of Watzlawick, Haley, and especially Gregory Bateson. Following Bateson (1979), they stressed that troubled families appear to be following an outdated or erroneous "map," which they confused with the "territory" of reality; and that therapeutic interventions should center on providing the family new connections or distinctions which would alter these maps. Also, with Bateson (1979), they emphasized that "mind is social" and that therapeutic efforts should focus on patterns of interaction between persons rather than toward specific individuals or symptoms he/she may be showing (Tomm, 1984a). They used the term *epistemology* in the way that Bateson (1979) did to refer to the way we know and understand the world around us. They tried to move themselves, and their clients, from a lineal epistemology to a circular epistemology, which emphasizes recursiveness in the interaction between parts of the system and attention to holistic patterns (Tomm, 1984a).

They worked with severely disturbed families, which they described as constrained by powerful homeostatic forces embedded in a complex web of transgenerational and cultural forces. In order to counteract the therapeutic impasses typically experienced with these kinds of families, the team originally relied heavily on the use of paradoxical interventions. This early Milan approach emphasized the therapist as expert, who out-maneuvered recalcitrant families. Another hallmark of the early Milan approach was the devising of elaborate therapeutic rituals by the treatment team, which were to be enacted by the families between sessions, typically spaced four weeks apart.

In 1980, the team split and created separate centers with separate staffs. The two men (Boscolo and Cecchin) went on to emphasize training, and the two women (Selvini Palazzoli and Prata) went on to emphasize research. The latter turned their attention to the "destructive games," which they believed characterized highly disturbed families (Nichols & Schwartz, 2001).

Boscolo and Cecchin's work (Boscolo, Cecchin, Hoffman, & Penn, 1987) involved in directions that actually repudiated several of the emphases found within *Paradox and Counterparadox*, and it is the work of this branch of the original Milan Associates that forms the backdrop of the ideas to be presented in the remainder of this chapter. Specifically, they warned that paradoxical interventions could be highly problematic and/or in-effective, and they started to rebel against blatant therapist manipulation. They began to describe therapy as more a collaborative enterprise in which the family finds its own solutions. They also began to place a greater emphasis, in the process of change, on the role of the helping the family to discover new meaning regarding what is happening within their lives and about their problems. That is to say, they moved toward the position that developing new meaning is more likely to change behavior than focusing on behav-ior directly. More specifically, they believed that helping families examine the systemic evolution of their problems (helping them change the "viewing" of their problems) al-lowed family members to relate differently.

Perhaps most importantly, for our purposes here, Boscolo and Cecchin came to rely less on directives and more on asking questions as the staple of their therapeutic arma-mentarium. This emphasis was in keeping with their emphasis on collaboration and cli-ent involvement. Presumably questions, as opposed to directives, call for a greater level of client participation and are more in keeping with the belief that clients are ultimately responsible for finding their own unique solutions. The interview process itself, not tell-ing clients what to do, is curative since it enables families themselves to choose new solutions to old problems.

One of their major tools in this process was the asking of circular questions, or ques-tions specifically designed to help family members view problems as interactional rather than in linear cause-and-effect terms. At the outset of therapy, most family members tend to view problems non-systemically, frequently blaming individuals or outside factors and assuming little personal responsibility. By asking circular questions (the process will be explained in great detail, below) Boscolo and Cecchin actually sought to change the family members epistemology or way of viewing their worlds. The technique of circular questions was based on Gregory Bateson's (1979) notion of the double description, or an alternate way of describing reality. Boscolo and Cecchin used circular questions to help clients view their problems in a relational context and also to see that context from the perspective of other family members (Boscolo, Cecchin, Hoffman, & Penn, 1987).

Because of this heavy emphasis on questions, the model evolved into an approach whereby (perhaps more than any other approach in psychotherapy) assessment and intervention become one. One assessed the family primarily through the process of asking questions and (especially thought the medium of reflexive questions, to be described below) the therapist also intervened though the process of asking more questions, which, in turn, generated more information and more questions. Thus assessment and intervention were themselves circular, recursive processes, so that all assessments were interventions and all interventions were assessments.

Several North Americans have become interpreters of the Boscolo/Cecchin branch of the Milan model, including Colette Fleuridas and colleagues at the University of Iowa (Fleuridas, Nelson, & Rosenthal, 1986), Peggy Penn (1992) at the Ackerman Institute in New York, and, perhaps it's most influential proponent, Karl Tomm (1984a, 1984b, 1987, 1988) at the University of Calgary Medical School, Alberta Canada. The Milan Associates strong emphasis on asking questions also influenced the narrative (White & Epston, 1990; Freedman & Combs, 1996), solution-focused (DeShazer, 1991), and collaborative language systems (Anderson, 1997) models of therapy that were to evolve later. The theory and techniques of Fleuridas et al. (1986) and Tomm (1987, 1988), as they pertain to the art asking questions, will be explicated in considerable detail later in this chapter.

Key Concepts/Techniques of the Milan Associates

A very influential paper was written by the Milan associates prior to their split (Selvini Palazzoli, Boscolo, Cecchin, & Prata, 1980), which contains several key concepts that were further elaborated by Boscolo and Cecchin later (Boscolo et al., 1987). The paper was entitled "Hypothesizing – Circularity – Neutrality" and was a kind of meta-framework for their approach. These terms also provide a guiding framework for the art of asking questions, which the current author considers to be the heart of the systemic approach.

Hypothesizing

This refers to the therapist's thoughts about the alternative explanations or "maps" which might be applied to the family's difficulty. The therapist's own hypotheses will orient him/her to the kinds of questions to be asked and therefore give order to the interview. Family members, of course, will have their own maps of the problem, which they often confuse with "the territory" (that is, they assume that their maps represent "The Truth"). Typically, these maps will be lineal and simplistic and center on blaming individuals or outside forces. The therapist should learn about the family member's hypotheses both for the purposes of "joining" and also because these hypotheses will help the therapist to confirm or refute his/her own hypotheses. The Milan associates believed that it is best not to ask about the therapist's own hypotheses directly, at least initially, because the family is likely to reject them (Tomm, 1984b). The therapist, rather, should present ideas that are related to, but sufficiently different from the family's ideas, so as to create "news of a difference" (Bateson, 1979), while at the same time not alienating the family. The therapist should try to ask questions that will elicit descriptions of specific events or behaviors that would tend to either confirm or refute the therapist's own hypotheses.

One type of question that is useful for helping clients to begin to change their maps (or hypotheses) is "what-if" questions. These refer to speculations about how things might be if existing conditions were different. Let us take the example of a 10-year-old boy, Johnny, whose parents (Alice and Sam) present as alternating between "being depressed" and "acting aggressive." Furthermore, let us assume that they disagree vehemently on how Johnny should be managed and that they blame their problems as a couple on Johnny's condition. A what if question (described below as a particular type of circular question) might be, "What would your relationship as a couple be right now if Johnny had not been born?" (adapted from Tomm, 1984b). If, for example, Alice and Sam were to realize that they would still be fighting about something else, they might begin to look at their situation differently.

Circularity

Circularity refers to the epistemological assumption, rooted in the ideas of Gregory Bateson (Bateson, 1979), that behaviors and ideas do not occur in isolation and that individuals are best understood within their ecological context. Furthermore, the notion of linear causality, which is a good map for the physical world, is a poor map for the social world. There is huge difference, Bateson (1979) reminded us, between kicking a stone versus kicking a dog, since the response of the latter would be quite unpredictable. Furthermore, the dog would give feedback to the kicker and might likely modify his behavior. Therefore, there is almost always mutual or circular causality in the social world. (However, as the feminist critique of family therapy has reminded us, circularity should not be confused with mutual responsibility and this notion should never be used to excuse excesses of power by perpetrators of any stripe).

In terms of conducting interviews, a circular perspective emphasizes paying attention to cyclical sequences of behaviors, which also interconnect with family beliefs. Furthermore, these patterns of relating and believing are important because they recursively tend to perpetuate dysfunctional ways of thinking and behaving (Fleuridas et al., 1986).

Another important aspect of circularity is to highlight the interactional relationship between the therapist and the treatment family. As previously noted, therapists develop hypotheses through their own interactional relationship with the family, and these hypotheses change based on the families' responses to these questions. Since the therapist himself/herself is part of the system being described, he/she is not some kind of objective outside observer who notes some static truth or who acts upon the family in the same way a person might kick a stone.

As noted previously, one of the main contributions of the Milan associates was to devise what they called circular questions. These were employed both to ferret out recursive family patterns and also to help the family understand the circular nature of its predicament. One of the major purposes of circular questions, then, is to help family members to begin viewing their problems (and strengths) systemically. A more exact definition of circular questions (and how they differ from other types of questions), and examples of circular questions, will be offered later in this paper.

Neutrality

Probably the most controversial of the triumvirate of key Milan concepts is neutrality. Basically, it refers to the attitude on the part of the therapist regarding the positions taken by the various family members. The neutral therapist tries to give each person a fair hearing and tries not to blame anyone. He/she assumes that given the family's history and circumstances, things make sense as they are and family members are not judged to for being who they are. According to Karl Tomm (Tomm, 1984b) neutrality suggests that the therapist takes a meta-position with regard to the individual family members, their patterns of interaction and their beliefs. By being neutral, the therapist attempts to remain at a higher logical level. At the same time, neutrality does not suggests inactivity or the therapist's remaining aloof, distant, or cold. However, unlike a structural family therapist, a systemic therapist would not intentionally "join" a specific family member for the purpose of unbalancing the system (Tomm, 1984b).

Therapist neutrality is controversial since it may be argued that therapists neither are nor should be neutral (Machal, Feldman, & Segal, 1989), especially when it comes to matters like violence and other abuses of power or privilege. Out of concern for these potential problems, Cecchin (1987) suggested using the term *curiosity* rather than neutrality. This term emphasizes the therapist's intent to understand the recursive processes within the family and the therapist's being open to multiple hypotheses regarding client behavior (Piercy & Wetchler, 1996).

Karl Tomm's Typology of Questions

Karl Tomm has been a highly creative and articulate interpreter of the later Milan approach. One of his major contributions has been to both refine and expand the systemic approach to asking questions. The reader will recall that, within this model, the very act of asking questions has the potential to change the family's viewing of the problem and thereby precipitate their finding solutions.

Philosophical Assumptions

Tomm (1987a) takes the position that there are advantages for the therapist to ask mainly questions, especially in the early and middle part of an interview. Questions, as opposed to statements, increase client engagement and reflection on their own process of problem solving. However, he also acknowledges that statements are necessary since the therapeutic alliance rests, in part, on client's experiencing the therapist as someone with integrity and beliefs. Also, for clients only to answer questions might feel like an imposition or interrogation. Therefore, some balance is necessary, although the systemic approach relies more heavily on questions than, say, the structural or strategic approaches (Tomm, 1988).

Tomm's 2 × 2 Meta-Typology of Questions

Tomm has created an interesting and influential meta-typology of questions. He believes there are two different types of *intent*" and two different types of *assumptions*, which underlie the questions that therapists ask. In the early parts of an interview, the therapist asks predominately *orienting questions*, where the clinician's intent is to develop his/her own understanding of what is happening. The therapist also asks *influencing questions* when his/her intent is more directly to change the client or family (as opposed to primarily gather information for himself/herself). Rather than seeing these two types as discrete categories, Tomm believes that a continuum exists between predominately orienting and predominantly influencing intent.

Tomm believes that another important continuum exists between *lineal assumptions* (when the therapist's own internal cognitive map is guided by cause and effect assumptions) and *circular assumptions* (when the therapist is guided by cybernetic/interactional assumptions).

By putting these two dimensions together (therapist intent and therapist assumptions), a 2 × 2 table is created (see Table 1), which creates a meta-model of four basic types of questions. In Figure 1, the horizontal axis depicts the degree to which a clinician's intent is *predominantly* focused on gaining information for himself or more overtly trying to bring about change. The vertical axis depicts the degree that the therapist's mental process is being *predominantly* guided by linear or circular assumptions.

Quadrant 1 is called *lineal questions*. These are a meta-designation for questions when the therapist has an orienting intent and also assumes that the events he/she is exploring occur predominantly in a lineal or cause and effect manner. Tomm (1988) believes that such questions typically have, overall, an "investigative intent" since the

Table 1: Sequence of Interaction Questions: Temporal Dimension (Past, Present, Future) by Content Dimension (General, Differences/Changes, Agreement/Disagreement, Explanation/Meaning)

Temporal dimension	General	Differences of changes	Agreement/ disagreement	Explanation/ meaning
Present	(1) Alice and Sam, when you fight, what is Johnny's reaction?	(2) Does Johnny's reaction to your fights vary, or is it always the same?	(3) Who else agrees that Johnny's aggression coincides with Mom's and Dad's fighting? Who disagrees?	(4) What (to sister Sue) does Johnny's showing depression mean to you?
Past	(5) When you fought in the past, what was Johnny's reaction?	(6) In the past did your reactions to his fights vary ...?	(7) Six months ago, did you agree that Johnny's aggression coincides ...?	(8) Sue, what did Johnny's showing depression mean to you a year ago?
Future/ hypothetical	(9) If your fights continue like this into the future, what effect do you think this will have on Johnny?	(10) Will your reactions to his fights continue to be different in the future?	(11) A year from now, do you thing you will disagree on whether Johnny's fighting coincides ...?	(12) What will Johnny's showing depression mean to you next year if it continues?

therapist is acting like an investigator, detective, or newspaper reporter. Lineal questions often take the form of "who did what?," "where?," "when?," and "why?." Tomm (1988) hastens to add that linear questions are often necessary in order to "join" family members who themselves tend to have lineal assumptions.

To return to the previous illustration of Johnny, who is presented to a therapist as both depressed and aggressive by his parents, the therapist might ask lineal questions like the following: "Have you taken Johnny to a general physician or psychiatrist for his depression?" "Who took Johnny, when, and why did you believe this was important?" By asking these questions the therapist is trying to orient himself/herself to what has happened and how the family views the problem. Such questions may, of course, at least temporarily reinforce the (non-systemic) belief that Johnny's depression is simply intrinsic to him as a person.

Quadrant 2 is called *circular questions.* As in the case of quadrant 1, the therapist still has an orienting intent, but now his/her assumptions are circular. The therapist assumes that everything is somehow linked to everything else and questions are formulated in order to draw out the patterns that connect persons, ideas, actions, feelings, and so forth. Tomm (1988) believes that the overall intent of circular questions is to be exploratory. Here the therapist is acting more like an explorer or a researcher who is out to make a new discovery. Circular questions are marked by a curiosity more about the possible connections or ramifications or reverberations of problems rather than a need to know specifically what caused a problem.

Returning to our example, the therapist might ask questions like "Who worries most about Johnny?" "Alice and Sam, do the two of you react differently to his showing depression versus his showing aggression, and what emotions do each bring forth in you?" "Do each of these upsetting behaviors bring you closer together or drive you further apart?" "If Johnny showed neither depression or aggression, what would your relationship be like then?" "Has Johnny's behavior always affected you the same way, or have your reactions changed over time?" Here the therapist is exploring, non-judgmentally, the reverberations of the presenting problem throughout the system. The therapist assumes there is a complex web of recursive connections and does not assume that there is any simple linear explanation for the problems presented. Therefore, the therapist does not think in terms of what "caused" the depression, but instead focuses on its systemic reverberations.

Quadrant 3 is called *strategic questions.* Unlike questions in the first two quadrants, these have an "influencing" intent (see the horizontal axis in Figure 1). In asking strategic questions, the therapist is intentionally trying to change the clients as opposed to predominantly learning more himself/herself. These questions also have, like Quadrant 1, lineal assumptions. Tomm (1988) says that the overall intent behind strategic questions is to be corrective. The therapist behaves like a teacher, instructor, or judge, and uses the guise of questions to tell the clients how they ought to behave. The therapist assumes there is a linear relationship between some aspect of client thinking or behavior and some undesirable outcome. While expressing concern about the impact of such questions on the therapeutic alliance, Tomm (1988) indicates that strategic questions are sometimes necessary in order to mobilize a system that is stuck.

Turning to our example, the therapist might ask strategic questions like "Don't you think it would be better for Johnny if the two of you worked better together as a team?" "Alice, would you be willing to talk with Sam directly about your concerns with Sam rather than expressing these to Johnny?" Here the therapist is using the vehicle of questions to correct the parents and influence them in more constructive directions.

Quadrant 4 is called *reflexive questions.* As in Quadrant 3 the therapist asks these questions with the intent of influencing the clients, but does so from the vantage point of circular assumptions. Tomm (1988) asserts that the overall intent behind reflexive questions is to be facilitative. Here the therapist acts like a coach who tries to bring forth the family's own problem-solving resources. These questions are kinder and gentler than Quadrant 3 strategic questions since they invite change rather than attempt to force it. Furthermore, they do so by opening space for the clients to see new possibilities since, as with Quadrant 2 circular questions, reflexive questions invite clients to make new connections and to see paths that they had hitherto missed.

To turn again to our example, the therapist might say, "Alice, if you were to share with Sam directly how worried you are about Johnny and how the situation is getting you down, what can you imagine he might think (or feel or do)?" "If you could imagine, for a moment, the two of you working cooperatively together as a team to deal with Johnny's problems, what would be different in your relationship, and how would that feel?" "Sam and Alice, if you had a chance to replay that conflict that you had the other night, and you knew in advance that it would turn out to be successful, what do you believe that each of your would have done differently? Notice that these questions cause the family members to reflect on the implications of their current behaviors, feelings, and perceptions, and to explore new options. Tomm (1988) believes that this is a more "neutral" method of inquiry than strategic questions since clients are given greater freedom to choose their own options.

Before leaving these definitions, it is important to note that the therapist's words alone may not be sufficient to distinguish among the four types of questions. Nonverbals, including the therapist's emotional tone as he/she asks the questions, may determine how the questions are experienced (Tomm, 1988) and whether, for example, they seem to invite or force change.

Tomm's Biases

It seems clear to this author that Tomm, while acknowledging the value of lineal and strategic questions under some circumstances, is advocating that therapists cultivate the art of asking good circular and reflexive questions. That is, the best chance for hitting therapeutic pay dirt comes from time spent in Quadrant 2 and Quadrant 4. Since family members already tend to view their issues linearly, it is unlikely that they will hear "news of a difference" by responding to Quadrant 1 (lineal) questions. Again, however, these questions may be helpful in both joining and orienting the therapist to the client's views. Since Quadrant 3 (strategic) questions tend to be confrontational, they may precipitate reactions of guilt, defensiveness, or shame; and are certainly less likely to representative of the core Milan values of circularity and neutrality.

Circular and Reflexive Questions in More Detail
On Not Missing the Forest for the Trees

The art of asking good circular and reflexive questions requires considerable skill and practice. They are also more complex and varied than the previous explanations might suggest. For this reason, we will now present more detail regarding both of these types of questions. Lest the reader feel overwhelmed by the detail, it will be helpful to keep Tomm's (1988) meta-model in mind, so that the "forest" is not lost as we now turn attention to the "trees." As we now explore the subtleties of circular and reflexive questions, keep in mind that both types of questions are designed to focus on the ecology of the family's issues, and hopefully to get the family members to think differently about them. The major difference between the two types of questions is that circular questions have more of an orienting intent for the therapist, and that reflexive questions have more of an influencing intent. Recall, however, that "orienting" and "influencing" represent a continuum and are not discrete categories. Therefore circular questions are, to some extent, influencing. They not only provide information to the therapist, but influence family members to make new connections that may lead to change. Conversely, reflexive questions are, to some extent, orienting. By hearing and observing the family's responses to these questions, the therapist gains valuable new information about the clients' system.

A Typology of Circular Questions

Several authors have created typologies of circular questions (Fleuridas et al., 1986; Penn, 1992; Tomm, 1988). Unfortunately, the terms created by these authors are not uniform – for example, Freuridas et al. (1986, published before Tomm, 1988) label what Tomm called reflexive questions as a form of circular questions – specifically, interventive circular questions."

The following typology, which draws heavily on the definitions by Feuridas et al. (1986), restricts itself to types of circular questions that do not overlap with those questions which Tomm would classify as reflexive. Greater detail on reflexive questions will be offered in the section that follows.

There are two basic types of circular questions: 1) sequence of interaction questions and 2) comparison/classification questions. Each of these two basic types can, in turn, be placed into a 4 × 3 table (see Tables 1 and 2). The vertical (row) dimension is a content dimension, and the horizontal (column) is a temporal dimension.

Note also that these questions may be asked in a way that is "triadic." This was a manner of questioning developed by the Milan Associates, whereby one family member was asked to comment on the interactional behavior of other family members. For example, "Johnny, how would you describe how your parent's fight?" This was believed to create a fuller systemic picture since it tapped perceptions of members of the system about the interactions of two or more other members. Of course, Alice and Sam, either as a couple or as individuals could also be asked questions about their own fighting. It is not required that circular questions be triadic, and the current author believes that families would likely become annoyed if all circular questions were asked in a triadic manner.

Sequence of interaction questions. These questions focus on interactional *behaviors*. They may relate to general reactions to interactions, perceptions regarding how interactions change, agreements and disagreements about interactions, and what the behavioral interactions mean; and how these interactions reverberate (or might reverberate in the case of future/ hypothetical questions) throughout the system. These are attempts to discover the full cycle or sequence of family behavior which may interact recursively with the problem, concern, or symptom, thereby perpetuating it.

The four content (columns in Table 1) dimensions are (using examples from our ongoing illustration):

- *General.* As the name implies, these are general questions about family member's responses (or other member's perceptions of member's responses) to sequences of behavioral interaction. "Alice and Sam, when you fight, what is Johnny's reaction?"
- *Differences or Changes.* These are questions about differences or changes in reactions/perceptions to sequences of interaction. "Does Johnny's reaction to your fights vary, or is it always the same?"
- *Agreement/Disagreement.* These are questions which highlight variability in family member's responses to sequences of interaction. "Who else agrees that Johnny's aggression coincides with Mom's and Dad's fighting? Who disagrees?"
- *Explanation/Meaning.* These are questions which ask members about the meanings they attribute to sequences of interaction. "What, (to sister, Sue) does Johnny's showing depression mean to you?"

Table 2: Comparison/Classification Questions: Temporal Dimension (Past, Present, Future) by Content Dimension (General, Differences/Changes, Agreement/Disagreement, Explanation/Meaning)

Temporal dimension	General	Differences of changes	Agreement/ disagreement	Explanation/ meaning
Present	(13) Who is more worried about Johnny, Alice or Sam? Please rank order the family members from most worried to least?	(14) How is Alice's worry about Johnny different from Sam's worry about Johnny? Has the way Alice and Sam worry about Johnny changed?	(15) Sue, do you agree or disagree that your mother's worry about Johnny is different from your father's worry?	(16) Sue, what does it mean to you that your mother and father worry in a different way about Johnny?
Past	(17) Who used to worry most about Johnny, Alice or Sam?	(18) In the past, was Alice's worry about Johnny different from Sam's worry about Johnny?	(19) Sue, several months ago, did you agree or disagree that your mother' worry is different ...?	(20) Last fall, what did it mean to you that your mother and father worried in a different way about Johnny?
Future/ hypo- thetical	(21) In the future, who will worry most about Johnny, Alice or Sam?	(22)In the future, do you think that Alice's worry about Johnny will be different than Sam's?	(23) Sue, a year from now do you think you will agree that your mother's worry is different than your father's ...?	(24) What would it mean to you if next year at this time your mother and father still worried in a different way about Johnny?

The three temporal dimensions (rows in Table 1) indicates that the four content sub-categories of sequences of interaction questions can all be asked with regard to the present, the past, or the future (hypothetical). If the present/general circular question (cell 1 in Table 1) is "Alice and Sam, when you fight, what is Johnny's reaction?" The same question in the past temporal dimension might be (cell 5), " Alice and Sam, when you fought in the past, what was Johnny's reaction?" The same question in the future temporal dimension (cell 9) might be, "Alice and Sam, if your fights continue like this into the future, what effect do you think this will have on Johnny?" The "what if" questions, described earlier in this chapter, fall into this cell.

The reader is referred to Table 1 to see how the differences/changes, agreement/disagreement, and explanation/meaning subcategories can be asked from the vantage point of the present, past, and the future. This temporal dimension adds contextual richness in that family member's beliefs about the evolution of problems/concerns affects their view of the present, which, in turn, affects their slant on the past and expectations for the future. So important is this dimension of time that Boscolo and Bertrando (1993) brought it to the systemic model as a major later addition.

Comparison/Classification Questions. These are questions asked of family members about other family members (so they are often triadic questions), with a view toward making comparisons and classifications regarding behaviors, beliefs, values, traditions, feelings, and relationships. The clinician asks the family members to compare, contrast, and rank order similarities and differences; investigates coalitions and alignments, and probes for patterns in the family members' responses. This is a broader category than sequence-of-interaction questions since the focus is not just on behaviors but also cognitions and feelings.

Fortunately, for ease in learning this model, the content and the temporal dimensions are the same for comparison/classification questions as for sequence of interaction questions (see Table 2). Turning again to our example:

- *General.* These are general (global) questions about comparisons ("Who is more worried about Johnny, Alice or Sam?") or classifications ("In terms of worry about Johnny, please rank order the family members from most worried to least?"). "Who is more attached to Johnny, his sister, Sue, or his grandmother?" "Classify the members of the extended family, from most to least in terms of their attachment to Johnny?"

- *Differences or Changes.* These are questions about variability in the general comparisons/classifications, which specifically highlight differences or changes. "How is Alice's worry about Johnny different from Sam's worry about Johnny?" Do Alice and Sam worry about Johnny in the same way every time, or is the worry different depending on whether he is showing depression or aggression?" "Sam, do you think that Alice's worry about Johnny has changed over the years?"

- *Agreement/Disagreement.* These are questions about variability in the general comparisons/classifications, which specifically highlight agreement or disagreement. An example would be if sister, Sue, were asked about her parents' worry about Johnny: "Sue, do you agree (or disagree) that your mother's worry about Johnny is different from your father's worry about Johnny?" (The reader will note that this is also a triadic question since one member of the family is being asked about the patterns of worry of two other members of the family).

- *Explanation/Meaning.* These are questions which focus on the meanings attributed to comparisons/classifications. To follow up on the previous question, if Sue had said she believed her parents did worry in a different way, the therapist might ask, "Sue, what does it mean to you (or what is your explanation for your belief) that Mom and Dad worry in a different way about Johnny?"

Once again, (see Table 2) a temporal dimension can be added; and each of these types of comparison/classification questions can be asked with reference to the present, the past, and how family members might (hypothetically) compare or classify cognitions, feelings, or behaviors in the future.

In Case You are Feeling a Bit Overwhelmed

Before leaving this section on the details of circular questions, the reader is reminded of the previous warning not to miss the forest for the trees. The reader will be forgiven if he or she does not remember all the 24 different subtypes of circular questions found in Tables 1 and 2! If all the details escape you, try to recall that the purpose of circular questions is to orient the therapist (and family members) to the systemic reverberations of what brought them to therapy. Fleuridas et al. (1986) note that they sometimes use the term "relationship" questions interchangeably with circular questions. So, if you don't remember all the details, do remember the mantra (phrased, of course, as a question), "How can I ask questions so that I, myself, and my clients will see things interactionally?" If you keep this in mind, you will (hopefully, naturally) start asking about sequences of interaction (Table 1). Then, if you can just remember three more key words: "differences, agreements, explanations," you might even master the important details since these form a template for the rest of what you will ask about sequences of interaction. The author's experience is that once you start asking these questions, the temporal dimension takes care of itself. You will also (hopefully naturally), if you keep in mind the interactional mantra, start asking about comparisons/classifications (Table 2). The same key words (differences, agreements, explanations) apply here too. So, take an interactional perspective and ask about differences, agreements, and explanations, and you will be well on your way to mastering the art of asking circular questions.

Reflexive Questions in More Detail

Recall that reflexive questions add clear intentionality on the part of the therapist to influence change in clients. Remember that Fleuridas et al. (1986) actually call them "interventive circular questions." They are interventive (like strategic questions) but they maximize self-healing and client choice.

Given this intentionality, it is ironic that Tomm (1987) claims to have stumbled on this type of question accidentally through an experience in Rotterdam, Holland in 1981. He was working with a team that was treating some children from a single parent family. Questions asked to the children about a hypothetical absence of their mother opened space for the children to break a malignant pattern of blame of their father, and to view him as a caring parent (Tomm, 1987). This experience awakened Tomm to the power of timely, well-crafted questions to bring forth a new vision of old maps and to effect change. He borrowed the term, reflexive, from the communication theorists, Pearce and Cronen (1979), where the term had the connotation of communication that brings forth new meaning and new action.

Tomm lists more types of reflexive questions than can be enumerated here. It is this writer's opinion that some of his categories are overlapping, so what follows are this writer's synopsis of what he considers to be the most distinctive major types, again using the illustration that we have followed throughout this chapter.

- *Future-Oriented Questions.* Here clients are urged, though questions, to reflect on some future possibilities (but with the clear intention of effecting change, which is what separates these questions from "future," temporal dimension, circular questions). The current author particularly likes to use future-oriented questions to instill hope or to trigger optimism (Tomm, 1987). For example, to Johnny's parents, a therapist might ask "Alice and Sam, after you have found ways to work together well as a team, list the ways in which that will positively affect how you feel about your marriage? Or, "Sam and Alice, when Johnny is happy again and functioning like what you want for a 10 year old, how will you celebrate the changes that have occurred in the family?" (adapted from Tomm, 1978). It is also possible to add circular dimensions to reflexive questions – for example, you could add a comparison/classification dimension to the last question by asking " ... who will be the first person to celebrate the changes that have occurred in the family?"
- *Observer Perspective Questions.* These are reflexive questions which urge clients to take a position meta to themselves about some behavior, event, cognition, feeling, or pattern for which change may be desirable. These questions may heighten awareness of self. For example, "Sam, did you notice how you said that to Alice? If you had a chance to make that statement over again, what would you do differently that might get a different result?" Observer perspective questions may also heighten awareness of other. "Sam, when you said that, did you notice Alice's reaction? What do you think you would notice in her if you said that again in a way that got through to her?" Such questions help family members to see the circular patterning in their interactions (recursiveness) and get beyond their own lineal reactiveness (Tomm, 1984b).
- *Embedded Suggestion Questions.* Tomm (1987) has a separate category for embedded suggestion questions, although the astute reader may have noticed that almost all of the reflexive questions described thus far contain embedded suggestions – statements within the questions that nudge the clients to change in some way. Embedded suggestion questions can take the form of *embedding an alternative action* (which is what was done in the question in the previous paragraph where the therapist said to Sam, "... what would you do differently that might get a different result?"). Perhaps somewhat more distinctive are *embedded reframes.* For example, "Alice and Sam, instead of thinking of Johnny as stubborn, if you were to think of him as 'confused,' so confused that he sincerely did not know what you wanted of him, how do you imagine that you might treat him differently?" (adapted from Tomm, 1987). Tomm has a separate category for what he calls "questions introducing hypotheses" but for the purpose of simplicity, the current author believes these can be conceptualized as another form of the embedded suggestion/reframe. "Sam and Alice, do you see any connection between the intensity of your fights and Johnny's aggressiveness?"
- *Normative-Comparison Questions.* These questions seek to capitalize on the desire of many families to move from seeing themselves as deviant or abnormal to seeing themselves as healthy and normal. If the therapist made the assumptions that Alice and Sam had this desire, and also believed that they tended to suppress

their underlying feelings, the therapist might say, "Sam and Alice, do you think that you are more open about sharing your feelings than most families, or less?" (The astute reader will also note that this question also contains a circular dimension of comparison, see Table 2). Do you know of some healthy families who are better able to express their underlying feelings?" (adapted from Tomm, 1987). Of course, this question might not be constructive if Sam and Alice did not aspire to be more like these "normal" families.

- *Distinction-Clarifying Questions*. These reflexive questions help to clarify internal struggles that are being experienced by clients. If the therapist expected, for example, that Sam was torn between his devotion to his career and the investment another part of him wished to make in his son (or marriage), the therapist might say, "Which do you think is more important to you, being highly successful in your career or having a rewarding family life?" If you had to choose between one of the these, where do you think that you would devote your limited time and energy?" (adapted from Tomm, 1987). Again, this question would not be effective if Sam was unambiguous about the time that he was devoting to his career. Recall that therapist questions should offer "news of a difference" to clients but not be so different that the client thinks that the therapist is "off on some other page." Alternatively, there may be times when the goal of the therapist might be to inject more ambiguity into the system. Often clients are rigid and hold on to positions with too much certainly. For example, if the therapist thought Sam's position were too rigid he/she might say, "Sam, how long have you held that position? When did your first begin to believe that way? If you happened to be mistaken, how do you think that you would find out?" (adapted from Tomm, 1987).

Research Evidence for the Model

Two studies have been published which offer promising yet tentative evidence for the value of circular and reflexive questions. Both were published in one of the most prestigious journals in the field (*Family Process*), and the second study builds on the first. Both studies, especially the second, show some evidence of methodological sophistication. On the other hand, these were analogue studies (they used a simulated therapist and clients) and had other limitations (noted below), which render their conclusions as less than definitive.

Dozier, Hicks, Cornille, and Peterson (1998) investigated a sample of 40 family triads (mother, father, and high school age son) drawn from a developmental research high school whose population was representative of the State of Florida. Seventy-five percent of the subjects were White, 21% were Black, and the rest self-described as "other." Family triads were randomly assigned (10 families in each condition) to watch a videotape of a therapist (who was White) interviewing a family in which the therapist asked predominantly questions that were either lineal, strategic, circular, or reflexive. The researchers had Karl Tomm himself approve the videotapes as good representations of the four styles of questions. "Blind" outside experts also correctly identified the tapes and certified that they were comparable in terms of credibility of presentation. The same therapist and family members (actors) were used across all condition to control for personal appeal and these persons were blind to the purposes of the study. Family members were told that the presenting problem was the father's depression, and they were asked to identify with the person in the corresponding role (father, mother, and son). After watching five minutes of tape, subjects were asked to rate the quality of the alliance between the therapist and the person in their role, using a therapeutic alliance measure with established reliability and validity (Pinsof & Catherall, 1986). Since Tomm (1988) had hypothesized that circular and reflexive questions elicited a sense of freedom/acceptance among clients, and linear and strategic questions elicited constraint and judgment, the investigators reasoned that the circular and reflexive interviews should produce higher alliance ratings.

Data analyses showed there were no differences in alliance ratings that were related to any demographic characteristic of the sample. The only difference was a highly significant main effect: alliance scores were higher ($p < .001$) for subjects who watched the interview with circular and reflexive questions versus subjects who watched the interviews with lineal and strategic questions. In terms of the meta-model described previously (see Figure 1), there were differences between the two styles with circular assumptions versus the two styles with linear assumptions. There were no significant differences between the alliance scores of the circular versus reflexive subjects and between the linear versus strategic subjects. Therefore the orienting versus influencing intent dimension did not discriminate.

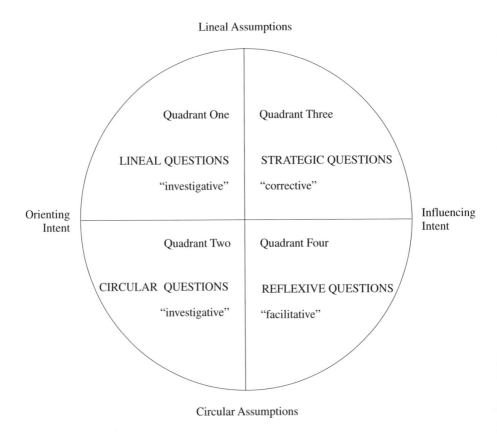

Figure 1. Four Types of Questions by Intent and Assumptions

Dermot and Carr (2001) replicated the same study using the same tapes, but with some modifications. First, the study was completed in Ireland, which allowed the researchers to determine whether the results held across another culture. Second, each subject not only rated the alliance for the person in his/her corresponding role but also completed an alliance rating for the family as a whole. Third, after each subject viewed the interview type to which he/she was randomly assigned, he/she also watched the other three tapes and did a comparative rating. Fourth, two additional alliance-rating scales were employed to check that results were not instrument specific. Fifth, the researchers used statistical procedures that accounted for the lack of independence of measures (a repeated measures design) and controlled for the order in which the tapes were presented to the subjects (a Latin Square design).

Results indicated that the outcomes originally reported by Dozier et al. (1998) are quite robust. The circular and reflexive interviews, once again, led to higher alliance scores, but this time on all three measure of the therapeutic alliance. As with the previous study, there were no differences that could be linked to demographic characteristics, or other significant differences in alliance scores for subjects who viewed the various types of interviews.

Taken together, the two studies demonstrated that, across two cultures, clients rated the therapeutic alliance as stronger when the therapist asked predominantly circular and reflexive questions. Since there is powerful evidence that the quality of the therapeutic alliance is itself a major predictor of therapeutic outcome (Hubble, Duncan, & Miller, 1999), these findings are potentially very important. Dermot and Carr (2001) concluded: "The present study underlines the importance of training therapists to include circular and reflexive questions." (p. 75)

As noted earlier, however, these studies have some limitations that render these conclusions tentative. In addition to their being analogue studies, measures were only taken during the engagement (beginning) phase of therapy. Future research will be needed to determine if the same relationships hold up during the middle and late phases of therapy. Also, it is possible that certain characteristics of the simulated therapist and family, or characteristics of the vignettes themselves, biased results in unknown ways. It is unclear if the same results would have been achieved with real therapists and clients in actual clinical settings.

Critique of the Systemic Approach to Assessment

The approach explicated in this chapter has a number of strengths as well as potential limitations. On the plus side, a method of assessment which relies on carefully crafted questions, and which elicits systemic connections, has a number of advantages. First, a high reliance on questions stimulates higher levels of client involvement and participation, which research suggests is strongly related to client change (Hubble et al., 1999). This is an approach that gets clients to become keen observers of their own process and discourages passivity. Second, it is a method which privileges client experience (Sprenkle, Blow, & Dickey, 1999). Since clients are encouraged to come up with their own unique insights and actions, client resistance and reactivity to therapists' imposing solutions is minimized. Therefore, it capitalizes on what may be the most important common factor in therapeutic change – the client's unique ability to take whatever is offered in therapy and to use it for his/her own purposes (Tallman & Bohart, 1999). Third, perhaps more than any other of the family therapy models, it is designed to bring forth, both for the therapist and clients, a systemic/interactional perspective. Sprenkle et al. (1999) have stressed that a systemic conceptualization of problems is one of the few truly unique common factors that distinguishes family therapy from other treatment modalities. Circular and reflexive questions may be among the most potent methods yet devised to bring this perspective into focus. Fourth, there is some promising empirical evidence that the use of circular and reflexive questions has a significant impact on clients' ratings of the therapeutic alliance, and therefore these questions may also contribute to therapy outcome.

On the negative side, the method has a number of potential disadvantages. First, it is not adequately researched. With the notable exception of the studies reviewed, most of the literature on the systemic perspective relies exclusively on personal testimony and clinical examples offered by its proponents. While these examples are often compelling, in this age of accountability, this is no substitute for more rigorous forms of evidence.

Second, it is much easier to describe these methods than to practice them effectively. Specifically, it is difficult to ask good circular and reflexive questions. Many novices ask circular questions in ways that come across as formulaic, stilted, and irrelevant to clients. This author has witnessed sessions in which clients found it mostly annoying to be barraged by strange sounding circular questions, to which they did not connect. Therapists need to pay attention to client feedback and to use words which sound natural and meaningful. Good reflexive questions, in turn, require a high degree of therapist creativity. In this author's experience, persons who have become skillful at asking circular and reflexive questions have received close supervision, and have engaged in disciples like writing reflexive questions down before sessions. Also, as noted previously, these questions need to be sufficiently different from the clients' perspectives to offer "news of a difference," but also to be close enough to the clients' perspectives so they are not summarily dismissed. The ability to walk this therapeutic fine line is an art.

Third, therapy and assessment is more than asking questions. Persons who use this method would be wise to consider supplementing it with other approaches like the use of questionnaires and assessment instruments. Also, as noted previously, the therapeutic alliance is also based on clients' perceptions that the therapist is a person of integrity with values and beliefs. This entails that the therapist share about himself/herself, which requires making statements as well as asking questions. Balancing statements with questions, therefore, is another therapeutic fine line that must be walked.

Fourth, and finally, the systemic method, as delineated by Boscolo and Checcin, and interpreters like Karl Tomm, seems strongly to privilege the role of cognitions in the process of change. While the current writer agrees that "changing the viewing" of clients is an important dimension of the change process (Sprenkle et al., 1999), the model may give somewhat short shrift to the role of affect in the process of change (Johnson, 1996) Interestingly, the later version of the Milan approach, emphasized in this paper, also pays less attention to the role of behavior in the process of change than the early Milan treatment model. The current writer believes there is sufficient evidence that the process of change is an affective, and cognitive, and behavioral process. All of these processes need to be emphasized approximately equally to get the greatest impact across the greatest range of clients, since clients vary considerably in the approach that best matches them.

Conclusion

This chapter has described the systemic approach to assessment and treatment. While there is promising evidence for its efficacy, more research will need to be done in actual clinical settings with real therapists and real clients. It is not at all clear whether this treatment works best for certain types of clients under certain circumstances and what therapists variables fit into the equation. Future research will also need to address if the model is as valuable for the later phases of therapy as it appears to be for the engagement phase.

A final strength of the model is that, since it is primarily about the process, not the content, of therapy; and since the ideas can be easily adapted to supplement other views, it can be used by clinicians who espouse almost any theoretical orientation. The reader is therefore encouraged to try out this approach to assessment, which is also an approach to intervention. The author both hopes that the art of asking questions described here, especially if practiced diligently and supervised, will enrich the reader's current approach to clinical interviewing.

References

Anderson, H. (1997).*Conversation, language, and possibilities*. New York: Basic Books.

Bateson, G. (1979). *Mind and nature*. New York: E. P. Dutton.

Boscolo, L., & Bertrando, P. (1993). *The times of time: A new perspective in systems therapy and consultation*. New York: Norton.

Boscolo. L., Cecchin, G., Hoffman, L., & Penn, P. (1987). *Milan systemic family therapy: Conversations in theory and practice*. New York: Basic Books.

Cecchin, G. (1987). Hypothesizing, circularity, and neutrality revisited: An invitation to curiosity. *Family Process, 26,* 405–413.

Combs, G., & Freedman, J.(1998). A response to Minuchin. *Journal of Marital and Family Therapy, 24,* 405–410.

Dermot, R., & Carr, A. (2001). A study of the differential effects of Tomm's questioning styles on the therapeutic alliance. *Family Process, 40,* 67–77.

DeShazer, S. (1991). *Putting differences to work*. New York: Norton.

Dozier, R. M., Hicks, M. W., Cornille, T. A., & Peterson, G. W. (1998). The effect of Tomm's therapeutic questioning styles on the therapeutic alliance: A clinical analogue study. *Family Process, 37,* 1–12.

Fleuridas, C., Nelson, T., & Rosenthal, D. (1986). The evolution of circular questions: Training family therapists. *Journal of Marital and Family Therapy, 12,* 113–127.

Freedman, J., & Combs, G. (1996). *Narrative therapy*. New York: W.W. Norton.

Hubble, M. A., Duncan, B. L., & Miller, S. (Eds.) (1999) *The heart and soul of change: What works in therapy*. Washington, DC: The American Psychological Association.

Johnson, S. M. (1996). *Creating connection: The practice of emotionally focused marital therapy*. New York: Brunner Mazel

Machal, M., Feldman, R., & Segal, J. (1989) The unraveling of a treatment program: A follow-up study of the Milan approach to family therapy. *Family Process, 28,* 257–470.

Minuchin, S. (1998) Where is the family in narrative family therapy. *Journal of Marital and Family Therapy, 24,* 397–404.

Nichols, M. P., & Schwartz, R. C. (2001). *Family therapy: Concepts and methods*, 5th Edition. Boston: Allyn and Bacon.

Pearce, W. B., & Cronen, V. E. (1980). *Communication, action, and meaning: The creation of social realities.* New York: Praeger.

Penn, P. (1992). Circular questioning. *Family Process, 21,* 267–280.

Piercy, F. P., & Wetchler, J. L., (1996) Structural, strategic, and systemic family therapies. In F. P. Piercy, D. H. Sprenkle, & J. L. Wetchler, *Family Therapy Sourcebook*, 2nd Ed. (pp. 50–71). New York: Guilford.

Pinsof, W. M., & Catherall, D. R. (1986). The integrative psychotherapy alliance: Family, couple, and individual scales. *Journal of Marital and Family Therapy, 12,* 137–148.

Selvini Palazzoli, M., Boscolo, L., Cecchin, G., & Prata, G. (1978). *Paradox and counterparadox.* New York: Jason Aronson.

Selvini Palazzoli, M., Boscolo, L., Cecchin, G., & Prata, G. (1980). Hypothesizing-circularity-neutrality: Three guidelines for the conductor of the session. *Family Process, 19,* 3–12.

Sprenkle, D. H., Blow, A. J., & Dickey, M. (1999). Common factors and other nontechnique variables in marriage and family therapy. In M. A. Hubble, B. L. Duncan, & S. Miller (Eds.), *The heart and soul of change: What works in therapy* (pp. 329–360). Washington, DC: The American Psychological Association.

Tallman, K. L., & Bohart, A.C. (1989). The client as a common factor: Clients as self-healers. In M. A. Hubbell, B. L. Duncan, & S. Miller (Eds.), *The heart and soul of change: What works in therapy.* Washington, DC: The American Psychological Association.

Tomm, K. (1984a) One perspective on the Milan systemic approach: Part Overview of development, theory, and practice. *Journal of Marital and Family Therapy ,10,* 113–126.

Tomm, K. (1984b) One perspective on the Milan systemic approach: Part II. Description of session format, interviewing style, and interventions. *Journal of Marital and Family Therapy,10,* 253–272.

Tomm, K. (1987) Reflexive questioning as a means to enable self-healing. *Family Process, 26,* 167–184.

Tomm, K. (1988) Interventive interviewing, Part III: Intending to ask circular, strategic, or reflexive questions. *Family Process, 27,* 1–16.

White, M., & Epston, D. (1990). *Narrative means to therapeutic ends.* New York: Norton.

12

Psychodynamic Assessment

Günter Reich & Manfred Cierpka

Summary
We begin with a description of the psychoanalytical theory of object relationships. Its aim is to clarify the interlocking of internal and interpersonal conflicts and the problems and symptoms they may cause. Following on from this, the psychodynamics of relationships between partners, parents and children, brothers and sisters, and finally between the therapist and the family system are examined.

What is the Aim of Psychodynamic Assessment?

A family assessment based on psychodynamics tries to make a connection between the internal and interpersonal conflicts within the family. These are largely dependent on the interplay of unconscious and preconscious intrapsychic and interpersonal forces, currently effective wishes, fears and defense mechanisms, and the resulting transactional patterns within the family. These manifest themselves during therapy as conflicts between family members and in the relationship between the therapist and the family system. Thus, psychodynamic assessment is first and foremost an assessment of relationships.

This definition relates to three dimensions of psychodynamic assessment:
- The currently effective unconscious and preconscious conflicts within the family. Here we refer to Sandler and Sandler's (1985) "present unconscious" and "past unconscious."
- The transferences within the family (Stierlin 1977), i.e., the actualizations (Sandler 1982) of wishes within a relationship – arising from earlier, internalized object relationships – in family interactions.
- The dynamics of transference and countertransference as encountered during therapy in an actualized form between therapist and family members.

The Interlocking of Past Relationship Experiences with Present Transactional Patterns: Explanatory Concepts

Past Unconscious and Present Unconscious

In order to differentiate between the present psychodynamic assessment and the multi-generational perspective, it is helpful to make a distinction between the past unconscious and the present unconscious (Sandler & Sandler, 1985). The past unconscious represents the wishes, fantasies, impulses, forms of defense, and conflict resolution that have arisen in the early stages of the individual's life; these are initially consciousness syntonic and become consciousness dystonic with the first censorship (when defense sets in).

The processes of the present unconscious serve to maintain internal balance in the present. The impulses (wishes, fears, memories, and fantasies) that emanate from the past unconscious are regarded as obtrusive, unfitting, and disturbing. In order to deal with them, two kinds of adjustment mechanism are used – first, the past must be brought into line with the present and adapted to form an up-to-date version. If this does not fully succeed, a "second censorship" is required in order to distort this updated wish (or fear, memory, fantasy) by means of defense operations, or to completely repress it. This second censorship is directed against current experience, which is so heavily burdened with early conflicts, in an attempt to avoid disappointment, humiliation, offence, and shame. These signal affects are also frequently defended against by means of, e.g., externalization or transformation into the opposite.

For example, when the conversation turns towards his relationship with his son, a man draws therapists into an argument about the "principles of bringing up children." This turns out to be a defense maneuver to mask a deep insecurity in this area. The man wonders if he has more loving feelings towards his son than he ought to have: he suspects that their relationship may have "homoerotic undertones." He is ashamed. The current censorship is directed against this conflict. The shame is defended against by the transformation of passive to active. He argues with the therapists, unconsciously anticipating their criticism. The underlying historical conflict that emerges here is based on the defense of close Oedipal bonds with his mother. She abused him in an eroticized manner for comfort because the father, an officer, was away at war and was finally killed. Consequently the man developed a deep "father-hunger" and wished to free himself from the guilty feelings arising from the close relationship with his mother, which at the same time he enjoyed. His son was seen as the liberator, as the next man in the sequence of generations, reminding him of his feelings towards his father. On the other hand, because of the oedipal ambivalence transferred to the son, the father developed feelings of guilt towards him, currently masked by feelings of shame that were initially also denied.

The past unconscious of the family comprises the multigenerational perspective and the dynamics at work here, such as identification processes, unconscious loyalty dynamics, the development of family myths, etc. The denied, disturbing past remains highly effective, but only appears in an updated version. It is expressed in current wishes and conflicts within relationships. The present unconscious manifests itself in current interpersonal processes of defense, collusive patterns in partnerships, interaction between parents and children, interaction with the extended family, and interaction within therapy, the level of "psychosocial compromise formation."

Psychoanalytic Object Relationship Theories and Family Assessment

Psychoanalytic object relationship theories form a bridge between psychoanalysis and family therapy. They stress the human being's basic need for relationships that go beyond the satisfaction of instincts and exist independently of this (see Balint, 1968; Eagle, 1988; Fairbairn, 1952; Kernberg, 1976, 1980; Modell, 1988). Even a baby, from birth onwards, seeks relationships with other people – so-called "objects" (Dornes, 1993; Lichtenberg, 1983, 1987; Stern, 1985).

The term "object relationship" is used in a double sense:
- firstly it means the interpersonal relationship between two people,
- secondly it refers to internalized ideational images, for example, the parents (in psychoanalytical language the "representations").

Object relationship theories represent models in which unconscious internal object relationships interact dynamically with current interpersonal experiences (Ogden, 1983; Sandler, 1982). In terms of developmental psychology, they describe early ego development as the differentiation between the self and the primary object (the mother). Initially, the family provides the child with a material, nourishing foundation and security, the so-called "holding function" of the mother during the first years of life (Winnicott, 1974). The detachment and individuation processes during the first four years of life are of vital importance for infantile development, for they allow the personality and mental structure of the child to develop both in harmony with the mother and at counterpoint to her (Mahler et al., 1975). An important outcome of this psychic development is the formation of self and object representations and a differentiated intrapsychic structure (Jacobson, 1964).

Recent infant research stresses the primary intersubjective relatedness of the baby; it actively seeks contact with the people who look after it and differentiates between them (Dornes, 1993; Lichtenberg, 1983, 1987; Stern, 1985). Children are not only the receivers of care and attention. They do not only identify with familial relationships and functions, but also actively change these from the very beginning.

The regulation of individual needs, fears, and conflicts in adulthood also functions within the framework of internalized relationship experiences with the parent figures in early childhood. Interaction patterns influenced by the child itself are internalized in dyads, triads, tetrads, and so on, as well as "family representations," i.e., pictures of the family as a whole (Cierpka, 1992); the emotional coloring of the respective experiences has an important influence on these patterns (Kernberg, 1976). These internalized schemes represent the subjective processing of interpersonal experience and interactions and not "objective reality" (Thomä & Kächele, 1985, p. 300). In this way they are compromise formations and can also be employed in the defense of unpleasant emotions and conflicts connected with relationships.

Dyads, Triads and Relationships Involving Several People

Human relationships have a basic triangular form, as every person is born as the extension of a couple, as a number three (Bauriedl, 1994; Buchholz, 1993; Cierpka, 1992; Reiche, 1992). At just a few weeks old, a baby is able to form separate relationships with both of its parents and other people and store these in the form of memory available to him/her. However, babies do not begin to symbolically represent these differences and gradually connect them with an internal concept of gender difference until the second half of the second year of life. A child's close bonding with or fixation on the mother should be seen as a result of its more frequent or exclusive early interactions with her and not as a "natural stage of development" (Dornes, 1993; Lichtenberg, 1983; Papousek, 1987; Stern, 1985).

How an individual comes to terms with the basic triangular structure of human relationships largely depends upon how he or she copes with the Oedipal conflict. The Oedipus conflict represents a "summary of the human condition, of the eye of a needle we all have to pass through, simply because we are procreated by a father and born by a mother" (Reiche, 1992, p. 57). This forces us to come to terms with the parents as individuals and as a couple, whether we want to or not. These processes do not depend on the type of family in which children grow up. Also in single-parent families children develop fantasies and questions about the absent parent and the relationship between both parents.

Parents who enjoy erotic satisfaction and generally harmonize with one another give their child a feeling of security and ease its Oedipal conflicts. It does not need to fantasize about its parents' sexual life as a violent act and perpetuate its wishes to own the parent of the opposite gender, with all the feelings of guilt this implies. Marital conflicts, on the other hand, can cause such fantasies to arise (see Dicks, 1967, p.38).

The theory of the Oedipal conflict makes it easier to understand why conflicts and discontent are to a certain extent unavoidable, even within successful, stable partnerships. In every marriage, an unconscious identification with our own parents' marriage, our most deeply internalized prototype of a partnership, is revived. The man and the woman now follow in the footsteps of her mother and his father. Incestuous wishes and fantasies, which have been successfully denied up until that point, are now brought back to life, accompanied by superego anxiety (Horney, 1927, p. 398).

The Oedipal conflict both drives the subject into the marriage and out of it. This is an important reason for the lapse of sexual desire within marriage – eroticism often appears to be difficult to combine with permanency in relationships (Reich, 1987). It also helps to explain why many couples find that their sexual relationship is disturbed or completely broken off following marriage or even more frequently after the birth of the first child – the partners are now sleeping with a "husband" or a "wife" or a "mother" and "father"; the partnership is superimposed by the internal images of the parents (Reich, 1987).

When further children are born, the pre-Oedipal or Oedipal triangular structure changes for the first child as well as for the parents; it becomes an extended relationship involving several people. An additional new subsystem is created within the family, with an interactive structure that is independent from the relationships between the parents and their child and between the two parents. There is also an increased possibility of forming complex internal structures and object representations (Diepold, 1988). Some psychoanalysts attribute a great deal of clinical significance to envy and rivalry between siblings in the development of psychic disorders, disconnected from the Oedipal triangular relationship (see Wurmser, 1987). Intact sibling relationships can make oedipal conflicts easier to withstand, just as they can encourage the development of a post-oedipal internal structure that no longer relates to the family in adolescence, e.g., within peer groups (Blos, 1962).

Sibling relationships and sibling transference often considerably influence the choice of partner, partnerships, and parent-child relationships, in which sibling relationships and conflicts are often restaged (Cierpka, 2001; Kreische, 1998; Sohni, 1998; Toman, 1974).

Assessment Questions

- Do the relationships within the family consist mainly of relationships between two people, or do important dyadic relationships, for example between the identified patient and the parents, exist in a network of multipersonal relationships?
- Which triangular relationships or relationships involving several individuals can be observed?
- Do these seem to be mainly based on conflicts, e.g., rivalry or envy, or do they appear to be positive, "holding"? Concerning which aspects and topics is this the case?
- Which deeper current conflicts are regulated by these relationships?
- What form does the erotic and sexual relationship between the couple take? Which conflicts and fantasies does this bring to light?
- Is there a sibling subsystem with its own interactions that are not dependent on the parent-child relationship?
- Do the parents transfer conflicts with their own brothers and sisters to one another or to the children?
- What possible conflicts in the multigenerational perspective do the above aspects indicate?

Object Representations, Internal "Map," and Primary Relationship Wishes

The various internalized object relationships take the form of an internal "map" (Friedman, 1980) of interpersonal and intrapsychic reality, which can be different for each member of the family. Internal maps are individual, personal theories on relationship forms or personal life plans (Cierpka, 1989b). They have three functions:
- They serve as an internal system of reference (Stierlin, 1975), for example, for the image a person has of the world and of others. This allows the subject to categorise experiences, make comparisons and estimates, find his or her way around in the world, and make decisions.
- They have a gyroscopic (i.e., guiding) function for present and future interpersonal relationships (Stierlin, 1975). This guides individuals, e.g., in the forming of partnerships.
- They contribute to autonomy, as they enable the individual to tune in to his own self and carry out an internal dialogue.

In accordance with their internal object relationships and the resulting individual life plans, people form primary relationship wishes with corresponding wishful fantasies (Luborsky, 1984; König & Kreische, 1992; Sandler, 1982). The differentiation of forms of object choice according to the "narcissistic type" and the "anaclitic type", as defined by Freud (1914b), appears to be of fundamental importance here. According to the first type, one loves what one is oneself (the self), what one has been, what one would like to be (the ideal ego) or the person that is or has been part of one's own self (e.g., one's own child). According to the latter type one loves the "nourishing woman" or the "protective man."

Individuals try to realize their wishes and wishful fantasies in their internal reality (in fantasies, daydreams, and dreams) or in their external reality, in order to create a "perceptual identity": a uniformity between the wishful image or fantasy and reality. Such realization attempts are generally modified to conform with one's sense of reality, the need for security and the demands of the superego and the ego ideal. When attempts are made to transform these wishes into external reality, "test signals" are given to other people and their answers are continually evaluated. The test signals are either reinforced, changed, or stopped. Wishes and wishful fantasies can change during the course of development, but they retain a lasting essence with a specific meaning for the individual.

For example, people may develop strong wishes for their attractiveness to be confirmed. They develop these wishes in their fantasy. They also try to find someone in the real world to admire them. They seek the company of men or women who seem to give them the confirmation they crave. They intensify relationships with such people, in the hope of receiving still more confirmation. They consider other people to be less interesting, as they provide little or no confirmation. They reduce contact with them or let it peter out. If these realization attempts often or continually fail to succeed in the actual field of relationships, the fantasy with its promises of wish fulfillment may become more and more important. These people may withdraw from social contact to a large degree.

The most intense relationship wishes are usually directed at the partner, children, and the family as a whole; thus these are the areas where the conflict-ridden dynamics of internal images of relationships are most strongly actualized and confirmation, disappointments, and offence most strongly experienced.

The Tension between Individual Life Plans and the Family

Internalized object relationships and relationship wishes contribute considerably to the life models of the various family members. Tension can arise here in two different ways:
- The relationship wishes and life plans of individual family members are incompatible.
- The demands of the family unit and the wishes of the individual family members, for example, the need for individuation and individuality, contradict one another.

Such tense conditions can promote the functionality of the family in a positive way; however, they can also impair it. The higher the discrepancy between individual internalized object relationships along with resulting relationship wishes and the interpersonal field of relationships within the family, the more probable it is that conscious or unconscious conflicts will exert a negative effect on the functionality of the family; the difference becomes so great that the fulfillment of mutual expectations and wishes is rendered extremely difficult. The systems are no longer in a state of balance.

For example, a high-spirited and sometimes impulsively aggressive child seeks relationships that offer him or her holding and firm limits, thus regulating violent emotions. Intrafamilial relationship patterns must also be relatively secure, so that the child is not left with the feeling that she or he bears responsibility for the breakdown of relationships. If the family cannot offer this kind of security in its network of relationships (e.g., due to serious marital conflicts or because the parents are afraid of impulsive behavior or unconsciously admire it and encourage it), the discrepancy between the relationship wishes of the child and the actual familial environment becomes too great. The consequence can be that expulsion tendencies arise or a scapegoat is looked for in an attempt to reduce the tension.

When the maps become too alike, the minimization of differences stands in the way of lively and constructive confrontation. Although the internal and external systems are in a state of balance, they are upheld rigidly in interpersonal and intrapsychic defense mechanisms, so that the liveliness and also the functionality of the family suffers.

Framo's (1992) comments on defense mechanisms in families is particularly true of such cases – i.e., that it is extremely difficult for anyone, however mature, to avoid the family role assigned to him if he stays within the sphere of the family – he will behave according to his role, against his will. Such families have much greater difficulties in adapting to changes in the life cycle than others.

Interpersonal Defense

Mentzos' (1990) concept of interpersonal defense outlines basic mechanisms for the actualization of relationship wishes and internalized relationship patterns. Here he refers to "organized interactive forms of defense in which one partner's real modes of behavior, characteristics, actions, and reactions encourage, allow, or stabilize the other partner's neurotic conflict defense or neurotic compromise formation in the satisfaction of needs. Often the procedure is reciprocal, so that the first partner's defense is also consolidated by the second partner. Of course, this assumes the existence of complementary modes of neurotic behavior. This sometimes occurs spontaneously; however, it is more often produced secondarily through the assignment of roles, delegation, unconscious seduction, and provocation (unconscious-manipulative). Naturally, such complementary interpersonal defense constellations are particularly stable" (p. 26).

Here, partners are either "chosen to actually take over the required function in the defense formation, or they are manipulated into doing so, e.g., via role assignment" (p. 27).

For example, a man withdraws increasingly into himself and is silent when conflicts arise with his wife, his children, or his parents, who live in the same house. This begins to annoy his wife more and more. After speaking to him several times about it, she finally explodes. He now criticizes her "aggression" and "lack of objectivity". She is ashamed of her "lack of self-control." The man is completely unaware of his own aggression, expressed in passivity and denial. It is masked to a large degree through isolation of affect and rationalization. He experiences it vicariously through his wife, who he is able to reproach according to the superego demands they both share ("be objective," "stay calm"). This represents a subtle form of aggression that conforms with the superego. He first gained access to his own aggression, which he had defended against due to a fear of being punished, during the course of treatment.

Interpersonal defense is basically the interactive actualization of internal relationship patterns (externalization), whereby one individual looks for or creates object representations or self representations in another. Wangh (1962) refers to this as an "evocation of a proxy."

Interpersonal defense plays an important part in the structuring of partnerships and relationships between parents and children. In recent times there has been a trend towards classifying the various processes involved in interpersonal defense and the accompanying actualization of relationship wishes and relationship experiences under the general term of "projective identification." The actions of one person induce particular modes of experience and behavior in another person. This person intermittently identifies with these induced modes of experience and behavior; the initiator also continues to identify with them in "empathic association." The initiator now feels that he can control his partner (Kernberg, 1987; Ogden, 1979). The global nature of this concept has been criticized; there is a movement towards using it as an "omnibus concept" in place of a differentiated description of the many and various unconscious interpersonal exchange processes (Heimann, 1975; Thomä & Kächele, 1988; see also Grefe & Reich, 1996). All of these processes usually comprise identification with the aggressor and transformation from active to passive, translated into corresponding behavior (Porder, 1987; see also Grefe & Reich, 1996).

For example, a father identifies with his own prohibiting, powerful parents and treats his child in the same way as he was treated by his parents. So he accuses the child of being malicious and proceeds to punish it or complains about how much the child makes him suffer.

A single-parent mother complains bitterly about her seven-year-old son, whom she describes as a "monster." The son is disruptive at school, singing loudly and walking around during lessons. At home he regularly demolishes the household when the mother is not there. "Whenever I break something, I say 'I'm on duty'" he commented to therapists, who could at first hardly believe their ears.

In the family of origin, the mother's brother was considered aggressive and "wayward;" at the same time he was spoiled and favored by the parents. For example, he was allowed to qualify for further education, while his sister was steered towards intermediate secondary education. She suffered a great deal at the hands of her brother's aggressive attacks and often had to "wait on" him. She could not allow herself to experience her envy and anger as she was afraid of disapproval and punishment. She denied these feelings and covered them by adopting altruistic characteristics. Through therapy it became clear that she was now re-enacting her relationship with her brother with her son. Primarily she accomplished this by suffering from his tyranny. However, she was radiant whenever she talked about his destructive habits, thus unconsciously reinforcing his behavior. At the same time, her son had now taken over the role of the person experiencing difficulties at school, almost on the brink of failure, which meant that she could take on a stance of moral judgment and punishment. She had assigned herself the strongest role and could now unconsciously revenge herself on her brother under the cloak of moral indignation.

Assessment Questions

- Which modes of behavior or symptoms of certain family members, e.g., the identified patient, partners, or "healthy" siblings, may be assumed to stem from the internalized relationship patterns of other family members?
- Which conscious and which suspected unconscious relationship wishes and internal relationship patterns are at work here?
- What effect do the tensions between individual relationship wishes and life plans and the demands of the family as a whole have on the functionality of the family?
- Which interactive processes can be observed where these relationship wishes and internalized relationship patterns are actualized?
- Which conflicts and unpleasant emotions are family members trying to block out with these actualizations?
- Do these relationship patterns infer processes that should be examined more closely from a multigenerational perspective?

The Psychodynamics of the Partnership

The Partnership as a Contract

Partnerships may be seen as expressions of an unconscious contract (Lederer & Jackson, 1967; Sager, 1976, 1981; Walster et al., 1977). They "are linked with expectations concerning what the partners put into the relationship and what they wish to receive. Crises and conflicts arise when these expectations are disappointed and one or both remain dissatisfied" (Reich, 1988a, p. 29). According to Sager (1981), partners' expectations of one another are experienced and communicated interpersonally on three levels – they can be conscious and declared, conscious but not declared, or undeclared and unconscious. In the long term, the unconscious level is the most important part of the contract. Here unrealistic and contradictory expectations often exist, which can even also sometimes stand at odds with conscious expectations.

Dicks (1967) distinguishes between three major levels of a couple's relationship, which together form a dynamic balanced system:
- The subsystem of sociocultural values and norms. This includes the social status and shared ideas of society as a whole, e.g., views on gender roles, political and social rights and duties, religious and political ideas and values;
- The subsystem of the "central ego" (Dicks follows Fairbairns's model of object relationships here, see also Eagle, 1988). This includes, e.g., the partners' conscious expectations from their life together and their lifestyle, their personal norms, judgments, interests (sport, cultural, or intellectual), habits, and taste. These expectations originate from the object relationships and social learning before marriage, e.g., from the parents' homes and lifestyles. Deviations from the parental model are also always linked with early object relationships that were emotionally important;
- The subsystem of unconscious "transactions". This refers to unconscious internalized relationships between the subject and important early objects, which now take effect between the partners, e.g., unconscious wishes for oral satisfaction, unconscious Oedipal wishes and conflicts.

The first two levels of the system, as well as the third, are often linked with affects and ideas on what is good, right, or vital that lie deep in the unconsciousness.

In order for a partnership to remain stable, at least two of the three subsystems must function to the satisfaction of both partners. In this concept, the unconscious internalized object relationships form only a part of the marriage conflict (see Reich, 1988a). Conflicts on the level of transactions, for example, unconscious childhood wishes, can be evened out, lessened, or even suppressed through mutual cultural (e.g., religious) and personal norms, so that altogether satisfaction outweighs dissatisfaction. On the level of the central ego, deviations from the parental model, i.e., from the norms and lifestyle of the parental home, can lead to a conflict between the now internalized "subcultural pressure" (from the parental objects) and own ideas. Such conflicts can be balanced out by the other two levels.

The importance of this view can hardly be stressed enough, as the level of unconscious transactions is often considered to be the only area of relevance – therapists often place too much focus upon it in assessment and treatment. This means that considerable resources in partnerships remain unnoticed or their importance is undervalued.

Assessment Questions

- On which level is the conflict in the partnership located (sociocultural norms, personal norms and lifestyle, internalized object relationships and unconscious transactions)?
- What possible sources of concurrence and satisfaction exist on the other levels?
- Are resources for the partnership available that could help to balance out conflicts?
- Which important early experiences and affects are the three levels associated with?
- Which multigenerational traditions and conflicts do the norms, lifestyles, and relationships point towards on the three levels?

The Collusion Model

Dicks describes the level of unconscious transactions (1967) by means of his model of collusion. Collusion describes an unconscious interplay between the partners on the basis of a mutual basic conflict in polarized positions or roles. For both partners this represents a joint self-healing attempt in the name of "the restoration of the whole personality." An individual seeks aspects of his own personality that have been suppressed through interaction with the parents in the partner. A "healing of the split-off" takes place, whereby parts of the individual's identity or fears – that have been suppressed by means of projection or projective identification – are discovered or induced in the partner. The conflict-ridden, unavailable aspects of both partners' personalities and potential are now shared out between each other, so that one partner forms the counterpole of the other in manifest behavior. For this reason, collusion represents a form of interpersonal defense. If the progressive and regressive patterns are divided up too rigidly, a flexible interchange of these positions can no longer take place in important areas of the relationship. Individual growth and differentiation is then avoided. Self-object boundaries and identities remain fluid. If the repressed parts of the personality are not reintegrated, conflicts involving two factors arise:

- One or both partners are disappointed that the other does not behave according to their expectations, i.e., "after the manner of a preconceived model or a figure from their fantasy world" (Dicks, 1967, p.50). For example, one partner can be experienced in the same disappointing way as a parent during childhood, whereas the other can be transported back into the role of a disappointed child who has got the worst of the deal. The experience of this similarity between the partner and a rejecting parent figure has probably been denied in the initial phases of partnership, when the partners idealized one other (see chapter on choice of partner). The discovery of being disappointed by the partner is often made simultaneously by both parties. It often results in a regression to infantile modes of behavior towards the partner and an escalation of conflicts.
- Certain characteristics or modes of behavior in the partner that were found attractive or even idealized at the beginning of the relationship are now criticized or fought against. This phenomenon, which often occurs in conflicts between partners, at first appears paradox. However, it can be explained as follows – the characteristics of the partner that are admired at the beginning and later rejected often represent elements of one's own personality that cannot be "lived" as they are prohibited by internalized parental figures. The fact that the partner gives free

expression to these suppressed parts of oneself causes the internal parents (the superego) to be summoned. The rejecting partner identifies with them (identification with the aggressor). The other partner, who was living out the suppressed tendencies of the first one, is now brought into the position of the rejected, punished, accused child. He or she feels the same way as the partner used to feel. The outcome is not only an externalization of an internal conflict-ridden object relationship but also a reversal of roles.

For example, a man complains about his wife's untidiness. This often leads to arguments, as he is constantly tidying up after her, checking her purse and bank account, etc. When he is asked what he initially found attractive about her, he replies "she didn't take things too seriously, she was so relaxed." The conflicts gradually broke out when the couple got married after completing their studies and starting work. Before this they had lived together quite happily. The man had had a strict upbringing, but he was afraid of confronting his parents. His wife took over this task for him; he had now taken on the role of his own strict parents.

Both forms of the "return of the repressed" are complementary to one another and often occur concurrently when a couple is experiencing massive conflicts. König & Kreische (1985) describe this in their concept of "crossover collusion," in which each partner takes over the roles of parent and child for the other.

Willi (1975) extends the collusion concept by describing the positions of progressive (overcompensatory, active) and regressive defense behavior along the lines of the classical psychoanalytic developmental theory.

- In narcissistic collusion there is a wish for fusion and extreme harmony, but at the same time the partners are afraid of this. This means that they can never reach their goal and are destined to remain deeply disappointed.
- In oral collusion, which is based on "taking care of one another," conflicts arise when the oral needs of the "carer" and "provider" can no longer be suppressed. The "charge" mistrusts the "provider;" his self-esteem is continually undermined by being taken care of.
- Anal-sadistic collusion is centered around the theme of "belonging to one another completely." There is a fear of the partner's autonomy, which is equated with the ruin of the relationship. Any step towards autonomy taken by the regressive partner is fought against. Power struggles, games involving infidelity and jealousy and masochistic transactions serve to maintain mutual dependency.
- Phallic-oedipal or hysterical collusion is focused upon "male strength" and "female weakness." On the surface, the woman desires the "strong, potent man," but on the other hand she undermines his position, "castrates" him or renders him impotent because of her own aspirations to the "male" role. Consequently, suppressed "passive" "female" tendencies emerge in the man to a greater degree.

The collusion patterns described by Willi are developed and reinforced according to their chances of actualization within the partnership to form an "interaction personality" (Willi, 1975). A mixture of the types is usually found in disturbed couples' relationships.

For diagnostic purposes these patterns offer a prototype for describing transactions, albeit not an exhaustive one taking the complexity of these processes as described by Dicks (1967) into consideration. Particularly when we explore the process of mate selection, of how the couple met, their situation, perception, wishes, and conflicts at that time, we are often provided with a very clear picture of the later dominant patterns of collusion here described in the cover memory (see Reich 1987, 1988a and the literature quoted there).

Assessment Questions

- What are the main manifest themes of the conflict between the partners?
- What possible unconscious themes can be inferred?
- How do the partners describe the process of mate selection, their meeting, and the first phase of their partnership?
- What did the partners find attractive about one another?
- In what way do the former elements that were found attractive reoccur in the conflict?
- Which internalized relationship patterns are actualized or externalized here?
- What possible multigenerational conflicts do these patterns point towards?

The Psychodynamics of the Relationship between Parent and Child

Couples who are in a relationship that they consider to be long-term probably always develop a family fantasy; they feel like a family. Even if they have no children, these possibly exist in a mutual fantasy world (see Cierpka, 1992).

Children are often conceived and born in the imagination of their parents before their real conception has taken place. The parents have probably also already fantasized about their further development.

The parents' unsolved problems stemming from the multigenerational level and severe tensions in the parental dyad can lead to children being manipulated into neuroticizing positions as object or self representations of the parents and furthermore identifying with these (Richter, 1963). Richter describes the following role patterns:

- If object representations are transferred to the child, her or she becomes a substitute for another person, e.g., a parent (parentification, reversal of the generations, see Chapter 12). Here, parents behave in a "childish" way towards the child, viewing it as a "source of love" or completely submitting to its demands at an early stage. If the child becomes a partner substitute, this generally points towards unsolved sexual conflicts between the parents or insufficient grieving over the loss of a partner. Unfulfilled needs for sexual, erotic satisfaction, or affection are directed towards the child in a more or less neutralized form. In the unconscious or preconscious fantasy system, the incest barrier breaks down. Parents can adopt jealously dominant or seductive, compliant behavior towards their children, fathers pushing their daughters into the position of "close companions" and "trusted accomplices." Freud (1905b) already declared marital conflicts to be an important prerequisite for neurotic developments, as they perpetuate Oedipal conflicts.
Sibling relationships, especially unsolved rivalry problems, can also be transferred to children. For example, oral or narcissistic collusion can be brought out of balance by the birth of a "newcomer" who demands and receives mother's or father's attention. This can culminate in envy and elimination impulses (Sohni, 1994).

- In the case of self representations being transferred to the children, Richter (1963) refers to "narcissistic projections" in accordance with Freud (1914b), and partly anticipating certain later developments (Kohut, 1971). The main function of these projections is to stabilize self-esteem (Mentzos, 1990).

Here the child can be made into an image, an extension of the individual's own person, to satisfy a narcissistic fantasy of immortality (see Freud, 1914b). The individual's own self-representations, his own characteristics, either imaginary or real, are projected onto the child. The child identifies with these and thus its psychic development (organization of instinctual drives, ego and superego structure) stops at the level reached by the parent concerned.

If the child acts as a substitute for the ideal self, it is seen as the parent would have liked to have become according to ego-ideal demands. His own feelings of failure, guilt, and shame are suppressed. This can prove too much for the child, who can react by developing many kinds of symptoms. In its fantasy, it remains nothing more than a part of the parent. If it acts as a substitute for the "negative self" of the parents, the child is pushed into the role of scapegoat. In the first stages it is given subtle signals or massive attributions encouraging it to enact the suppressed impulses of the parents. The child identifies with the attributions according to the maxim "better this identity than none at all" (see Erikson, 1956). In this way, parents can act out their unconscious impulses through identification with the children, enjoying guilt-free substitute satisfaction. They can also externalize their self-punishment tendencies, with the "naughty child" on the receiving end (see also the case history in the paragraph Interpersonal Defense and the first interview outlined in Chapter 6, where the identified patient's symptom allows her to act out her parents' anal protest).

– Unresolved conflicts between parents can be widened and displaced if both parents attempt to pull the child on to their sides. The child becomes a contested ally. This tendency is observed over and over again in cases of divorce, where children are made into witnesses, referees or set to work as spies against the other parent (Reich, 1991). In extreme cases, children can be given the feeling that they will be loved only if they take one parent's side against the other. This happens, for example, when the parents' affection is inconstant and depends upon certain statements being made by the child. This form of exploitation can lead to a corruption of the ability to form relationships, to self-hatred, which is often externalized, and to dissocial modes of behavior (see also Boszormenyi-Nagy & Krasner, 1986).

Richter (1970) divides neurotic familial processes into "symptom neurotic" and "character neurotic" developments. In familial symptom neurosis, a member of the family is declared unhealthy and becomes a "case". This often serves to calm the tense atmosphere; the displacement allows the other members of the family to consider themselves as "normal."

In familial character neurosis, the family members have become stabilized in mutual defense against the outside world, often with the help of a neurotic ideology. Absorbed in their own world, they experience the environment as anomalous or threatening; on the other hand, the family members' experience and behavior is ego-syntonic for all concerned. They are like a wrong-way driver, wondering why all the cars coming towards him are traveling in the wrong direction. Although the boundary between the family and the outside world is rigid, boundaries within the family are fluid. Richter describes

– the anxiety neurotic *sanatorium family*, which exteriorizes intrafamilial tension and defends against this in a symbiotic attitude of conservation;

- the paranoid *fortress family*, whose members experience the outside world as hostile and threatening; and
- the *hysterical family*, whose life together is organized like a theatre production, avoiding seriousness and sincerity with extreme displays of emotion. On the other hand, affects of a depressive nature threaten to break out from beneath the surface.

The distinction between familial symptom neurosis and character neurosis provides information on how far families are able to distance themselves from their patterns of experience and behavior and reflect upon themselves, i.e., whether they are capable of achieving a "therapeutic splitting of the ego."

Assessment Questions

- How are the children involved in the parents' unsolved conflicts?
- Do they appear to represent internal "objects" or parts of the parents' selves?
- To what extent does the child's symptom represent a compromise formation for these conflicts?
- To what extent has the family gained stability as a result of the symptom?
- Which "neurotic ideologies" does the family use to gain stability?

The Psychodynamics of Sibling Relationships

Siblings as an Independent Subsystem with its Own Dynamics

Siblings form an independent subsystem within the family with its own relationship experiences, conflicts and solutions. A good relationship between brothers and sisters helps to stabilize the boundary between the generations and offer resistance against coalitions, alliances and parentification. Sibling relationships can provide support and maintain equilibrium in conflicts within and outside of the family (e.g., with peers) (Reich et al., 2002; Sohni, 1994).

Differences between Siblings

Siblings grow up in the same family, which means they have a great deal in common. However, there are also considerable differences between them. Not only differences in age, gender, or serial order in the sibling constellation contribute to the differences between children but, more importantly, their individual experiences. The concept of the "non-shared environment" (see Joraschky & Cierpka, 1990) applies if children develop in different ways and differ greatly from one another in their sibling relationships or specific peer relationships. Interactions between siblings that reinforce the differences between them are known as deidentification. If brothers and sisters take on complementary roles that are further reinforced by the parents, their differences are emphasized rather than the common ground between them. These differences are already present in the serial order in the sibling constellation (Sulloway, 1996). The non-shared environment and experience seem to be more relevant for the personal development of the child than the family reality that is shared by everyone (Hetherington et al., 1994, Reiss et al., 2000).

It is well known that parents bring up some children differently from others. For example, one child must be treated firmly and given clear guidelines, while another needs more support and praise, etc. Parents emphasize these differences, but do not often speak of the things the children have in common. If too much emphasis is placed upon the differences, conflicts between the children and (indirectly) between the parents can be reinforced.

Differences Due to Different Identification

A child can be strongly identified with a parent or grandparent and differ from their brothers and sisters because of this. If similar differences and tensions exist in the relationship between the parents, the children can be fairly easily drawn into coalitions and alliances with one parent. It is also sometimes observed that a parent reproaches a child that is dissimilar (i.e., identified with the other parent) in lieu of the partner.

Assessment Questions

- To what extent have the brothers and sisters formed their own subsystem?
- How do the brothers and sisters interact with one another?
- In which areas are the sibling relationships supportive, where do conflicts exist?
- How do the parents interfere in this interaction?
- How can the differences between the brothers and sisters be understood? What identifications lie behind the similarities?
- To what extent are factors relating to the children important?
- To what extent are parental projections at work?

The Psychodynamics of the Therapist–Family System

Motives for Therapy, Working Alliance, and Resistance

Patients with all kinds of disorders, problems, levels of ego development and differentiation ask for family therapy.

The motivation within the family can diverge greatly. The less family members have profited from the pre-therapy relationships, the more willing they will be to change. Family members often anticipate these connections and oppose "either the psychotherapy of any member of the family or the family setting," as the family setting already implies the assumption that the symptom or problem has "something to do with the family." Consequently resistance is commonly encountered in the initial stages of family therapy (Reich, 1990b, p. 116).

Assessment Questions

- How motivated is the family and how do levels of motivation vary among family members for undergoing therapy?
- How far does this go?
- Which family members have profited in some way from the relational arrangements up until now?
- Which members are interested in change?
- What resistances against family sessions can be observed?

Transference in Family Therapy

In psychoanalysis, a tendency to actualize wish fantasies or reanimate object relationships from the past is described as transference. Transferences are generally not simple "reprints" of past relationships, but "new editions" that have been revised in the imagination (Freud, 1905a), compressions and compromise formations arising from wishes, fears, commands and prohibitions, and external perceptions (Sandler, 1982).

They do not have a simple repetitive character but also represent an attempt to change and come to terms with painful experiences from the past (Sandler, 1982; Sandler & Sandler, 1985; Weiss & Sampson, 1986). The resulting relationship patterns may be seen as a joint construction created by the parties involved (e.g., therapists and patients), to which both make considerable contributions (Balint, 1957; Fenichel, 1941; Thomä & Kächele, 1985; Waelder, 1956).

Stierlin (1977) describes two forms of transference – intrafamilial and transfamilial – that are relevant in family assessment:
- In intrafamilial transference, object and self representations are transferred from parents to children. However, children can also transfer attitudes from early childhood to their parents when they themselves have reached adulthood. Even helpless and frail ageing parents are often still experienced as powerful and frightening or strong and protecting (see Sperling & Sperling, 1976).
- In transfamiliar transference, patterns of behavior and experience from the family are relived in other relationships.

In family interviews, the persons who would normally be reanimated in other relationships as revised internal images are actually present (i.e., for children and young people the parents; in multigenerational sessions also the grandparents for the parents). This changes transference patterns considerably. Images of internal relationships not represented in the group of people present are now transferred to the therapists. Generally, these are idealized helper and rescuer figures or threatening figures; both possibilities can exist side by side as the family members' unspoken expectations with corresponding interactive signals. These transference patterns are also reflected in the family members' fantasies concerning the process of therapy (Buchholz, 1990; Reich, 1990).

Initial Transference Patterns

Transference becomes immediately apparent, during the first interview at the latest. Families closely observe every signal from the therapists that might serve to confirm or negate their transference patterns. This comprises a considerable proportion of the present unconscious in the therapy system. The following patterns are typical here (see also Buchholz, 1990a, b; Reich, 1990b):

- In their fantasies, families or family members see therapists as external rescuers, appointing them with idealized expectations. This usually serves to fill a "vacancy" in the family system.

  The family may expect the therapists to be like idealized grandparent or parent figures, possessing the exact abilities and knowledge that they lack, understanding everything and knowing exactly what to do. This transference of ideal objects may come from single family members, while others feel more anxious. Children can sometimes see the therapists as ideal parents, making the real parents feel belittled or fearing criticism. A partner can see the therapists as an ideal partner or parents, which offends the real partner or puts him or her to shame, causing aggressive behavior towards the therapists.

- If family therapy sessions can cause repressed separation conflicts and fantasies to become mobilized.

  If family members feel existentially bound to one another in a close fusion and completely defend against differences or aggressive conflicts, the following mutual fantasy can arise: "Either we stick together as we have up until now and survive, or we go our separate ways and perish." This is often connected with a system based on reciprocal exploitation, blackmail, and restriction. The family members are afraid that family therapy may result in the realization of their suppressed wishes for separation and the catastrophe they feel this implies.

- Family therapy can make a guilt problem within the family become virulent.

  Family members, particularly parents, often wonder if the child's symptom is their fault, may pass the blame to one another, and feel indirectly accused. Often, the question of blame has already played an important role in the family's past (in the past unconscious). In these cases, the therapist is seen as the condemning instance, as the detective, the prosecutor, judge, or priest, the therapy setting as the confessional, the court, the interrogation room (Reich, 1990b, p. 117/118). Sometimes, the tables are turned and the therapist is placed under interrogation.

- The fact that the family has allowed outside observers to enter their private world can produce a feeling of shame as a "guardian of internal boundaries" (Wurmser, 1990).

  This happens when a discrepancy is perceived between the real situation and an "intended ideal" (Seidler, 1994). This discrepancy is experienced as a flaw or defect. Therapists are often seen as representations of a social ideal the family cannot achieve, before whom they are obliged to expose their abnormality, the flaw or defect. According to how strong this fear is the therapist's every word may be scrutinized to see if it hints of exposure or depreciation. Or the tables are turned and therapists are expected to disclose whether they have children, how they get along with their parents, etc.

- Family therapy may be experienced as a seductive situation; the therapists are seen as more powerful and potent in the oedipal sense, a better, more attractive couple, ideal parental figures. The partners may try to win them over, wishing to be wooed by them in return. Additionally, therapists may be seen as Zeitgeist representations who break into the family, in the adolescent sense, with the intention of alienating the young people from their parents or the family's moral views.

- A further important aspect is the transference of the family's defense against affects and conflicts. Here the family, as a well-established team, draws the therapists into the "transactional whirlpool" of familial processes in an automatic, unconscious play of interactive loops. In this way, dealing with explosive or painful affects, fear, grief, or helplessness can be avoided or deflected. Burdensome events and traumata are denied, either in their affective significance or globally: "We've never experienced anything like that," "Well, everyone has a little difference of opinion now and then, don't they?" or "Who doesn't drink the odd glass of wine?," etc.

Assessment Questions

- What are the family members' implicit ideas on the assessment and therapeutic process?
- Which transference pattern is most evident?
- What form of defense against conflict and affects is shown by the family?
- How do the family members attempt to draw the therapists into these patterns?

The Dynamics of Transference-Countertransference as Collusion

Transference and countertransference represent a systemic interaction between the therapists' system and the family; as such they are compromise formations that require careful analysis (Brenner, 1985; König, 1993).

This can be seen on several levels:
- the therapists' transference from their own family history to families, their unsolved conflicts and relating defense mechanisms;
- the therapists' explicit and implicit models concerning healthy family development, the cause of disorders, and therapy-related processes of change;
- tensions between the team of therapists, resulting in a reduced level of receptiveness for the family's conflicts and affects.

Transference from Therapists to Families

In general, families represent more powerful and multiple triggers for transference for therapists than individual patients.

Therapists can see their own parents in the parents or themselves as parents; in the children they can see themselves as children or their own children. These levels of experience are often addressed simultaneously.

In family interviews, therapists usually develop a mild transference neurosis (Buchholz, 1982) – and often more. Due to multiple transference triggers and the transactional pull of defense in family therapy, there is a much greater danger of therapists becoming "reinfected" with their own unsolved family problems (Whitaker et al., 1965). It is not uncommon for therapists to give way to a compulsion to reorganize families according to fantasies and wishes relating to their own families, reconstructing their own family battles so as to work them through again and come to terms with them in the present (Framo, 1965, 1992; Reich, 1982, 1984).

Together with the "interactive pressure" exerted by the family, this "role-responsiveness" (Sandler, 1976) can lead to therapists either becoming too involved with families or remaining at too great a distance, entering into one-sided alliances and losing sight of "multidirectional partiality" (Boszormenyi-Nagy & Spark, 1973; Reich, 1990).

Collusive defense patterns are also observed again and again.

For example, if therapists are inclined to be extremely active, this may support an existing pattern within the family based on the defense of unpleasant things by means of activity. Just like the family, they divert unpleasant topics by changing the subject when emotional tension within the family rises, rationalizing, avoiding, or downplaying.

Models of Disorders and Therapy–Related Change

Explicit, but still more preconscious and unconscious models relating to the cause of disorders and healthy developments can result in collusion with the initial transference patterns of the family as described above, or unproductive interaction patterns. The more ego-syntonic the therapists' internal models are, the more difficult these are to overcome.

For example, if suppressed separation problems exist, the premise "disorders result from a lack of individuation" on the part of therapists can cause them to unconsciously concentrate on one side of the separation conflict, stressing the advantages of separation and unconsciously adopting a pedagogic, critical, or disparaging tone when this topic is discussed.

Therapists' unconscious premises on the etiology and change of disorders are often linked with their personal history, their own conflicts and positive experiences of change (see Reich, 1982, 1984, 1990; also Bauriedl, 1994).

Tensions Within the Therapeutic Team

Teams who work on the therapy and supervision of families are predestined to reanimate and restage family feelings and unresolved family conflicts. These feelings and conflicts often affect the various team members in different ways. However, it is common for sibling rivalry or gender rivalry to be revived in teams of family therapists (see Bauriedl, 1994; Framo, 1965).

If the tensions between team members become too great and therapists stand in the way of one another, a paralyzing effect on the therapeutic process may be observed. Affective resonance to the family's problems may be impaired. Important conflicts may remain untouched upon. The assessment process remains shallow because the therapists are unable to become involved with one another; consequently they remain at a distance from the family.

Strong transferences from therapists to families and resulting team conflicts cannot be fully resolved in supervision teams, as they function as working groups and not as groups for self-experience. If team conflicts cannot be resolved, it may be advisable for a team consultation to be held and/or for only a single member of the team to continue working with the family.

Countertransference Analysis

How Can Entanglements with the Family Be Identified?

There are many signals that point towards collusive entanglements with families. They are not "faults" but – when closely analyzed – can provide important assessment information.

Here are a few of the typical signals that should be more closely examined:
- Family members are not included in the conversation, or if so only rarely.
- Themes suggested by the family or clear emotional reactions are not followed up on.
- The subject is changed at important stages in the conversation; however, this remains unnoticed or is not mentioned.
- Important themes or feelings are dealt with in a routine fashion, without giving family members an opportunity to develop emotional reactions.
- Therapists "forget" to mention something they intended to speak about (e.g., routine procedures such as defining the interview time).
- Therapists experience violent affects (fear, guilt, humiliation, inadequacy, disgust, distaste, anger).
- Therapists react in an aggressive, critical, judgmental, or tactless way.
- Therapists feel paralyzed, tired, or bored.
- Therapists express themselves unclearly or inarticulately.
- Therapists are overly preoccupied with families in their spare time and in their dreams.
- Therapists speak about different things at the same time or interrupt one another.

Working with Countertransference

If the above-mentioned signals or other signs of collusive entanglement are observed, a closer look should be taken at therapists' models relating to the development and change of disorders and team conflicts. Both give indications of personal transference from therapists to families based on the therapists' own biographies (Framo, 1965; Reich, 1984).

It is essential for therapists to continue work on the analysis of patterns and conflicts arising from their own families of origin – not only during the training period, but also for as long as they work in the field of therapy. This personal analysis must be continually adapted, taking the changing phases of the personal life cycle, career development, and difficult therapy situations into consideration. It goes far beyond self-experience on the couch (see Framo, 1992; Massing et al., 1999; Reich, 1982, 1984, 2004; Titelman, 1986).

Assessment Questions

- What signs of collusive entanglement with the family are experienced by the therapists?
- What implicit or explicit models relating to the cause and treatment of psychic illnesses are manifest?

- Do difficulties within the team affect family interviews? If so, how?
- What patterns from their own family histories are team members reminded of by their interaction with the family and the team?

The Condensation of Collusive Patterns in the Family Scene

Family interviews are interactive plays involving several characters in which unconscious conflicts are staged verbally, non-verbally, and paraverbally. The therapists play an active role. Unconscious scenes are played out just as much in interviews based on systems therapy as in psychoanalytically oriented therapy. When viewing the scene as a form of unconscious communication between therapists and family, we must take into consideration transference patterns, forms of the actualization of unconscious wishes and fears, collusive patterns between the partners, transference from the parents to the children and interpersonal defense, e.g., in the form of displacement or avoidance. Important events from the family's history, unconscious family fantasies or family secrets may be expressed in family scenes (Buchholz, 1982).

At the beginning of a family interview, a therapist gives a twelve-year-old girl a small child's chair to sit on. He has previously completed the registration procedure with the family and heard the mother's initial report on her daughter's aggressive behavior and the violent, sometimes physical conflicts between them. Therefore, he ought to be aware of how old she is. When he notices that the daughter looks completely out of place on the small chair, he gives her several other chairs to "try out." Ultimately, the daughter chooses the small chair that was given to her in the first place.

Important elements for the dynamics of the scene are not only the therapist's fear of aggressive behavior in the consulting room but also the fact that the parents still treat their daughter as a small child, giving her far less freedom than other children of her age. She reacts to this treatment by displaying helpless rage and passive denial at school, and neglecting her room at home. Sometimes she also reacts with encopresis. The message is: "If you treat me like a baby in one area, I don't want to grow up at all." The scene involving the chairs does not only symbolize the question of age, but also the anal character of the conflict involving a regression to anal patterns of aggression. In this family, a close alliance exists between the father and the daughter, from which the jealous mother is excluded. The father is reluctant to part from a small "pre-oedipal" daughter who stays with him and acts as an "antidepressant." The mother is also afraid of the daughter growing up and becoming a rival. She increasingly draws comparisons between her daughter and her own "tyrannical" mother.

Assessment Questions

- How can the typical initial scene of the family interview be described?
- How are therapists and family members integrated in the scene?
- Which conflict-ridden relationship wishes between the family members and what forms of defense are expressed in the scene?

References

Balint, M. (1957). *Problems of human pleasure and behaviour*. London: Hogarth.

Balint, M. (1968). *Therapeutische Aspekte der Regression. Die Theorie der Grundstörung* [Therapeutic aspects of regression: The thoery of base disorders]. Reinbek: Rowohlt.

Bauriedl, Th. (1994). *Auch ohne Couch. Psychoanalyse als Beziehungstheorie und ihre Anwendungen* [Also without couch: Psychoanalysis as relationship theory and its application]. Stuttgart: Verlag Internationale Psychoanalyse.

Blos, P. (1962). *On adolescence. A psychoanalytic interpretation*. Stuttgart: Klett-Cotta

Boszormenyi-Nagy, I., & Krasner, B. R. (1986). *Between give and take. A clinical guide to contextual therapy*. New York: Brunner/Mazel.

Boszormenyi-Nagy, I., & Spark, G. (1973). *Invisible loyalties*. New York: Harper and Row.

Brenner, C. H. (1985). Countertransference as compromise formation. *Psychoanalysis Quarterly, 54*, 155–163.

Buchholz, M. B. (1982). *Psychoanalytische Methode und Familientherapie* [Psychoanalytical methods and family therapy]. Frankfurt/M: Verlag Fachbuchhandlung für Psychologie.

Buchholz, M. B. (1990). Die Rotation der Triade [The rotation of the triad]. *Forum der Psychoanalyse, 6*, 116–134.

Buchholz, M. B. (1990). *Die unbewußte Familie. Psychoanalytische Studien zur Familie in der Moderne* [The unconscious family: Psychoanalytical studies of the modern family]. Berlin: Springer.

Buchholz, M. B. (1993). *Dreiecksgeschichten* [Triangular histories]. Göttingen: Vandenhoeck & Ruprecht.

Cierpka, M. (1989). "Persönliche Lebensentwürfe" und familiärer Kontext ["Personal life plans" and the familial context]. *Prax.Psychother. Psychosom, 34*, 165–173.

Cierpka, M. (1992). Zur Entwicklung des Familiengefühls. *Forum der Psychoanalyse, 8*, 32–46.

Cierpka, M. (2001). Geschwisterbeziehungen aus familientherapeutischer Perspektive – Unterstützung, Bindung, Rivalität und Neid [Sibling relationships from a family therapy perspective – Support, attachment, rivalry, and envy]. *Prax. Kinderpsychol. Kinderpsychiat., 50*, 440–453.

Dicks, H. V. (1967). *Marital tensions*. London: Routledge and Kegan Paul.

Diepold, B. (1988). Psychoanalytische Aspekte von Geschwisterbeziehungen [Psychoanalytical aspects of sibling relationships]. *Praxis der Kinderpsychologie Kinderpsychiatrie, 37*, 274–280.

Dornes, M. (1993). *Der kompetente Säugling. Die präverbale Entwicklung des Menschen* [The competent baby: The preverbal development of humans]. Frankfurt/M.: Fischer.

Eagle, M. N. (1984). *Recent developments in psychonalysis. A critical evaluation*. New York: McGraw-Hill Inc.

Erikson, E. H. (1956). Das Problem der Ich-Identität [The problem of ego identity]. In E. H. Erikson, (1979), *Identität und Lebenszyklus* (pp. 123–212). Frankfurt/M: Suhrkamp.

Fairbairn, W. R. D. (1952). *Psychoanalytic studies of the personality*. London: Tavistock Publications/Routledge & Kegan Paul.

Fenichel, O. (1941). *Problems of psychoanalytic technique*. New York: The Psychoanalytic Quarterly Inc.

Framo, J. L. (1965). Beweggründe und Techniken der intensiven Familientherapie [Motivations and techniques of intensive family therapy]. In I. Boszormenyi-Nagy & J. L. Framo (Eds.), *Familientherapie* (pp. 169–243). Reinbek: Rowohlt.

Framo, J. L. (1992). *Family-of-origin therapy: An intergenerational approach.* New York: Brunner/Mazel.

Freud, S. (1905a). Bruchstück einer Hysterie-Analyse [Fragment of an analysis of a case of hysteria]. *Gesammelte Werke, Band 5* (Vol. 5, pp. 161–286). Frankfurt: Fisher.

Freud, S. (1905b). Drei Abhandlungen zur Sexualtheorie [Three essays on the theory of sexuality]. *Gesammelte Werke, Band 5* (Vol. 5, pp. 27–145). Frankfurt: Fisher.

Freud, S. (1914). Zur Einführung des Narzißmus [On narcissism: An introduction]. *Gesammelte Werke, Band 10* (Vol. 10, pp. 137–170). Frankfurt: Fisher.

Friedman, L. J. (1980). Integrating psychoanalytic object-relations understanding with family systems intervention in couples therapy. In J. K. Pearce & L. J. Friedman (Eds.), *Family therapy* (pp. 63–79). New York: Grune und Stratton.

Grefe, J., & Reich, G. (1994). *Eine Kritik der Konzeptes der Projektiven Identifikation und seiner klinischen Verwendung* [A critique of the concept of projective identification and its clinical application]. Presentation, Göttingen, Germany.

Heimann, P. (1975). Sacrificial parapraxis: Failure or achievement? In P. Heimann (1989), *About children and children-no-longer. Collected Papers 1942–80* (pp. 276–295). London: Tavistock/Routledge.

Hetherington, E. M., Reiss, D., & Plomin, R. (1994). *Separate social worlds of siblings. The impact of nonshared environment on development.* Hillsdale, NJ: Lawrence Erlbaum.

Horney, K. (1927). Die monogame Forderung [The problem of the monogamous ideal]. *Internationale Zeitschrift für Psychoanalyse, 13,* 397–409.

Jacobson, E. (1964). *The self and the object world.* New York: International Universities Press.

Joraschky, P., & Cierpka, M. (1990). Von der geteilten zur nichtgeteilten Konstruktion der Realität [From the shared to the not shared construction of reality]. *Familiendynamik, 15,* 43–61.

Kernberg, O. F. (1976). *Object relations theory and clinical psychoanalysis.* New York: Jason Aronason.

Kernberg, O. F. (1987). Projection and projective identification. *Journal of the American Psychoanalytical Association, 35,* 795–819.

Kohut, H. (1971). *The analysis of the self.* New York: International Universities Press.

König, K. (1993). *Gegenübertragungsanalyse* [Countertransference analysis]. Göttingen: Vandenhoeck & Ruprecht.

König, K., & Kreische, R. (1985). Partnerwahl und Übertragung [Partner choice and transference]. *Familiendynamik, 10,* 341–352.

König, K., & Kreische, R. (1992). *Psychotherapeuten und Paare* [Psychotherapists and couples]. Göttingen: Vandenhoeck & Ruprecht.

Kreische, R. (1998). Paarbeziehungen und Geschwisterbeziehungen [Couples' relations and siblings relations]. *Kontext, 29,* 32–41.

Lederer, W. J., & Jackson, D. D. (1967). *The mirages of marriage.* New York: Norton.

Lichtenberg, J. D. (1983). *Psychoanalysis and infant research.* Hillsdale, NJ: The Analytic Press

Lichtenberg, J. D. (1987). Infant studies and clinical work with adults. *Psychoanalytical Inquiry, 7,* 311–330.

Luborsky, L. (1984). *Principles of psychoanalytic psychotherapy.*. New York: Basic Books.

Mahler, M. S., Pine, F., & Bergmann, A. (1975). *The psychological birth of the human infant.* New York: Basic Books.

Massing, A., Reich, G., & Sperling, E. (1999). *Die Mehrgenerationen-Familientherapie* [Multigenerational family therapy] (4th ed.). Göttingen: Vandenhoeck und Ruprecht.

Mentzos, S. (1990). *Interpersonelle und institutionalisierte Abwehr* (rev. Ed.) [Interpersonal and institutional defence]. Frankfurt/M: Suhrkamp,.

Modell, A. H. (1988). Psychoanalysis. In A. H. Modell, *A New Context.*, Madison CT: International Universities Press.

Ogden, T. H. (1979). On projective identification. *International Journal of Psychoanalysis, 60,* 357–373.

Ogden, T. N. (1983). The concept of internal object relations. *International Journal of Psychoanalysis, 60,* 318–327.

Papousek, M. (1987). Die Rolle des Vaters in der frühen Kindheit [The role of fathers in early childhood]. *Kind und Umwelt, 54,* 29–49.

Porder, M. S. (1987). Projective identification: An alternative hypothesis. *Psychoanalyses Quarterly, 56(3),* 231–451.

Reich, G. (1982). Tabus und Ängste des Therapeuten im Umgang mit der eigenen Familie [Taboos and fears of therapists in their contact with their own families]. *Zeitschrift für Psychosomatische Medizin und Psychoanalyse, 28,* 393–406.

Reich, G. (1984). Der Einfluß der Herkunftsfamilie auf die Tätigkeit von Therapeuten und Beratern [The influence of the family of origin on the activities of therapists and advisors]. *Praxis der Kinderpsychologie und Kinderpsychiatrie, 33,* 61–69.

Reich, G. (1987). Das sexuelle Erleben von Paaren auf dem Hintergrund ihrer Familiengeschichte – Beobachtungen in Familientherapien [The sexual experiences of couples with view to their family histories – Observations from family therapy]. In A Massing & I Weber I (Eds.), *Lust und Leid. Sexualität im Alltag und alltägliche Sexualität* (pp. 187–221). Berlin: Springer.

Reich, G. (1988). Trennungskonflikte: familiendynamische und zeitgeschichtliche Aspekte [Separation conflicts: Family dynamics and time history aspects]. *Wege zum Menschen, 40,* 194–208.

Reich, G. (1990). Psychoanalytische und systemische Familientherapie – Integrative Aspekte und Differenzen in Theorie und Praxis [Psychoanalytical and systemic family therapy]. In A. Massing (Ed.), *Psychoanalytische Wege der Familientherapie* (pp. 97–144). Berlin: Springer

Reich, G. (1991). Kinder in Scheidungskonflikten [Children in divorce conflicts]. In H. Krabbe (Ed.), *Scheidung ohne Richter. Neue Lösungen für Trennungskonflikte* (pp. 59–85). Reinbek: Rowohlt.

Reich, G. (2004). Psychotherapeuten und ihre Familien [Psychotherapists and their famileies]. In O. F. Kerberg, B. Dulz, & J. Eckert (Eds.), *WIR. Was wir Psychotherapeuten schon immer über uns wissen wollten* (pp. 127–135). Stuttgart: Schtaauer.

Reich, G., & Bauers, B. (1988). Nachscheidungskonflikte – eine Herausforderung an Beratung und Therapie [Post divorce conflicts – A challenge for adivse and therapy]. *Praxis der Kinderpsychologie und Kinderpsychiatrie, 37,* 346–355.

Reich, G., Killius, U., & Yamini, A. (2002). Familienbeziehungen als eigenständiger Erfahrungsraum im familiären Kontext [Sibling relationships as an autonomous realm of interpersonal experience in the family]. *Kontext, 33,* 99–109.

Reiche, R. (1992). *Geschlechterspannung. Eine psychoanalytische Untersuchung* [Gender tension: A psychoanalytical investigation]. Frankfurt/M: Fischer.

Reiss, D., Neiderhiser, J. M., Hetherington, E. M., & Plomin, R. (2000). *The relationship code: Deciphering genetic and social influences on adolescent development*. Cambridge, MA: Harvard University Press.

Richter, H. E. (1963). *Eltern, Kind und Neurose* [Parents, children, and neurosis].Stuttgart: Klett

Richter, H. E. (1970). Patient Familie [Patient families]. Reinbek: Rowohlt.

Sager, C. J. (1981). Couples therapy and marriage contracts. In A. S. Gurman & D. P. Kniskern (Eds.), *Handbook of family therapy* (pp. 85–130). New York: Brunner/Mazel.

Sandler, A. M., & Sandler, J. (1985). Vergangenheits-Unbewußtes, Gegenwarts-Unbewußtes und die Deutung der Übertragung [Past unconsciousness, present unconsciouness, and the interpretation of transference]. *Psyche, 39,* 800–829.

Sandler, J. (1976). Gegenübertragung und Bereitschaft zur Rollenübernahme [Counter transference and role transfer tendency]. *Psyche, 30,* 297–305.

Sandler, J. (1982). Unbewußte Wünsche und menschliche Beziehungen [Unconscious wishes and human relationships]. *Psyche, 36,* 59–74.

Seidler, G. H. (1994). Der Sog in die Monade. Die Elimination der "dritten Position". Klinische Bilder und psychodynamische Abläufe beim "destruktiven Narzißmus" [The undertow in the monad – The elimination of the "third position": Clinical pictures and psychodynamic processes in "Destructive narcissism"]. In G. H. Seidler (Ed.), *Das Ich und das Fremde. Klinische und sozialpsychologische Analysen des destruktiven Narzißmus* (pp. 9–23). Opladen: Westdeutscher Verlag.

Sohni, H. (1994). Geschwisterbeziehungen. Die Einführung der horizontalen Beziehungsdynamik in ein psychoanalytisches Konzept "Familie" [Sibling relationships: The implementation of the horizontal relationship dynamic in a psychoanalytical concept "family". *Praxis der Kinderpsychologie und Kinderpsychiatrie, 43,* 284–295.

Sohni, H. (1998). Geschwister – ihre Bedeutung für die psychische Entwicklung im Familiensystem und in der Psychotherapie [Siblings – Their importance for pyschic development in family systems and in psychotherapy]. *Kontext, 29,* 5–31.

Sperling, E., & Sperling, U. (1976). Die Einbeziehung der Großeltern in die Familientherapie [The intergration of grandparents in family therapy]. In H. E. Richter, H. Strotzka, & J. Willi (Eds.), *Familie und seelische Krankheit* (pp. 196–215). Reinbek: Rowohlt.

Stern, D. N. (1985). *The interpersonal world of the infant. A view from psychoanalysis and developmental psychology*. New York: Basic Books.

Stierlin, H. (1975). *Von der Psychoanalyse zur Familientherapie* [From psychoanalysis to family therapy]. Stuttgart: Klett-Cotta.

Stierlin, H. (1977). Familientherapeutische Aspekte der Übertragung und Gegenübertragung [Family therapeutic aspects of transference and counter transference]. *Familiendynamik, 3,* 182–197.

Sulloway, F. J. (1996). *Born to rebel*. New York: Random House Inc.

Thomä, H., & Kächele, H. (1985). *Lehrbuch der psychoanalytischen Therapie. Bd 1 Grundlagen* [Handbook of psychoanalytical therapy: Vol. 1: Fundamentals]. Berlin: Springer.

Thomä, H., & Kächele, H. (1988). *Lehrbuch der psychoanalytischen Therapie. Bd Praxis* [Handbook of psychoanalytical therapy: Vol. 2: Praxis]. Berlin: Springer.

Titelman, P. (1986). *The therapists own family. Toward the differentiation of self.* Northvale, NJ: Jason Aronson.

Toman, W. (1974). *Familienkonstellationen. Ihr Einfluß auf den Menschen und sein soziales Verhalten* [Familial constellations: Their influence on humans and their social behavior]. München: Beck.

Waelder, R. (1956). Introduction to the discussion on problems of transference. *International Journal of Psychoanalysis, 37,* 367–368.

Wangh, M. (1962). The evocation of a proxy. *Psychoanalytic Study of the Child, 17,* 451–472.

Weiss, J., & Sampson, H. (1986). *The psychoanalytic process.* New York: Guildford.

Whitaker, C. A., Felder, R. E., & Warkentin, J. (1965). Gegenübertragung bei der Familienbehandlung von Schizophrenie [Countertransference on the familial treatment of schizophrenia]. In I. Boszormenyi-Nagy & J. L. Framo (Eds.) *Familientherapie – Theorie und Praxis, Bd 2* (Vo.2, pp. 90–109). Hamburg: Rowohlt

Willi, J. (1975). *Die Zweierbeziehung* [The couple relationship]. Hamburg: Rowohlt.

Winnicott, D. W. (1974). *Reifungsprozesse und fördernde Umwelt* [Maturational processes and the facilitating world]. München: Kindler.

Wurmser, L. (1987). *Flucht vor dem Gewissen. Analyse von Über-Ich und Abwehr bei schweren Neurosen* [Flight from conscience: Analysis of the superego and defences in severe neurosis]. Berlin: Springer.

Wurmser, L. (1990). *Die Maske der Scham. Die Psychoanalyse von Schamkonflikten und Schamaffekten* [The mask of shame: The psychoanalysis of shame conflicts and shame affects]. Berlin: Springer.

13

Family Sculpture Procedures

Gary H. Bischof and Karen B. Helmeke

"Family sculpting is a potent process for concretizing and exploring relationships with the ability to condense meaning into an evocative, efficient image which is easier to store, retrieve, and relate to than equivalent verbal descriptions."
(L'Abate, Ganahl, & Hansen, 1986, p. 166)

Summary
Family sculpture offers a creative and active means of assessing and treating families. This chapter provides a historical background and describes how to conduct various types of family sculpture. Techniques include use of family sculpture with actual families, training groups, and the use of figurines or objects to spatially depict relationships and interactions in a family system. Research findings involving these techniques are also presented.

Introduction

Family sculpture emerged in the late 1960s as a vibrant, active way to assess and to intervene with families. This method involves positioning family members in physical space to represent the relationships and roles within the family system. In this chapter we begin with an overview of the major assumptions of experiential family therapy, as family sculpture is considered to be a procedure within this wider domain of experiential family techniques. Next we review the historical development and key contributors of family sculpture. Three primary types of sculpture are described in detail. These are family sculptures with actual family members, boundary sculptures with dyads, and sculptures of families conducted in training, educational, or therapy groups. Case examples are used throughout to illustrate concepts and techniques. The chapter then addresses some variations of family sculpture called simple spatializations, which center on a specific issue or construct. We also discuss the use of sculptures using symbolic figures such as dolls or wooden figures, both as assessment techniques and as therapeutic interventions. We conclude by considering the limited research related to family sculpture techniques, and invite the reader to experiment with these fun and creative procedures.

Major Assumptions and Concepts

Experiential Family Therapy

Experiential family therapy was influenced by popular humanistic, existential therapies of the 1960s, such as gestalt therapy, psychodrama, client-centered therapy, and the encounter group movement (Piercy, Sprenkle, & Wetchler, 1996). Two pioneers of family therapy are considered to be the founders of experiential family therapy: Virginia Satir and Carl Whitaker. Fred and Bunny Duhl, who were integrally involved in the development of family sculpture, are considered as being among the early experiential family therapists. Though the styles of experiential therapists vary greatly, certain theoretical assumptions are held by most proponents. These major assumptions, drawn primarily from Piercy et al's review of experiential family therapy are briefly described next.

Primacy of Experience

The experience of living comes first; our thoughts and intellectualizations are our attempts to make sense of our experiences. Firsthand experiential data is paramount. Experiential family therapists are especially interested in the experience of families, and thus facilitate here-and-now experiences in the therapy room, perhaps focusing on dreams, fantasies, feelings, or sensations.

Spontaneity and Creativity

Creative, non-rational, right-brain experiencing is promoted. Spontaneity is desired for both therapist and family. Active techniques such as family sculpting, puppetry, drawings, psychodrama, and family choreography are applied to free family members to experience each other and life more fully.

Affect

Honest, open, emotional expression is considered crucial in successful experiential family therapy. Evocative procedures are used to unblock constraints to direct communication of feelings. Affective expression, itself, is considered therapeutic and growth-producing.

Present-Centeredness

Immediate experiencing and direct emotional expression can occur only in the present, clearly the time orientation of choice in this type of therapy. Living in the moment, being aware of the here-and-now, and avoiding attempts to dwell on the past or future are regarded as crucial.

Global vs. Specific Goals

Goals for experiential therapy are global, such as congruence, awareness, self-esteem, independence, and connection, etc. Such vague, non-operationalized goals make it difficult to conduct research of these approaches, and inhibit attempts to prove efficacy. As we shall see later, this is true for family sculpture procedures too.

Space as a Key Dimension of Families

Family sculpture directly utilizes the dimension of space in the lives of families. In 1950, David Kantor had begun to explore the significance of space in human relationships, and became preoccupied with the use of space as a metaphor for understanding family relationships (Papp, 1976). Kantor and Lehr (1975) later articulated these ideas and identified space as one of three key dimensions of family process, along with time and energy. They saw space as crucial in the development of family identity. "If a family system fails to develop a territory, it virtually ceases to exist, for it becomes indistinguishable from the larger space. It is in this working out ...[of] how it is the same or different from those around it that a family defines itself to the community" (Kantor & Lehr, p. 68). This process of defining itself spatially, termed "bounding" occurs at the perimeter of a family. One may note the similarity of this concept to the notion of boundaries from structural theories of families. Kantor and Lehr identified two other spatial regulation concepts occurring within the family: linking and centering.

Linking is the regulation of distance of all persons within the family's interior (Kantor & Lehr, 1975). Linking operations involve movements of family members either to closer proximity or greater distance, and directly affect interpersonal relationships. Examples include a family member inviting another to "sit here next to me," creating movement closer into one's space, or as one family member enters a room, another leaves, thus resulting in moving farther apart. Centering for Kantor and Lehr involved the family's generation of general guidelines for organizing the total space in which it lives. "Centering consists of the developing, maintaining, and transmitting of spatial guidelines for how traffic should flow within and across its borders" (p. 74). This is akin to family "rules" particularly applied to the spatial realm.

These views on the dimension of space were echoed a few years later by Maurizio Andolfi (1979, p. 76) who saw space as an "innate and universal dimension of human expressive and social behavior. Space defines the individual's territory ... where one can find oneself and at the same time negotiate relationships with others." Andolfi distinguishes interactional family therapy from traditional psychodynamic therapies that rely on the spoken word as the principal therapeutic instrument and means for understanding inner states. In interactional therapy, physical contact, movement, action, and the presence of others (all related to the dimension of space) simultaneously produce associations, meanings, and behavior within the given context. Consistent with experiential family therapies discussed above, family sculpture places an emphasis upon "enacting and dramatizing emotional states and conflicts in the present, in order to verify the family's capacity to change with the help of the therapist's active intervention" (Andolfi, p. 76).

It is not surprising that family sculpture developed within the field of family therapy, rather than within frameworks of other forms of therapy existing at that time (Papp, 1976). Family therapy's focus upon inter-relatedness involving space, time, energy, and movement is inherent to a systems concept of human behavior. In addition to the concept of space, family sculpture also includes a sense of action and movement within that space. Indeed, use of the term "sculpture" may actually be a misnomer, as sculpture evokes images of a solid, unchanging art form that connotes a static representation. While some forms of family sculpture may include static, non-moving features, early proponents suggested the use of gestures and movement in this technique. Now that we have considered the major assumptions of experiential therapy and the concept of space in family process, let us proceed with an overview of the development of family sculpture and its early proponents.

Historical Developments and Early Proponents

Historically, family sculpture began with Kantor's attempts to translate systems theory into physical form through spatial arrangements. Family sculpture is related both historically and in method to psychodrama, (Moreno, 1946) and to experiential exercises used in human relations training (Constantine, 1978). It differs principally from psychodrama in that it portrays symbolic processes, relationships, and events through spatial analogies, whereas psychodrama often involves reenacting actual events. In addition, psychodrama promotes recall of expressed and unexpressed affect, with strong emotional re-experiencing and catharsis as primary aims of this technique. Family sculpture, on the other hand, intends to help the client distance from the emotional experience, and through this disengagement, enables new insight into complex relational determinants of past and present situations (Constantine). This is not to say that family sculpture is devoid of emotion. In fact, such active, process-oriented activities may elicit strong emotions, but emotional expression and catharsis are not viewed as ends in themselves. Instead, sculpture aims to help clients develop awareness and insight into their personal participation in ongoing interpersonal patterns.

The mainstream of family sculpture was originated in 1969 by David Kantor, a disciple of Moreno's psychodrama work and one of the founders of the Boston Family Institute. Bunny Duhl, Fred Duhl, and their colleagues at Boston State Hospital and the Boston Family Institute made important contributions and elaborations of Kantor's original methods (Constantine, 1978; Duhl, Kantor, & Duhl, 1973). The Duhl's were early trainees of Kantor, and Bunny Duhl credits Kantor's development of family sculpture as a key in her early training (Duhl, 1999).

Larry Constantine (1978), who also trained at the Boston Family Institute, and has offered several variations of sculpting, reports that the earliest experiments with sculpture utilized the placement of objects rather than people. The actual use of people was catalyzed by a visit by Virginia Satir, who demonstrated the use of people to metaphorically represent specific abstract types of family configurations and roles. Satir (1972) popularized an active, hands-on approach that utilized space and movement with families. Using her impressive personal presence and intuition, she often took the lead and suggested various positions and movements of family members. Other methods of family sculpture developed by Kantor, the Duhl's, Constantine, and others emphasized having various family members themselves sculpt the family based upon their own perspective and experience of the family.

Other pioneers in the use of family sculpture include Peggy Papp and colleagues from the Ackerman Family Institute in New York, who in another early article described the use of family sculpture in a multi-family group prevention project (Papp, Silverstein, & Carter, 1973). Papp went on to develop and write further about the symbolic use of space, action, and movement in work with families in what she termed "family choreography," emphasizing the active, moving nature of this technique (Papp, 1976).

The methods and techniques of the early developers of family sculpture have stood the test of time. Clinicians who utilize sculpture continue to use the general procedures they outlined. Later in the chapter we will describe these methods in detail. More recent developments have described the use of family sculpture with specific populations, such as psychosomatic families (Onnis et al., 1994), or premarital couples (Lesage-Higgins, 1999), and the integration of family sculpture with current popular therapeutic approaches, such as brief solution-focused therapy (Bischof, 1993).

Family Sculpture

We now consider the steps involved in executing a sculpture with a family when family members are present. These steps are similar for sculpting with individuals, for example in training groups, or in boundary sculptures which will be discussed later. Duhl et al. (1973) and Constantine (1978) identify three basic elements included in all types of sculpture:

(1) *Establishing the mapping between physical and metaphorical space*. This involves introducing the exercise and defining the space and context to be utilized. For example, typically the physical distance between two objects or people in the sculpt is used to depict the level of emotional closeness or distance. The family and therapist define a specific time or event for the family, perhaps a key life cycle transition or nodal point for the family.

(2) *Placing the players in space, constructing the actual sculpture*. During this step one person moves around in the space and positions family members to represent their relationships and roles in the family. The sculptor, assisted by the therapist, adjusts people until it feels "right" from the sculptor's perspective.

(3) *Processing or debriefing the experience*. Once the actual sculpting is complete, family members return to the here-and-now and process their experiences, whether as the sculptor or family member. The sculpture is explored from multiple points of view and thoroughly discussed for its meaning, impact, and implications.

In family sculpture, each of the three general stages may involve several specific steps (Constantine, 1978; L'Abate, Ganahl, & Hansen, 1986). Constantine identifies seven steps for a complete family sculpture, while L'Abate and colleagues suggest fourteen distinct steps that are possible, but not always necessary. A composite of these is offered here.

Introduction and Warm up of Family

The therapist introduces the sculpting exercise, describes the process, and gives a rationale for its use. Language understandable to all should be used. Comparing the exercise to the children's game "statues" can be helpful. It is beneficial to have family members get up out of their chairs and move around, perhaps moving furniture to create space for the sculpture. This facilitates an orientation to movement and space and differentiates the activity from a typical session. Normalizing discomfort and apprehensions, especially for persons who tend to intellectualize, while underlining the benefits, can help to bypass initial resistance.

Select a Sculptor

The next step is to select one family member to do the first sculpture. Some simply ask for a volunteer at this stage, assuring the family that all will get a chance. Others may be more intentional, selecting a family member such as a child who may be more willing to be expressive and may have some keen insights into the family system. Some advise that the identified patient and those entrapped in significant triangles in the family should be avoided initially. L'Abate and colleagues (1986) suggest it may be wise to avoid parents at first, as they might set a destructive precedent that the children may not feel free to challenge. Going with a child or adolescent is a good bet if no one comes forward.

Defining the Focus

Once you have a sculptor, next the therapist helps to define the focus of the sculpture. One can choose a specific time in the family's history, certain family situations or problems, or specific places the family inhabits. One can also sculpt abstract properties or family processes, such as power or boundaries. Examples may include the family dinner table, a typical evening at home, or a scene of a characteristic problem the family is facing. Often the sculpture begins with a focus on the family in the present, as it is currently. The therapist might assist the sculptor in getting into and re-experiencing the scene by suggesting he/she walk around in the space, or close one's eyes and imagine several possibilities, which can serve to enrich the sculpting experience.

Placing Family Members in the Sculpture

In this step, the sculptor places family members as he/she desires. The therapist establishes a ground rule that there should be limited talking, and family members should not challenge the instructions of the sculptor, but can clarify the sculptor's instructions if needed. One by one, family members are added to the scene, and the sculptor makes adjustments and refinements as needed. This process itself becomes a vivid example of systems theory, as previously arranged interactions between family members may be altered when new players are added to the scene. Gestures, nonverbals such as facial expressions or body posture, sounds, and movement can also be included. The sculptor is encouraged to continue to make alterations until the sculpture feels right and accurately portrays that person's experience of the family. Props or objects can be used to represent absent family members, or if available, a co-therapist or therapy team member can stand in for a missing family member. Usually family members play themselves, but it is also possible to have the sculptor assign each person to play the role of another family member. This strategy can be useful if family members are argumentative with the sculptor about their positions, or if the therapist is attempting to promote empathy and understanding for other family members' experiences. The sculptor should be encouraged by the therapist for working at the sculpture, regardless of the content or sophistication.

Detailing the Sculpture

After each person has been put in place, or after the completion of the initial sculpture, the sculptor should be helped by the therapist to sharpen the detail to increase expressiveness. The therapist may intervene to encourage elaboration or detailing, or to remind the sculptor of interactions that may be missing. L'Abate and colleagues (1986) suggest this comes with experience and the therapist's sense that something is missing or incomplete. One might remind the sculptor that gestures, movements, sounds, etc. may be added if they have not done so. The therapist may question or clarify what is intended by the sculptor, but should not influence the content of the sculptor's representation. For example, the therapist might point out that the sculptor has positioned two siblings quite a distance from one another, and may ask if the sculptor intended to portray them as distant emotionally. A helpful approach is to point out an area or body part that has not been detailed and invite the sculptor to add detail there. For instance, "What would you like Dad to show with his expression?" or "Your sister is standing still; could you add a gesture or movement for her that would help to capture her place in the family?"

It is also important that the sculpture is systemic. Some sculptors might place family members in relation only to him or herself, failing to portray the relationships of all family members and the web of interactions therein (Duhl et al., 1973). In these cases, the attentive therapist invites further detailing to enhance the systemic quality. Constantine (1978, p. 19) suggests at this point that the therapist should assist the sculptor to "assemble the action of each person into a composite 'strategic sequence' representative of the family's operation." This helps to identify and underline key sequences of interaction for the family and aids in the understanding of the family as a system.

Sculptor Adds Self

Once other family members are in place and the sculpture has been adequately detailed, the sculptor adds her- or himself. The sculptor now becomes part of the scene, and things may look or feel different from this new perspective. Additional changes or adjustments may be made. The therapist may help sharpen the details of the sculptor and the interactions with other family members. As above, the family as a whole should be maintained, with particular focus at this point on the various relations with the sculptor.

Choice Point

Once the addition of the sculptor is accomplished, several options are available, depending upon the time available, the goals of the therapist, the dynamics of the family, and other factors. Various proponents of family sculpture present different suggestions. L'Abate et al. (1986) identify four options suggested by key originators of this technique. These will be briefly described next.

a) Put in motion and ritualize. In this option, motion is added to the sculpture and key sequences are repeated to deepen their impact and value. A static sculpture gives one an idea of boundaries and relationships, but less so the rules of interaction or sequences in a family. With dynamic or moving sculptures, one can more readily see patterns of interaction and repetitive sequences, producing a more dynamic representation of the family. Duhl et al. (1973) and Constantine (1978) emphasize the importance of adding movement and having the family repeat the primary sequence at least three times. One might also have the family repeat the pattern in slow motion to accentuate automatic interactions (Papp, 1976). These serve to "ritualize" the sequence and lead to greater learning and frequently result in additional discoveries and insights into how a family system operates. It can be helpful to instruct the players to continue longer than might feel comfortable to ensure that the full impact of the sculpt can be experienced.

The value of adding movement is illustrated by a case example from Papp et al. (1973) of a 9-year-old boy who was brought in due to concerns about his habit of walking around in circles. In a sculpt, the boy depicted his two sisters playing jacks in one corner of the room, while the parents quarreled in another. Neither group paid attention to the boy, and he positioned himself alone in the center of the room. This quiet boy was then asked to show in movement what he did about this situation. He described first going to his sisters, but they tell him to go away, so he then would go to his parents, but was told not to bother them, so he returned to his sisters, and so on. As he described his predicament, he began walking in circles, going round and round between his sisters and parents. The connection between the presenting problem and family dynamics was not lost on the family, and they were made aware for the first time of his isolation and frustration in trying to find a place in the family.

b) Give a descriptive title. In this option, the sculptor or family is invited to generate a title or metaphor for the overall sculpture. This title captures the essence of the experience and can be a shorthand way to refer to the sculpt as well as a resource for possible therapeutic themes. Examples include "a cage of tigers, with everyone pacing and alone" (Duhl et al., 1973) or "the queen for a day family" for a family engaged in an ongoing contest to see who deserved the most sympathy (L'Abate et al., 1986). Authors differ on when to ask for such a title. Some suggest it occur just after the sculpting is finished, while others use titles after the entire process has been completed and debriefed.

c) Explore solutions to improve problem situation presented. Once the repetitive pattern is firmly embedded in the family's awareness, one can work on changing it. The therapist should be cautious about moving too quickly toward solutions. Some suggest it is quite enough simply for the family to experience itself in a new way through the process of sculpting their patterns and viewing themselves more wholistically, and that solutions can be explored later. Others encourage the sculptor or other family members to create an "ideal" sculpture of the family, or how the family would look after small steps of change. Sculpting allows for the exploration of many new alternatives in a short period of time. The option of moving toward preferred states for the family may be guided by time constraints or a desire to allow others to sculpt their representations of the family. Therapists can also suggest families think about how they would like to change their sculptures as a homework task and explore alternatives in subsequent sessions.

d) Sculpt other relevant situations until a pattern emerges. A final alternative is to sculpt additional scenes which are related to the one just completed, before any processing. One would look here for patterns that cut across multiple scenes, for a common theme or interactional process. The authors have found it helpful at times to direct the sculptor to sculpt the family at key stages of the family life cycle, for example, before, during, and after a divorce, or a few years before and after a significant death. This can quickly help the family to see their progression through time and perhaps to identify previous stages that were not negotiated well, contributing to current difficulties.

De-role and Debrief Sculptor and Participants

In this step, the sculptor and family members leave their roles and return to the present. The therapist facilitates a debriefing of the experience. This may take place while the individuals are in place, or they may move to a different place, perhaps sitting down again. Helping the family members come out of their roles and the associated feelings is important, especially when the sculpt involves the past. This can help one to separate from past unhealthy roles. Constantine (1978) suggests debriefing the family members first, and finally the sculptor, while Duhl et al. (1973) prefer to get feedback from the sculptor first, then the other participants, and finally from observers, if applicable. Questions such as these might be asked:

To the sculptor:
"What was it like for you to position your family?
You seemed to struggle with how to portray Dad; what was going on for you?
How did you feel as you saw your family acted out in this way?"

To the family members:
"How was it for you to be placed in your position?
What, if anything, did you want to change about the role you were asked to play?
What struck you about your family from this exercise?"

How one processes the sculptures and makes interpretations depends upon the form of sculptings and the therapeutic goals. If one is interested in differentiation, the unique perspective of each individual might be emphasized. Boundaries, coalitions, and hierarchy might be the focus of a structural therapist. A solution-oriented therapist might be especially interested in changes the family made from past or present sculpts to a preferred reality for the family in the future. A focus on the system as a whole or the place of the symptomatic behavior as demonstrated in the sculpt might also be highlighted. Some suggest it is the therapist's role to abstract meaning and feed it back to the sculptor or family (Papp, 1976). Others tend to avoid interpretation and elicit the family's reaction first before biasing them with their own (L'Abate et al., 1986). An exception for this group is if the family begins to focus on a negative aspect of the experience while ignoring other aspects, they will intervene more actively. Ideally, the therapist's contributions during the processing of the sculpting should be either elaborations of a family theme or alternative visions to be considered by the family. One should be cautious about imposing his or her view on the family's experience.

Begin Again with New Sculptor

Processing may be quite limited if other family members are to be given a turn at sculpting the family. The process begins anew here, with another family member assuming the role of sculptor and progressing through the steps outlined above. Of course, attention must be given to time limitations. There may be adequate time to have several family members sculpt their view of the family in one session. In other instances, additional sculpts may need to be done in later sessions.

Variations of Family Sculpture

Constantine (1978) cautions that two of the most common errors made by therapists are rushing the sculpture or pushing for premature closure. He advocates the use of a "mini-sculpture" in some cases when a brief assessment through sculpture is desired. The sculptor may simply be asked to position other members in ways that represent his or her view of the relational dynamics of the family. This type of sculpture is generally limited to a static representation and may only take a few minutes, but brevity is achieved by limiting the sculpture experience in some way.

Another variation of a mini-sculpture developed by Kantor (in Constantine, 1978, p. 19) is a three-dimensional sculpture in which physical closeness or distance represents emotional involvement, vertical displacements symbolize power differences (higher being more powerful), and facial expression, gestures, and body orientation show the general nature of the relationships among family members. Key dimensions of family process – affect, power, and meaning – are all captured, and this type of sculpture "approaches the richness of a 'full' sculpture in a fraction of the time."

Finally, there are a few other types of family sculptures (Constantine, 1978). A "typological" sculpture portrays various types of family structure, and the sculptor then chooses one to build upon for their respective family. This type, though, may impose a pre-conceived notion, thus limiting the creativity of the sculptor. Sculpting the families of origin of the adult members of the family can be very productive, yielding insight into connections from previous generations to current patterns and roles. Lastly, there is the "multiple" sculpture, also called a "consensus" or "composite" sculpture. In this variation, all family members simultaneously attempt to place themselves in relation to each other. Usually this would be around a single dimension or issue, such as emotional closeness. Each member tries to place him or herself in correct relation to all other members. This final one would be especially fun to videotape and play back to the family. Indeed, having family members watch portions of video playback of their family sculpting can be quite instructive and provide additional distance in order to see one's family more from an outsider perspective.

Boundary Sculpture

Family sculpture helps to define the processes and dynamics between a group of people, which involves a larger set of more complicated interactions. It is also possible to sculpt a smaller, two-person system. This type of sculpt is referred to as dyadic or boundary sculpture (Duhl et al., 1973). In this type of sculpt, the goal is to clarify the rules that govern each participant's personal space, for the purpose of increasing the awareness of and responsibility for understanding the boundaries of the other person. The premise of this type of sculpt is that without making the processes overt, each member of a two-person system is able to remain ignorant of the different rules governing personal space by which the other member operates. When one member remains ignorant of the other's rules, then what typically happens is one judges the other person's behavior by one's own set of rules. Thus, in boundary sculpting, both participants are encouraged to reveal, describe, and enact their own personal boundaries.

The originators of this type of sculpt emphasize that boundary sculpture can be done with any dyad, not just a couple. It could be done with any two family members, co-therapists, co-leaders, co-students, co-workers, etc., in which issues involving emotional closeness and distancing, availability and turning away from, and an inability to interpret accurately the actions of the other are at stake. This sculpt, which often reflects real physical distance, also typically functions as a metaphor of the boundaries of one's self. This involves the ability or lack thereof to set boundaries and to keep people from entering when necessary, or to allow people to enter one's personal space when appropriate (Constantine, 1978).

The following are the steps involved in a boundary sculpture:

Defining One's Own Personal Space

Each person takes a turn in mapping out his or her own perception of one's personal boundaries. The person graphically displays the sense of closeness, distance, intrusion, inclusion, and exclusion in real physical space. (Constantine, 1978). The therapist invites the sculptor to move around the room, to explore the actual physical setting, and to get a feel for one's personal space, and to become aware of "the space you always carry with you. The edge of that area which feels as if it was you or yours, where your space leaves off and the rest of the world begins" (Constantine, p. 18).

The sculptor is asked to describe physical characteristics of this space, such as size, shape, and variability. In addition, metaphorical characteristics of this space are explored, such as color, texture, thickness, firmness, transparency, and penetrability. The therapist then summarizes, and gives the sculptor an opportunity to confirm or correct the summary. Next, the therapist inquires about any entries and exits in one's personal space, and asks how the sculptor can leave their personal space, one more indication of a healthy control over one's own space.

Describing and Enacting the Rules for How Someone Enters the Individual's System

Next, the therapist works with the sculptor to determine who and under what circumstances someone can enter the sculptor's personal space. Using subjects of various ages, both sexes, and a range of emotional closeness, a variety of scenarios are considered. Thus, the sculptor enacts the reaction to the entrance of a male or female stranger, acquaintance, or intimate of a certain age and taking a certain approach, such as cautious, fast, slow, suspicious, aggressive, submissive, or seductive. One person, playing a specific subject, tries to enter the sculptor's space without using any words. Obviously, there are limitless combinations, so the therapist intuits which type of subject is selected, or the requests of the sculptor are honored. For this dynamic exploration, the other member of the dyad is usually an observer to the process, but at the therapist's discretion, may be called upon to play the role of one of the subjects.

The variety of subjects, means of entry, approaches, and the sculptor's reactions to each allows for a clearer picture of where the sculptor's boundaries are, how clearly they are defined, and how strongly defended they are. Throughout this process, the sculptor is given feedback, about what the sculptor did or looked like, how the sculptor is perceived by the subjects, etc.

Describing and Enacting How the Individual invites Others into his or her Space

Finally, the sculptor is asked to demonstrate how others are brought into one's space. Using the same subjects as in the previous part of the sculpture, the sculptor approaches the subject and without using words tries to get the subject into the sculptor's space. At the time, the subject can be minimally to heavily engaged in his or her own activities when the sculptor approaches. Again, various aspects of the sculptor's actions are informative. Does one give up easily? Does the sculptor become aggressive or physical? Are they creative in trying alternative approaches, or do they become more rigid? Is eye contact used? Humor? Seduction? Persistence?

Once, again, the participants give feedback to the sculptor about what it was like to interact with the sculptor, giving the sculptor further opportunity to learn new information on how one's behavior affects another.

Involving the Second Member of the Dyad

This information can be used not only by the sculptor for his or her own awareness, but also by the other member of the dyad who has been observing the entire process. The therapist now asks the other person to enter the sculptor's space, again without using any words, as one is typically accustomed to doing. Then the therapist asks the other person to enter the sculptor's space using the new information gleaned from observing the partner's sculpting of their interpersonal boundaries. Typically, the sculptor responds in a more accepting manner.

Next, the whole process is repeated, with the second member of the dyad becoming the sculptor, and the previous sculptor becoming the observer. At the end of this process, the therapist asks each member of the dyad to "go get the other person" and bring them back into their space. This is done first as they have typically done, and second in the way that they now know the other person wants. If deemed desirable, the therapist can give a paradoxical directive for each of them to approach the other in the way that they used to. This procedure allows for covert processes to become overt, so that neither member of the dyad can continue to act as though they were not aware of the other's rules, preferences, and wishes, making each one more responsible for the systemic interactions in the relationship. The hope is that as each member of the dyad learns, respects, and validates the personal boundary rules of the other, and that the need for rigid, impermeable boundaries intended to protect against intrusion or violation will fade away.

Sculpture Used in Groups

Both the family sculpting and the boundary sculpting exercises can be adapted for use with a variety of groups, whether they be training, educational, or therapy groups. A wide variety of applications of sculpting can be made, limited only by the ingenuity of group leaders and members. Some training programs make use of a live supervision session, in which the client gives permission for the observing team to role-play various members of his or her family. Often, the therapist has experienced some type of stuckness with the client, and the supervisor and therapist have mutually agreed that such a family sculpture could be beneficial for the process of therapy, the therapeutic relationship, and/or the client. When using this format, all members of the observing team have received some type of instruction on family sculptures, whether and when they are to offer interpretations, what type of comments the therapist is hoping for or thinks is important to avoid during the feedback period, etc. Such a format allows for other therapists-in-training to experience an application of sculpting to therapy, and helps them to decide if and how they might make use of such experiential exercises in their own clinical work.

Others sculpt the relationships among a group of trainees, or the relationship between the trainee and supervisor (Andolfi, 1979). Marchetti-Mercer and Cleaver (2000) propose a training method that combines genograms and family sculpting as a way to improve cross-cultural understanding among psychology master's students in a training program in South Africa. After presenting their genogram to the class, students then sculpted their family, and were given the opportunity to change any of the relationships within the family. Sculptors, other participants, and observers of these family sculptures were then asked to write about their experiences. Their reactions reflected an increased awareness of the similarities between their families, despite having different cultural and racial backgrounds.

The most commonly used form, however, is for a member of the group to make sculptures of their own families of origin, using other group members to role-play members of their family. Many of the same steps that are used in family sculpting apply to sculpture in groups, although there are several important differences. As with family sculpting, the three general stages apply to training sculptures: 1) establishing the mapping between physical and metaphorical space, 2) placing the players in space, constructing the actual sculpture, and 3) processing or debriefing the experience (Constantine, 1978; Duhl et al., 1973). Similarly, the specific steps for a family sculpture outlined above are also followed in training sculptures. The following paragraphs set forth some of the distinctions between a sculpture used with groups of non-family members and a family sculpture.

In group sculptures, it is very important to allow the sculptor to select who will role play each family member of his or her family. Often there are subtle characteristics, previously unknown to the sculptor, that the family member and role player have in common, that shed light both on the family member being role-played, and on the relationship between group members. This is not always the case, however, as sometimes there might be only one older female in the group who is asked to play the mother, for instance. But often one result of the sculpt is for the sculptor to have increased awareness that his or her attitude toward a certain group member (ranging from warmth to apathy to hostility) may be due to some resemblance to a family member.

A second difference is the presence and role of the group of observers or audience. It is not unusual in sculptures with groups for there to be more group members than family members to be role-played. The observers are asked to notice body language, facial expressions, themes and patterns, as well as their own emotional responses that emerge from witnessing the sculpture. Typically during the debriefing period in training sculptures, the observers are asked to give their impressions first, followed by the people role-playing the family members, then the person role-playing the sculptor gives his or her impressions, and finally the sculptor shares his or her experiences. The significance of this order lies in the impact that is made when the observers, who are more removed from the experience, give feedback to the sculptor that so accurately reflects the perspectives of the sculptor and/or the family members. By giving their feedback first, it is clear that they have not been influenced by the comments of the participants. Similarly, the sculptor is often able to gain new empathy for a family member, by hearing colleagues voice their experiences of playing a certain family member. If the family members themselves had conveyed the same message, it would have had less credibility. But hearing group members voice sentiments almost identical to those expressed by the real family members allows the sculptor to grasp the systemic nature of the family members' behaviors. Finally, the observers and participants are given an opportunity to check their impressions against the perceptions of the sculptor, as the sculptor more fully explains the situation being portrayed in the sculpture.

It is important for the facilitators of group sculptures to consider beforehand whether they will ask the sculptors to select someone else to role-play themselves. In some cases, it might be important for the sculptor to observe someone else in their role. In other cases, there might be reasons that it would be helpful for the sculptor to become a part of the sculpture, and in other situations, the decision may be left to the sculptor. An example of a situation when it was better for the sculptor to select someone else to role-play her own position was a student who became very absorbed in her own role. While role-playing her family, it became apparent that the emotions surfacing from the sculpture were of such intensity that it was more beneficial for her to have someone else stand in her place. This student indicated in the debriefing period that while she was engaged in the sculpture herself, she was not able to focus on any of the other members of the family, because she was too flooded by her own visceral reactions to being in that role. Once she stepped out of that role to observe, however, she was able to notice what was happening to and between other family members.

During the debriefing stage of the group sculpture, it is critical to have a ritualized way of group members to distance themselves from the role they played. This allows for intense feelings that are aroused between family members to be diffused. If this is not done, it is not unusual to notice the sculptor to continue to call the group member by the name of the family member he or she role-played, and to continue to relate to that person as if he or she was the family member. In some cases, group members are asked to play family members with negative or other powerful characteristics, and they need a way to separate themselves from such a role. Some simple ritual can be used, such as having the sculptor face each family member, and for each to thank the other for the role-play and to re-identify themselves as group members:

Sam: Thank you for selecting me to play Frank, your brother. It was an honor to role-play someone who is so loyal to his younger brother. But I am not Frank any longer. My name is Sam.
Sculptor: Thank you, Sam, for being my brother Frank today, and for the insights you gave me into what it was like for him to be the oldest in my family.

There are different purposes for a training sculpture compared to one that is used in therapy. As with a family sculpture, sculptors in a training sculpture can gain greater understanding of their own family system, and their and other family members' role in that system. In addition, they often gain insight into their relationships with other group members, and become more aware of the influence of family-of-origin issues in their own clinical work. Besides the benefits gained by the sculptor, the other participants and observers learn more about the systemic nature of systems, perhaps making connections to their own family of origin. They are also exposed to the experiential impact of such an exercise in a way that just merely describing the exercise could not do. They also gain first-hand knowledge about conducting a sculpture.

That accounts for a final distinction between a family sculpture and sculpture conducted with a training group: the didactic nature of a training sculpture. Trainees learn through demonstration the technique of sculpting, a process that is assisted by occasional pauses and asides, in order for the facilitator of the sculpture to explain a certain aspect of sculpting. For instance, the facilitator can stop at certain key points in the sculpture and explain the options that are available at that point, such as requesting further detail in a sculpt, adding motion or language, offering or withholding interpretation, etc., and suggesting a rationale for each choice. Also, different types of sculpts can be demonstrated, such as linear sculptures, boundary sculptures, and polar sculptures (Constantine, 1978), so that trainees can explore the benefits, disadvantages, and challenges of doing each type of sculpture.

Case Study

The following is a case example of a training sculptor used in an introductory marriage and family therapy course. The sculptor, Gwen, was a second year student in a marriage and family therapy master's program, who was in her second semester of practicum. The professor/facilitator had contacted her prior to the class to inquire whether she would be interested and willing to do her family sculpture for class, and was asked to think of some key event in her family's life. She also discussed with Gwen whether she wanted to play herself in the sculpt, or whether she would select someone else. Together they decided that she would select someone else and observe the sculpt from that perspective, giving her the option to switch places with that person if she thought it might be beneficial, and step into the sculpt herself. During class, the facilitator asked her to visualize the setting in which this event took place, and to rearrange the room as necessary, describing to the class what she was doing. She was instructed to give details to the class about the setting, but not about the specific situation she had in mind. Gwen moved several chairs into place to form a couch, and another chair became the television set. Two other chairs represented rocking chairs in her family's living room, where the scenario was to take place. The facilitator then asked her to draw a brief genogram on the chalkboard, diagramming her immediate family members, their names, ages at the time, and birth order. She drew her father Peter, 34, her mother Diane, 32, her older sister Tina, 11, and herself, at age 8.

Next, the facilitator had Gwen select members from class to portray her parents, her sister, and herself. As she selected each one, she told them where in the living room they were to go, and whether they were to sit, stand, or lay down. She also gave them brief directions about what pose they were to take, where they were looking, etc. She placed her father Peter outside the walls of the living room/house, with his back turned away from the rest of the family. She placed her mother Diane on one side of the couch, sitting with her arms crossed in front of her, staring straight ahead at the TV. Next to the TV, looking at her mother, she put her sister Tina. Finally, she placed the person playing herself on the couch right next to her mother.

The facilitator instructed her to stand back and look over the scene and decide if it looked right, or if any changes needed to be made. She also asked Gwen to provide a few more details about posture, attitudes, and facial gestures. Gwen looked it over, and moved her father a bit farther away from the rest of the family members, and moved his arms so that they were extended out in front of him. She told the person playing Diane that she should look tired, and had her slump over a bit more on the couch. She told Tina that she would be perky and energetic, and was always busy. She told the other Gwen that she needed to look smaller, and positioned her so that she would be more tucked into the couch. The person playing Gwen wondered where she would be looking, and after a brief pause, Gwen decided that she would alternate between looking down at her hands, looking up at her mother, and watching TV.

This was a nice segue into the next part of the sculpture, which was to ask Gwen to give each person a short movement along with a short phrase. The phrases and gestures were to be representative of that person. Gwen started with her sister, and had her bounce into the room, take her hands out of her pockets, and hold up her hands, saying, "What are we going to do now?" For her mother, Gwen had her uncross her arms, rest her chin on her hand, and mumble, "Give me strength." The father was to look up in the air, and stretch out his arms, and say, "It's a great day for a baseball game." Gwen had the person playing herself bury her head in her arms and say, "I'm so small." The family members were instructed to continue to repeat both the phrases and the gestures, in random order.

Next, the sculpture was put in place, and the movements and verbal phrases began. After a couple of rounds, the family members stopped, and the facilitator encouraged them to continue. The facilitator explained that the continued repetitions were a crucial component of an effective sculpture, and that even though it might feel uncomfortable or ridiculous to continue, insights often emerged only after repeated cycles. The tenor of the interactions changed noticeably as the sculpture played out for about 2-3 minutes. At the end of this time, the facilitator asked Gwen if she wanted to repeat the sculpture playing herself this time. Gwen decided that she did not wish to do so, and would rather spend more time processing what had just happened.

The next step was to debrief the process. First the observers were asked to give their comments and impressions. Some commented on how the mother and two daughters seemed like their own subsystem, and the father was his own separate unit. Another observer said the following:

Observers: At first Gwen was saying "I'm so small, but at some point it changed, and she started saying, "I'm too small." It was like she was saying that about both her father and her mother. She was too small to go with her dad to the baseball game, and too small to provide any strength to her mother.

Next, the facilitator asked the persons playing the family members for their reflections. The following were some of the comments made:

Tina/Oldest sister: I started out feeling happy-go-lucky, my usual self, ready to see what we were going to do next. But then I would look back and forth between my mother and father, and I started feeling really torn and confused. I'd feel happy when I heard my dad say we were going to a ballgame–at first it sounded like he was going to take me along with him. Then I would look at my mom, and I started feeling worried. After a while, it was like I was saying, "What are we going to do?" in a nervous kind of way, like, how were we ever going to cope, instead of just wondering what we were going to get to do next. After it kept going on, it felt like Dad wasn't even talking to me. If I was going to the ballgame with him, why was I way over here?

Diane/Mother: I feel so tired right now, like I don't want to take my chin off my hand. I just want to lie here, and not have any other responsibilities. I don't feel any connection to my husband – he's been off in his own world for so long, and it's been up to me to take care of all of the household responsibilities, and everything else around here. I just don't know how I am going to do it anymore. I found myself looking to Tina when I said, "Give me strength." At first, that was just like I was just saying it to myself, but pretty soon it seemed like I was depending on Tina for strength, even though that didn't really feel appropriate. I didn't really look much at Gwen, but it was comforting just having her sitting so close next to me. I liked having her there, and wanted to give her the impression that she could lean on me, even though I felt so weak.

Peter/Father: I really didn't feel much towards any of the rest of them. It was like I was in my own world. Sometimes it felt like I was a little kid myself, and I was excited at this beautiful day, and I was going to get to go to the baseball game and do what I wanted. There were times I didn't even really hear what any of them were saying. It was sort of an annoying interruption when I kept hearing Tina ask what we were going to do.

The last person to offer comments about the experience was the person playing Gwen. She talked about the sadness she felt playing Gwen, and how alone and scared she was. She also found herself looking to Tina to help hold things together, and how good it was to hear a happy voice when her mother sounded so weary. She could relate to the comments from the observers about feeling "too small," because she felt so powerless in this role. She had no way of getting her father's attention, she didn't feel like she could do anything to help her mother, and she found herself feeling smaller and smaller as the sculpting continued to play out.

Finally, Gwen herself responded to some of the comments made by the observers and participants, and talked about what it was like to see her family portrayed. Only after all of this discussion did the facilitator ask Gwen to reveal the circumstances behind the sculpture. Gwen told the class that the scene was meant to portray her family at the point when she was 8 when her father announced that he was divorcing her mother and leaving the family. As they found out later, he had been having an affair with another woman, and within a year had remarried to her. She, her sister, and her mother struggled along for many years, trying to get by.

She talked about how interesting it was to hear comments about what it must have been like for her sister, because she had always resented her because it seemed like her dad favored her, and she acted as though everything came so easily to her. She hadn't thought about how rejected her sister might have felt when her dad left, which was reasonable to conclude since her father had little contact with either sister after the divorce. She had often felt jealous of the special relationship Tina and her mother seemed to have. She also hadn't thought about how much pressure her sister might have felt to be the strong one in the family.

Gwen also commented on feeling less angry towards her mother. For so many years, she had blamed her for so many of the bad things that had happened to their family. She had viewed her father as this easy-going, happy-go-lucky kind of man, and had never really felt much anger towards him, but the sculpture and her classmates' comments made her rethink her attitudes towards each parent. Maybe there was another side to her father that was irresponsible, leaving her mother overburdened with caring for both children, the house, and her job. She had built up this image of a wonderful father that was chased away by an overbearing wife, but the comments from the person who played her father startled her. It was painful to think that her father might have cared so little, but that was more in keeping with his actions of the last 24 years. And she had a new appreciation for what it might have been like to be in her mother's shoes, and was moved to tears when she heard the comments from the person playing her mother about feeling connected to Gwen as they sat together. It was reassuring to think her mother maybe wanted a closer relationship with her, but was so overwhelmed with everything else. She also thanked the person playing Gwen and told her that she had felt so small and powerless for so long, and it was strange to hear the role-playing Gwen say the same things she had felt in her family.

By this time, it was necessary to conclude the sculpture, and so each of the family members was asked to face Gwen, and to remind her that they were not her family members, but members of her class; friends and colleagues, but not family. Gwen thanked each one in turn for their willingness to become her family for a brief time. The facilitator reminded all of those present that such an experience has the potential to stir up some powerful emotions, and that they would process further the following week if necessary. In addition, the facilitator gave permission to Gwen and the members of class who played her family to contact her during the week if they experienced any disturbing or upsetting reactions to the sculpture.

Simple Spatializations

In addition to the primary types of sculpture described above, there are other uses of space that have been reported in the literature related to family sculpture (Constantine, 1978). Spatialization is a "direct use of physical space to map a simple or limited personal or interpersonal construct" (p. 16). Space is used to map the concept, and the sculpting is converted into a living graph by people placing themselves in the space in relation to the concept. Three types of simple spatialization include (1) linear, (2) matrix, and (3) polar sculptures. Each is briefly described below.

Linear Sculpture

People place themselves along a line representing a unipolar (one-way) dimension (such as powerfulness) or a bipolar dimension (such as "head vs. heart"). After the dimensions are defined, clients are invited to walk silently along the line to find a place that feels right to them. Clients could be asked to take before/after positions to highlight progress or to clarify goals. The first author has found the use of linear sculpts to be helpful in assessing and highlighting change near the end of treatment. A continuum also lends itself nicely to scaling questions from solution-focused therapy and can be used with clients reluctant to be nailed down with numbers (Bischof, 1993).

The first author was a team member on a couple therapy case; early attempts at using scaling questions were met with strong resistance to the use of numbers to quantify feelings and progress. The same couple, though, was quite willing to do linear sculptures that covered such themes as organized vs. spontaneous, laid back vs. worrying, commitment to the marriage, and comparisons of beginning of treatment and current functioning for several areas. Both partners placed themselves on the line concurrently for some of the sculptures, resulting in rich discussion of their acceptance of differences (a theme developed during therapy). The couple commented immediately after, and again in a subsequent session, about how much they gained from doing these sculptures. While reluctant to quantify progress in numbers, they "experienced" their progress by placing themselves along continua, which helped them underline the progress they had made. Part of their explanation of the usefulness involved the necessity to "take a stand" that was more powerful and insightful than simply talking about things.

Matrix Sculpture

The matrix sculpture is an extension of the linear sculpture into two dimensions. The two "lines" are at right angles to each other. The client places him/herself on one continuum first, and then the other, or the person may select a spot where it feels right for both dimensions. This is an efficient way to explore the relationship between two variables. An example of a matrix sculpture is "frequency of arguments" on one line and "intensity of arguments" on the other. In this variation of sculpting, two factors could be considered simultaneously, which of course, would not be possible if one was limited to verbal discussion.

Polar Sculpture

In a polar sculpture, people place themselves or others at some distance from a single reference point, which may be a person, an object, or an abstract concept. The thing or concept may be in the center of the room or a side of the room, and participants walk around the space and orient themselves in a spot that feels comfortable to them. They then process in place why they picked that particular position, and perhaps are invited to share if they were content with that, or if they desired to change their orientation in some way. Additionally, in a family or group situation, the people can be asked also to position themselves in relation to each other as well. Another possibility is to have people sculpt themselves in relation to a value-laden statement, perhaps one written on a dry erase board or piece of paper. The first author used a variation of this in an anger management group, with group members indicating their agreement or disagreement with various statements that contained myths about gender roles and domestic violence. Participants enjoyed the exercise, and found it helpful to have to take a position and explain it, and also to see where their fellow group members positioned themselves.

Constantine (1978, p. 16) describes an example of a polar sculpture with a family, around an object representing "head of the household." The children were able to express their awareness of their mother's ambivalent desire to be "head of the house," yet to leave responsibility with her husband. The father in turn was adamant in occupying the center, however ineffectively. All were able to relate this pattern to an overall struggle between the parents and to use this awareness to explore alternative strategies for themselves.

Two other variations of spatializations described by Constantine (1978) that capture developmental issues warrant mention. In the *developmental sculpture* a succession of concentric circles are defined on the floor, each space representing a significant period or life cycle stage in the sculptor's life. The sculptor enters each space and describes its quality, significant features, and important people in that space. The nature and circumstances of the transition to the next stage may also be explored. The *life line sculpture*, a living time line, involves having the person traverse along a line that runs the length of the room from birth to the present. The person describes whatever occurs to him or her in terms of people, events, relationships, and feelings at selected points on the line. Allotting a specific amount of time for the traversal helps to focus this sculpture for maximum benefit.

Symbolic Figure Placement Techniques

The sculpting procedures we have discussed thus far have all involved the placement of actual people to represent relationships and family dynamics. Symbolic figure placement techniques (SFPT) involve the use of figurines, dolls, or other physical objects to represent the members of a family (Gehring & Schulteiss, 1987). Many of these techniques began as assessment devices, typically using actual distances in the representations of people's families as a measurement of emotional closeness or cohesion.

Mutter (1999) writes about the cinical use of wooden figures on a chessboard, and identifies three advantages of using SFPT over traditional family sculpture. One is that many clinicians' offices do not have the room to allow for a full family sculpture. Second, it is not always possible to have all the family members present due to distance, death, or refusal to be involved in sessions. Third, there are some clients who feel too self-conscious to do something active like sculpting in therapy. Mutter has the client place him or herself anywhere on the board first (which itself can be revealing), and then add figures that represent other family members, much the same as is done in traditional sculpting. The therapist processes the symbolic representation of the family similarly to other types of sculptures. Of course, gestures and movement are difficult to portray with these static figures, but they provide an excellent alternative when the family is unavailable or unwilling to be involved in treatment. These techniques also provide a quantifiable alternative to map and measure the relationships within a family system. A few prominent SFPT are reviewed here. See Gehring and Schulteiss (1987) for a more detailed review of SFPT.

Kvebaek Family Sculpture Technique (KFST)

The KFST was created by David Kvebaek in 1968 (interestingly, around the time David Kantor was developing ideas about family sculpture) in Norway as a way to present complicated family situations in clinical team meetings. He later introduced his idea to leading family therapists and researchers in the USA and was well received, as people were excited about the KFST as a means to measure family dynamics (Cromwell, Kvebaek, & Fournier,1980). Thi technique ses a chess-like board (1m × 1m) blocked off into alternating black and white squares. Wooden blocks or figures represent family members, and these are placed on the board to indicate emotional closeness/distance in "real" and "ideal" portrayals of family relationships. One might also have the subject portray one's family during a time of high conflict or tension. The technique has been used primarily as an assessment device, calculating dyadic and triadic distances between family members based upon a Pythagorean formula. A discrepancy score is calculated by measuring the deviance of each person's representation from the average represented distances of all family members. Differences between the "real" and "ideal" depictions are assumed to indicate a desire for change in family relationships. A score assumed to measure each family member's influence is calculated by comparing the degree of similarity between individual and group representations (Gehring & Schulteiss, 1987).

In two separate studies of families of adolescents, the KFST showed convergent and construct validity for cohesion as measured by versions of the Family Adaptability and Cohesion Evaluation Scale (FACES; Berry, Hurley, & Worthington, 1990; Russell, 1980). A Norwegian study of psychosocial factors in children with recent onset of rheumatic disease ($N = 72$) yielded mixed results when comparing FACES III cohesion measures with family closeness as measured by the KFST (Vandvik & Eckblad, 1993). FACES III cohesion sum scores and KFST family mean interpersonal distance were not correlated, whereas the cohesion sum scores were related to the mother-father distance on the KFST. They concluded that these results support the usefulness of a distinction between cohesion as a family characteristic and dyadic closeness, especially between the parent figures. This Norwegian study also found a linear relationship between the KFST and semi-structured interview assessments of child and family psychosocial function. For more information on the history and use of the KFST, one can visit their website (www.healthyhumansystems.com).

Modification of the original instructions for the use of the KFST as an assessment technique and processing as family members place the blocks on the board increase clinical usefulness (Bischof, 1993), and provide a means to assess and enhance emotional intensity in couples and families (Hernandez, 1998). The first author has used the KFST therapeutically with good results. An adult mother of two school-age boys who had survived ritualistic abuse and cult involvement by her former partner found the technique quite helpful in briefly depicting several stages of their life together as a family. Illustrating family dynamics during the time she and the boys lived with this abusive man evoked strong emotions. She then felt empowered as she progressed through depictions that showed her movement toward independence and protection of herself and her family. She used some other material in the room to build a barrier between her family and him to accentuate the firm boundaries she had put into place and intended to maintain. The KFST helped her to tell her story succinctly and powerfully, and she was rather amazed at her ability to do this through the use of this technique.

Family Distance Doll Placement Technique (FDDPT)

Similar to the KFST, the FDDPT, developed by Gerber and Kaswan (1971), assesses psychological distance in the family. Subjects are asked individually and as a group to think about positive and negative family events and then to depict those situations by arranging dolls on a board. Family closeness is categorized by eight "grouping schemata." Psychological distance is measured by the distance between the figurines and their orientation through four "focus categories" (Gehring & Schulteiss, 1987). In families of preadolescents, closer doll placement occurred in positive situations, and parents tended to portray their family as more unified than did their children.

Family System Test (FAST)

Another type of SFPT, the FAST, developed by Gehring (Gehring & Wyler, 1986) measures the quality of subsystem boundaries in terms of cohesion and power. Wooden figures with modestly structured faces are placed on a monochromatic board. Power is depicted by placing figures on cylindrical blocks of various heights (higher = more power). Subjects individually represent their perceptions of cohesion and power in their family in "typical," "ideal," and "conflict" situations. Following the individual assessments, the family as a group is instructed to create joint representations consensually. There are two cohesion scores, one based on the Pythagorean calculation of dyadic distances, and the other on the mutual focus between figure pairs (orientation). Power, defined as the ability to influence other family members, is measured by the height of the blocks as well as dyadic height differences (Gehring & Schulteiss, 1987). In a study of families with adolescents, conducted following completion of therapy, mean values on all three parameters varied as a function of the situations depicted (Gehring & Wyler). The family members' ideal representations showed the closest distances, the most orientation between the figures, and the least use of power blocks. In the typical, and even more so in the conflict representation, a considerable shift in less cohesion (distance and orientation) and an increase in the use of power blocks was shown.

Finally, other types of SFPT used for clinical purposes have been identified. Mutter's (1999) use of a chessboard and wooded figures was mentioned above. Another alternative is to use a flannel board with felt figures of various sizes to represent adults or children, and colors to depict oneself, and nuclear or extended family members (Lawson & Hebert, 1991). The authors found that using a flannel board and figures was less threatening and more manageable for many family members, compared with traditional family sculpture. An additional option is to use a checkerboard and checkers, which are accessible and inexpensive. Power could be depicted by increasing the number of checkers for a specific family member, and the black and red colors could also symbolize some aspect of family dynamics. Before concluding, we consider the limited research of family sculpture techniques.

Research on Family Sculpture Techniques

With the exception of a few studies mentioned above on SFPT and on FAST, empirical research on family sculpture techniques is sparse and generally limited to studies of European families. As was mentioned above, experiential family activities are difficult to research due in part to the spontaneity and variability inherent in such techniques and an emphasis upon global goals. Many published works on family sculpture attest to the clinical value of these procedures, supported through anecdotal evidence and case examples of families who responded well to the use of sculpting techniques. A common outcome is that families became "unblocked" or "unstuck" with the help of family sculpture, and that an awareness of systemic qualities of the family was enhanced. Family members and trainees also routinely report that they learn much from such exercises, and identify engaging in family sculpture as some of the more memorable and helpful aspects of therapy or training. Two specific studies using family sculpture procedures and recommendations for further research on SFPT are discussed next.

One study of psychosomatic families was found that attempted to investigate empirically the use of family sculpture (Onnis et al., 1994). The authors of this study report on the use of sculpture with 41 Italian families with psychosomatic problems (e.g., asthma, enuresis, anorexia, gastritis). It was hypothesized that the symbolic nature of sculpture would be a good fit with the nonverbal language of psychosomatic symptoms. Onnis et al. (p. 341) were also interested in restoring "temporal dimensions into family systems that seem to have lost their evolutionary potential and to be in a sort of 'time lock'." The inclusion of time was accomplished by asking each family member to represent the family as it now is, and how it will be ten years into the future. They report that 38 of the 41 families (therapy was interrupted in 3 cases) showed either improvement or disappearance of the presenting symptom, and that the family evolutionary process resumed. In all the cases, the sessions dedicated to family sculptures represented a therapeutic turning point. They caution that the results are incomplete and that follow-ups will need to be conducted.

An extension of the Norwegian study mentioned above using the Kvebaek FST also warrants mention. Eckblad & Vandvik (1992) report on the development of a computerized scoring procedure for the KFST with 92 mothers of children with recent onset of rheumatic diseases. They identified four family types based upon distance and structural parameters of the mothers' "real" and "ideal" sculpts of their families: close, hierarchic, unspecified, and skewed. The four types differed with regard to the childhood environment of the mother, chronic family difficulties, and the psychosocial functioning of the primary patient. Families of the mothers who reported greater discrepancies between their real and ideal portrayals (indicating a desire for change) differed in regards to configuration types, distance variables (especially greater distance between the parents), and psychosocial characteristics. They also differed on the basis of the childhood environment of the mother, chronic family difficulties, and satisfaction with the sharing of household chores, but not on disease severity or psychosocial functioning of the child. The significance of the parental dyad for this population is underscored by the findings of this study. It should be noted, though, that only the perspective of the mother was taken into account.

In their review of Symbolic Figure Placement Techniques, Gehring and Schulteiss (1987), conclude that SFPT are well suited for research and suggest that further research is needed in four areas. One is to validate SFPT with other self-report methods and observed family interactions. A second effort is to clarify the concept of power as either individual properties or as a property of a system. Third, the interrelationship between the individuals' perception of various subsystems and the whole family needs further investigation. Fourth, it should be determined whether all family members are equally good informants. In summary, future research will reveal the extent to which these tools can be useful as projective tests and family tasks in clinical practice, and how they can contribute to structural research on family functioning.

Conclusion

This chapter has presented various kinds of family sculpture, a type of experiential family therapy activity. The procedures developed by the originators of family sculpture have remained viable and useful over the past thirty years, and continue to be utilized by therapists and trainers. We have discussed techniques for use when family members are present, such as the family sculpture, boundary sculpture, and simple spatializations. The use of sculpting methods with groups has also been addressed. Symbolic figure placement techniques, which can be quite helpful with individuals or when family members are inaccessible, have been offered as a creative alternative.

We have considered the limited research on family sculpture techniques. Certainly, more research is needed to verify clinical impressions about the effectiveness of these procedures. Existing studies show promise for the use of sculpting as a valid assessment of family dynamics, especially family cohesion at the dyadic and family levels. Limited investigations have shown positive outcomes associated with the clinical use of family sculpture, interestingly with medical problems. As mentioned earlier, sculpting has also been integrated with other more recent developments in the field of family therapy.

Like most experiential activities, reading about family sculpture is no substitute for actually engaging in these techniques with families, groups, or individuals. We invite you to experiment with various family sculpture procedures, and conclude with the encouraging words of Larry Constantine (1978, p. 22), a key contributor in this area:

> Real comfort and creativity with sculpture techniques comes only from trying them out, from liberal experimentation. Experimentation can take place in almost any setting. One of the delights of sculpture is that it so seldom fails to liberate and to supply fresh ideas to almost any process.

References

Andolfi, M. (1979). *Family therapy: An interactional approach*. New York: Plenum Press.

Berry, J. T., Hurley, J. H., & Worthington, E. L. (1990). Empirical validity of the Kvebaek Family Sculpture Technique. *The American Journal of Family Therapy, 18,* 19–31.

Bischof, G. (1993). Solution-focused brief therapy and experiential family therapy activities: An integration. *Journal of Systemic Therapies, 12,* 61–73.

Constantine, L. L. (1978). Family sculpture and relationship mapping techniques. *Journal of Marriage and Family Counseling, 4,* 13–23.

Cromwell, R., Kvebaek, D., & Fournier, D. (1980). *The Kvebaek family technique: A diagnostic and research tool in family therapy*. Jonesboro, TN: Pilgrimage.

Duhl, B. S. (1999). A personal view of action metaphor: Bringing what's inside out. In D. J. Wiener (Ed.), *Beyond talk therapy: Using movement and expressive techniques in clinical practice* (pp. 79–96). Washington, DC: American Psychological Association.

Duhl, F. J., Kantor, D., & Duhl, B. S. (1973). Learning, space, and action in family therapy: A primer of sculpture. In D. Bloch (Ed.), *Techniques of family psychotherapy: A primer* (pp. 47–63). New York: Grune & Stratton.

Eckblad, G., & Vandvik, I. H. (1992). A computerized scoring procedure for the Kvebaek Family Sculpture Technique applied to families of children with rheumatic diseases. *Family Process, 31,* 85–98.

Gehring, T. M., & Schulteiss, R. B. (1987). Spatial representation and assessment of family relationships. *The American Journal of Family Therapy, 15,* 261–264.

Gehring, T. M., & Wyler, I. L. (1986). Family System Test (FAST): A three-dimensional approach to investigate family relationships. *Child Psychiatry and Human Development, 16,* 235–248.

Gerber, G. L., & Kaswan, J. (1971). Expression of emotion through family grouping schemata, distance and interpersonal focus. *Journal of Consulting and Clinical Psychology, 36,* 370–377.

Hernandez, S. L. (1998). The emotional thermometer: Using family sculpting for emotional assessment. *Family Therapy, 25,* 121–128.

Kantor, D., & Lehr, W. (1975). *Inside the family.* San Francisco: Jossey-Bass.

L'Abate, L., Ganahl, G., & Hansen, J. (1986). *Methods of family therapy.* Englewood Cliffs, NJ: Prentice Hall.

Lawson, D. M., & Hebert, B. (1991). Family sculpting using a flannel board. *Journal of Mental Health Counseling, 13,* 405–409.

Lesage-Higgins, S. A. (1999). Family sculpting in premarital counseling. *Family Therapy, 26,* 31–38.

Marchetti-Mercer, M.C., & Cleaver, G. (2000). Genograms and family sculpting: An aid to cross-cultural understanding in the training of psychology students in South Africa. *Counseling Psychologist, 28,* 61–80.

Moreno, J. L. (1946). *Psychodrama.* New York: Beacon.

Mutter, K. F. (1999). Helping families see themselves. *Journal of Family Psychotherapy, 10,* 83–86.

Onnis, L., DiGennaro, A., Cespa, G., Agostini, B., Dentale, R., & Quinzi, P. (1994). Sculpting present and future: A systemic intervention model applied to psychosomatic families. *Family Process, 33,* 341–355.

Papp, P. (1976). Family choreography. In P. J. Geurin (Ed.), *Family therapy: Theory and practice* (pp. 465–479). New York: Gardner Press.

Papp, P., Silverstein, O., & Carter, B. (1973). Family sculpting in preventive work with "well families." *Family Process, 12,* 197–212.

Piercy, F. P., Sprenkle, D. H., Wetchler, J. L., & Associates (1996). *Family therapy sourcebook* (2nd ed.). New York: Guilford.

Russell, C. S. (1980). A methodological study of family cohesion and adaptability. *Journal of Marital and Family Therapy, 6,* 459–470.

Satir, V. (1972). *Peoplemaking.* Palo Alto, CA: Science & Behavior Books.

Vandvik, I. H., & Eckblad, G. F. (1993). FACES III and the Kvebaek Family Sculpture Technique and measures of cohesion and closeness. *Family Process, 32,* 221–233.

List Of Contributors

C. Everett Bailey, Ph.D.
Psychological Counseling Services, Ltd.
7530 W. Angus Drive
Scottsdale, AZ 85251
USA
E-mail: CEverettBailey@msn.com

Dieter Benninghoven, Dr. phil.
Medical University of Lübeck
Clinic for Psychosomatics and Psycho-
therapy
Ratzeburger Allee 160
D-23562 Lübeck
Germany
E-mail: benningh@med.inf.mu-luebeck.de

Gary H. Bischof, Ph.D., LMFT
Western Michigan University
3102 Sangren Hall
Kalamazoo, MI 49008
USA
E-mail: gary.bischof@wmich.edu

Adrian J. Blow, Ph.D., LMFT
Associate Professor
Saint Louis University
Department of Counseling & Family
Therapy
3750 Lindell Blvd.
St. Louis, MO 63108
USA
E-mail: blowaj@slu.edu

Uta Bohlen, Dipl. Psych.
Offener Marktplatz
D-22765 Hamburg
Germany

Manfred Cierpka, Prof. Dr. med.
Medical Director of the Institute of
Psychosomatic Cooperative Research
And Family Therapy
University of Heidelberg
Bergheimerstr. 54
D-69115 Heidelberg
Germany
E-mail: Manfred_Cierpka@med.uni-
heidelberg.de

Silvia Echevarria-Doan, Ph.D.
Associate Professor
Department of Counselor Education
University of Florida
P.O. Box 117046
Gainesville, FL 32611
USA
E-mail: silvia@coe.ufl.edu

Diane Estrada, Ph.D.
Assistant Professor
Couples & Family Therapy Coordinator
Division of Counseling Psychology &
Counselor Education
University of Colorado at Denver and
Health Sciences Center
Campus Box 106
PO Box 173364
Denver, CO 80217-3364
USA
Email:diane.estrada@cudenver.edu

Gina N. Harvey, M.A.
Private practice
234 Oak St.
Dayton OH 45410
USA
E-mail: ggutenkunst@woh.rr.com

Karen B. Helmeke, Ph.D., LMFT
6346 Cypress St.
Portage, MI 49024
USA
E-mail: khelmeke@juno.com

Sabine Krebeck, Dipl. Psych.
Schröderstr. 49
D-69120 Heidelberg
Germany

A. Peter MacLean, Ph.D., P.Eng.
School of Psychology
University of Ottawa
Ottawa, Ontario
Canada K1N 6N5
E-mail: macleanp@uottawa.ca

Martha Marquez
Private Practice
879 Falling Water Rd
Weston, FL 33326
USA
E-mail: mgmarquez@att.net

Almuth Massing, Dr. med.
Hanssenstr. 6
37073 Goettingen
Germany

Dr. Günter Reich, PD. Dr. phil.
University of Göttingen
Department of Psychosomatics and
Psychotherapy
Family Therapy
Humboldtallee 38
D-37073 Göttingen
Germany
E-mail: greich@gwdg.de

Douglas H. Sprenkle
Professor and Director
Marriage and Family Therapy Program
Department of Child Development and
Family Studies
Purdue University
201 Fowler Memorial House
1200 West State Street
West Lafayette, IN 47907-2055
USA
E-mail: Sprenkled@aol.com

Volker Thomas, Ph.D.
Associate Professor
Marriage and Family Therapy Program
Department of Child Development and
Family Studies
Purdue University
Fowler Memorial House
1200 W. State Street
West Lafayette, IN 47907-2055
USA
E-mail: thomasv@purdue.edu

Tina M. Timm, Ph.D., LCSW
Assistant Professor
Director of Field Education
Saint Louis University
School of Social Service
3550 Lindell Blvd.
St. Louis, MO 63103
USA
E-mail: timmtm@slu.edu

Joseph L. Wetchler, Ph.D.
Professor
Marriage and Family Therapy Program
Purdue University Calumet
Hammond IN 46323
USA
E-mail: wetchler@calumet.purdue.edu

Subject Index

Author Index